W9-CMT-635

THE LEVANT AT THE BEGINNING OF THE MIDDLE BRONZE AGE

AMERICAN SCHOOLS OF ORIENTAL RESEARCH DISSERTATION SERIES

Number 5

THE LEVANT AT THE BEGINNING OF THE MIDDLE BRONZE AGE

by
Patty Gerstenblith

THE LEVANT AT THE BEGINNING OF THE MIDDLE BRONZE AGE

by
Patty Gerstenblith

Published by
American Schools of Oriental Research

Distributed by

Eisenbrauns
Winona Lake, IN 46590

THE LEVANT AT THE BEGINNING OF THE MIDDLE BRONZE AGE

by
Patty Gerstenblith

Library of Congress Cataloging in Publication Data

Gerstenblith, Patty.
The Levant at the beginning of the Middle Bronze Age.

(Dissertation series/American Schools of Oriental Research; no. 5)
Bibliography: p.
Includes index.
1. Near East—Antiquities. 2. Bronze age—Near East. I. Title. II. Series: Dissertation series (American Schools of Oriental Research); no. 5.
DS56.G47 1983 939'.4 82-24515

Printed in the United States of America

In Memory of My Father

TABLE OF CONTENTS

LIST OF FIGURES

LIST OF TABLES

NOTE ON TRANSCRIPTIONS

Transcription of Akkadian words follows the system of *The Chicago Assyrian Dictionary*. The spellings of place names transcribed from Hebrew and Arabic and of place names and personal names from Akkadian have been made as consistent as possible, although these may not be entirely uniform due to the use of more familiar spellings for some names.

Acknowledgments

The idea for this project developed as a result of the disruptions in the Eastern Mediterranean during the summer of 1974 which caused my travels through the countries which form the subject of this study. Among the people who were influential in the formulation of this work, I would especially like to mention Professor William Dever, who first introduced me to the problems of the Middle Bronze Age in Syria-Palestine. This study originally formed the subject of my Ph.D. dissertation, "The Levant in the Middle Bronze I and its Connections with Anatolia and Mesopotamia: A Study in Trade and Settlement Patterns," which was completed in May, 1977, at Harvard University. I would like to acknowledge the help of Professors D. G. Mitten, G. M. A. Hanfmann, R. Tringham, C. C. Lamberg-Karlovsky, and M. Coogan both for reading and criticizing the original dissertation and for their support of my interdepartmental doctoral program at Harvard.

I would like to thank the Fulbright-Hays Doctoral Dissertation Research Abroad Program and the Mrs. Giles Whiting Foundation for their support of the research and writing of this manuscript in dissertation form in Ankara, Jerusalem, and Cambridge. Mrs. Elizabeth Pattullo, the Harvard University administrator of these programs, was most understanding of the wanderings of an archaeologist. The American Council of Learned Societies through their Grant to Recent Recipients of the Ph.D. aided in the preparation of this manuscript for publication. I would also like to express my appreciation to the Turkish Department of Antiquities for permission to conduct research in Turkey in 1974-75 and to the staffs of the British Institute of Archaeology in Ankara in 1974-75 and the Albright Institute of Archaeological Research in Jerusalem in 1975-76 for the use of their facilities. I would also like to thank several individuals, including R. Amiran, P. Beck, E. Eisenberg, and S. Gitin, for discussing with me their ideas and material.

For providing assistance in the revision of this manuscript, I would like to thank Ms. R. Burbank, Archivist of the Oriental Institute Museum, for permission to utilize the unpublished plans of the Megiddo excavations, and the library staffs of the Hebrew Union College-Jewish Institute of Religion (Cincinnati) and the Classics Department of the University of Cincinnati. In the final preparation of this manuscript, the care of the typists, Jan Dupont and Miriam November, is sincerely appreciated. Special thanks must be expressed to Professor James Weinstein for his positive contribution to this project as editor. Many friends, too numerous to be mentioned, in Ankara, Jerusalem, Cambridge, and Cincinnati have helped in discussing the problems of this study and in many other ways.

This acknowledgment, however, would not be complete without an expression of my deepest gratitude to my parents, who have always given guidance and understanding, and to my husband, Sam Gordon, whose loving patience and support helped me to complete this.

Cincinnati
April 1980

Chapter I
Introduction

Throughout much of its history, the region of the Levant has played a significant role as a crossroads in trade and communication between the Mediterranean and Asian worlds and as mediator between the two major cultural spheres of Mesopotamia and Egypt. As a result, the Levant has often experienced struggle between Egypt and Mesopotamia or Anatolia for control through political, economic, military, or even cultural domination. During certain periods, however, the Levant attained independence, and, although still the recipient of cultural elements from both the south and the north, sustained its own individual and distinctive culture. Such a period was the Middle Bronze Age when city-states, concentrated on the large tells which were inhabited intermittently from the 3rd to the 1st millennium B.C., flourished, and the influence of Levantine culture was apparent from the Egyptian Delta to southern Anatolia. The inception of this Middle Bronze Age culture in the Levant marks a sharp break from the culture which immediately preceded, especially in the southern Levant, and the beginning of technological and social phenomena which dominated the Levant throughout the rest of the 2nd millennium B.C. The purpose of this study is to investigate the development of this Middle Bronze Age culture, particularly in its formative stages.

Two main methodological objectives underlie this study. The first is an attempt to synthesize textual and artifactual evidence. The Levant of the Middle Bronze Age is a region from which there is minimal extant textual evidence, but which is mentioned in documents from contiguous regions. Such a situation permits the application of methodologies developed independently in the analysis of cultures of prehistoric and historic regions but which are not often utilized in combination. This study therefore presents an example of the synthesis of these different types of evidence and permits an even greater understanding of cultural development than would be achieved through the use of only one type of evidence and methodology. Such a synthesis also encourages the application of these methodologies to different aspects of archaeological inquiry.

The use of these different types of evidence, however, also leads to certain methodological difficulties—primarily caused by the dichotomy between study of the artifactual evidence and study of the human and social organization which produced the artifacts. The limitation imposed by the character of the available evidence (primarily as a result of excavation and publication methods) often restricts the scope of the conclusions which may be drawn from the artifacts themselves. The texts, on the other hand, although another type of artifact, may inform more directly concerning human behavior, although they are not without their problems of reading and translation. As a result, the synthesis of methodologies is not always as complete as one might wish. Nonetheless, it is hoped that this study will demonstrate at least the beginning formulation of such a synthetic approach to the study of Bronze Age archaeology in the Near East.

The second objective of this study is the analysis of different facets of the overall culture of a particular time and place. "We can regard the men in society as nodes in a lattice connected in numerous different ways, each way corresponding to one of the various dimensions of the environment. . . . we may picture the incredible complexity of a cultural system, acting in several dimensions and with several different kinds of connections between its components which are itself of different kinds" (Renfrew 1972: 21-22). Each of the ways in which the components of a culture interact may be termed a subsystem. Several subsystems which are relevant to the study of prehistoric and protohistoric cultures include subsistence, technology, trade and communications, and social and projective or symbolic institutions (Renfrew 1972: 22). The subject of this study—the culture of the

Levant at the beginning of the Middle Bronze Age—involves several developments and radical changes from the preceding culture. The subsystems outlined here and their interactions will be studied in order to attempt to understand these changes and the mechanisms by which they were effected.

Much emphasis will be placed in this study on ceramic evidence and, to a lesser extent, metal artifacts. While the study of a cultural system should include all categories of artifactual evidence (and one might particularly point to such areas as glyptic art and funerary practices which deserve additional attention), pottery is perhaps the most ubiquitous artifact type and has served as the prime chronological and cultural measure in the study of the Levantine Bronze Age. Since it has been the most studied artifact type, ceramics are used here as one of the main tools in the analysis and definition of the Middle Bronze I culture in the Levant.

I.1 Terminology

The first problem which must be considered in attempting to synthesize the archaeological evidence of the early 2nd millennium B.C. from the Levant is that of terminology. The question of the designation of the subdivisions of the Middle Bronze Age is still unresolved and has led to much confusion in the literature. This problem, however, does not concern only the Middle Bronze Age but, in fact, involves the end of the Early Bronze Age and, particularly, the character of the transition between the two periods.

Albright first defined the Middle Bronze I and Middle Bronze II periods as a result of his excavations at Tell Beit Mirsim, with the latter period divided into two phases, "A" and "B." He had previously established an "EB IV" period on the basis of surface pottery from the site of Bab edh-Dhra in Transjordan, but he subsequently divided comparable material from Tell Beit Mirsim and Bethel into the EB III and MB I periods (Dever 1973: 38-39). Wright continued to use the term "EB IV" in the late 1930s, but it later fell out of use with a sequence of EB III-MB I-MB IIA-MB IIB (and MB IIC at some sites) established as the traditional terminology of Albright.

Several other systems have since been proposed, generally reflecting the interpretation that the MB I of the Albright system is an intrusive culture in Palestine and should therefore be linked with neither the Early Bronze Age nor the Middle Bronze Age by terminology. The main proponent of this system has been Kenyon, who adapted Iliffe's use of the term "Intermediate" in her "Intermediate Early Bronze-Middle Bronze" period and thus relabelled the subdivisions of the Middle Bronze Age as MB I and MB II (Kenyon 1971: 567-68). Variations of this system have since been devised by several scholars, for example, Lapp and Kochavi (see Dever 1970: 132-35; 1973:38-41, fig. 1 and n. 6 for bibliography; and Richard 1978: 3-15; see here table 1).

Two lines of research which have appeared in recent years argue for a revision of both these terminological systems. The first of these involves the study of Albright's MB I period and, in particular, the recognition of Albright's original "EB IV" as a closely related precursor of his MB I. Dever has argued for a system which recognizes this relationship, as follows: "The adoption of a single terminology to cover the period under discussion [EB IV-MB I] emphasizes properly that the major breaks are those which set it off from EB III and MB II, and *not* the break between former EB IV and MB I" (Dever 1973: 60; see also Richard 1978: 275-77). In recognition of divisions within this period, Oren proposed two phases (Oren 1973: 58-60), while Dever has proposed three.

The second line of research involves Albright's MB IIA phase and has, through recently excavated evidence and reexamination of previously known material, shown that the major break in fact occurs between the MB I and MB IIA (in Albright's system) and that the MB IIA period should now be recognized as a complete and independent, although formative, phase of the Middle Bronze Age. To quote Dever again, "The point is now almost beyond dispute: the MB I period has few if any links with MB IIA and Middle Bronze proper. . . . the break between the two in terms of their material culture is one of the most abrupt and complete in the entire cultural sequence of Palestine" (Dever 1976: 5).[1] This break is easily observed whether one studies ceramic forms, metal technology, patterns of urbanization, or even burial practices.[2]

The terminology which will be used in this study will therefore take into account the recognition of the EB IV and Middle Bronze periods as proposed by Oren and Dever and will consist of a sequence

Table 1. Proposed Terminologies for the Middle Bronze Age in the Levant (adapted from Dever 1973: fig. 1)

Wright/Albright/Glueck	1930s	EB IV	MB I		MB IIA	MB IIB
Kenyon	1951/56/60	Intermediate EB-MB			MB I	MB II
Tufnell	1958	EB IV	Caliciform		MB I	MB II
Amiran	1960	MB I (A B C) - - - - →			MB IIA	MB IIB
Wright	1961	EB IIIB (EB IV	MB I EB IV)		MB IIA	MB IIB
Albright	1962	MB I	MB I		MB IIA	MB IIB
Albright	1965	EB IIIC/IV	MB I		MB IIA	MB IIB
Lapp	1966	IB I	IB II		MB IIA	MB IIB
Kochavi	1967/69/75	Intermediate Bronze			MB IIA	MB IIB
Mazar	1968	Middle Bronze I			MB IIA	MB IIB
Lapp	1968	EB IVA	EB IVB			
Amiran	1970	EB IV	MB I		MB IIA	MB IIB
Lapp	1970	EB IV	MB I			
Dever	1970/71	EB IV	MB I		MB IIA	MB IIB
Oren	1971/73	EB IVA	EB IVB		MB I	MB II
General Consensus Is./Am.	1972	EB IV	MB I		MB IIA	MB IIB
Dever	1973	EB IVA	EB IVB	EB IVC	MB IIA	MB IIB
Williams	1975	Palestine: Syria: EB III	EB IV MB I		- - - - - - } MB IIA1-2 }	MB IIB-C & MB IIIA-B
Proposed terminology		EB IV (to be divided)			MB I	MB II

of EB IV (undivided since the question of its phasing is not germane to the subject of this discussion and is still controversial), MB I, and MB II, the latter two as approximate equivalents of Albright's MB IIA and MB IIB. It is hoped that the use of this terminology will help in the eventual adoption of a uniform terminology by all archaeologists concerned with the problems of the Levant during the Middle Bronze I period and in a clarification of our concept of this formative phase.

I.2. Topography of the Levant

"Three geographical factors determine the character of this country: its position within the Mediterranean zone, on the crossroads of three continents and two oceans, and on the boundary of the desert and the sown" (Orni and Efrat 1976: xiii). Geography and location are perhaps the explanation of two persistent characteristics of the Levant. First, the region has functioned as an important cross-roads for trade and communication in the Eastern Mediterranean area. Second, its generally favorable geographic and climatic conditions have been conducive to agricultural exploitation, despite the proximity of arid desert regions and the shifting marginal zones between the agricultural and the pastoralist populations.

The main topographic features of the Levant began to form during the Lower Miocene in connection with the Alpine-Himalayan revolution which produced the major east-west mountain chains of Anatolia, southern Europe, and central Asia.[3] In the Levant, the folding was less intense and followed a primarily north-south orientation. This mountain-building phase produced the Amanus, Lebanon, and Anti-Lebanon ranges of the northern Levant and south-central Anatolia as well as the hill region of Judaea, Samaria, and the Upper Galilee in the southern Levant.

At the same time, the Great Rift Valley, which extends from the ᶜAmuq plain, through Syria and Lebanon, through the Huleh, Galilee, Jordan Valley, Dead Sea, and Arabah, and into the Red Sea and, finally, Africa, began to form. The formation of the Rift was accompanied by faulting on both sides which produced east-west oriented valleys, such as the Jezreel, the Zebulon (near Haifa), and Beth-shan valleys. The north-south Rift Valley, which was crossed by several east-west valleys permitting cross-communication, was a major transportation route between Mesopotamia/Anatolia and Egypt/Africa throughout history. The central north-south ranges, including the Lebanon in the north and the hill country in the south, tended to confine north-south transit to either the Rift Valley or the coastal plain, although the central hill country of Judaea and Samaria was used in some periods as another route of communication.

The coastal plain, which narrows progressively towards the north and is almost negligible in Lebanon and Syria, was the other main route of communications, especially in the south. Its unusually straight outline (except for Haifa Bay) limited the number of good harbors. In antiquity, important coastal ports and cities tended to be in the north, for example, at Ugarit, Byblos, Tyre, and Sidon, while in the south it was less common for important cities to be located immediately on the coast. The southern coastal plain was therefore even more important as a means of overland communications, and some of the larger and continuously inhabited sites were located in the plain just east from the coast, for example, Gezer, Beth-shemesh, and Aphek. Megiddo, whose location in the Jezreel Valley was comparable in terms of agricultural potential and facility of communication, displayed a similar continuity of settlement. The coastal plain is also characterized by an accessible supply of fresh water, both as ground water which is often close to the surface and as springs which tend to be located along the western fringe of the plain, such as that at Aphek (Ras el-ᶜAin).

The soils of the coastal plain are also conducive to agriculture: the "red sands" (or hamra soils) of the western plain allow permeability and aeration of the soil as well as plant growth and thus are ideal for citrus cultivation; the alluvial soils composed of terra rossa deposited by the streams from the hill country in the eastern part of the plain are also suitable for agriculture (such as vegetables, fodder, and grain). This terra rossa also makes the hill country itself conducive to farming, although it is easily eroded as the result of wheat cultivation, deforestation, and overgrazing. The hill country also includes rendzina soils which, while less liable to erosion than terra rossa, can support crops such as fruit trees, vine, and grains. The basalt soils of the lower Galilee, when occurring in plateau regions, can also support grain and other field crops. The Biqaᶜ Valley in the northern Levant, which follows the Rift Valley there, is also one of the most agriculturally suitable regions of the Levant.

The preagricultural vegetation of the Levant consisted of subtropical, evergreen and coniferous woodland with tropical shrubs and thorn forest in the south. It probably also included the natural habitats of the wild olive tree, and, coinciding with this, the subsequent cultivation of olives, dates, grapes, and possibly citrus fruits (Butzer 1970: 39-45). The Levant was also the natural habitat of the wild prototypes of emmer, einkorn, and barley.

The modern vegetation pattern, however, has been drastically altered because of erosion, deforestation, and overgrazing and has reached varying degrees of impoverishment, particularly in the more mountainous regions. The typical "Mediterranean agriculture" is restricted in the Levant to the coastal plain and interior valleys, the hill regions depending on altitude, and sections of the Rift Valley, such as the Biqaᶜ, Huleh, and Galilee, where the climate is near-tropical and there are sources of fresh water. Mediterranean farming of the Levant includes three main branches: field crops (primarily wheat), fruit (olives and grapes), and sheep and goat herding (in the marginal zones) which provides milk, meat, and other raw materials.

The mineral resources of the Levant are, however, limited, with the exception of the modern exploitation of the salt, sulfur, phosphates, and other minerals of the Dead Sea and Negev regions (Orni and Efrat 1976: 473-75). Only the copper of the southern Negev seems to have been exploited in antiquity, and the evidence of such mining activity in the prehistoric periods is difficult to date precisely.

The next two chapters will present summaries of the textual and artifactual evidence concerning the Levant during the MB I and its relations with the contiguous areas of Mesopotamia, Anatolia, and

Egypt. Following these, several studies of particular groups of artifact types will be presented in order to demonstrate certain characteristics of the MB I culture and, in particular, the technological innovations of this period and the influence of Anatolian and Mesopotamian cultural elements upon the development of the MB I culture. After a consideration of the chronological placement of the MB I period with particular respect to the comparative chronologies of Egypt and Mesopotamia, patterns of urbanism and settlement during MB I are studied in order to elucidate certain phenomena of the MB I period. These studies should define the innovations in the various cultural subsystems which mark the beginning of the 2nd millennium and thereby add to our understanding of the formation of the Middle Bronze Age culture of the Levant.

NOTES

[1]Even in 1970 Dever had stated this position when he wrote, "it is clear . . . that there is virtually no continuity between the two periods [the MB I and MB IIA in Albright's terms]; there is not, for instance, a single demonstrable ceramic link, and even the bronzes are only distantly related, if at all" (Dever 1970: 144).

[2]An entirely new terminology has recently been proposed by Williams (1975: 840-42). However, the complications inherent in his system are too many to be presented here (but see comments in Chapters III and VII).

[3]For much of the following description, see Orni and Efrat 1976: 3-14; Aharoni 1974: 19-38. See fig. 1 for the main topographic features of the Levant mentioned here.

Chapter II
The Textual Evidence

In this chapter a discussion will be presented of the textual evidence relevant to the study of the Levant during the first quarter of the 2nd millennium B.C. The purpose of this discussion is to provide some of the types of information which are not always discernible in the archaeological record. This information can be used to demonstrate the extent of contact which the Levant had with neighboring areas at that time and to explore the economic and political natures of this contact, its motivation, its mechanisms, and the types of influence which it may have had upon the development of the Middle Bronze Age culture of the Levant. Although this presentation is not intended to be exhaustive of all the available material, it should demonstrate the extensive external relations between the Levant and the regions of Anatolia and Mesopotamia and their economic interdependence.

The paradox of attempting to use textual evidence to elucidate our study of the Levant during this period is that few texts of the early 2nd millennium are so far known from the Levant itself.[1] For contemporary written evidence, it is therefore necessary to rely upon texts and inscriptions from the neighboring areas of Anatolia, Mesopotamia, and Egypt. The "Cappadocian" texts, most of which were found at the site of Kültepe in central Anatolia, document an extensive trade system which operated between Assyria and Anatolia and provide some references to the Levant. Although such references are rare, the Assyrian trade with Anatolia is also studied in order to provide a chronological framework for the early 2nd millennium and as background for connections between the Levant and Anatolia which may be apparent in the material culture. The Mesopotamian textual evidence shows the complex economic and political relationships which existed between Mesopotamia and the Levant, while the Egyptian material is studied in order to evaluate the hypothesis that the Levant was part of an Egyptian hegemony during the Middle Bronze I period.

II.1. The Anatolian Textual Evidence

The Anatolian textual evidence attests to an extensive trade network stretching from Assur to Kaniš and other towns of the central Anatolian plateau during the Old Assyrian period. This trade system, which was administered by Assyrian merchants living in both Assur and Anatolia, was primarily involved in the exchange of certain metals, textiles, and a few other commodities. The "Cappadocian" texts, written in an Old Assyrian dialect, are primarily records of financial transactions, caravan lists, and accounts of traded commodities, but they also contain much indirect evidence concerning economics, social customs, legal structure, and the history and chronology of Assur and the Anatolian kingdoms. Since several studies have presented comprehensive syntheses of the textual and archaeological material,[2] the following summary is limited to information concerning the existence of this trade network, its chronological framework, the commodities which were traded, and the evidence for contact, although minimal, between Mesopotamia and the Levant, and between Anatolia and the Levant, in the Old Assyrian period.

The trade network of the Old Assyrian period is generally considered to have begun in the middle or late 20th century B.C. and lasted, with perhaps a break corresponding to the archaeological gap between Levels II and Ib of the *kārum* area at the site of Kültepe, the source of most of the known "Cappadocian" texts (T. Özgüç 1959: XIX-XXI), until approximately the late 19th century B.C. (Balkan 1955: 41-101; H. Lewy 1971a: 708-15). Several references to Kaniš, Ḫattuša, and Ḫarsamna in the Mari texts from the time of Zimrilim (Balkan 1957: 48-49; *infra*, section II.2) and to Kaniš in texts from Tell al-Rimah (Dalley *et al.* 1976: 31; Dalley 1977: 159) may indicate a need to lengthen the Assyrian Colony period into the 18th century B.C. N. Özgüç has assigned some cylinder seals of the Kültepe repertoire to the time of Samsuiluna, Hammurabi's successor, thus providing a late 18th century B.C. date for the end of the Assyrian colonies (N. Özgüç 1968: 319; see also Buchanan 1969: 758-62). It has also been suggested that the Assyrian colonies were actually established earlier, perhaps even as early as the late 3rd millennium B.C.,[3] although there are no documents extant from Kültepe which attest to such trade. Whatever chronological fluctuations and further refinements are suggested for the "Cappadocian" texts, it is apparent that they correspond to the period of this study—that is, from the middle or late 20th century B.C. to at least the time of Hammurabi.

The picture of the trade between Assyria and central Anatolia as depicted in the texts is perhaps somewhat one-sided because virtually all the texts were found in Anatolia. Assur itself has so far yielded few comparable texts of this period (Larsen 1976: 48-80), although the practice of keeping duplicate copies of letters still enables the reconstruction of both ends of the trade system. The exports from Anatolia consisted primarily of silver and, in smaller quantities, gold. The imports from Assur into Anatolia included various types of textiles, most of which are not clearly identified (see also Dalley 1977: 155-59), and a substance, *annaku*, perhaps to be translated as tin.[4] Other unidentified metals involved in the trade include *aši'u* and *amūtu*; these were dealt with in small quantities and may represent some form of iron (Maxwell-Hyslop 1972: 159-62). Copper was traded on a fairly large scale but only in an internal Anatolian trade network in which both Assyrians and Anatolians participated; it was rarely exported to Assur and apparently only for special purposes (Veenhof 1972: 350). Other commodities, also traded but not of great significance, included wool and wheat.

The geography of sites mentioned in the texts is not directly relevant to this study except in terms of the attempt to identify various routes used by the caravans. Eleven *kārum*-settlements are attested in the texts as located in different Anatolian towns, and ten lesser organizations, *wabartu*-settlements, are also mentioned (Larsen 1976: 236-41). The only colonies so far identified are Kaniš (Kültepe), Ḫattuša (Boğazköy), possibly Am/nkuwa (Alişar—Larsen 1976: 53), and possibly Purušḫaddum (Acemhüyük?—N. Özgüç 1966: 29-30), although much has been written concerning the localization of other places mentioned in the texts (especially Bilgiç 1945-51: 20-32; Garelli 1963: 97-125).

The texts seem to indicate that two routes were available for the part of the journey within Anatolia, but a single route in northern Mesopotamia was commonly used. Most analyses, with some modifications, trace a route from Assur northwards along the Tigris, then west around or through the Jebel Sinjar and across the upper drainage of the Ḫabur and Balikh rivers, then north again to the Euphrates and, finally, via either Maraş or Malatya to the Plain of Elbistan and then west to Kaniš (for variations, see Goetze 1953: 68-70, 72). Another possibility—to follow the Tigris directly north to the Diyarbakir and Ergani Maden region (a possible source of copper), then to Elaziğ, Malatya, and the Plain of Elbistan and Kaniš—has also been suggested (Orlin 1970: 36-43). The possibility of another route, via northern Syria, not directly attested in the texts, will also be discussed later (see fig. 2 for locations of sites and routes mentioned).

The question of whether the "Cappadocian" texts give any indication of an extension of the Assyrian-Anatolian trade system into the region of the Levant is important in the attempt to show contact between these regions in this time period. Indications of such contact do exist, although they are relatively few and brief. The first such indicator is the use of the term, *kaspu amurru* ("Amorite silver"). The term *amurru*, although often translated as "Amorite," may actually mean "western" (for fuller discussion of this term, see Thompson 1974: 67-88). Since, as Lewy explains, a precious metal may be named after the area where it was first produced, traded, or used as currency, it may be suggested that this silver came from or in some way was associated with the "western lands," perhaps the Levant. That such silver was highly valued in both Kaniš and Assur is also implied in the texts (J. Lewy 1961: 69-70).

A second factor is the specific mention of places located in the Levant: (1) Tadmur/Palmyra, a man from which is mentioned in a text (J. Lewy 1961: 69-70), and (2) Ebla (Tell Mardikh, located in the Orontes Valley) whose merchants are mentioned as purchasing copper with *kaspu amurru* (J. Lewy 1961: 70). As previously discussed, 3rd-millennium-B.C. texts excavated at the site of Ebla may also mention the town of Kaniš, thus leading to the possibility that trade between Ebla and Kaniš dates at least to this period (Pettinato 1976: 48).[5] The reference to Ebla in the "Cappadocian" texts documents the direct extension of Assyrian trade into the Levant and leads to speculation that another form of transit trade toward the west was in existence in the Old Assyrian period and was comparable, although perhaps on a smaller scale, to the trade documented in the Mari texts. It also helps to substantiate the hypothesis, presented later in this chapter, that the information from the Mari texts can be used to illustrate the type of trade which may have existed between Mesopotamia and the Levant in the period immediately preceding the date of the Mari texts themselves.

Additional evidence for contact with the Levant in this period is more tenuous but still worthy of mention. First is the presence of people with West Semitic names in Kaniš, as deduced from prosopographic evidence presented by J. Lewy (1961: 34-35, 66; Orlin 1970: 27; see also H. Lewy 1971a: 721), as well as in Assur and in some of the stations along the caravan route. Lewy specifically suggested that "Amorites" may have been involved in the organization and assembling of caravans departing from Assur and that they provided the donkeys used in the caravans. Furthermore, he proposed that these donkeys were of a certain breed imported from the area of Damascus (J. Lewy 1961: 73-74, but this suggestion, in particular, has not been accepted (Veenhof 1972: 1-2, n. 4 and also Larsen 1976: 45-46).

Finally, one might consider the possibility of additional trade routes to the west of those generally suggested. Several towns which have been located in northern Syria (Garelli 1963: 95) are mentioned along with Ebla as places visited by the Assyrian merchants. Since Ebla has been identified, a trade route leading from the Orontes region directly north through the ᶜAmuq Valley, past Sakcegözü, and then to Maraş should also be considered. The existence of early 2nd-millennium-B.C. occupation in this region at Sakcegözü has been substantiated (Waechter, Gögüs, and Seton Williams 1951: 193-201), and the route through the ᶜAmuq plain would have been easily accessible (Seton Williams 1954: 131-33). Furthermore, one is tempted to hypothesize a route from Cilicia through the Cilician Gates to Kaniš and the central Anatolian plateau. Such a route is marked by sites with distinctive early 2nd-millennium-B.C. pottery (see Chapter IV.2), as is also the pass through the Anti-Taurus near Bahçe linking the ᶜAmuq with the Tarsus/Adana region. There is, however, no textual evidence for this second route, although some of the place-names mentioned in these texts have been located in the southern part of the central Anatolian plateau. In addition, Garelli suggested that Wahšušana, which he located in the southwestern part of the plateau region, may have been the center of commerce between Kaniš and Syria via the Cilician Gates (Garelli 1963: 125).

The "Cappadocian" texts contain a wealth of information concerning the extensive trade system between Mesopotamia and Anatolia as well as a small amount of information concerning direct contacts from Mesopotamia and Anatolia to the Levant during the Assyrian Colony period. The latter information, while meager, does show that this contact did exist, and thus it opens the possibility that influences from Mesopotamia and/or Anatolia reached the Levant from almost the beginning of the 2nd millenium B.C.

II.2 Textual Evidence from Mesopotamia

The written evidence from Mesopotamia which concerns contact with the Levant will now be summarized in order to demonstrate from contemporary sources that such contact existed and that it was not haphazard but organized with a specific economic and sometimes political purpose. This discussion will be restricted, however, by a few considerations. First, it makes no pretense to cover all the textual evidence available from Mesopotamia, since this is not necessary for the purposes of the present study. Second, no attempt is made to enter into the various controversies concerning specific problems of Mesopotamian geography in the Old Babylonian period, and only those ancient place names whose locations are generally accepted will be considered. Third, although not all the texts discussed date from the exact time period of this study, it is usually possible to do a limited amount of cautious extrapolation from different periods.

The fourth limitation of this discussion is that primary reliance will be placed on evidence relating to the economic interaction between Mesopotamia and the west. The political relationships, which were more complex and are now more fully synthesized by the various editors of the individual texts and by Mesopotamian historians (see Kupper 1973: 1-41 and H. Lewy 1971b: 752-62), will only enter the discussion insofar as they influenced trade and economic relations between Mesopotamia and the Levant.

The types of textual sources available will first be discussed, and the more relevant of these will be considered later in the context of the types of information which may be gleaned from them. The most important source of literary evidence is the Mari archives which contain the correspondence of the rulers of Mari with their fellow rulers, servants, or political dependents. These documents[6] span the reigns of three kings and cover a wide range of subjects, including politics, administration, trade, economics, and law.

Three additional archives are also of interest, although they do not provide as much information concerning contacts with the west. The first of these to be found was the group of tablets from Chagar Bazar (Gadd 1937: 178-85; 1940: 22-26) which date from a period in which Chagar Bazar was under the political rule of Iasmaḫ-Adad of Mari. The texts are primarily lists of names and allowances, and most of the geographical connections indicated are with the east. Iamḫad, however, is mentioned twice, showing that some contact with the west did exist.

The second archive consists of two groups of tablets from the site of Tell Shemshara, located in the northeastern section of the Dokan plateau and now identified as ancient Šušarra (Ingholt 1957: 214-15; Laessøe 1957: 216-18; 1959a; 1959b: 85-94; 1960: 12-19; and 1965: 189-96). The earlier group has been assigned to the time of Šamši-Adad I, while the second group should belong to the latter part of the rule of Hammurabi (or even later) since Babylonian influence or control seems to be indicated. The first group consists primarily of letters concerning local political developments but also includes business and economic texts (Laessøe 1959a: 67-71), some of which concern the use of copper and tin. The main interest of the Shemshara tablets here, however, is that the contrasts between the political background of the two sets of texts (Laessøe 1960: 15) show that the political developments in the main government centers of Assyria and Babylon were reflected at the provincial level as well.

The last group of texts comes from the site of Tell al-Rimah (Oates 1968: 136-38; Page 1968: 87-97; Dalley *et al.* 1976), located in the northern plain of Iraq and to be identified with the town of Karana or located within the state of Karana, which is mentioned in the Mari texts (Oates 1970: 5-6; Dalley *et al.* 1976: 34-36; Dalley 1977: 157, n. 14). The majority of these texts have been dated to the Old Babylonian period (Dalley *et al.* 1976), and the prosperity of this site has been associated by the excavator with the Assyrian-Cappadocian trade which may have passed through this region (Oates 1965: 79). These texts also concentrate on administrative and economic (especially agricultural) matters. Contact with Mari is attested in the Tell al-Rimah texts, and Kaniš appears in probably two texts (Dalley *et al.* 1976; text nos. 33:16 and 122:4(?), 16), once apparently in connection with the textile trade between Assur and Kaniš.

The second type of textual evidence consists of descriptions of the conquest of western lands by Mesopotamian rulers, namely Sargon of Akkad, Iaḫdunlim, Šamši-Adad, and possibly Zimrilim. Sargon claims to have had dominion from the "Upper Sea" (the Mediterranean) to the "Lower Sea" (the Persian Gulf) and may also have conducted a major campaign in Anatolia (Malamat 1965: 365-67; Güterbock 1964: 1-6; Mellink 1963: 101-15 and H. Lewy 1971a: 707). The description of Iaḫdunlim's conquest of the Lebanon-Amanus region is contained within a foundation inscription found in the Šamaš temple at Mari (Dossin 1955: 1-28; Malamat 1965: 367-70) and is especially significant since it seems to imply some economic motivation for his expedition. A building inscription of Šamši-Adad concerning his temple of Enlil in Assur also implies at least some temporary control of the Lebanon area (Malamat 1965: 370-71; Munn-Rankin 1956: 81).

Finally, the "itinerary" texts describe the specific geographical routes used. One of these itineraries is known from two copies in the Oriental Museum of the University of Illinois, Urbana, and from a more complete version of the "outbound" portion of the journey in the Yale Babylonian Collection (Goetze 1953: 51-72; Hallo 1964: 57-88; Leemans 1968: 210-13; and Goetze 1964: 114-19). These texts have been variously dated, most recently by Hallo and Leemans to the reign of Rim-Sin of Larsa (1822-1763 B.C.). This itinerary describes a round-trip journey from Larsa to Emar covering the Upper Mesopotamian region and the drainage areas of the Balikh and Ḫabur rivers and also mentions possible routes from Mesopotamia to central Anatolia (Goetze 1953: 60-70) and to the Levant (Hallo 1964: fig. 6). Another type of itinerary, referred to as the "dream book route," is contained within texts of the Assyrian Dream-Book, the relevant version of which is dated to the Middle Babylonian (Kassite) period but may relate to the period of the Mari correspondence. This route probably reflects commonly used routes, since, as Oppenheim (1956: 260) writes: "It stands to reason that the names of cities and countries to which a person sees himself travel in his dreams may shed a revealing light on the geographical horizon of the period."

The list of specific towns which are mentioned in the texts and whose identification with known archaeological sites is accepted demonstrates the geographical extent of Mesopotamian contact with the Levant. Beginning with Upper Mesopotamia, we find Harran (Prag 1970: 72-73, 76), Tuttul (although this identification is less certain, Goetze 1953: 60; 1964: 118-19), and Emar mentioned in the Larsa-to-Emar itinerary (Birot 1964: 41, for discussion of the location of Emar in the region of Eski-Meskene, presumably within the kingdom of Aleppo). Harran is also mentioned in the Tell al-Rimah texts (Page 1968: 95) and in the Mari texts (*ARMT* VII, 219), while Emar appears in the Assyrian Dream-Book (Oppenheim 1956: 260) and in the Mari archives (*ARMT* II, 134; XII, 747; XIII, 35; and XIV, 27, 33 and 91). Carchemish, located on the upper Euphrates, appears several times in the Mari archives (for example, *ARMT* XIV, 31, 52 and 86), and two of its kings, Aplaḫanda and Iatar-Ami, are also well known (see fig. 3 for these and the following mentioned places). A "man of Carchemish" is also mentioned as the recipient of a pair of shoes in a Mari tablet belonging to a group of texts which are dated before the reign of Iaḫdunlim (*ARMT* XIX, 299; for the date of these texts, see the Introduction, pp. 7 and 10).

The kingdom of Iamḫad and its capital, Aleppo, appear quite frequently. Two of its rulers, Iarimlim and Hammuraḫi, are also mentioned as are often products which are called "Iamḫadian." In addition to the many references in the Mari archives (for example, *ARMT* XIV, 30, 33, 55, 65, 92; XVIII, 16), Iamḫad is also mentioned in the Chagar Bazar texts (Gadd 1940: 43) and in the Assyrian Dream-Book itinerary. The other important western principality which appears almost as frequently in the Mari archives (for example, *ARMT* XIV, 65, 69; XVIII, 61) and is also in the Assyrian Dream-Book is Qatanum, with its rulers Iški-Adad and Amutpiel. The identifications of Qatanum with the site of Qatna-Mishrife and of Iamḫad with Aleppo were both established by Dossin (1939c: 46-54). Qatna, in particular, had extensive political and military connections with Mari during the period of the Assyrian interregnum, while Zimrilim took refuge in the court of Aleppo. It is interesting to compare the frequency of references to Qatna in the correspondence of Šamši-Adad and Iasmaḫ-Adad to that of references to Iamḫad in the letters of Zimrilim—a factor which is the obvious result of the political alliances of the respective eras.

The site of Ebla is apparently not mentioned in any of the published Mari texts (Edzard 1976: 9-13) which may accord with the suggestion of Matthiae (1976: 97) that, by the Mari period, Ebla had been eclipsed by the kingdom of Aleppo. There is, however, a reference in a text dated to the 18th year of Išbi-Erra (2017-1985 B.C.), founder of the First Dynasty of Isin, to the men of Ebla and Mari (Crawford 1954: 60, pl. LXXI, No. 417: 2-3). This reference may be an additional indication of contact between Mesopotamia and the west during the time of the Assyrian Colony period.

The southwestern limit of geographical references is the town of Hazor located in the Upper Galilee. In addition to the Dream-Book reference, Hazor is mentioned five times in the published Mari texts—twice in connection with trade and the other times in connection with what seem to be diplomatic missions. One text (*ARMT* VI, 23) is particularly tantalizing since the list, which includes Iamḫad, Qatna, and Hazor, is in geographical order but is incomplete, so that one may assume that another town south of Hazor (possibly Megiddo?) was mentioned. A sixth Mari letter, not published in the *ARMT* series but referred to by Malamat (1970: 165), is written by Šamši-Adad to his son Iasmaḫ-Adad and refers to diplomatic messengers from Qatna and Hazor. Yet another Mari text, A. 1270 (Dossin 1970: 97-106; Malamat 1970: 168-69; 1971: 31-38), includes a reference to Hazor and its king, Ibni-Adad, Laiš and its king, Waritaldu (which, according to Malamat [1971: 35-36], should be identified as a Hurrian name), and Muzunnum (located by Malamat in the Hauran, Bashan, or Damascus region). Laiš has been identified with the site of Tel Dan (Malamat 1971: 35-36), located approximately 30 km. north of Hazor.

This same Mari text (A. 1270) also contains two references to Ugarit in connection with the tin trade—the second time mentioning tin consignments to three private individuals at Ugarit, including the "Caphtorite," the "Carian" and the "dragoman" (or interpreter). This text is therefore important not only for its possible references to Crete and Caria (in southwestern Anatolia), but also for the clear indication that Ugarit was serving as a western trade emporium for the exchange of goods between east and west, that is, Mesopotamia and the Aegean-Anatolian world (see Heltzer 1978 for discussion of the role of Ugarit in the trade of the second half of the 2nd millennium B.C.). This role is parallelled by that of Mari as an exchange center between the east (Susa, Elam, and eastern Mesopotamia) and the western, coastal Mediterranean lands. Byblos is also recorded several times in connection with diplomatic messengers and with clothing (Dossin 1939a: 111, and in an unpublished text, S. 143, no. 36, see *ARMT* XVIII, p. 112, n. 10, and p. 128). Dossin mentions four references to Cypriote copper (that is, copper from "Alašiya") and several to items described as "Caphtorite," including a vase, a statue, and some other, unidentified object sent by Zimrilim to Hammurabi in Babylon (Dossin 1939a: 111-12). These references are, however, difficult to evaluate since the texts themselves are not fully published.

Additional references to geographical locations in this region begin to raise more problems, either with identifications or with text readings. The identification of ᵓApum, which appears in the Mari texts (for example, *ARMT* XIV, 102, 125), with the land of Damascus (Albright 1941b: 35) might permit the reconstruction of an inland, in addition to the coastal, trade route via the Damascus region to Hazor and the Jordan Valley, if Muzunnum is to be located in this area. The question of the location of the "land of Amurru" (mentioned in the Mari texts) will not be raised here (Chapter II.1 *supra*; Malamat 1960: 16-17), nor the various linguistic and geographical problems associated with the Amorites and the various nomadic tribes which figure in the Mari archives (see Thompson 1974: 58-88).

The region of northern Syria, specifically the Lebanon and Amanus Mountains, is alluded to in the inscriptions of Iaḫdunlim and Šamši-Adad. The Iaḫdunlim inscription refers to "the Cedar and Boxwood Mountain, the great mountains," which are probably to be identified with mountains of the Lebanon or Amanus ranges or both (Malamat 1965: 368). The inscription of Šamši-Adad specifically refers to the "land of Lebanon on the shore of the Great Sea," the usual name for the Mediterranean in later texts. A fragment of the Assyrian Dream-Book also mentions "Laban" which Oppenheim, however, hesitates to identify with Mount Lebanon (Oppenheim 1956: 268, n. 36). Malamat, however, accepts the identification since he also reads "Opis" (in the next line) as referring to ᵓApum or Damascus (Malamat 1960: 16, n. 19; see also Albright 1941b: 35).

Finally, there are some interesting references to Anatolian sites in the Mari texts (see *ARMT* VII, Commentary, p. 333), while Kaniš is also mentioned in the Tell al-Rimah tablets (Dalley *et al.* 1976: text nos. 33 and 122; Dalley 1977: 159). Only one of the Mari letters is fully published (Dossin 1939b: 70-72). This letter, assigned to the time of Zimrilim on the basis of the orthography, was probably written by a dependent ruler either in northern Mesopotamia or in the vicinity of the route from Mari to Anatolia. This ruler would seem to have acted as an intermediary in the trade between Mari and Anatolia since he writes: ". . . all the magnificent things which can be brought to me from Kaniš, from Ḫarsamnâ, and from Ḫattuša, objects of art, works, precious objects . . . I will have taken to you" (lines 7-11). It is interesting to note the form of Ḫattuša which presumably represents the proto-Hittite form, Ḫattuš, rather than the Hittite form, Ḫattušaš (Dossin 1939b: 74; Bittel 1970: 18).

The mention of Kaniš here is matched by another reference to it in an incompletely published Mari text (Dossin 1939b: 73-74; see also Dossin 1938: 115), also assigned to Zimrilim. In this text, a caravan of 50 donkeys "and their men" set out from the town of Aškur-Adad, king of Karana (see Dalley *et al.* 1976: 32-33), in the direction of Kaniš. Since the town of Karana is probably to be identified with the site of Tell al-Rimah, this reference provides direct evidence for a route from northern Mesopotamia to central Anatolia during the Mari period. Finally, Ḫarsamna, which is known from later Hittite documents and was presumably located somewhere between Kaniš and Ḫattuša, is also mentioned in another Mari text—a letter to Zimrilim from his ambassador to Carchemish responding to Zimrilim's request for white horses. Aplaḫanda replies that he had none then to send, but "while waiting, I shall have sent to him some white ḫarsamnite horses" (Dossin 1939b: 75). These texts therefore indicate that horses and various exotic objects were imported from Anatolia into Mesopotamia in the time of Zimrilim. Such trade is, of course, extensively attested in the earlier "Cappadocian" texts, but it is significant to note that both Kaniš and Ḫattuša were still actively trading in the time of Zimrilim, and, as previously discussed (Chapter II.1), this provides a *terminus post quem* for the end of the *kārum* Ib period.

Information concerning the types of contact between Mesopotamia and these western areas shows that this contact was primarily of two kinds—political and economic, the latter usually related to the functions of trade. These different types of contact will be discussed in order to demonstrate the political and, in particular, the economic interdependence of these regions, with emphasis upon the evidence for movements of people and objects between these regions.

Travel by diplomatic missions and messengers between the various kingdoms demonstrates the mobility of individuals, while foreigners were also often required to dwell in different cities for an extended period of time. Diplomatic protocol apparently even demanded that the host country provide an escort for a messenger returning home (for example, *ARMT* V, 58 and 80; Munn-Rankin 1956: 99-108). As a possible result of this or simply because it was safer or easier to do so, groups of messengers from various states often travelled together. An interesting example of this is *ARMT* XII, 747, in which a group of men (possibly envoys or even artisans) from various cities as far apart as Hazor, Iamḫad, Carchemish, Emar, Elaḫut, and Ešnunna stay together in a special quarter of the palace at Mari and are apportioned special commodities (*ARMT* XII, pp. 4-5; Malamat 1970: 165; Sasson 1968: 53). Additional sites which are mentioned in this context in the correspondence of Baḫdilim include Babylon, Ekallatum, Qatna, Arrapḫa, and Karana and attest to direct travel between such far-distant cities as even Hazor and Babylon (*ARMT* VI, 14, 15, 19, 23, and 78; see also the discussion of various travellers and their provisions in Birot 1964: 36-37).

The trade or exchange of goods and services attested in the textual evidence may be grouped as follows: (1) the exchange of royal gifts; (2) goods which have either arrived at Mari or are being dispatched from there, which, it may be assumed, imply organized trade in the sense of an exchange of commodities under the supervision of designated individuals or "merchants"; (3) the employment of individual artists or artisans from foreign countries to perform specific tasks requiring special skills; although this is not an exchange of commodities, the exchange of services and labor may be considered as a form of trade, especially since it would have contributed to contact between individuals from different towns.

The exchange of gifts between rulers of different kingdoms was related to the general political situation and was, to some extent, regulated by the demands of diplomatic etiquette (Munn-Rankin 1956: 96-99; also *ARMT* XVIII, p. 128; cf. North 1975: 490-91). Such exchange is also usually considered to be a form of trade since the giving of gifts often went in both directions, thus constituting an "exchange" of goods. The gifts were often in such large quantities that they were apparently intended not only for the ruler's consumption, but probably also for division among royal retainers, dependents, and perhaps other individuals. An interesting series of letters concerning this exchange of gifts was written by Aplaḫanda, the king of Carchemish, to Iasmaḫ-Adad and includes the exchange of wine, food, honey, and clothing (*ARMT* V, 5, 6, and 13). From the archaeological viewpoint, it is interesting to note that in one letter alone (*ARMT* V, 13) the movement of 100 jars (presumably storage jars) of wine and honey from Carchemish to Mari is attested.

The hiring of foreign artisans is exemplified by the following: *ARMT* XIII, 42: a servant of Zimrilim discusses the payment of a carpenter from Iamḫad, who has produced a *lamassu*; *ARMT* I, 46: Sasson (1968: 52) interprets this text as possibly indicating that a Mari citizen living or employed in Qatna produced a silver bracelet, although Dossin's translation differs; *ARMT* I, 83: Šamši-Adad tells Iasmaḫ-Adad to send singers, whom Aplaḫanda had requested, to Carchemish (see also Sasson 1968: 53); *ARMT* XII, 747: Sasson (1968: 53) interprets this text as referring to skilled workers living in special quarters in Mari. Although singers and artisans are also mentioned as recipients in the text, it might be argued that such a diverse list recalls the lists of messengers previously discussed (cf. Birot *ARMT* XII, pp. 4-5).

The next point to be considered concerns the types of goods which were exchanged between Mesopotamia and the west (see table 3, *infra*). This trade seems to have involved at least the following items: various types of food, clothing, wood, precious stones, and metals (presumably both the raw materials and, in some cases, the manufactured objects).

(1) Food: (a) Wine: The letters from Aplaḫanda to Iasmaḫ-Adad already discussed above show that wine was sent from Carchemish to Mari, in large quantities and usually as a royal gift. This may indicate either that Mari usually imported its wine from the west or that the Carchemish wine was considered to be of special value. Wine, when

mentioned in the texts, is often implied to have been imported from elsewhere, presumably the west, as in *ARMT* VII, 256. In *ARMT* XIII, 126, Kibri-Dagan, the governor of Terqa, mentions the shipment of wine to Atamrun in the boats of men from Emar (see also Kupper 1964: 115). *ARMT* VII, 238, lists 100 jars of wine as sent by Iarimlim and approximately 100 sent from elsewhere, the name of which is not preserved. In *ARMT* IX, 33, Hammurabi of Aleppo is recorded as having sent wine "for the cellar" and, finally, in *ARMT* IX, 17, is a record of "2[9]3 (?) jars of wi[ne] which, from Iatar-Ami, Darii̯[a] . . . (?) has broug[ht.]" Although this might also sound like another royal gift, because of the quantity involved and because the transaction was handled by a merchant previously known (*ARMT* VIII, 80) to have been involved in dealings with both wine and wood, it may be implied that this was also a commercial transaction (see *ARMT* IX, p. 271).

(b) Oil: Oil, sometimes specified as olive oil, also seems to have been imported from the west. Whether this was used for consumption or for other purposes is not clear. *ARMT* IX, 9, mentions "277 j[ars of oil (?)] were received . . . oil which Nur-Sin sent from Alaḫtum," a place which has been identified as part of the Aleppo kingdom; furthermore, Nur-Sin, the individual responsible for the delivery of the oil, seems to be known as Zimrilim's representative in Aleppo (*ARMT* IX, p. 269). In *ARMT* IX, 6, a quantity of oil is imported apparently from a great distance under the auspices of Kutkutum, who seems to have been either a merchant or caravan chief, although the source of the oil is not specified (*ARMT* IX, p. 268). *ARMT* VII, 238, lists various commodities sent from the different western kingdoms, including perhaps 18 jars of olive oil sent by Iarimlim and probably another 18 sent from someone whose name has not been preserved. *ARMT* VII, 256, also lists the receipt of 46 jars of olive oil from an unspecified place, while in *ARMT* VII, 257, Aplaḫanda again sends ten jars of oil.

(c) Honey: The other frequently mentioned food commodity is honey which is sent, for example, by Aplaḫanda (*ARMT* VII, 257—ten jars) and by Iarimlim (*ARMT* VII, 238—ten jars).

(d) Grain: An interesting letter from Iasim-Sumu to Zimrilim (*ARMT* XIII, 35) explains that there is an insufficient number of boats to transport the grain harvest from Emar to Mari, and another letter from Iaqqim-Adad (*ARMT* XIV, 33) mentions boats which were sent to Emar to take grain. These indications of the importation of grain to Mari may be significant since grain is generally a staple, as opposed to the other goods discussed above which might be considered as luxuries (for a discussion of shipments by boat along the Euphrates, see Burke 1964: 68-100).

(2) Clothing: Various types of clothing, for which the exact meaning is usually unknown, are sent from different rulers to Mari, while garments qualified by toponymics, such as Iamḫadian or Byblite, are also mentioned. It is unclear whether this indicates a garment from that city, one manufactured of material from that city, or simply one in the fashion or style of that city. This problem of interpretation would relate to the suggestion that Mesopotamia may have imported raw materials, manufactured the item and then reexported the finished product. Examples of such references may be found in: *ARMT* VII, 238 and 251, *ARMT* IX, 102, and *ARMT* XVIII, 12 and 41. In all these cases, garments are sent from Aplaḫanda or Iarimlim to Mari, while Iarimlim even sends garments which are designated as of a different origin (*ARMT* XVIII, p. 128). In *ARMT* I, 54, the export of garments from Mari to Qatna is also recorded.

(3) Woods: The import of woods from the west is attested in a letter from Šamši-Adad to Iasmaḫ-Adad (*ARMT* I, 7) and in the inscription of Iaḫdunlim which describes his conquest of the Lebanon and Amanus regions. In the Mari letter, Šamši-Adad discusses various types of wood brought from Qatna (lines 4-14): "The palms, the cypress, and the myrtle wood which were brought from Qatanum, are deposited at Subrum. Send to Subrum Mašiya and the men with him and they may divide into three the palms, the cypress, and the myrtle wood. Send a third of the palms, the cypress, and the myrtle wood to Ekallatum, a third to Nineveh, a third to Šubat-Enlil." This text not only shows the importation of these woods from the west but also demonstrates Mari's role as a transit station for products passing from west to east and the interdependence which extended from eastern Mesopotamia to the Mediterranean coast.

Iaḫdunlim, in his description of the Lebanon region, claims: "To the Cedar and Boxwood Mountain, the great mountains, he [Iaḫdunlim] penetrated, and boxwood, cedar, cypress, and *elammakam*[7] trees, these trees he cut down. He stripped (the forest) bare, established his name, and made known his might" (Malamat 1965: 367). Although there has been some discussion regarding the translation of the names of the trees, there is no doubt that one of the major purposes of the expedition was the exploitation of the plentiful wood resources of the Lebanon-Amanus region. Iaḫdunlim's further claim to have imposed a "permanent tax" upon these lands may imply that this exploitation continued for at least part of his reign. Malamat, in fact, gives even greater emphasis to the economic aspects of Iaḫdunlim's campaign and writes: ". . . it seems most probable . . . that Iaḫdunlim really did carry out an extensive military campaign in the Mediterranean coastlands but that this expedition must be viewed as an ephemeral episode which did not lead to a permanent subjugation of the coastal region but, rather, opened up the coast for economic activity" (Malamat 1965: 370).

(4) Precious Materials: Various precious materials are mentioned in the Mari texts, although none of these references specifically relate to contact between Mari and the west. Because of the limited natural resources of Mesopotamia, however, it may be assumed that these materials were imported into Mesopotamia and, in some cases, possibly reexported. This is yet another example of the role of Mari as a transit trade center. Among the precious materials mentioned are silver (*ARMT* VII, 10) and gold in various forms (*ARMT* VII, 4 and 10), alabaster and rock-crystal (*ARMT* VII, 4 and 247). In *ARMT* I, 58, Šamši-Adad writes to Iasmaḫ-Adad that an individual, Sin-idinnam, should be sent to him with the gold and silver which were brought from Qatna. There are at least two references to lapis lazuli which are significant because Afghanistan may have been the only source of lapis lazuli in the Near East (Herrmann 1968: 21-22). In *ARMT* IX, 279, 102 beads of lapis lazuli are mentioned, while in *ARMT* IX, 254, 1/3 mina and three shekels of lapis and then 15 shekels of lapis are brought from Ešnunna—a logical route if the lapis is imported from the east.

(5) Vessels: The exchange of vessels, both as containers for oil, wine, and honey (as previously discussed) and for their own sake, is frequently recorded. It may perhaps be assumed that when vessels or jars (*karpatu*) were used as storage containers and therefore not traded for their own value, they were probably the typical ceramic storage jars used for transport of commodities (*ARMT* VII, Commentary, p. 314). However, vessels of less common materials are also listed in the texts (although not specifically mentioned as exchange items) and would have been valued because of the metal from which they were made and the artistry involved in their production (*ARMT* VII, 218, 219, 237, 239, and 265). Rhyta of silver and bronze in the form of the heads of various animals (*ARMT* VII, 218, 219, and 239) are compared by Bottéro with the excavated rhyta from Anatolia (Commentary, pp. 309-13).

(6) Metals: The discussion of the trade in metals is very complex and raises many questions of translation and interpretation (see Chapter VI.2). Those metals mentioned include copper, iron, tin (*annaku*: see Chapter II.1 and Chapter VI.2; also Laessøe 1959b: 83-84, 91-94; Leemans 1968: 201-15; Muhly 1973: 243-44; and Heltzer 1978: 108-11) and bronze. Bronze is generally only mentioned as a material from which other objects are made (*ARMT* VII, 119, 194, 219, 238, and 249; Commentary, p. 300). Iron is mentioned in texts of *ARMT* VII (Nos. 244 and 247), once in the earlier texts of the *šakkanakku* period, perhaps contemporary with the Third Dynasty of Ur (*ARMT* XIX, 337), and possibly in *ARMT* V, 5, in which Aplaḫanda sends Iasmaḫ-Adad a bracelet of iron. Bottéro suggests on the basis of this last reference and one in the Alalakh texts that iron may have been more common in the west than in Mesopotamia (*ARMT* VII, Commentary, p. 301). The sources of copper are not generally discussed, although there are references to "Copper of the Mountain" (*ARMT* VII, 135) without any further localization. This is sometimes, however, assumed to refer to a mountain range in northern Syria or southern Anatolia (the Taurus or Amanus, see Sasson 1966: 168-69). There are also references to Cypriote copper (for further discussion of the relations between Syria and Cyprus in the context of this copper trade, see Sasson 1966: 168-70).

Finally, and perhaps of most interest, is the problem of the trade in tin (or *annaku*) which is well attested in several of the Mari letters (*ARMT* VII, 86, 87, 88, 233, and 236; A. 1270), a letter from the Shemshara archives (Laessøe 1959b: 83-94) and a group of texts referring to the Babylonian tin trade (Leemans 1968: 201-10). There is considerable uncertainty concerning the source of tin, although it may have been located somewhere to the east of Mesopotamia—Elam, Iran, and points further east have been suggested (see Chapter VI.2).

Whatever the source of the tin, the Mari texts give much information concerning its reexport from Mari to the west, again demonstrating Mari's role as a transit trade center. Several texts record western destinations for tin: *ARMT* VII, 86 lists: 50 minas for Iarimlim and 10 minas for other men from Iamḫad, 1 talent for Aplaḫanda and 2 1/2 minas for another man from Carchemish; No. 87 shows 50 minas for Iarimlim and 50 minas for Amutpiel. No. 88 records 1 talent 53 2/3 minas exchanged for 11 minas and an uncertain number of shekels of silver (?) to be sent to Iamḫad and Qatna; No. 233 lists 19 minas, 2 shekels of tin for Iarimlim and, later, another 3 bars of tin also for Iarimlim; No. 236 lists 10 minas for Hazor and 19 minas, 2 shekels for Iarimlim; A. 1270 lists 16 talents, 10 minas of tin at Mari, some apparently sent by Hammurabi of Babylon and by Šeplarpak of Susa; 20 minas are sent to two individuals at Ugarit, a large quantity to various members of the royal family in Aleppo, 10 minas to Muzunnum, 8 1/3 minas to Waritaldu, king of Laiš, 30 minas to Ibni-Adad, king of Hazor, 20 minas to Amutpiel of Qatna, and unknown amounts to the Caphtorite, the Carian, and the "dragoman" at Ugarit. There was obviously a regularized export of tin to the west from Mari, thus completing the picture of commercial interdependence between Mesopotamia and the west. Although the balance of trade seems weighted towards more imports into Mesopotamia (foods, cloth, woods, and probably some metals), Mesopotamia was at least able to reexport the relatively valuable and quite necessary tin to the west (see also the comments of Crawford 1973: 232-41).

Finally, the last problem to be considered on the basis of this textual evidence concerns the possible routes utilized to carry out this trade. The texts seem to indicate that there were two principal routes between Mesopotamia and the west (see fig. 3). The first of these, called the "dream book route," is described in the Assyrian Dream-Book and follows the logical geographical order of Sippar, Rapiqum, Mari, Emar, Aleppo, Qatna, and Hazor (Oppenheim 1956: 260). This route may also have been advisable in order to avoid the desert west and south of Mari, even when travelling from Mesopotamia directly west to the Mediterranean coast.

The second route, however, ignores this principle and seems to have gone direct from Mari (or Terqa) across the desert to Qatna. The route is attested in *ARMT* I, 66, when Šamši-Adad writes to Iasmaḫ-Adad: "I am sending to you a caravan which brings the oracle to Qatanum. Do not seize this caravan . . . and write to Terqa that they should give them what is needed [referred to by Albright 1940b: 25, as "skin-bottles"] for ten days, which permits them to reach Qatanum." The omission of any mention of intermediary towns, and, as Albright points out, the emphasis which Šamši-Adad puts on the need to supply the caravan with provisions sufficient until it reaches Qatna, indicates that the route from Mari to Qatna was direct and avoided Aleppo. It might be possible to ascribe the use of the desert route, which was evidently more difficult and dangerous, to either a need for haste or a lack of friendly relations between Aleppo and Mari during the Assyrian interregnum, although there were still extensive trade relations between the two even at this time.

That the less obvious route (or longer or more difficult route) might be chosen due to political considerations (or other reasons not necessarily demonstrated in the texts) is also shown in the choice of route taken by the expedition described in the Larsa to Emar itinerary. It would have been more direct and presumably easier for the expedition to have followed the Euphrates River valley direct to Emar, rather than crossing to the Tigris at Mankisum and then having to cut due west across the Ḫabur and Balikh rivers and then south again to Emar (Hallo 1964: 86, fig. 6). Hallo attributes this detour to the existence of an independent and presumably hostile kingdom at Mari (for example, during the reigns of either Iaḫdunlim or Zimrilim) and writes that this dating of the text "in fact suggests as a motive for the mission the assertion of Babylonian control over an alternate route to Aleppo and the West (and to Anatolia) in the face of a blockade of the Euphrates by an independent Mari" (Hallo 1964: 86). Regardless of the exact date and attribution of the text, it is clear that the expedition chose a longer and perhaps more difficult route, presumably as the result of political and/or economic considerations.

Thus, in summary, we can see that there was communication between Mesopotamia and the west, and even between the west and points further east, such as Elam, for both diplomatic and economic purposes (see table 3). That the precise routes followed or specific areas which had trade connections at any particular time might be subject to various political pressures has also been demonstrated. However, this symbiotic relationship, in which the western principalities provided some of the natural resources which Mesopotamia lacked, while Mesopotamia acted as the center for the

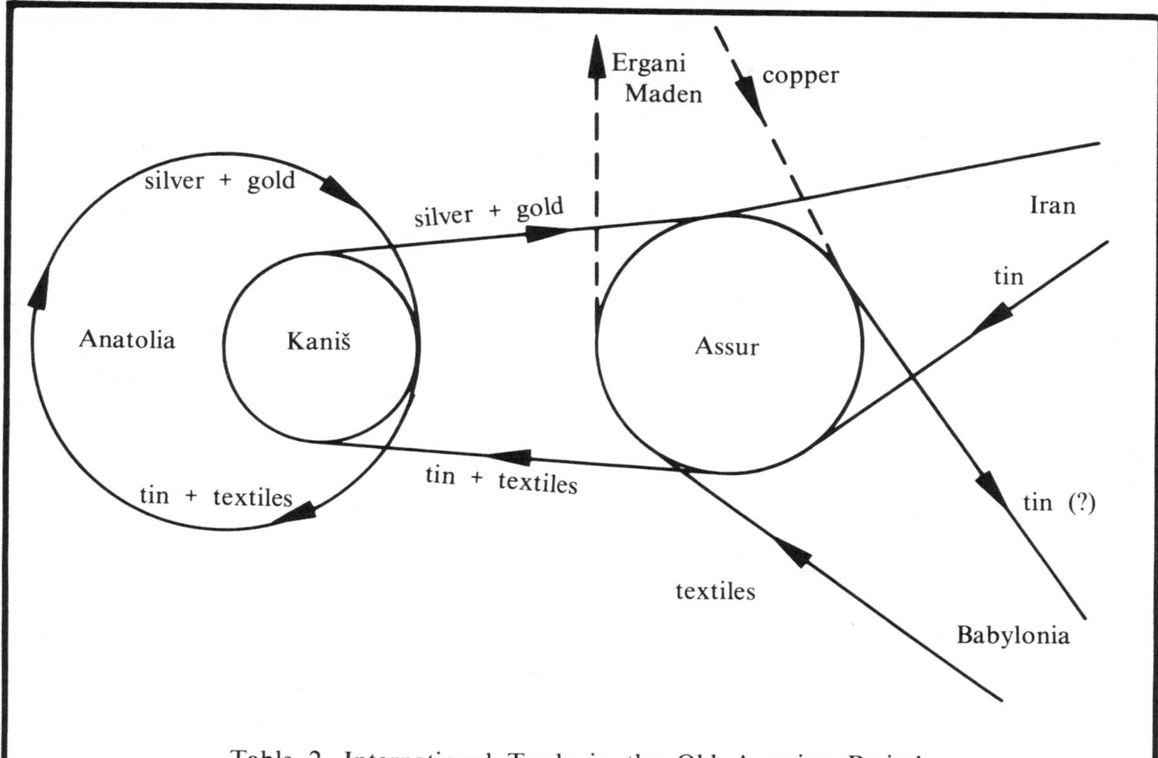

Table 2. International Trade in the Old Assyrian Period.
(adapted from Larsen 1967: 172)

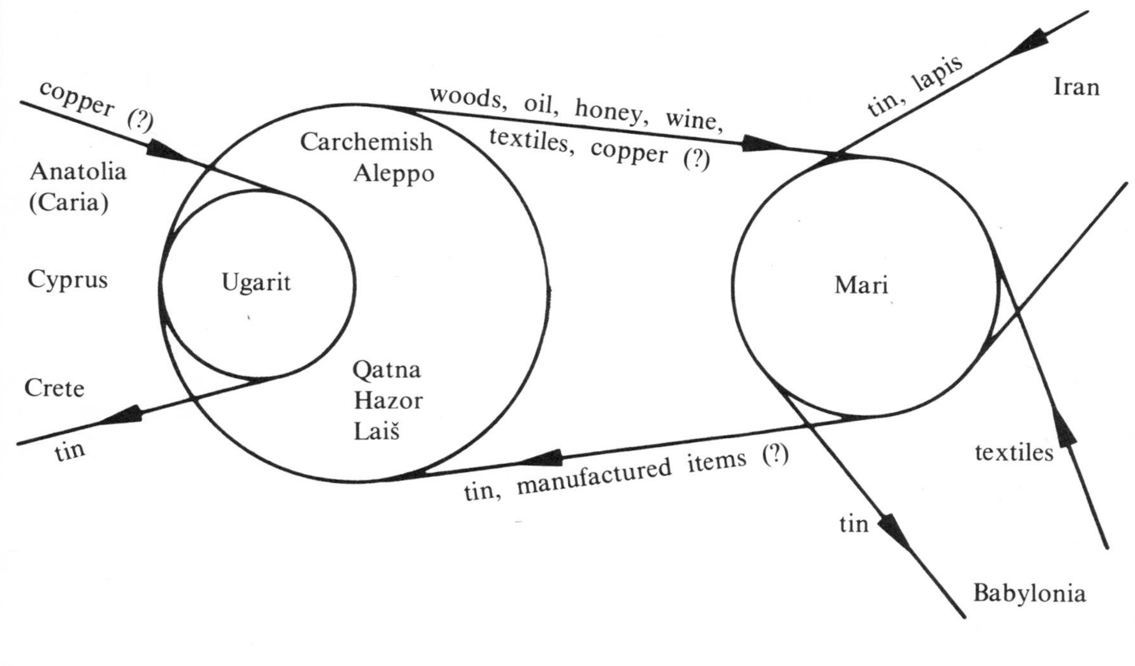

Table 3. International Trade in the Mari Period.

transit trade of certain commodities to the west, continued throughout the Mari period and may have existed during most of the Assyrian Colony period as well. The background for the connections which will be demonstrated in the artifact evidence is therefore well represented in the literary evidence from Mesopotamia.

II.3 Egyptian Textual and Epigraphic Evidence

The Egyptian evidence has traditionally been linked closer to the MB I period than has the extensive textual information available from Mesopotamia. The Egyptian material is important for two reasons: (1) in evaluating the extent and especially the mechanisms of trade, it is important to remember the role which Egypt may have played as an agent in the commercial contact of the Levant with such areas as Cyprus, Anatolia, and possibly even the Aegean; (2) the MB I period has often been interpreted as one of nearly complete reliance upon, if not actual domination by, the Egyptian 12th Dynasty. The possibility of strong Egyptian domination of, or influence over, parts of Syria or Palestine during MB I could invalidate the hypothesis that the complex of relationships previously described as existing with Mesopotamia in a slightly later period also existed at an earlier time. Evaluation of the Egyptian evidence might indicate whether one can extrapolate from the period of the Mari texts to the preceding period or whether the role of Egypt would have eclipsed any potential trade relations with Mesopotamia in MB I.

The types of epigraphic evidence for contact between Egypt and the Levant include the two major groups of Execration Texts, scarabs, and other inscribed material found at various sites in the Levant, and Egyptian stories which indicate contacts with the Levant, the most famous of which is the Tale of Sinuhe. The information from these sources is well summarized by Posener (1971: 545-58); the inscribed materials in the Levant are compiled by Porter and Moss (1951: 369-96).

The Execration Texts have perhaps been the greatest source of controversy on this subject. The texts may be divided into two major groups. The first, inscribed on sherds in the Berlin Museum, was published by Sethe in 1926; additional texts, also on potsherds as well as statuettes, were excavated in 1962-63 at Mirgissa in Nubia and were dated, on paleographic and other stylistic grounds, to either the time of the Sethe group or slightly earlier (Posener 1966: 279-80). The second major group, which is larger and was dated by Posener approximately a generation later than the Sethe group, is inscribed on fragments of statuettes of captives. Some of these figurines were presumably found at Saqqarah and are in the Cairo Museum (Posener 1939: 313-17), while another group is in the Brussels Museum (Posener 1940). These texts give lists of cities or regions and their rulers who were cursed by the King of Egypt—presumably because he either feared them or wanted to ward off some potential threat—and have been variously dated to the end of Dynasty 11 and, more usually, Dynasty 12 (Albright 1928: 249-50; Weill 1939: 947; Posener 1940: 31-35).

The lists of cities mentioned in the texts are assumed to give some picture of the political geography of the Levant at that time—at least as seen through Egyptian eyes—and the differences between the "Sethe group" and the "Posener group" are supposed to reflect changes in the political organization of the Levant between the dates of the two groups. Among those places mentioned in the texts for which a modern identification has been proposed are (Albright 1941b: 33-34; 1928: 235-47; 1941a: 18-19; Dussaud 1927: 217-30) *Skmỉmỉ* = Shechem; *Ḥḏw(ỉ)ꜣỉ* = Haṣûra, Hazor; ᵓ(a)pwm = ᵓApum, Damascus or that region; *ꜣwšꜣmm* = Urušalimum, Jerusalem; *ꜣws(i)* = Laish, Tel Dan; *ᵓ(a)pqwm* = Apǐqum, Aphek (Ras el-ᶜAin); *ᶜky* = Acco, Acre; *Isqꜣnw* = Ashkelon; *Kbn(i)* = Gubla (Kubni), Byblos.

The interpretation of the political significance of these texts has varied considerably. The first implication which has been drawn from these texts concerns the social organization of the individual towns or cities as a function of the number of "princes" or chieftains mentioned. For example, since the Sethe group of texts record that ᶜArqatum had only one chief, while Ashkelon had three and Jerusalem two, Albright (1928: 250) concluded that such towns had a "normal clan system." He further suggested that the coastal cities did not have a tribal organization while the inland cities did. Posener (1940: 39-40) proposed that the multiplicity of rulers suggests either a collective type of political organization or a territorial fragmentation, so that there may have been a ruler for the northern area and one for the southern, or for the "high" and "low" countries.

The contrasting evidence from the two groups of texts was also used by Albright (1941a: 18-19) to demonstrate a change in the settlement pattern system of the Levant based on the greater number of towns mentioned in proportion to the smaller number of princes assigned to an individual town in the later texts (Posener 1940: 40). The earlier (Berlin) texts list only five known cities (Byblos, ᶜArqatum, Ullaza, Jerusalem, and Ashkelon; the identification of a possible sixth, that of Rehob, has been questioned, Albright 1928: 241-42), while the other names presumably refer to tribal groups or districts. The later (Brussels) texts add at least ten more towns or cities, thus supposedly showing a process of increasing urbanization during the MB I period. Posener (1971: 555-56) basically agreed with this line of interpretation and wrote:

> This multiplication of princes under the same heading suggests a tribal type of organization, as it is known among nomads. In certain cases it seems possible to detect evidence of the break-up of small city states, which had existed previously, into still smaller political units. The Saqqara figurines, which are slightly later in date, name only one ruler for most of the countries. This change may reflect an historical development, either the reconstitution of the old principalities or the merging of related groups. . . . These comparisons [between the two groups of texts] give an idea of the confusion produced by the arrival of nomads, or semi-nomads, and of the fairly rapid return to a certain degree of stability.

This view, however, reflects a change in the opinion which Posener had expressed in his publication of the Brussels texts, where he pointed out that the Sethe texts seem to try to give as long a list of princes as possible, while the statuettes give a longer geographical list, presumably at the expense of the list of princes. He suggested that the Brussels texts mention only the most important or the best known of the rulers in a region which had more than one ruler and chose to omit the others, so that no particular significance should be attached to the number of rulers mentioned for a specific town (Posener 1940: 40). It is therefore apparent that several interpretations may be considered as possible, and no definitive explanation may be assumed.

Another question which needs to be considered is whether these texts present the extent of the Egyptian Empire during the early 2nd millennium B.C. Albright's conclusion (1928: 224) seemed to be that "the complete catalogue corresponds roughly to the extent of the Egyptian Empire," that the places mentioned were considered by the Egyptians as either actual or potential rebels against the empire, and that the Egyptian Empire, although extending along the Levantine coast at least as far as Byblos, did not include the Syrian hinterland (Albright 1928: 250).

Posener, however, presents a very different line of interpretation. While not denying the considerable cultural and probable political influence which Egypt had on the Levant during the 12th Dynasty, he nonetheless concludes that this area was not then subject to Egypt. He reads the texts as referring not to the actual extent of the empire, but "to the dogmatic belief in universal domination by the pharaohs, according to which every human being, wherever he might be, must submit to him and owed him obedience. We cannot therefore base our ideas on these lists in determining the extent of the empire belonging to the 12th Dynasty pharaohs, nor in determining which part of it was causing disquiet as to its loyalty" (Posener 1971: 548).

Finally, the interpretation proposed by Weinstein (1975: 13) should also be considered. He does not attach much specific significance to the Execration Texts because of the uncertainties of the dates of the texts and of the identifications of many of the toponyms mentioned. Second, he equates the increase in the number of places mentioned in the Brussels Texts with an increase in Egyptian cognizance of the Levant and therefore associates these texts with the end of MB I, which he attempts to show as a period of increased contact between Egypt and the Levant. Finally, he discounts an Egyptian fear of attack by the Asiatics since the relatively small, generally unfortified MB I sites would not have been likely to pose a serious threat to Egypt, although they would have been capable of hindering Egyptian trade with the Levant. His general interpretation of the nature of Egyptian-Levantine contacts will be more fully considered below, but his cautionary approach to a source of evidence about which so little is known is a useful alternative. The many uncertainties involving these texts, including their date and the fact that they may only represent an Egyptian view of the situation in the Levant, would seem to invalidate their use as a definitive source of information concerning the Levant during the MB I period.

Various Middle Kingdom Egyptian objects, including scarabs, stelae, and inscribed statuettes, have been found at many sites in the Levant (Porter and Moss 1951: 369-96), and these are also often interpreted as indicating extensive Egyptian influence or control. Many objects were found in Syria, especially at Byblos, whose close connections with Egypt during the 3rd millennium as well as in the Middle Kingdom are not doubted. In addition, a diorite sphinx of Amenemhet IV was found in Beirut, although not in original context; a sphinx of Princess It, the daughter of Amenemhet II, was found in the Temple of Nin-Egal at Qatna, and a seal impression, apparently attributable to Dynasty 12, was found at Alalakh. An inscribed Egyptian scepter or mace, possibly attributable to a pharaoh of Dynasty 13, was found in the tomb of the "Lord of the Goats" at Tell Mardikh (Matthiae 1980a: 16-17; 1980b: 17).

A large quantity of objects, including scarabs, statuettes, seals, and plaques, many with inscriptions, have been found at sites in Palestine (Porter and Moss 1951: 369-82), but, as Weinstein (1975: 1-10) points out, relatively few are from secure MB I contexts. Those found in MB I contexts include: three scarabs and one scaraboid from MB I tombs on the tell at Megiddo (Tombs 3143, 5090, and 5106; also Tufnell 1973: 71-73) and 14 from Tomb 912B which was reused in the Late Bronze Age, scarabs from mixed EB III/IV to MB II contexts at Beth-shan, two unpublished scarabs from MB I/II tombs at Safed, three scarabs from Tell el-ᶜAjjul Tomb 1406 (Tufnell's Group 4) and Tomb 1410B (Group 5—MB II), scarabs from graves near Tel Aviv which have been assigned to late MB I or MB II, one scarab possibly from Stratum 2 of Aphek, one design scarab from Tomb AN at Tell el-Farᶜah (N.), and seven scarabs from Jericho Tomb B 48, MB II. The only other admissible evidence for contact between Egypt and the southern Levant during the early 2nd millennium B.C. is that for a military campaign by Senusert III in the area of Shechem. This campaign is recorded on the stele of the Inspectors of Retainers, Khusobk (Wilson 1969: 230) and may be interpreted (Weinstein 1975: 11) as a raid against Asiatics who were perhaps hindering Egyptian trade along the Via Maris route. Possibly another raid in the reign of Amenemhet I is recorded on Louvre Stele C 1 (Weinstein 1975: 11, n. 90).

Several Egyptian statuettes of the Middle Kingdom and early Second Intermediate Period have also been found in the southern Levant (4 from Megiddo, 3 from Gezer, 3 from Tell el-ᶜAjjul, and one from near Ein ha-Shofet) and have been used to demonstrate close ties between Egypt and this region. None of these statuettes, however, was found in clear MB I context, and Weinstein (1974: 53-56) has suggested that they are indicative of post-MB I contacts between Egypt and the southern Levant.

The discussion surrounding these finds centers on the question of their significance. The interpretations range from one extreme in which Egypt is considered to have had political domination over much of Palestine and at least the Syrian coast to the other extreme according to which these finds are only indications of commercial and economic activities. As representative of the former view, Yadin has proposed that "there was an Egyptian domination, albeit a loose one, whose main objective was the exploitation of the country's agricultural products" (Yadin 1978: 20, n. 77; 1977: 104, n. 77; 1972: 206). Posener has suggested that the statuettes of officials found at Ugarit and Megiddo should be interpreted as indicating that "Egypt maintained more or less permanent missions in the two towns" (Posener 1971: 549; for a different interpretation of the Megiddo statue, see Weinstein 1974: 56). If one recalls the places where Egyptian statuettes have been found which were certainly not part of the Egyptian Empire, such as Anatolia and Crete,[8] it would seem likely that the statuettes indicate close diplomatic or economic relations, not political or military domination, during whatever period they were actually brought to these sites in the southern Levant.

Weinstein takes the argument a step further and concludes, in judging from the archaeological evidence found in Palestine, that ". . . the supposed Egyptian 'empire' in Palestine appears to be a complete fiction, and an alternative explanation for the occurrence of these Middle Kingdom objects in MB II B-C Palestine is that they were part of the loot from the Hyksos plundering of Middle Kingdom cemeteries in Egypt" (Weinstein 1975: 9-10). He interprets the quantity and type of Egyptian objects found in Syria, especially at Byblos, differently and believes that these, in contrast to those found in Palestine, do indicate extensive political and commercial ties during the MB I period (Weinstein 1974: 56; 1975: 13).

Finally, one should also consider the Tale of Sinuhe (Wilson 1969: 18-22) which is usually interpreted as demonstrating the presence of resident Egyptians in the Levant during the reigns of Amenemhet I and Senusert I. The land of Upper Retenu where Sinuhe dwells in exile can only be located by references in the text to Byblos and to "Qedem" (the East), although the area is characterized in the story by figs, grapes, wine, honey, olives, fruit trees, barley, emmer, cattle, and relative proximity to both the desert and a main route to Egypt, so that one may be tempted to think of the Biqa^{c} Valley. The explanation for the presence of Egyptians in this land is not clear, but they certainly would not seem to be on official missions since they receive the exiled Sinuhe. The furthest that one can push the evidence would be to propose that there were friendly relations between Egyptians and Asiatics and that there were unofficial Egyptians dwelling peacefully in parts of the Levant during the time of the Middle Kingdom.

In conclusion, then, one must return to the original question of whether a possible Egyptian hegemony in the Levant during MB I would have precluded commercial contact between the Levant and Mesopotamia, as described in the slightly later Mari texts and hinted in the contemporary "Cappadocian" texts. When one considers the lack of specific textual evidence for such an Egyptian hegemony or domination, it would seem possible to conclude that direct Egyptian influence in the Levant, with the possible exception of the Syrian coast (particularly Byblos), was minimal and can just as reasonably be attributed to commercial as to political ties. The influences on the material culture of the Levant which can be ascribed to contact with the north and the east cannot then be rejected on the basis of an assumption of exclusive contact with Egypt during the MB I period.

The literary evidence culled from texts and epigraphic material from the regions contiguous to the Levant—Mesopotamia, Egypt, and Anatolia—help to establish the following points:

(1) An extensive trade network existed in the 20th-19th centuries B.C. (that is, during the *karum* Kaniš Level II period) between Assyria and Anatolia. The major commodities traded included silver from Anatolia and probably tin and textiles from Assyria. Assur acted as a transit trade center since the tin, and at least some of the textiles, were first imported into Assur from elsewhere (that is, Iran or further east, and Babylonia, respectively; see table 2), although Assur was also a major textile manufacturing center. There is, as well, some evidence for direct contact with the Levant at this time.

(2) In the Mari period (that is, *kārum* Kaniš Level Ib), the Anatolian-oriented trade continued, although on a greatly reduced scale, as evidenced by both the "Cappadocian" and Mari texts. The tin trade seems to have been controlled through different trade centers, possibly reflecting changes in political, administrative, production, and/or marketing centers.

(3) The Mari texts document extensive political and trade relations between Mari and the major sites in the Levant, including Qatna, Aleppo, Ugarit, Hazor, and Laiš. The major commodities traded included foods, wood, and possibly copper from the west, and tin and possibly manufactured items from Mesopotamia, with Mari taking over the role of a major transit trade center (see table 3). Ugarit may also have been a trade center for the west since other foreigners (possibly from Cyprus, Crete, and Anatolia) are mentioned as residing there and receiving tin shipments from Mari.

(4) The Egyptian material is insufficient to support the hypothesis of an Egyptian hegemony in the Levant in the early 2nd millennium B.C., although there undoubtedly was Egyptian influence and presence, especially in such centers as Byblos. Whatever the extent of this Egyptian influence, it would not have isolated the Levant from other influences, such as from Mesopotamia and Anatolia.

(5) A clear background of relations between the Levant and Mesopotamia—at first minimal but then increasing into the Mari period—is established through the literary evidence, thereby providing the framework for other evidence of contacts, which will be discussed in the following chapters.

NOTES

[1]Only 15 of the approximately 15,000 texts which have so far been excavated at the site of Tell Mardikh (ancient Ebla) have been assigned to the first quarter of the 2nd millennium B.C. (Pettinato 1975: 362). The 3rd-millennium texts shed some light on the situation in northern Syria (Pettinato and Matthiae 1976: 1-30) but are almost entirely unpublished. The sites of Hazor, Lachish, Megiddo, Gaza, Sinai, Jaffa, Mari, Tuttul, Naḫor, and Ursu are apparently mentioned in these texts (Pettinato 1975: 365; 1976: 46) while Pettinato (1976: 52, n. 7) also claims that all the cities mentioned in texts from the Mari, Alalakh, Ugarit, and El-Amarna archives occur in the Ebla archives. Pettinato has even hypothesized that the *kārum* Kaniš is referred to in some of the ecomomic texts (Pettinato 1976: 48) and that commercial relations were well established with sites of

central Anatolia in a system which may recall that of the later Old Assyrian period. It seems necessary, however, to await further publication of individual texts before discussing extensive political and economic contacts. (For disagreement with Pettinato's reading of many personal and place names, especially the identification of Kaniš, see Archi 1979: 556-66; for a more general critique, see Biggs 1980: 76-87.)

A juglet with an inscription incised after firing was found at the site of Hazor (Yadin *et al.* 1960: 115-17, pl. CXII:9) and assigned to the MB II period, although its exact stratigraphic position was uncertain. The inscription was read as Akkadian, perhaps a theophoric personal name, which was associated by its grammatical form to the Mari period. Clay liver model fragments were also found at Hazor in a 15th-century-B.C. context and dated to the Old Babylonian period (Landsberger and Tadmor 1964: 201-18). Finally, a fragment of a clay envelope with cuneiform signs and impressions of signs from the tablet which it had held was found at the site of Gezer in fill of a level dated to the 14th century B.C. (Shaffer in Dever *et al.* 1970: 111-12). On the basis of the ductus style, Shaffer dated the fragment to the Old Babylonian period, probably in the 17th century B.C. None of these examples of writing from the southern Levant, however, can be associated with the MB I period and, therefore, these do not give any additional information concerning the period under consideration here.

[2]For further information concerning the Assyrian Colony period, see: Garelli 1963: 391-406; Veenhof 1972: XV-XIX; Larsen 1967: 7-57; 1976: 50-55; H. Lewy 1971a: 707-28; J. Lewy 1956: 1-79; 1958: 89-101.

[3]Such suggestions are based on legends concerning Sargon of Akkad and Naram-Sin, those of the latter including a reference to the city of Purušḫanda, which is sometimes identified with the *kārum* of Purušḫaddum (H. Lewy 1971a: 707, but see Larsen 1976: 277-78, who doubts the historical value of these legends). Relations between Anatolia and Ebla in northern Syria in the 3rd millennium B.C., as discussed above, may now be indicated by texts from Tell Mardikh (*supra* n. 1; Pettinato 1976: 48).

[4]Both Lewys had supported a translation of *annaku* as lead and hypothesized a system in which the lead was desilvered or used in a process of desilvering copper ores in Anatolia, with the silver then being exported back to Assur (J. Lewy 1958: 91-93 and n. 11; H. Lewy 1971a: 724-25). For reasons which will be presented in Chapter VI.2, where this controversy will be more extensively discussed, a translation of *annaku* as tin is here favored, although the issue cannot yet be completely settled.

[5]This evidence might further support the hypothesis that such complex trade relationships as depicted in the "Cappadocian" and Mari texts are not limited to the Old Assyrian or Mari periods, but rather that it is the survival of the documents describing the trade which is unusual. A better understanding of the trade situation in the 3rd millennium B.C. must await fuller publication of the Ebla texts and excavation and publication of the 3rd-millennium levels at Kültepe.

[6]Most of the published Mari texts appear in a series of volumes, *Archives royales de Mari, Transcription et Traduction*, hereafter referred to as *ARMT* and cited by text number.

[7]Dossin (1955: 14) suggests th at the name of the fourth tree, *elammaku*, may be translated as sandalwood, but Malamat (1965: 368) disputes this.

[8]Two Middle Kingdom statues found in Anatolia, along with a statue found in the central courtyard of the Palace at Knossos (Evans 1921: 286-89, fig. 220), demonstrate that such statues cannot possibly be used as an indication of the extent of Egyptian political dominion, although they may show the extent of commercial contact. W. S. Smith (1969: 279; also 1965: 14-15, and n. 48) has suggested that Egyptians who travelled abroad (possibly either as ambassadors or perhaps even as merchants residing in foreign countries) took with them small statues to be placed in their tombs in case they should die abroad. The two statues found in Anatolia were not, however, in proper context. The first was found in Adana in a classical context (Allen 1929: 67); it is a black granite, kneeling statuette of Sitsnefru, probably a contemporary of Senusert II. The second was excavated in a Roman and Byzantine necropolis at the site of Kirik Kale (or Kürigan Kale) along with some presumably "Hittite" (that is, red-slipped) pottery. It is of black granite and belonged to Keri, also of the Middle Kingdom (Allen 1929: 66-67). Since Kirik Kale is located near the Kizil Irmak, north of Kayseri, this inland discovery may show that Egyptian contact was more than just a coastal manifestation. One might still, however, question the exact circumstances under which the statue found its way to this particular site or suggest that both these statuettes could have been brought to Anatolia after the Middle Kingdom.

Chapter III
The Artifactual Evidence of the Levant

This chapter is not an attempt to present a complete summary of our current state of knowledge concerning the MB I period (for discussion of the main characteristics of MB I, see Dever 1976: 3-38; Mazar 1968: 65-97; Kenyon 1971: 567-94; and 1973: 77-116). Rather, it is a synthesis of certain features of the material culture, primarily the ceramic materials but also certain other types of artifactual evidence, in order: (1) to place the ceramic material in a stratigraphic and developmental sequence which will allow a finer chronological subdivision of MB I; (2) to show the general patterns of relationships of sites within the Levant based on similarities in the material culture; (3) to identify certain features which indicate connections with Anatolia and with Mesopotamia; and (4) to place the appearance of these foreign-related features within the chronological phasing proposed here for the MB I period.

In attempting to accomplish the first of these goals, it is not only necessary to study the groups of artifacts as published and assigned to MB I, but also to determine the stratigraphic associations of particular pottery groups and, if possible, to devise a chronological sequence which shows the ceramic development of MB I types into the MB II repertoire. Indication of typological subdivision has already been given in some publications in which an MB I-MB II transitional period is recognized, as, for example, in Kenyon's typological study of the Megiddo pottery (Kenyon 1969: 26-28), Tufnell's groups of the Tell el-ᶜAjjul Courtyard Cemetery pottery (Tufnell 1962: 1-23), Yadin's classification of the pottery in the burial cave found in the Hazor Area L cistern (Yadin 1975: 269), and Epstein's discussion of the pottery from Kfar Szold and Ginosar (Epstein 1974: 13-39). All of these classifications were, however, based on typological analysis and, although these will generally prove to have been justified, it would seem to be even more advantageous to base such refinements on stratigraphic analyses.

MB I stratified sites are not numerous and in the southern Levant may be limited to the sites of Megiddo, Tell Beit Mirsim, and Aphek (Ras el-ᶜAin). The last of these, Aphek, which is currently being excavated, has the greatest potential for providing a stratified sequence for the MB I period, and any ceramic typology for this period must be based on these results. The site of Megiddo may also be used on a limited basis to provide a stratified sequence and supplies in its ceramic repertoire additional features which are not found at Aphek. It is therefore necessary to attempt to correlate the evidence from these two sites in formulating a stratigraphically-based typology for the MB I period. In the following discussion, the evidence from Megiddo, with its limitations, is presented first and then checked against the evidence from Aphek.

III.1. Stratified Sites of the MB I Period

A. MEGIDDO

The site of Megiddo was excavated by the Oriental Institute of the University of Chicago from 1925 to 1939. As is now commonly recognized, the published strata do not represent coherent stratigraphic levels since tomb groups and all finds from the same absolute level were grouped together, and no account was taken of such factors as differences in topography and later cuttings for pits and wall foundations. Despite the resulting confusion, since it is possible to reconstruct the individual locus groups, several attempts have been made to rework the stratigraphy and to reassign the structures and find groups to coherent architectural and ceramic phases. In addition to the attempts to do this on paper (Kenyon 1958: 51*-60*; Thompson 1970: 38-49; Williams 1975: 907-34), subsequent excavation by Dunayevsky and Kempinski (1973: 161-75) further defined the Early Bronze Age sequence of the temples in Area BB, but, despite their discussion of the MB II strata, did little to permit a relative chronological ordering of the Megiddo loci.[1]

It does, however, seem possible on the basis of the Chicago publication to define three phases, and perhaps a fourth, which can be ceramically assigned to MB I. These phases are not intended to imply the existence of three entirely discrete architectural strata throughout the site, but they do demonstrate a sequence of use in a given area. If the reconstruction of these phases is correct, then two important conclusions can be drawn from the existence of these phases: (1) the MB I period must have lasted, at least at Megiddo, for a long enough period to allow for these phases; (2) this stratigraphic phasing should permit a loose, sequential, chronological ordering of the ceramic material—on which, along with the Aphek evidence, may subsequently be built a more extensive typology of the MB I period.

The stratigraphic phasing may be demonstrated in the western section of Area BB (see fig. 9 for a plan of the superposition of these loci and figs. 1018 for the pottery from these loci). The two sectors, east and west, of Area BB need to be considered separately since the structures in each half do not join and therefore are not necessarily related.

A structure in Square N 12 (on the Stratum XII plan, Loud 1948: fig. 398) is associated with Loci 5043, 5048, 5038, 5037, and 5044. Of these, 5038 has no pottery, while 5037 and 5044 (shown on the Stratum XI plan, Loud 1948: fig. 399, but associated with this structure on the original excavation plan, plan 56 "Stable") contain pottery which is probably MB II in date (5044: Loud 1948: pl. 38:4; 5037: Loud 1948: pls. 33:29 and 36:3); these three loci are also shown as belonging to structures which are at higher elevations (plan 56 "Stable") and so provide no conclusive evidence of stratification. The other loci (5048 and 5043), however, are associated with the walls of the structure in Square N 12 and contain a Cypriote White Painted III-IV juglet (5048: Loud 1948: pl. 26:16) and a goblet (5043: Loud 1948: pl. 26:18) which can be assigned to MB I (compare the goblet with the example from Aphek, Iliffe 1936: 125:76).

The walls of this structure from Stratum XII overlie the following loci (shown on the plan for Statum XIIIA, Loud 1948: fig. 397; plan 59 "Stable") and their associated pottery: 5049 (Loud 1948: pl. 17:25), 5054 (Loud 1948: pl. 18:6), 5063 (no pottery), 5064 (Loud 1948: pl. 17:3 and 17), T. 5097 (Loud 1948: pl. 17:5 and 21), and T. 5103 (Loud 1948: pls. 17:13 and 24, 18:3, 19:4 and 7). Locus 5064 and the wall immediately south of Locus 5064 cover a pavement shown on the Stratum XIIIB plan (Loud 1948: fig. 396; plan 61 "Stable") which has no locus number (and, presumably, no associated pottery) but which may be identified by T. 5166 located next to it. The walls of this building, with which Loci 5064, 5063, and 5049 are associated, also overlie T. 5180 (shown on the plan of Stratum XIV, Loud 1948: fig. 395; plan 61 "Stable"; with pottery, Loud 1948: pls. 10:14 and 11:13) which therefore should be stratigraphically equivalent to this pavement. According to the published plans, this pavement next to T. 1566 from the Stratum XIIIB plan seals T. 5181, shown on the plan for Stratum XIV and containing pottery (Loud 1948: pls. 10:12 and 17, 11:17, 12:20 and 22, 14:17) which can be assigned to MB I as well. On the original plans, however, T. 5181, although sealed by the structure associated with Locus 5064, is adjacent to the pavement (plan 61 "Stable"). Although the elevations for the tomb (59.30 and 58.60) are lower than those of the pavement (at 59.95 and 59.70) and it is therefore likely that T. 5181 represents a still earlier phase of MB I, direct stratigraphic superposition is lacking. Therefore, although a Phase 1 of stratigraphy for this area can be suggested, it cannot be proven, and those loci assigned to both Phases 1 and 2 are grouped together on tables 4 and 5 and fig. 10.

With less certainty, it is also possible to assign T. 5149 to this same Phase 1/2. This tomb (elevation 58.90, plan 61 "Stable") is sealed by a wall fragment (elevations 60.60 and 60.20, without locus number, but shown on the Stratum XIIIA plan, Loud 1948: fig. 397, and 59 "Stable" plan). This wall fragment, although not connected to the structure of Loci 5064, 5063, and 5049, is at the same absolute elevation as this structure and could be stratigraphically equivalent to it. If this association were accepted, Tomb 5149 would be placed in the same phase as Tombs 5180 and 5181. Pavement 5034 (Stratum XIIIA plan, plan 59 "Stable") has an elevation of 60.25 and is associated with the structure to which this unnumbered wall fragment also belongs. Pavement 5076, which appears on the same plans, is at an even lower elevation (59.65), so that while it may be earlier, both pavements may be conservatively considered as associated with the structure of Loci 5064, 5063, and 5049. In summary, then, one can propose the following table of approximate stratigraphic sequences (see Table 4 on p. 25).

Several loci appearing on the plans for Strata XIV-XII may tentatively be added to the Phase 3 and 4 groups. Tombs 5183 (Stratum XIV plan,

Table 4. Superposition of Loci in Area BB, West, Megiddo.
(see also fig. 9)

Phase	Loci (with associated pottery plate references to Loud 1948) NP = no pottery	
4	Structure—5048 (26:16), 5043 (26:18)	
3	Structure—5064 (17:3, 17), 5063 (NP), 5049 (17:25), 5054 (18:6), T. 5097 (17:5, 21), T. 5103 (17:3, 24; 18:3, 19:4, 7)	Pavements 5076 (19:6) and 5034 (17:11)
2 }	T. 5180 (10:4, 11:13)	T. 5149 (8:8)
1 }	T. 5181 (10:12, 17; 11:17; 12:20, 22, 14:17)	

Loud 1948: pls. 11:18, 14:12) and 5275 (Stratum XIV plan, Loud 1948: pls. 11:6 and 8, 12:3) and Wall Fragment 5101 (Stratum XIIIA plan, Loud 1948: pl. 19:14; plan 59 "Stable") are sealed by structures shown on the plan for Stratum XII, although these are not joined to the building of Loci 5048, 5043, and 5038. Their placement in Phase 3 is therefore tentative. Several tombs may be added to Phase 4 since they appear to be sealed by the same structure of the Stratum XI plan (Loci 5035, 5037, 5044) which seals the structure of Loci 5048, 5043, and 5038. These tombs include: T. 5088, 5134, 5137, 5142, 5152, 5178, 5179, 5186, 5241, 5242, 5252, 5254, 5259, 5261, and 5274. The group of pottery included in Phase 4 would form the latest group of MB I pottery at Megiddo and is transitional to MB II, as demonstrated by the flaring bowl from T. 5259 (Loud 1948: pl. 28:13).

In turning to the southeast sector of Area BB, one first observes that there is less stratification of structures and, as a result, only two phases of use can be clearly defined. One must begin by adopting Kenyon's conclusion that the city wall and the building just to the west (shown on the plan of Stratum XIIIA) cannot be contemporary since the east walls of the building have been truncated by the construction of the city wall (Kenyon 1969: 44, but see also Harif 1978: 27-29, who disagrees). The city wall, as shown on the plan for Stratum XIIIA, seals only one tomb, T. 3162 (Stratum XIV plan, Loud 1948: pls. 10:13, 11:9, 12:12, 12:14, 14:7, and 15:15), which is MB I, thus giving only a *terminus post quem* for its construction. The buildings associated with the city wall shown on the Stratum XII plan, as well as buildings on the Stratum XI plan, seal a mixture of MB I and MB II tombs and so all that can be said is that these structures must be later than MB I. The following tombs may be assigned to either Phase 3 or 4 of MB I on typological grounds but should be considered as stratigraphically placed in late MB I: T. 3109, 3140, 3141, 3125, 3168, 3147, 3144, 3155, 3093, 3157, 3146, 2151, and possibly 3130 and 2146. This group of tombs does not, however, prove a sequence of habitation in the southeast sector since the tombs might belong to the occupants of structures located elsewhere on the tell.

The only building phase, therefore, is represented by the "truncated building" (shown on the Stratum XIIIA plan) which, in its turn, also seals a group of tombs (T. 3171, 3148, 3143, and 3150), the pottery of which can be termed "early MB I." This pottery shows several features similar to the pottery of the earliest phase from the west sector, such as the jugs with neck ridge to which the handle is attached (or collarette juglet), the simple rounded bowl from both T. 5181 and T. 3148, and the handleless, flat-based store jar.[2] Tomb 3162 can be assigned to either Phase 3 or Phase 4 since it should be later than this last group of tombs. While the bowl and most of the juglets seem to belong to the earlier phase, the painted juglet might argue for a placement in Phase 4.[3]

The relative paucity of material from Area AA prevents almost any definitive assignment of loci or levels from this area to a particular phase. Only five of the loci assigned to Stratum XIII (Loud 1948: fig. 378) are sealed by Stratum XII (4087, T. 4095, 4085, T. 4105, and T. 4088); in addition, Locus 4092 is perhaps partially sealed. The sealed loci seem easily attributable to the MB I period, but it is difficult to correlate them stratigraphically with the loci of Area BB.[4] Two vessels from the sealed T. 4088 (the two-handled store jar, Loud 1948: pl. 21:3, and the flaring carinated bowl, Loud 1948: pl. 21:12) would also seem to place this group in MB II, but parallels from the site of Aphek (*infra*) show that these forms existed at the end of MB I as well. Of the two unsealed tomb groups, T. 4112, which included a juglet with pinched rim

(Loud 1948: pl. 20:4), can be assigned to MB I, while T. 4110 is uncertainly dated since none of the forms is distinctly MB I. Of the pottery appearing in loci shown on the Stratum XII plan, most of the groups should be assigned to MB II since there is little which is distinctively earlier, although some forms do repeat from the late phase of MB I from Area BB, such as bowl Type 53 (Loud 1948: pl. 29:19).

It is also possible to assign many of the other tomb groups from Strata XV to XII either to one of these phases of MB I or to the MB II period on purely typological grounds. Such assignments, which are basically subjective in nature and therefore cannot be used as definitive proofs of a typological sequence, still confirm in various respects the original sequence seen in the relatively small group of loci which were assigned to these phases for stratigraphic reasons. Table 5 suggests a possible phasing for these loci but should not be taken as a rigid division of these pottery groups which often shade from one phase into the next.

Of the tomb groups excavated in the "Stages" area southeast of the mound (Guy 1938), several have already been assigned to the MB I period by Wright (1961: 89, chart 5). These include Tombs 911A1 (Guy 1938: pls. 28 and 29), 911D (Guy 1938: pls. 31:8-21 and 32:1-3), 912B (Guy 1938: pl. 35:1-13), and 912D (Guy 1938: pl. 35:14-19). Of the other tombs assigned in the publication to MB II, most may be placed in that period or even later. It may also be possible to add to Wright's MB I group T. 234 (Guy 1938: pl. 26:5-9).[5]

The material from T. 911A seems to represent the entire span of MB I, but the only vessels of interest include the handleless store jar which is early MB I (Guy 1938: pl. 29:9), the juglets with painted horizontal bands (Guy 1938: pl. 29:2-5) which relate most closely to Phase 3, and the somewhat unusual elongated store jar with two red painted horizontal bands, probably of either Phase 3 or 4 (Guy 1938: pl. 29:11). The jugs of T. 911D with painted horizontal bands (Guy 1938: pl. 31:18, 19, and 21, the last two with stripes on the handle) also recall the painted jugs of Phase 3. All but one of the bowls from this tomb are decorated with red wash on both the rim interior and exterior (Guy 1938: pl. 31:8-12, 14, and 15), and these forms, with the jugs, would seem to indicate a Phase 3 dating. The remaining two tomb groups (912B and 912D) do not add to the features already noted. We should, however, mention another band-painted, handleless store jar (Guy 1938: pl. 35:5, T. 912B) and the unusual pointed mug from T. 912D (Guy 1938: pl. 35:19).[6]

The only vessels still to be considered are those which are listed in the publication as "associated" with a locus, although not actually found in that locus. This group should therefore be considered as without stratigraphic provenience and, since many of these vessels were found individually, there is little value in attempting to phase them. Of the more unusual types represented, there are two more examples of the flat-based, handleless store jar, one of which has a design of painted concentric circles on the body in red and black. Additional vessel types include a juglet with red and black painted circles, a bowl with S-curved profile and black and red painted decoration, and a store jar with a thickened, flattened rim forming a "hole-mouth," which may be compared with the kraters of the prepalace phase at Aphek and which also has painted bands and triangles on the exterior. Finally, two examples of pinched-rim pitchers should be placed early in the Megiddo sequence.[7]

Some of the conclusions concerning each phase which may be drawn from the typologically assigned as well as the stratified material may be summarized as follows:

Phases 1 and 2 (figs. 10-11): The handleless store jar with flat or slightly rounded base, sometimes with horizontal painted bands and sometimes with "moulded" rim (see Aphek material, *infra*, for explanation; for examples: Loud 1948: pls. 8:8, 12:17, 20, and 22) is common in this early phase. The collarette juglet (Loud 1948: pl. 10:16, 17, and 21) has been considered an early MB I feature and is present here as well. The tendency to flat bases or only low disc bases on the bowls is also found in this group. Finally, there seems to be a greater proportion of red slip and burnish decoration in this phase than in the later phases, but such a conclusion must be stated only tentatively because of the relatively small quantity of pottery available.

Phase 3 (figs. 12-14): The handleless type of store jar continues, but without painted bands, while a form which foreshadows the later type with handles (Loud 1948: pls. 18:3 and 21:1) and more piriform body tapering toward the base (Loud 1948: pl. 12:18) also appears. The pitchers, usually with flat or low disc base, are the only form which continues the painted band decoration. Some juglets begin to show connections with later piriform types (Loud 1948: pl. 19:30 from T. 3130). The small basket-handled pitcher (Loud 1948:

Table 5. MB I Loci at Megiddo by Phase. ("Strat." indicates that the locus was assigned to a phase by stratigraphic indications; otherwise, loci are assigned typologically.)

Locus	*Stratum*	*Phase*
T. 2146	XIII	4 (E) Strat.
T. 2151	XIII	4 (E) Strat.
T. 2152	XIV	2
T. 3092	XII	3 (?)
T. 3093	XIII	4 (E) Strat.
T. 3104-5	XII	3
T. 3109	XIII	3 (E) Strat.
T. 3117	XII	4
T. 3118	XIII	3
T. 3125	XIII	3 (E) Strat.
T. 3127	XIII	3
T. 3128	XII	4/MBII
T. 3130	XIII	3 (E) Strat.
T. 3134	XIII	3
T. 3138	XIV	2
T. 3140-1	XIII	3 (E) Strat.
T. 3143	XIV	1/2 (E) Strat.
T. 3144	XIV	4 (E) Strat.
T. 3146	XIII	4 (E) Strat.
T. 3147	XIV	3 (E) Strat.
T. 3148-9	XIV	1/2 (E) Strat.
T. 3150	XIV	1/2 (E) Strat.
T. 3151	XV	2
T. 3153	XIV	3
T. 3155	XIV	4 (E) Strat.
T. 3157	XIV	4 (E) Strat.
T. 3162	XIV	3/4
T. 3168	XIV	3 (E) Strat.
T. 3171	XV	1/2 (E) Strat.
T. 4016	XIV	4
T. 4046	XIV	3
4085	XIII	3/4
4088	XIII	3/4
4092	XIV?	3/4
T. 4095	XIII	3/4
T. 4105	XIII	3/4
T. 4112	XIII	3/4
5034	XIIIA	3 (W) Strat.
5043	XII	4 (W) Strat.
5048	XII	4 (W) Strat.
5049	XIIIA	3 (W) Strat.
5054	XIIIA	3 (W) Strat.
T. 5063	XIIIA	4
5064	XIIIA	3 (W) Strat.
5072	XIIIA	3
T. 5074	XIV	3
T. 5075	XIIIA	3 (?)
5076	XIIIA	3 (W) Strat.
T. 5084	XIIIA	4
T. 5088	XIIIA	4 (W) Strat.
T. 5090	XIIIA	3/4
T. 5094	XIIIA	3/4
T. 5097	XIIIA	3 (W) Strat.
5101	XIIIA	3 (W) Strat. (?)
T. 5102	XIIIA	3/4 (?)
T. 5103	XIIIA	3 (W) Strat.
T. 5104	XIIIA	4 (W) Strat.
T. 5106	XII	4
T. 5111	XII	4
T. 5112	XII	4
T. 5114	XIIIB	3
T. 5118	XIV	3
T. 5121	XIV	3
T. 5130	XIV	3/4
T. 5134	XII	4 (W) Strat.
T. 5137	XII	4 (W) Strat.
T. 5142	XII	4 (W) Strat.
T. 5147	XIV	2
T. 5149	XV	1/2 (W) Strat.
T. 5152	XIIIA	4 (W) Strat.
T. 5156	XIV	2
T. 5158	XIV	3
T. 5167	XV	2
T. 5171	XIV	3
T. 5175	XV	2
T. 5176	XIV	2
T. 5177	XIV	3
T. 5178	XIV	4 (W) Strat.
T. 5179	XIV	4 (W) Strat.
T. 5180	XIV	2 (W) Strat.
T. 5181	XIV	1/2 (W) Strat.
T. 5183	XIV	3 (W) Strat. (?)
T. 5185	XIV	2
T. 5186	XIV	4 (W) Strat.
T. 5188	XIV	3 (?)
T. 5202	XV	3
T. 5241	XII	4 (W) Strat.
T. 5242	XII	4 (W) Strat.
T. 5252	XIIIA	4 (W) Strat.
T. 5254	XII	4 (W) Strat.
T. 5259	XII	4 (W) Strat.
5260	XIIIB	3
T. 5261	XII	4 (W) Strat.
T. 5268	XIIIB	3
T. 5270	XIIIA	3
T. 5274	XII	4 (W) Strat.
T. 5275	XIV	3 (W) Strat. (?)

pl. 20:18) is similar to examples in late MB I groups, such as the transitional group from the Hazor burial cave (Yadin 1975: 271). Some bowls display higher bases (Loud 1948: pl. 14:7 and 39), and, in addition to the typical sharply carinated bowl, an S-shaped carinated type appears (Loud 1948: pl. 14:27). The introduction of foreign-related features is, however, perhaps the most significant aspect of this phase (see Chapter V.1 for a fuller discussion of these comparisons). First, relating to Mesopotamian ceramics are the goblet (Loud 1948: pl. 18:6) and the mug shapes (Loud 1948: pl. 11:6 and 8). Secondly, forms reminiscent of Anatolian types include the cut-away spouted pitcher (Loud 1948: pls. 16:2 and 25:12) and the trefoil-rimmed mug (Loud 1948: pl. 20:17, if correctly restored). Finally, an unusual deep bowl (Loud 1948: pl. 22:6) shows some relationship with examples from Ugarit (Schaeffer 1932: 18, fig. 12:10).

Phase 4 (figs. 15-18): This phase shows a continuation in the type of foreign relationships already demonstrated in Phase 3 with the important addition of the Cypriote painted juglets (Loud 1948: pl. 26:13, 14, and 16). Those features which are typical of late MB I include: juglets with "stepped" rim (Loud 1948: pls. 10:19, 19:31, and 24:24), "cylindrical" juglets (Loud 1948: pls. 11:4, 17:9, and 23:17), piriform juglets (Loud 1948: pl. 24:16 and 21), the elongated dipper jug (Loud 1948: pls. 12:7 and 11, 20:9 and 11), and the large jug with single handle (Loud 1948: pl. 23:7 and 8). The classic MB I simple and sharply carinated bowls continue (Loud 1948: pl. 14:34, 36, and 37), sometimes now with high ring base (Loud 1948: pl. 29:23). A carinated example, clearly a forerunner of the MB II type, may begin now (Loud 1948: pls. 15:9 and 21:12 from Area AA), as does the flaring carinated type (Loud 1948: pl. 28:12) which is associated with late MB I at Aphek.

Several more generalized conclusions, some with implications for our understanding of the relationships between the Megiddo repertoire and the ceramics of the rest of the Levant, will here be summarized:

(1) Several superposed occupation phases can be assigned to the MB I period at Megiddo, proving that (at least at Megiddo) MB I must have spanned a reasonable length of time in order to allow for these phases.

(2) The handleless band-painted store jars tend to occur early in the sequence (T. 5181 and T. 5149).

(3) The cup or goblet form, a Mesopotamian-related shape, appears in the two later phases (examples from Locus 5054, Phase 3, and Locus 5043, Phase 4).

(4) The pitchers with cut-away spouts or with strongly pinched rims, showing Anatolian influence, are primarily of the later phases of MB I and continue into the MB II period (examples from T. 4112 and T. 5252, although a pitcher with pinched rim and painted bands also occurs in Phase 2, from T. 5180).

(5) The foliated cup, which is usually attributed only to MB II, may have its origins as early as the third phase of MB I (Loud 1948: pl. 20:17 from T. 3109).

(6) The examples of Cypriote imported pottery (a White Painted III-IV jug from 5048, Loud 1948: pl. 26:16, and a Red-on-Black jug from T. 5134, Loud 1948: pl. 26:14) are from the last phase of MB I. The implications of these conclusions for chronological correlations and the spread of influences will be discussed more fully elsewhere.

While Megiddo is the only extensively excavated and published site in northern Israel, the site of Aphek now provides a typological ceramic sequence derived from stratigraphic excavations. A comparison of this phasing of MB I ceramics based on the material from Megiddo with the results of the current excavations at Aphek should therefore test the validity of this proposed sequence into which other sites may then be fitted.

B. APHEK (RAS EL-ᶜAIN)

Tel Aphek, strategically located near the sources of the Yarkon River and along the north-south route of the Via Maris, was first excavated by Ory in 1936 and 1937 (Ory 1936: 111-12; Iliffe 1936: 113-19; Ory 1937: 99-120) and then by Eitan in 1969 (Eitan 1969: 49-68). The site is now being excavated by M. Kochavi (Kochavi 1975: 17-42) on behalf of the Tel Aviv University Institute of Archaeology. Ory's excavations consisted primarily of a series of trial pits on the northeast slope with much of the ceramic material of the Middle Bronze Age coming from tombs and some from near the city wall (Ory 1936: 111, 1937: 100-4). Since this material was not excavated stratigraphically, it will be discussed after the material from Kochavi's excavations, which provide a stratified sequence of pottery types.

Most of the MB I material comes from Area A, located at the northwest corner of the mound, and was divided into three phases according to architectural strata: the prepalace, palace, and postpalace phases (Kochavi 1975: 22-34). It seems possible to propose that the Aphek material shows a development in its MB I ceramic repertoire similar to that of the phased Megiddo material, not necessarily in a direct correspondence of the phases but at least in terms of a relative ordering of earlier, middle, and later characteristics. Two additional factors, however, must be taken into account in order to explain certain differences between the two groups of material: first, the possibillity of regional differences, since Megiddo seems to represent a northern sphere, while Aphek shows a diminution in northern ties; second, a difference in function, in that a large proportion of the Megiddo material comes from tombs while most of the Aphek material from Kochavi's excavations is from living areas. The latter factor may account for the near or complete absence of certain features at one site, while the former might explain the tendency to a different orientation in foreign influences.

An analysis of the similarities and differences between the Megiddo and Aphek material will therefore be presented in order to demonstrate the general validity of the use of these phases.[8]

Aphek Prepalace Phase/Megiddo Phases 1 and 2: The Aphek carinated bowls (Beck 1975: fig. 1:10) are characterized by a pronounced gutter rim, red slip and burnish decoration. A Megiddo carinated bowl (Loud 1948: pl. 14:38, T. 3143) does not have the gutter rim but is similarly decorated. Simple rounded bowls occur at both sites. The open bowls with a ridge or knob below the rim and radial burnish from Aphek may be compared with a Megiddo bowl with a ridge below the rim, red slip and radial burnish and with another bowl with knobs and radial burnish. There is also at least one additional type of bowl present at Megiddo with an inverted bead rim which is perhaps a variant of the simple rounded bowl. All the bowls of this phase share a flat or very low disc base and a tendency to decoration of red slip and burnishing.[9]

The krater is more common at Aphek than at Megiddo and occurs in two varieties: the "hole-mouth" with thickened, everted rim and a type with flaring rim and usually a pronounced gutter. The latter is missing from the early phase at Megiddo, while the former is represented by only two unstratified examples. There are also two types of cooking pot present at Aphek: a wheel-made variety which seems to be missing at Megiddo, and the more typical MB I type, handmade with straight sides, holes below the rim, and plastic decoration below the holes. This latter type also occurs at Megiddo but only in unstratified context.[10]

Several types of store jars are present at Aphek, while Megiddo has only one basic variety in this phase. The Aphek examples include: an oval type with loop handles, flat base, and pattern combing (Beck 1975: fig. 1:3);[11] a large jar with flaring neck and often rope design or impressions (Beck 1975: figs. 1:6, 6:16, 3:1-3), whose only parallel at Megiddo is a neck fragment with rope decoration (Loud 1948: pl. 13:10, S=3154), but whose rim is of a different form; the special group of store jars with handles and painted decoration from Aphek Locus 463 (Beck 1975: fig. 3:7-10) which only resemble examples from Megiddo in the use of painted, generally monochrome, linear decoration; and a small- to medium-sized store jar without handles and often with painted decoration. All of these vessels have similar proportions with an oval body, relatively large, flattish base, and flaring neck. There are, however, two rim types: one externally thickened with a concave inner profile and the other a "moulded" rim, usually flattened on top.[12] This type at Megiddo is often decorated with monochrome painted bands on the upper part of the body, although the rim is sometimes also painted (Loud 1948: pl. 12:22). Only one example (Loud 1948: pl. 13:5), whose form is so similar to that of stratified examples that it must be placed with this group, has a more complex design with a zigzag line around the neck and a series of concentric circles in red and black on its body. As Beck points out (Beck 1975: 53-54), this type of vessel is related in both its form and decoration to similar examples from the Levantine coast to the north and probably also to forms from northern Mesopotamia. The frequency of this type of store jar at Megiddo and in the tombs of Ory's excavations in comparison with its relative scarcity in Kochavi's excavations might suggest that this type had a funerary-related function but was not used for domestic purposes.

As with the flat-based, band-painted store jars, juglets, which are so common at Megiddo, are relatively rare in the Aphek living areas. One Aphek juglet (the collarette type) from T. 43 has a ridge below the rim and painted decoration (Beck 1975: fig. 14:8). Its form would seem to place it with a group of juglets from Megiddo Phases 1 and 2.[13] The decoration of the Aphek juglet is closest to that of an unstratified Megiddo juglet (Loud 1948:

pl. 19:33), but there are also several examples of such decoration found particularly in northern Israel and the Lebanon (Beck 1975: 7682). This juglet seems to fit well with the painted juglets from Ory's excavation (Ory 1937: pl. XXV), suggesting that this may be a funerary type.

Aphek Palace Phase/Megiddo Phase 3: A new form of bowl with S-curved profile (Beck 1975: fig. 4:4-7) is introduced into the repertoire at Aphek in the levelling fill beneath floor A IVb, while the other vessel types basically continue from the prepalace phase. These same basic types also continue, with the introduction of jugs (Beck 1975: fig. 7:1), in the earlier phase of the palace floor. In the second palace-floor phase, the carinated bowls continue, and the Megiddo examples of this phase show a gutter rim which would relate them more closely to those from Aphek (Loud 1948: pls. 14:27, 16:14). At both sites and in several vessel types, the low ring base appears and is characteristic of this phase (Beck 1975: fig. 9:6; Loud 1948: figs. 21:19, 20:17, a mug form, and pl. 22:6).

An unusual, deep rounded bowl with four knobs was found at Aphek (Beck 1975: fig. 10:4), and, on the basis of this parallel, a locus with a similar bowl from Megiddo (T. 3118, Loud 1948: pl. 22:6) was also assigned to Phase 3. The incised cross decoration on the knobs of the Aphek bowl is compared by Beck to similar designs on seals from Karahöyük-Konya (Beck 1975: 64-65). Bowls with thickened or inverted rim appear at both Aphek and Megiddo (Beck 1975: fig. 8:10-12; Loud 1948: pls. 22:2, 21:19). Neither of the cooking-pot types characteristic at Aphek seems to appear at Megiddo. One deep, rounded cooking pot, apparently wheelmade, occurs in T. 3109 (Loud 1948: pl. 22:7). In Megiddo Phase 3, the more elongated store jar with two handles but with still relatively large base (Loud 1948: pl. 21:1) now appears, although the profile of the rim is quite different from that of the otherwise similar store jars from Aphek (Beck 1975: fig. 10:5-6).

The juglets from both sites begin to show an elongation in their shape which with an accentuation of the shoulder often becomes nearly piriform. The dipper juglet type from Megiddo (Loud 1948: pls. 20:15-16, 12:3 and 5) is paralleled at Aphek (Beck 1975: fig. 9:3 and 7), as is also the more piriform type with gutter rim and small base (Beck 1975: fig. 9:2; Loud 1948: pls. 17:5, 19:28). Although the Aphek jug (Beck 1975: fig. 9:5) with sharply carinated body has no direct parallel, it seems to belong to the same class with more rounded body at Megiddo (Loud 1948: pls. 10:1, 19:23). The basket-handled juglet makes its appearance now at both sites (Beck 1975: fig. 9:4; Loud 1948: pl. 20:18), although, as Beck points out, the body of the Aphek example is actually closer in form to that of another Phase 3 juglet from Megiddo (Loud 1948: pl. 13:8) which has an unusual cross decoration on its exterior. Finally, an Aphek jug (Beck 1975: fig. 10:3), although missing part of its rim, seems to have a diagonal slant which Beck suggests should be reconstructed as a slanted rim (Beck 1975: 68). If this reconstruction is correct, then the appearance of this type would parallel the introduction in this phase at Megiddo of the jug with cut-away slanted spout which shows northern influence.[14]

Aphek Postpalace Phase/Megiddo Phase 4: More of the Aphek material from this phase comes from tombs and therefore seems to show a distribution of forms closer to that at Megiddo. Two types of store jars occur at Aphek: a large elongated type (Beck 1975: figs. 11:5, 12:6) and a smaller, oval type (Beck 1975: fig. 12:10). Only the former type, with handles and a short constricted neck (Loud 1948: pl. 18:3), appears in this phase at Megiddo. Among the old bowl types, the carinated bowl with gutter rim, red slip and burnishing, and the open bowl, now usually unslipped, continue. There is also a tendency, however, to use a higher ring base.[15] A new type of bowl with high rounded carination and flaring neck appears at Aphek (Beck 1975: fig. 11:1, 2, 6-7) but not at Megiddo in this phase.[16]

Several types of juglets may be distinguished: the piriform juglet with button base and usually red slip and burnish is now fairly frequent; a juglet with pointed base and pinched rim; the dipper juglet, now also with pointed base; a biconical jug; the cylindrical jug with flat base (a new shape), and, finally, another new shape, the juglet with a folded or "stepped" rim, very likely a descendant of the collarette-rim juglets of the early MB I phase.[17]

Some of the pottery found during Ory's excavations at Aphek should be mentioned here because, although it is not stratified material, it represents a fairly homogeneous group of MB I pottery and adds several pottery types to the MB I ceramic corpus. This group can probably be placed in the early and middle phases of MB I on the basis of the flat-based store jars (Iliffe 1936: 123:23, 24, 29, 51), the goblet (Iliffe 1936: 125:76), and collarette juglets (Iliffe 1936: 125:36, 37, 69). Although the second season of excavations produced similar store jars (Ory 1937: 116:73-76), some later MB I types are also represented; for example, pointed juglets, a juglet with button base, and bowls with low bases. Additional vessels of particular interest include: two handled bowls, the lower part of a pitcher with red slip and burnishing, a bowl with a cross band in dark red paint on the interior, a red-slipped, handleless pitcher or bottle, a small handleless jar with pink painted zones on a white wash ground, and juglets with trefoil rim or painted horizontal bands.[18]

On the basis of this detailed comparison of the pottery from Aphek and Megiddo, it would seem possible to conclude that there is some correspondence between the phasing of these two sites, thus giving validity to the stratigraphic reconstruction of the Megiddo loci as originally devised on independent criteria. The differences seem explicable by the two basic differences in the nature of the sites previously discussed and also by the fact that we would not expect these two sites to be identical in all details of their ceramic sequences.

C. TELL BEIT MIRSIM

This site, where Albright first defined the ceramic chronology of Palestine (Albright 1932, 1933 and 1938a), has a typical repertoire of MB I pottery, but, perhaps because of its pioneering role in the development of the ceramic typology, it is now of somewhat limited use in our attempt to refine further this typology. The two levels assigned to MB I (Ṣtrata G and F) are not usually divided, primarily because of the poor preservation and relative paucity of Stratum F (Albright 1932: 17). These strata therefore show a mix of MB I phases as defined above, including carinated bowls, usually red-slipped and highly burnished, but sometimes a buff color (Albright 1933: 68), with bases ranging from flat and disc to high ring bases. The late form of carinated bowls, with rounded carination and flaring neck, is also represented at Tell Beit Mirsim. Of interest is a bowl with a decoration of a cross in red slip on the interior. Also illustrated is another unusual bowl type, or "teapot," with a side-spout and the rim form of a holemouth jar. The juglet is represented by several fragmentary examples, one with a pinched rim which would relate it to the numerous examples from Megiddo and which, Albright points out (Albright 1932: 15), becomes a much more popular type in the MB II period at Tell Beit Mirsim. There are also numerous examples of the typical flat-based cooking pot with a band of plastic ornament and a row of pierced holes.[19]

The store jar is represented by the double loop-handled type with elongated body and relatively pointed base (Albright 1933: pl. 5:6). There are also fragmentary examples of the upper part of what may be store jars with externally thickened rims and painted decoration on the neck and shoulders. There are many examples of painted decoration, although few which are complete, so it is difficult to discuss which shapes tend to be decorated in this way. The decorations tend to be linear, usually horizontal bands, sometimes alternating with zones of crosses or wavy lines, and are therefore similar in form to those of the Megiddo and Aphek store jars and jugs. The technique, however, is quite different in that the painting tends to be bichrome, dark blue and red, on a white wash ground (Albright 1933: 70). The painted decoration on the vessels from Megiddo is usually executed in a red or brown on the buff natural ground of the vessel. This difference would seem to show that although the decoration may have a common inspiration, there was also considerable regional variation, since the Tell Beit Mirsim variant occurs at other sites in the south and is even used for some of the painted pottery from Aphek. There is probably also one sherd of Cypriote White Painted ware, similar to some examples from Megiddo and other Levantine sites.[20]

III.2. Other Sites of the Southern Levant

Other sites of the southern Levant with material relevant to our study will now be considered by geographical regions (see figs. 1 and 4 for locations of sites). Two features will be sought: first, evidence for MB I presence (including both settlement and tombs) and, second, indications of foreign connections for influences on the development of the local ceramic repertoire. In the first region to be considered, that of the northern Negev, Shephelah, and Philistine Plain, it should be noted that although MB I occupation is present, the only sites which show foreign influence to any extent are those with easy access to the coast (primarily Tell el-ᶜAjjul and Dhahrat el-Humraiya). The second area is the hill country of Judaea and Samaria, which can be contrasted with the Jordan River Valley, where the MB I presence seems negligible. The third area is that of the north which can be subdivided into the Upper Galilee and the coastal region. This area is the richest both in MB I material and in evidence for foreign contacts.

A. NORTHERN NEGEV/SHEPHELAH/PHILISTINE PLAIN

Tell el-ᶜAjjul: This site, located along the Wadi Gaza, was probably an important coastal site in antiquity and may also have controlled a land route between Syria and Egypt. Tell el-ᶜAjjul was originally excavated and published by Petrie (Petrie 1931, 1932, 1933, and 1934), but some of the material has since been republished by Albright (1938b: 337-59), Stewart (1974: 9-16), and Tufnell (1962: 1-37). In addition to the tomb groups of the Courtyard Cemetery which Albright identified as comparable to Tell Beit Mirsim Strata G-F (Albright 1938b: 342-43), additional material which has been identified as possibly MB I includes: Tomb 1015 (Dever 1976: chart 2), Tomb 303B,[21] and stray vessels found in the excavation of the city levels which led Stewart to hypothesize an MB I occupation level which was overlooked or missed by Petrie (Stewart 1974: 10). Some of these vessels are the most interesting of the Tell el-ᶜAjjul material for our comparative purposes and include a trefoil jug with painted geometric decoration, a small jar with horizontal painted lines, and two teapots with beaked spouts, one of which is attached to the rim of the vessel by a bridge;[22] the two teapots are particularly significant in their similarity to examples from Byblos.

Tufnell republished the Courtyard Cemetery material and divided it into six chronologically ordered groups. Although Dever assigned the first five groups to MB I (Dever 1976: chart 2), only the first two groups (Tufnell 1962: figs. 9 and 10) seem to contain typical MB I material. The other groups (Tufnell 1962: figs. 11-14) both continue MB I forms and introduce MB II features, so that these should probably be considered either transitional MB I/II or early MB II. Group 1 (Tufnell 1962: fig. 9) contains dipper juglets with flat base (Nos. 4, 5c and 6, No. 4 with a pinched rim), simple cups with flat (No. 2) or low disc base (No. 5a), a one-handled mug (No. 3), and a two-handled store jar with an incised mark (No. 5). Although this group is clearly MB I, it cannot be directly compared with the typical early MB I phases of such sites as Megiddo and Aphek, since it is lacking the ubiquitous carinated bowls, the handleless store jars, and the other varieties of juglets.

Group 2 (Tufnell 1962: fig. 10) includes a carinated bowl (No. 20), large open bowls with disc base and inverted rim (Nos. 12, 15 and 19), juglets with flat or slightly rounded base (Nos. 8-10, 13, 14), and a double-handled store jar with flat base (No. 16); also typical in this group is the relatively high proportion of vessels with red-slipped and burnished decoration.[23] A group of metal objects placed in Group 2 includes a veined dagger, a socketed spearhead, and a torque, which, Tufnell points out, recalls the assemblage of Schaeffer's "porteurs de torques" (Tufnell 1962: 21). These specific objects—the metal weapons, the painted juglet, and the teapots—show a direct relationship to objects produced in the north. However, the lack of general northern influence on the local repertoire may indicate a regional diversity of MB I culture.

Lachish: Although the site of Lachish, located approximately 13 km. west of Tell Beit Mirsim, lacks any clearly defined MB I stratum or tomb groups, there are several stray vessels and sherds which can be assigned to this period and which may therefore indicate that there was MB I occupation. The only MB I sherds from the mound itself were found in the fill beneath the later MB II glacis (Tufnell 1958: 54-57, figs. 3 and 4). Fragments of MB I bowls with low disc bases, the rounded base of a store jar, and straight-sided cooking pots with pierced rim are all present. Of particular interest are several sherds, probably of store jars, with linear decoration in bluish black and red paint on a lime wash, comparable to examples from Tell Beit Mirsim G-F, a neck and rim fragment of a juglet with two bands of red paint, and a sherd of Cypriote White Painted IV ware.[24]

Of the tomb groups, only a few can be assigned to MB I. Tomb 1552 may overlap late MB I and early MB II and contains carinated bowls on low disc bases, a flaring carinated bowl, flat-based cylindrical juglets, and dipper juglets with flat bases. Tomb 1504 contains a juglet with trefoil rim and a spouted vessel with a decoration of zigzags and lines in red paint. Tomb 1513 has a mix of Early Bronze Age pottery with typical MB I carinated bowls, simple bowls, and flat-based store jars.[25]

In summary, the pottery of Lachish is, as might be expected, probably closest to that of Tell Beit

Mirsim. With the exception of a Cypriote sherd at each site, the pottery shows little influence from the north or west, but the flat-based store jar may be an indication of northern influence.

Tell el-Hesi and *Tell en-Nagila*: Both of these sites, located on the same wadi bed about 32 km. east of Gaza, show some indication of MB I occupation. In the excavations of Petrie and of Bliss at Tell el-Hesi, pottery with MB I features (carinated bowls, some with gutter rims, cylindrical juglets, sherds with red-slip and burnish decoration) was found,[26] but nothing that adds to our knowledge of external contacts. The current excavations at Tell el-Hesi have so far not found any remains of this period (Fargo and O'Connell 1978: 165-82). The excavations at Tell en-Nagila (Amiran and Eitan 1965: 113-23) have produced fairly extensive remains but only of the MB II period, including a fortified city with living quarters and public buildings.[27] Survey of the tell, however, also produced sherds probably belonging to the MB I period.

Dhahrat el-Humraiya: The cemetery site of Dhahrat el-Humraiya is located in the Wadi Rubin region, about 13 km. south of Jaffa and about 3 km. from the coast (Ory 1948: 75-89). Dever (1976: 35, n. 104) pointed out that many of the 63 tombs excavated there should belong to the period of MB I or transitional MB I/II. With the exception of those graves which can be assigned either to the Late Bronze Age (Nos. 8, 27, 28, 57) and probably to MB II (Nos. 45, 55, 63),[28] most of the remaining graves should probably be placed in a late MB I or transitional MB I/II phase (roughly equivalent to Megiddo Phase 4). Most of these graves, however, contain too small a number of vessels, particularly distinctive vessels, to allow any greater specificity. Several parallels, primarily between the material from Dhahrat el-Humraiya and Aphek, can be drawn in order to support this general conclusion.[29] Two vessels of interest come from Grave 21. One is a simple jar with long neck and deep red slip (Ory 1948: 82-83, fig. 21) whose best parallel, despite some differences in body proportions, is a jar found in Ory's excavations at Aphek (Iliffe 1936: 125:74, pl. LXVII). The other is a bowl with small knobs on the rim and a red cross painted on the interior (Ory 1948: 83, fig. 22) which has a parallel from Tell Beit Mirsim (Albright 1933: pl. 5:5) and is therefore placed in MB I (probably mid-MB I). The imported Cypriote pottery, probably the most interesting of the Dhahrat el-Humraiya material, will be discussed in Chapter IV.3 with the other examples of Cypriote pottery found in the Levant.[30]

Two other tomb groups located in the Wadi Rubin region near Dhahrat el-Humraiya were excavated in the 1920s. One of these, at Neby Rubin (Mayer 1926: 2-7, pls. I and II), presents a nearly homogeneous group of MB I material, including open bowls on low disc bases (one with a ridge below the rim), simple carinated bowls usually with gutter rim and disc or ring bases and some with traces of burnish, dipper juglets with flattened base and some with pinched rim, elongated store jars with two handles and flattened bases, and an alabaster vessel. This group can be assigned a mid-late MB I date.[31]

Beth-shemesh: Of the ceramic material excavated at Beth-shemesh, there is little which can be clearly attributed to the MB I period. The first expedition, led by Mackenzie, found nothing of MB I from the tell but excavated one tomb group, the "High Place Grotto Sepulchre," which contained primarily MB I pottery.[32] Of the areas excavated by Grant in 1929, Tomb 3 can be attributed to MB II, while Tomb 2 spans the period from MB I through the Late Bronze Age (Grant 1929: 148-60). In addition to the usual repertoire of MB I/II pottery, it is worthwhile to note a flat-based store jar (Grant 1929: 155, 141, No. 134) and a handleless jar with burnished decoration comparable to other MB I examples (Grant 1929: 139, 153, No. 239). In later seasons of excavation, Grant and Wright (1939: 95-99) were able to distinguish a stratum (VI) which predated the MB II architectural stratum and contained a mixture of EB IV and MB I sherds. The material identifiable as MB I includes fragments of cooking pots with molded band and pierced rim, several polychrome sherds with straight and wavy lines in red and black painted on a white lime wash, sherds of small store jars, juglets with pinched rim, flat-based carinated bowls with thick slip and burnishing, and a sherd of an imported Cypriote juglet.[33]

Gezer: Three tomb groups from Macalister's excavations at this site may be completely or partially assigned to MB I. The pottery from the tombs in III 30 (Macalister 1912a: 298-300, fig. 158) may be considered as MB I, and possibly early in the period because of the flat-based, handleless store jar (No. 3). Other vessels found here include two pitchers with painted decoration (Nos. 6 and 7), a jug with pinched rim (No. 1), a one-handled mug (No. 2), and two simple rounded bowls (Nos. 4 and 5). One of the extramural tombs (Macalister 1912a: 301-2, No. 1) seemed to span both MB I and early MB II, with, of particular interest, a Cypriote juglet and a red-cross bowl.[34] Finally, the deposits of Cave 15 I seem to span the period from at least MB I (and probably earlier) to MB II, but these are of little interest here.[35]

In recent excavations directed by Dever (Dever *et al.* 1971: 120-21, 124-26; and Dever *et al.* 1974: 26-31, pls. 11-14), Stratum XXI has been assigned to the MB I-MB II period, dated to the early 18th century B.C. Various fragmentary architectural structures from both Fields V and VI have been assigned to this stratum, which is typified by dark red-slipped pottery including carinated bowls (Dever *et al.* 1974: pl. 14:12, 13, 29, 30), flat-based store jars (Dever *et al.* 1974: pl. 11:2, 3, 5, 6), and a fragment of a handmade cooking pot (Dever *et al.* 1974: pl. 11:25).

B. JUDAEA/SAMARIA/JORDAN RIVER VALLEY

Wadi et-Tin: This cave burial, located approximately 5 km. southeast of Bethlehem (Vincent 1947: 269-82), contained a large group of pottery which spans both MB I and MB II, the majority of the vessels probably belonging to the later period,[36] but also with some MB I pottery. Of interest to note are: the handleless jar or bottle with parallels from Aphek and Dhahrat el-Humraiya, a small jar with two horizontal handles which has no apparent direct parallel from other Levantine sites, the bowl with a cross painted in black over a red slip on the interior, a red-slipped pitcher which seems to have a beaked cut-away spout, and a one-handled, wide-bodied flask which also has few parallels.[37] Although this group includes little painted pottery (except for the cross-painted bowl), there are a few indications of possible connections beyond the local area. This may seem unusual because of the relatively southern and inland location, but at least some of these features find parallels at sites in the same region, particularly the cross-painted bowl which also appears at Tell Beit Mirsim.

Khirbet Kufin: Another site in this region, Khirbet Kufin (Smith 1962), is located about 11 km. north of Hebron and consisted of several tomb groups, of which the upper strata in Chambers 3/4 and 6/7 of Tomb 3 can be attributed to MB I (with possibly some overlap into MB II in the latter group). The finds from this stratum in Chamber 3/4 (Smith 1962: 17, pl. XIII) include a simple carinated bowl on flat disc base, two juglets (one with a squared handle), a store jar with two handles, flat base, and incised bands, a ribbed dagger blade and two chisel-axe blades, apparently of bronze. The pottery would seem to fit well in the middle phase of MB I, while Smith draws parallels from Tell el-ᶜAjjul, Megiddo, and several Syrian sites. The Chamber 6/7 group (Smith 1962: pls. XIV-XVII) is somewhat more diverse; this group includes several typical MB I pottery types,[38] one limestone and three alabaster vessels which are of Egyptian manufacture or inspiration, three bronze dagger blades, and a bronze axe blade. This chisel-axe blade with two notches and at least the two pointed juglets should belong to MB II, while most of the other objects can be placed in mid-to-late MB I. This collection of objects is a good illustration of the penetration of both Syrian and Egyptian influences to this inland site.

Moza: The other known sites in the Jerusalem area, with the exception of ᶜAin es-Samiyeh, have produced little MB I material. The reused EB IV shaft tombs at Moza (Sussman 1966: 40-43; Dever 1976: 24, n. 35) contained a mixture of MB I and MB II pottery, but the notched axe (Sussman 1966: fig. 3:2) and carinated bowls with S-curved profile (Sussman 1966: fig. 2:4, 8-9) can be placed in MB I.

Gibeon (el-Jib): The necropolis at Gibeon yielded one or possibly two tombs with MB I material (Pritchard 1963: 42-43, 61-62; Tombs 31-31A and 58, respectively, figs. 34 and 64). Tomb 58 contained two flat-based, handleless store jars and a third, larger store jar of similar shape but with shorter neck and an incised band; this group probably dates to early MB I. Tomb 31 had a store jar with two handles and a flat base, which seems to fit well in the mid-MB I repertoire, and also a dagger and a notched chisel-axe.[39]

Shechem; *Bethel*: Although the American excavations at Shechem uncovered remains of two MB I phases in each of two fields (VI and IX, see Toombs 1976: 57-59)—including several architectural structures marking the MB I occupation—since none of the pottery has been published, this site does not yet add to our MB I ceramic corpus.[40] Some stray sherds from the excavations at Bethel have been identified as late MB I, indicating perhaps some slight occupation during this period (Kelso 1968: 23, 56-68; cf. Dever 1976: 25, n. 41).

Jericho: The site of Tell es-Sultan (Garstang 1932; 1933; Kenyon 1960; 1965) has yielded stratified tell material of the Neolithic period through Late Bronze Age, but since only the tombs from the most recent excavations have so far been published, this discussion will be limited primarily to this group of material. Eighty tombs were assigned by Kenyon to the Middle Bronze Age and divided into five groups; however, only one tomb, K 3, was placed in the MB I period (Kenyon 1965: 203-6). This tomb contained a ceramic group fairly typical of MB I.[41] The juglets with stepped rim, bowls with S-curved profiles, and large jugs associate this group with the palace and postpalace phases at Aphek and with Phase 4 at Megiddo (Beck 1975: fig. 11:4; Loud 1948: pls. 10:20, 17:6, 23:7-8, 24:24).[42] The Jericho material, along with that from the other sites in the Jerusalem area, may show a limit in the extent both of the MB I culture and of external influences, although one should still allow for the possibility of future discoveries.

ᶜAin es-Samiyeh; *Sinjil*: The exception to this scarcity of MB I material in the Jerusalem region is the group of tombs at ᶜAin es-Samiyeh and Sinjil, located approximately 24 km. north of Jerusalem. The pottery from this site (Dever 1975a: fig. 3:4-12) includes an open bowl with ring base and four projections on the rim, several simple cups on flat or disc bases, a handleless jar or bottle, a piriform juglet, and another juglet, related to the jar shape but with a handle and flaring neck; the last three vessels are decorated with red slip and burnishing. The weaponry is also typical of MB I, particularly the duckbill fenestrated axe and the socketed spearheads (Dever 1975a: fig. 1:2-4; fig. 3:2-3).

Tell el-Farᶜah (N.): The excavations at Tell el-Farᶜah (N.), conducted by R. de Vaux, revealed remains of this period from an occupation level consisting of houses just above the latest Early Bronze remains and below the foritifications constructed in MB II (de Vaux 1962: 236; Mallet 1973: 29-53, pls. 11 and 12). In addition, several tombs could be assigned to the MB I period. Tomb B (de Vaux and Steve 1948: 571-72, fig. 11; Mallet 1973: pl. 28) was the burial of a young child with a handleless store jar, a carinated bowl on low disc base, and the lower fragment of a jug with red slip and vertical burnish. The finds of Tomb 16 (de Vaux 1955: 544-45, fig. 2) included several juglets with pinched trefoil rims, a flat-based store jar with painted horizontal bands, piriform juglets, an elongated dipper juglet, an open bowl, and two somewhat unusual vessels (de Vaux 1955: 544-45, fig. 2: No. 8, a squat pot with four horizontal handles, and No. 9, a jar with two vertical handles). Tomb AN (de Vaux 1962: 240-43, fig. 3; Mallet 1973: 73-76, pls. 17 and 18) contained two juglets with ridge below the rim, a large jug with one handle, a store jar with two handles and a flat base, and a bowl with rounded carinated profile. The piriform shape of the juglets would seem to indicate a later MB I date, as would also the large jug and the store jar. Tomb AD (de Vaux 1962: 246-47, fig. 6; Mallet 1973: 65-72, pls. 15 and 16) should probably be dated as well in MB I. Its contents, which are similar to those of Tomb AN, included two large store jars with two handles; a stepped-rim juglet; two jugs with one handle, one of which is a triple handle with a knob at the rim attachment; a piriform juglet; and an ovoid dipper juglet. A two-handled store jar, open bowl with a cross painted in red on the interior and a piriform juglet were found in Tomb W, which should be of MB I date (de Vaux 1962: 249-50; Mallet 1973: 83-86, pl. 23). Tomb X contained a bowl with high, rounded carination, a simple carinated bowl, a tripodic vessel, a double-handled store jar, and a slightly piriform juglet (de Vaux 1962: 250, fig. 5; Mallet 1973: 87-90, pl. 25). Finally, Tomb Y, with a piriform juglet and a jug with slightly pinched rim (de Vaux 1962: 249-50; Mallet 1973: 91-92, pl. 26), should be placed fairly late in the MB I period.

Beth-shan: Of the EB IV shaft tombs at this site, one multichambered shaft tomb (Tomb 92) was reused in the MB I period (Oren 1971: fig. 2; 1973: 61-67). It contained a homogeneous group of MB I weaponry—a fenestrated duckbill axehead, a socketed spearhead, a dagger blade with two central ribs and two rivet holes, and a rounded arrowhead with short tang—but no pottery.

C. GALILEE AND NORTH COAST:

Ginosar; *Kfar Szold*: A series of tombs excavated near these two settlements north of Lake Kinneret was dated to the Middle Bronze Age (Epstein 1974). The most distinctive pottery form from these sites is the stepped-rim juglet (described by Epstein as a juglet with candlestick rim and marked neck ridge) which is placed here in a phase marking the end of MB I and transitional to MB II, thus correlating with those examples from the Aphek postpalace phase and Megiddo Phase 4. Several examples from Kfar Szold (Epstein 1974: fig. 1) have painted decoration of horizontal bands, concentric circles, and even hatched triangles. Other pottery from Kfar Szold includes piriform and dipper juglets, some with a gutter rim (Epstein 1974: fig. 1:17-18), and several types of bowls, both open (one with four knobs on the rim,

Epstein 1974: fig. 4:1) and deep globular types, some with burnishing on the exterior.

Of the tombs excavated at Ginosar, Tomb 1 contained both MB I and transitional MB I/II pottery. Several types of jugs and juglets were represented, including an ovoid jug with broad rim, gutter profile, and red burnishing.[43] The rolled rim of another jug from Ginosar (Epstein 1974: fig. 5:1) is also paralleled at Megiddo (Loud 1948: pl. 19:21, T. 3125, Phase 3). A collarette-rim juglet (Epstein 1974: fig. 5:9) relates to the earlier part of MB I, while the pinched-rim juglets with horizontal combing (Epstein 1974: fig. 6:4-5) and a mug (Epstein 1974: fig. 6:8) recall Phase 3 of Megiddo, and a rounded jug with pinched rim[44] and the several stepped-rim juglets, one with painted metope decoration (Epstein 1974: fig. 5:8 and 10), should correspond wtih Megiddo Phase 4. A juglet with a variant of the stepped-rim profile appears at both sites (Epstein 1974: fig. 5:7; Loud 1948: pl. 10:20, T. 3144, Phase 4). There is also a typical assortment of bowls, many carinated with S-curved profiles (Epstein 1974: fig. 7:4-13, the last with painted horizontal stripes), and some open bowls, one with a bar below the rim and another with four knobs attached below the rim (Epstein 1974: fig. 7:1-3). Finally, there are two bronze weapons (Epstein 1974: fig. 7:14-15): a spearhead with raised midrib and a chisel-axe.

Tomb 4 contains several stepped-rim juglets (Epstein 1974: fig. 14), most of which have painted purplish brown decoration on a white, slipped and burnished surface. The motifs include horizontal lines, concentric circles, and, on one (Epstein 1974: fig.14: No. 15), a scene of schematic ibexes and a bird between spirals. These juglets provide a rich range for comparisons with the painted pottery of Syria. Other pottery forms represented include a pinched-rim juglet, a foliated mug, a jug with candlestick rim, a cylindrical juglet, several globular bowls (one with painted purple bands), and a Cypriote juglet in the White Painted III-IV Pendent Line Style (Epstein 1974: fig. 15:1-3, fig.16:2 and 8, fig. 15:9). The similarity of this group to the pottery from Megiddo shows that this site fits well within the culture most extensively represented at Megiddo. The tombs of Kfar Szold and Ginosar, especially in the series of painted juglets but also in other forms present, show a marked relationship with the Syrian sites as well.

Hazor: The site of Hazor, located in the hills above Lake Kinneret and along the route leading to the Biqa[c] Valley, presents a puzzle in our analysis of the trade connections of the MB I period. As was discussed in the preceding chapter, Hazor is mentioned several times in the Mari archive documents, yet the extent of habitation attributed to the MB I period is meager. Some archaeologists, most notably Yadin (1972: 203-6; 1978: 21), correlate the MB II fortified settlement with the Mari period in order to explain this incongruity. Since this problem involves a question of the chronological correlations of this period, it will be considered in Chapter VII. The tell material attributable to the MB I period consists primarily of sherds found beneath the MB II level with which some structures and graves were associated and is placed in the "pre-XVII" stratum (Yadin *et al.* 1958: 145-47; 1960: 76-78; Yadin 1972: 121-22; see also Dever 1976: 24, n. 32). A corpus of pottery belonging to the transitional period between MB I and MB II was found in a rock-cut burial cave in the south slope of the upper city which, because of its position, had to predate the construction of the MB II fortification system (Yadin and Shiloh 1971: 230; Yadin 1972: 201-3; 1975: 269-71). The finds from this cave included two daggers, a spearhead, toggle pins, and approximately 150 vessels, with the following types represented: piriform juglets with candlestick rims and double handles, most with red-slip and burnish decoration (a few in black); a jug and juglet with linear painted decoration in red; a basket-handled juglet with horizontal painted lines in red; several carinated bowls of late MB I-early MB II types; jugs with pinched rim; and open bowls, at least one with a red cross painted on the interior.

Tel Dan; *Tel Kedesh*: Two other major tells in the region of Hazor have also produced material of the MB I period. Tel Dan, located to the north and identified with the Laiš of the Mari documents, has an extensive MB II fortification system beneath which were MB I and MB II stratified occupation levels (Biran 1975: 313-16). The pottery from the MB I level included typical MB I material: a store jar, a painted pitcher, other vessels with red-slip and burnished decoration, and a bronze duckbill axe. A stone chamber tomb of the MB I period, with typical red burnished pottery and a bronze dagger, was excavated beneath the earthen rampart.

The site of Tel Kedesh, to the west of Hazor, is perhaps the largest tell in the region; there is evidence for occupation probably from the Early Bronze Age through the Roman period. Stray finds from this unexcavated site include two carinated bowls of MB I type which are on display in the museum of Kibbutz Sasa. Both of these sites, along with Hazor, are located in an area where one could expect a major trade route from the Syria-Lebanon region and therefore also extensive habitation of the Middle Bronze Age. Despite these indications of MB I occupation, this area must remain largely unknown until further excavation. The finding of scattered MB I sherds in surveys of the Golan region may indicate MB I occupation in the Damascus region and inland Syria (Kochavi 1972: 245, 253, pl. III:7-11).

Turᶜan:[45] An unpublished group of pottery from a shaft tomb located approximately 15 km. east of Nazareth is comparable to the tombs at Ginosar and Kfar Szold. The repertoire ranges from early to late MB I including both the collarette-rim juglet and several piriform juglets with stepped-rim profile. Other vessel types represented are globular dipper juglets with small flat bases, juglets with pinched rim, juglets with broad rim and gutter profile similar to those mentioned above from Ginosar and Megiddo; carinated bowls, some with S-curved profile, some with red slip and burnishing and others with reddish brown painted bands; two open platters with red slip and burnishing; a tripod bowl with four handles; a small store jar with two handles and a flat base, and an unusual bird-juglet of Tell el-Yahudiyeh ware. While this group would seem to fit well within the MB I period, it may also indicate a considerable span of time (as the excavator suggested), both because of the development indicated by the ceramic typology and because the seven skeletons found in the tomb may represent sequential burials.

ᶜAffula: A group of tombs from the Early Bronze Age to Late Bronze Age was excavated at a tell near the town of ᶜAffula (Sukenik 1948: 8-17, pls. XIV-XV). Of these, Burial 3 from Pit A, Burials 11-14 from Pit E, and Burial 19 from Pit F can be attributed to MB I.[46] A fragmentary juglet with triple handle and a knob on the rim at the handle attachment can also be assigned to MB I (Sukenik 1948: pl. XIV:5). While only the ostrich egg shell from Burial 19, Pit F (Sukenik 1948: pl. XV:18) gives clear indication of external contact, probably with Egypt, this group still represents a typical MB I ceramic assemblage.

Tel Zeror; *Tel Poleg*: In returning to the region of Megiddo, several sites with MB I material have been identified. Two sites, Tel Zeror and Tel Poleg, both situated in the Plain of Sharon and therefore stratigically located to control traffic along the coastal corridor (Gophna 1964: 109-11; 1965: 553; 1973: 111-19, Ohata 1966: 1 and 28) had large fortifications which were dated to the MB I period (for doubts, see Yadin 1972: 203-6). Little of the pottery from Tel Zeror, however, can be attributed to MB I.[47]

At Tel Poleg, two levels with typologically similar pottery have been assigned to MB I. The pottery types represented include the carinated bowl with small disc base, gutter rim, and red-slipped and burnished exterior (Gophna 1973: fig. 5:1; pl. 21:1); the globular bowl with small disc base and also a red-slipped and burnished exterior (Gophna 1973: fig. 5:2); open bowls with disc or ring base and brown or red slip and burnishing (Gophna 1973: fig. 5:3—one example of this type with a cross painted on the interior in brown, fig. 5:4); and bowls of various types with bosses (Gophna 1973: pl. 21:2). Other vessels included store jars, cooking pots, jugs with brown slip and band burnishing, and a juglet with button base, red slip, and burnish (Gophna 1973: pl. 21:5). As Gophna points out, these forms have parallels with other MB I assemblages at Tell Beit Mirsim, Megiddo, Aphek, and Tell el-ᶜAjjul, and, if the stratigraphy linking these finds with the fortifications is correct, Tel Poleg may provide an example of an MB I fortification system (see Chapter VIII for a consideration of the fortfications).

Barqai: An EB IV shaft tomb near Kibbutz Barqai (Gophna and Sussman 1969), also in the Plain of Sharon and approximately 18 km. southwest of Megiddo, was reused in the Middle Bronze Age. Although the objects of these periods were mixed together, the second burial phase corresponds to MB I. The finds of this phase included socketed javelin heads (Gophna and Sussman 1969: fig. 4:13-14), two painted juglets with pinched rims, a collarette-rim juglet, and a flat-based store jar (Gophna and Sussman 1969: fig. 4:1, 3, 5, 12). Because of the last two vessels, this group should be placed in the early phase of MB I and provides several points of external influence. Also of interest to note is a bowl with a red cross painted on the interior and a red band on the rim exterior (Gophna and Sussman 1969: fig. 6:10) which, although placed in MB II, relates to similar examples from Tell Beit Mirsim, Wadi et-Tin, Gezer, and Aphek.

Akko; *Mevorach*; *Achzib*: Two large tells with evidence of MB I habitation, Tel Akko (Dothan 1975: 163-66; 1976a: 12) and Tel Mevorach, are being excavated on the coast in the Haifa region. Tel Mevorach shows typical MB I ceramic repertoires from stratified occupation areas but no imports of Cypriote pottery (Stern and Saltz 1978: 139). Tel Akko has revealed typical MB I pottery, especially carinated bowls (Dothan 1976b: 8-9, fig. 7:1-10), and a considerable quantity of imported Cypriote White Painted II-IV pottery (Dothan 1976b: 9, figs. 8-12), mostly of the Pendent Line and Cross Line groups, which may be an indication of fairly extensive trade between the coast of Palestine and Cyprus. Much of the MB I pottery, however, was found in the fill of the glacis which was therefore considered to be of post-MB I date. Subsequent excavations, however, revealed a city gate, dubbed the "Sea Gate," which, along with an associated *terre pisée* rampart, has been dated to the MB I period (Dothan and Raban 1980: 35-39).

The Plain of Akko was recently studied in a survey (Prausnitz 1975a: 23-30; 1975b: 202-10) which located several MB I sites and identified a pattern of settlement for the region consisting of three tiers of occupied sites: the first along the coast, the second in the coastal plain near fresh water sources and with the ability to control road junctions, and the third along the hill tops overlooking the plain and with a good defensive position. Some of these sites have been or are now being excavated, such as Tel Maᶜamer, Tel Bira, Tel Regev, and Kabri. Achzib, located on the coast, was sounded in two seasons and a system of fortifications found, the fill of which contained a fairly extensive corpus of late MB I and early MB II pottery (Oren 1975),[48] as well as a fragment of an imported Cypriote White Painted vessel with reddish purple bands (Oren 1975: fig. 4:90).

Nahariya: Another site in this coastal region, the Middle Bronze Age temple precinct at Nahariya, which is located along the coast about 8 km. north of Akko and less than 1 km. south of the ancient settlement at Achzib, was excavated by Ben-Dor in 1947 (Ben-Dor 1950: 1-41) and again by Moshe Dothan in 1954 and 1955 (Dothan 1956: 14-25). Ben-Dor's excavations concentrated on the main temple building, in which he distinguished seven successive floor levels, and on the area just to the north and west of the building. Dothan expanded the excavated area to the south of the main building and identified three building phases (Dothan 1956: fig. 1). While Dothan clearly states (1956: 22) that the presence of Cypriote Base Ring ware and White Slip ware as well as some bichrome sherds indicates that the use of the site must have continued into the 16th century B.C., neither he nor Ben-Dor attempted to establish a date for the beginning of the occupation of the area. Except for the publication of most of the pottery from Ben-Dor's excavation by floor level, it is not possible to deduce the chronology of the site on the basis of stratigraphy, but only on the basis of distinctive pottery types which can be dated by comparative material. Even here there is some difficulty in that so much of the pottery is unusual, consisting primarily of incense burners, multiple vessels and lamps, and handmade miniatures. The collarette juglet, however, is represented by three examples, one of them a miniature which is decorated with vertical and horizontal lines on the rim, handle and upper half of the body in brown paint (Ben-Dor 1950: fig. 16:325; pl. IX:22 and fig. 24c). The lower part of a typical rounded, handleless, small store jar is also present and is decorated with horizontal bands in red and black (Ben-Dor 1950: fig. 47); it and the collarette juglets should be placed in the early phase of MB I. Dothan (1956: fig. 8) shows a painted juglet, which may be compared with similar examples from Megiddo Phases 3 and 4.[49] Finally, it is interesting to note two fragmentary cut-away spouts of pitchers in greenish buff ware (Ben-Dor 1950: 31, fig. 25 and pl. IX:21) which Ben-Dor identifies as "probably Cypriote." Concerning this temple site, we can conclude that its beginning dates to early MB I and that its pottery fits well within the culture best represented at Megiddo.

III.3. Sites of the Northern Levant

The sites of Syria and Lebanon, some of which were the major centers of settlement during the 2nd millennium B.C., will be reviewed. The major characteristics of the material culture of MB I, which were discerned in the southern sites, will also be shown to the present at these northern sites, and it can be demonstrated that the MB I culture of the Levant was probably more homogeneous than it is often thought to have been.

A. LEBANESE COAST AND RELATED INLAND SITES

Byblos: The extensive material excavated at the site of Byblos has long been a source of controversy in the discussion of the dating and origins of the characteristic MB I culture of the Levant. The similarity of the assemblage of artifacts found in the Royal Tombs and in the "dépôts des offrandes" to the material excavated at other Levantine sites[50] was recognized soon after the publication of the first Byblos finds. Because many of these were found in apparently closed contexts along with datable Egyptian objects, especially in the Royal Tombs, it was thought that Byblos would establish an absolute chronology for the Levant in MB I. Albright, in particular, tended to interpret the Byblos material as representative of the earliest Middle Bronze Age culture and therefore used the Egyptian evidence to date the beginning of his MB IIA period. Despite the problems of date, the Byblos material provides some of the richest clues for cross-contacts between the Levant and Anatolia, Egypt, and Mesopotamia.

The Royal Tombs: Tombs I and II have been dated to the reigns, respectively, of Amenemhet III and IV on the basis of their cartouches which were found in the tombs. The date of Tomb III is not as certain, but it may belong to the beginning of Dynasty 13 (Tufnell 1969: 5-6), while, of the remaining tombs, Tomb IV was disturbed, Tombs VI-IX had little pottery and are probably to be placed later than the first three tombs, and Tomb V (the tomb of Ahiram) is considerably later (Montet 1928: 202-4, 214).

The metal vessels found in Tombs I-III include two silver teapots, one with a strainer spout, which are paralleled by two ceramic teapots from Tomb III at Byblos[51] and from Tell el-ᶜAjjul (Schaeffer 1948: fig. 122:11). Tufnell has suggested that this shape may have an Anatolian prototype (Tufnell 1969: 10). The presence of these similar teapot types (especially the two silver examples) in tombs which belong to different generations shows that these tomb groups cannot be used as closed units of vessel types representing a specific time. In this case (as probably with the offering deposits) vessels which were saved and considered heirlooms may have been buried much after the time when they or their types were in actual use.

There were two carinated bowls[52] in Tomb II which relate to the MB II type of carinated bowl with flaring rim and which should be dated, at the latest, to the early 18th century B.C. (according to Tufnell 1969: 5). Finally, the fragmentary bronze spouted pitcher from Tomb II (Montet 1929: pl. CXV: No. 782) has clear Anatolian affinities, although the lotus at the base of the handle (Montet 1928: 195) might argue for a local origin.

Of the pottery vessels discussed by Tufnell, most are of limited interest. The simple rounded cups and the U-shaped open bowls with flat or rounded base (Tufnell 1969: figs. 2 and 3) are common at sites in Syria and Lebanon during the Middle Bronze Age, while the first type is also common farther south. The dipper juglets (Tufnell 1969: fig. 4:32-43) with plain finish, rounded base, and pinched rims are generally considered a later Middle Bronze Age feature and, along with the store jars (Tufnell 1969: fig. 6:53-57) which had also perplexed Tufnell (1969: 15), were considered by Dever (1976: 11, 27, n. 69) to have general parallels with his MB IIC period.

The beakers (Tufnell 1969: fig. 4:46-47) may relate to the goblets of Phase 4 Megiddo but are an advanced form with ring base and therefore later than the flat-based type of late MB I. Also of this type but closer to the Megiddo examples and to one from Gezer (Macalister 1912b: pl. LXI:34) is Montet's No. 815 (Montet 1929: pl. CXVII, not drawn by Tufnell) which has a sharper profile than do Tufnell's examples. The goblets with loop handle near the base (Tufnell 1969: fig. 5:48-49) are matched by other examples from the Lebanon area (Chehab 1939: fig. 2a).

The juglets with pinched rim and ring base have parallels from central Anatolia (Tufnell 1969: 13) and may be the intermediary types for the Anatolian-influenced jugs with pinched rims at sites in the southern Levant.[53] The jug (Tufnell 1969: fig. 5:50) also shows strong northern influence but is paralleled by a juglet from Megiddo (Loud 1948: pl. 20:4, T. 4112) and, although less closely, by an example from Gezer (Macalister 1912a: fig. 158:1). The remaining vessel, the large jar (Tufnell 1969: fig. 5:51), has no direct parallels but may belong to a group of jars (generally with narrower bodies) from the southern Levant.[54]

In the other tomb groups, the "tombeaux des particuliers," also excavated by Montet, the first two tombs show a mix of MB II vessels, including several Tell el-Yahudiyeh juglets. The third tomb, however, seems to present a fairly homogeneous group of MB I pottery whose date is further indicated by the presence of two fenestrated duckbill axes. An unusual vessel from this tomb is an animal-headed juglet whose rim is so pinched as to form a figure eight. Other vessels include a shallow bowl with horizontal handle at the rim, juglets with flattened base and pinched rim, one example of which (Montet 1929: pl. CXLVII: No. 931) has painted horizontal bands, a one-handled mug with wheel-combing, and a biconical-shaped mug with handle.[55]

The Deposits: Of the many "dépôts des offrandes" excavated by both Montet and Dunand and whose dating and purpose are quite controversial, the best known is the so-called "Montet Jar." Because of the republication of the contents of the "Montet Jar" by Ward and Tufnell, it is possible to study these objects in greater detail than from Montet's original publication. For our purposes, the greatest interest lies in the three metal vessels (Nos. 207-209, Tufnell and Ward 1966: 212, fig. 9). The carinated bowl, No. 209, is a typical form which appears in both MB I and MB II, but the high ring base is usually an MB II feature, at least in the southern Levant. The other bowl, No. 207, has its closest parallel in another example in bronze from Byblos (Dunand 1939: 147: No. 2171; Dunand 1937: pl. LXVI) but no direct parallel from other sites, although it obviously falls into the same category of MB I/II bowls; it also has a high ring base. The third vessel, No. 208, has no parallels from the Levant, although Tufnell and Ward compare it to vessels from Iran and the Luristan area, and especially to examples from Tepe Hissar IIIC and B (Tufnell and Ward 1966: 213, n. 2). The authors suggest that, since the two bowls with their ring bases seem to belong to the MB II period, it might be necessary to raise the date for the beginning of MB II (Tufnell and Ward 1966: 214).

The "Montet Jar" itself (Tufnell and Ward 1966: fig. 1, pl. XI) is also of interest because of the manufacturing techniques and decorative motifs which clearly relate to both the EB IV period and to MB I. In terms of technique, the combination of handmade body with wheelmade neck is typical of EB IV, as also is the rope molding; the flattened base, however, relates to the MB I period (Tufnell and Ward 1966: 173). As Ward and Tufnell point out, the hatched triangles and the wavy and straight painted lines are clear links to the Syrian painted-ware styles of the early 2nd millennium (Tufnell and Ward 1966: 171-72; Schaeffer 1948: figs. 84:11, 86:2 and 4, right). This motif appears frequently in the Levant in MB I, although, with the exception of the "Montet Jar,"[56] it usually appears on various juglet types. The appearance of this motif on the "Montet Jar" and on another jar from Ugarit (Schaeffer 1932: fig. 12:10) provides a pivotal point in the relative date of this motif, since its appearance on a vessel which in technique is transitional between the EB IV and the MB I periods should provide a horizon for the occurrence of this motif in western Syria.

Because of the pivotal role of the "Montet Jar" in the ceramic sequence, it would be helpful if an absolute date could be determined for it and, by extension, possibly for the beginning of MB I ceramic features, at least in Syria. Tufnell and Ward concluded that the jar and all its contents, with the exception of the three cylinder seals, should be dated between 2130 B.C. (beginning of Dynasty 10) and ca. 2040 B.C. (the reunification of Egypt under Mentuhotep II). Porada, however, places the three cylinder seals, which she relates to Alalakh and Hama, Levels J2 and H4, and to the "Syrian Group" of cylinder seal impressions from Kültepe Level II, somewhat later, that is, the late 20th to the mid-19th century B.C., although she makes some comparisons with earlier, late-3rd-millennium material (Porada 1966: 243-58). Although it is impossible to resolve this apparent conflict, the evidence for the dating of the jar and its contents would seem to give a *terminus ante quem* for the beginning of MB I in Syria in the middle of the 19th century B.C. Since there is no reason, however, for assuming that all the objects in the Jar are the same date, no further chronological conclusions can be drawn.

In addition to the "Montet Jar," there were over 40 other offering deposits, most of them excavated by Dunand. Although these are of relatively little interest here, they should be mentioned so that they can be placed in their proper context. As with many of the finds from Byblos there is disagreement over their dating and their function.[57] The large majority of the offerings are metal objects, primarily human and animal figurines or weaponry. Their large number and the presence of molds and incomplete examples would argue for local manufacture. The weaponry also gives some indication of dating since there are several typical of the MB I repertoire, especially the fenestrated duckbill axes.[58]

The pottery found in the deposits consists primarily of the jars in which the objects had been buried. Most of these jars are of an unusual shape, often cylindrical and elongated, designed to fit the sizes of the jars' contents. However, there are also some examples of fairly typical store jar forms with flattened base, plump oval body, everted rim, and two handles. This shape would seem to place these store jars in an early-to-mid MB I context, although they are not exactly of the flat-based, handleless type.[59] The cylindrical store jars were usually painted with horizontal or vertical straight, wavy, or zigzag lines, cross-hatching, circles and herringbone patterns, usually executed in red or reddish brown paint, sometimes on a white ground.[60] Another vessel used as a container was a goblet which held a bronze juglet with a high ring base.[61]

Of the other pottery vessels found either in deposits or as stray finds which can be attributed to MB I, a few are of interest. A flat-based goblet, similar in shape to the goblets from the Royal Tombs, is decorated with horizontal straight and wavy lines painted in red. Of two juglets, one has a pinched rim and burnish decoration and the other horizontal lines painted in red. Two biconical mugs resemble those found in the third private tomb; one has red-painted undulating and straight lines. A collarette juglet is decorated with horizontal lines in red on the neck, rim, and handle and a large spiral on the body. Finally, one nearly complete and several sherds of vessels are Minoan imports, probably to be dated to the Middle Minoan I period.[62]

The conclusions concerning the development of MB I ceramics drawn from the Byblos material can be summarized. First, the presence of pottery with MB II affinities in the first three Royal Tombs would argue that the Egyptian material in the Royal Tombs cannot be used to date the appearance of MB I in the Levant;[63] if anything, this material should be used to argue a date for MB II in the beginning of the 18th century. This conclusion may be further supported by the presence of metal vessels with high ring bases among the contents of the "Montet Jar," the latest suggested date for which is in the 19th century B.C. The "Montet Jar" itself, as a vessel transitional between the EB IV and the MB I periods, can be used to suggest a date during the 20th century B.C. for the appearance of at least certain MB I features and especially for the appearance of certain painted motifs in western Syria. Finally, this assemblage shows direct parallels with both Anatolia and the southern Levant, including Megiddo, Aphek, and Tell el-ᶜAjjul.

Ras Shamra (*Ugarit*): Ras Shamra is one of the largest Bronze Age sites located along the Syrian coast, yet the finds and occupation attributable to MB I are relatively sparse, although this may not be an accurate reflection of the extent of MB I occupation. While several tomb groups spanning the Middle Bronze Age were published by Schaeffer in the 1930s and 1940s, very little of the tell material from occupation levels has yet been published (Courtois 1973: 296).

The entire Middle Bronze Age falls within Stratum 2 of the "Ugarit moyen" (hereafter abbreviated as U.M.), which is subdivided into: 1 = EB IV (2100-1900 B.C.); 2 = MB I (1900-1700 B.C.); 3 = MB II (1700-1550 B.C.). The dates were derived by Schaeffer from synchronisms with the Egyptian dynastic sequence. In some cases, however, Schaeffer changed his attribution of a tomb group to either U.M. 2 or U.M. 3 between the preliminary report and later publications.[64] Another difficulty is that Schaeffer often attributes vessels either to U.M. 2 or to U.M. 2/beginning of U.M. 3, which, by the criteria of the ceramic development established at other sites in the Levant, ought to be clearly attributed to MB II.[65]

The tomb material which may be attributed to MB I comes primarily from three sources (North 1973: 136-37): Tomb XXXVI (Level J) from Cut I, Tomb LV (the lowest level) from Cut II, and the cist graves from the tell area between the temples of Baal and Dagon, or Cut III. While additional material from the tell has been published (Schaeffer 1949), no ceramic material has yet been published from a recently excavated occupation area along the western edge of the tell (Courtois 1973: 293-97; 1974: 102).

Tomb XXXVI contained two juglets on ring bases with strongly pinched rims, two bichrome (red and black) juglets, one with pinched rim and both with relatively flat bases, several sherds (one belonging to a cup of Middle Minoan IIA Kamares ware), and a juglet with stepped-rim profile, low ring base, and a black burnished finish.[66] While the first four juglets should be placed in MB II, the last juglet may indicate some mix of late MB I or transitional MB I/MB II pottery.

Cave LV may also represent a mix of MB I-II pottery, with the majority belonging to the later period, including pointed dipper juglets, juglets with pinched rims and piriform bodies (one with bichrome decoration), carinated bowls on high ring bases, and a mug with trefoil rim. An open bowl on flat base, two Cypriote White Painted juglets, and one jug with flat base, ovoid body, pinched rim, and painted decoration in black could belong to late MB I.[67]

The material from the tell assigned to "Ugarit moyen" and excavated at a depth between 2 and 3 m. presents more difficulties because absolute levels were sometimes used to determine the dating of an object, thus causing confusion of material from different time periods (for example, see Schaeffer 1932: 19 and the graphic presentation, Schaeffer 1948: pl. XIII). Of the vessels which can be attributed to MB I, the following are of interest. A collarette juglet with painted concentric circles on the body may be compared with examples previously discussed from Aphek and Megiddo and thus dated to early MB I. A stepped-rim juglet with similar painted decoration is comparable to examples from Ginosar. Additional juglet types include undecorated stepped-rim juglets, juglets with painted decoration, usually horizontal lines, round bodies, sometimes flattened bases and either flat or pinched rims, a jug with cut-away spout, flat base and painted decoration of vertical and horizontal lines and cross-hatched triangles on the rim, neck ridge and body, and two plain juglets with flat rims. A two-handled krater with red and black painted decoration of cross-hatched triangles should be considered MB I as also various types of carinated bowls. A new type of bowl occurs with narrow base out of proportion to the width of the body and rim and sometimes with carinated shoulder and one or two handles.These may be comparable to some of the bowls from the Royal Tombs at Byblos (Tufnell 1969: fig. 3:17-28). Also represented were two pitchers with beaked spouts, incised line decorations, and red-slipped and burnished finish which are so similar to central Anatolian examples that Schaeffer considered one of them an import. The imported wares included many Cypriote White Painted juglets of various types and more Middle Minoan pottery. The metal objects included fenestrated duckbill axes and triangular dagger blades with rivet holes.[68] A more recently excavated group from the South Acropolis includes a stepped-rim juglet with painted decoration of concentric circles, a painted dipper juglet, an "eye" jug, and a black burnished vessel with a ring body (Schaeffer 1978: 208-9, figs. 4 and 4A).

While the MB I material from Ras Shamra is perhaps disappointing in its paucity and its inability to add to our understanding of the chronology of MB I, it is at least possible to establish an MB I horizon at the site and to show a continuity in the familiar forms, particularly the juglets and the bowls, along the Syrian coast. Many of the smaller ceramic groups, primarily from tombs, from the Syro-Lebanese coast will now be examined.

Kafer Djarra: The most extensive group of Middle Bronze Age tombs of this region was excavated in the area of Sidon on the Lebanese coast. The necropolis at Kafer Djarra was first investigated by Contenau (1920: 125-30; 1924: 124-25) who found a flat-based, handleless store jar (Contenau 1924: pl. XXXIV) in addition to several vessels of MB II. This necropolis was later excavated by Guigues who explored 74 burials at Ruweise. These tombs can be placed in different phases of the Middle Bronze Age, many to the last phase of MB I and/or the beginning of MB II. The finds of Tomb 6 were sparse but may belong to MB I because of two juglets with pinched rim and a neck ridge. Tomb 8 is probably partially MB I with a mug related to the "Ḫabur" goblet shape, a jug with horizontal rim, flat base, and painted bands, a globular jug with handle on the shoulder and red slip and burnish, a carinated bowl, a cylindrical juglet, and a tripod jar. Tomb 14 had several juglets (one with pinched rim, flat base, and red slip and vertical burnish), a flat-based store jar with red horizontal bands on the body and radiating lines on the neck, and a jar with basket handle with red slip and vertical burnish.[69] Tomb 15, with a tripod vase, cylindrical juglets, juglets with pointed base, and a small bowl with pointed carination (Guigues 1937: fig. 32), is probably transitional between MB I and MB II. Tomb 25 has primarily MB II material, but some of the carinated bowls may still relate to MB I (Guigues 1937: figs. 37K and 38q).

Tomb 33, with a carinated bowl (Guigues 1938: fig. 40), a cylindrical juglet, and a javelin head with median rib, may be late MB I, as also Tomb 37 with a similar group of vessels. Tomb 56 contained a flat-based carinated bowl, a cylindrical juglet, a juglet with pinched rim, and an ovoid juglet with handle on shoulder and horizontal bands in black and red.[70] This tomb should be placed in mid-to-late MB I.

Tomb 57 represents a fairly homogeneous MB I group, as shown by the presence of both a duckbill fenestrated axe and the chisel-type axe (Guigues 1938: fig. 51). The pottery includes juglets with both pinched and horizontal rims, carinated bowls, a jug with handle on the shoulder, a small jar with two lug handles, a jar with red slip, single handle, and spout (Guigues 1938: figs. 49 and 50),[71] and two mugs with small disc base, one with red slip and vertical burnish (Guigues 1938: fig. 53; compare with Loud 1948: pl. 17:12, probably of Megiddo Phase 3). Two juglet rims, one pinched and the other rounded, decorated with horizontal brown lines may either be fragments of imported Cypriote juglets or possibly local imitations of Cypriote pottery. The pinched rim is not as common on Cypriote juglets as on those produced on the mainland, but it is not possible to determine their place of manufacture (Guigues 1938: fig. 48). In addition to the axes, the tomb contained four javelin heads with marked midrib, four dagger blades, and a lapis lazuli cylinder showing a presentation scene which probably belongs to the style of the First Babylonian Dynasty (Guigues 1938: fig. 54; see also Schaeffer 1948: 73).

Tomb 62 represents the transitional MB I/MB II phase, including simple and flaring carinated bowls, many with red or brown slip and burnish, stepped-rim juglets, a cylindrical juglet, two handleless store jars, one with painted concentric circles and horizontal lines (Guigues 1938: fig. 59), and two large jugs with handle on shoulder (Guigues 1938: figs. 57-63). Tomb 66 contained 17 juglets and presents a range of MB I and MB II types. The most interesting are the two painted examples, one with concentric circles and the other with a herringbone pattern (Guigues 1938: pl. III:bl and X, restored with a stepped rim). As well as other juglet types, such as pointed dipper juglets, piriform juglets, and pinched-rim juglets (Guigues 1938: figs. 67-69), carinated bowls of MB II type, a goblet similar to examples from the Royal Tombs at Byblos (Tufnell 1969: fig. 4:46-47), three chisel-axes, two dagger blades with weak midrib, scarabs, and a cylinder seal in black steatite (which seems to relate to the later Mitannian style) were also present.

Tomb 73 includes several stepped-rim juglets with painted decoration (Guigues 1938: fig. 79) but, with pointed dipper juglets, MB II carinated bowls, and a late form of store jar, this tomb should probably be placed in MB II. Finally, Tomb 74 (Guigues 1938: figs. 84-93) had a similar group of mostly MB II vessels but also included a spouted bowl (*supra*, Tomb 57, n. 71) and a jug with close parallels from Megiddo Phases 3 and 4 (Loud 1948: pls. 10:5-7 and 7:15). While Guigues dated these tombs between 1725 and 1550 B.C. and thus within the traditional dates for MB II, the numerous parallels from other MB I Levantine sites argue for a date for some of the tombs beginning in that period.

Lebeᶜa: Two of the tombs excavated by Guigues at Lebeᶜa in the Sidon area also belong to the MB I period. Of these, Tomb 1 (Guigues 1937: figs. 3 and 4) contained a pinched-rim juglet, with burnishing and painted decoration of concentric circles in red between bordering lines in black,[72] a fenestrated duckbill axe, a dagger blade with medial veins and three rivet holes, and additional juglets with straight and pinched rims. Tomb 3 also contained a variety of MB I juglets: one, very close to the early collarette juglet, had a series of spirals and horizontal bands painted on the body in red (Guigues 1937: figs. 6 and 7).

Qraye: Another tomb at Qraye located near Sidon contained predominantly Late Bronze Age pottery (Guigues 1939: 53-63), but Schaeffer (1948: 76-77) suggested, on the basis of three vessels which seemed to belong to the Middle Bronze Age, that the tomb was originally cut in the Middle Bronze Age and then later reused. These three vessels include a Cypriote White Painted III-IV juglet of the Pendent Line style, which could be placed at the end of MB I or in MB II, a spouted jar which reminded Schaeffer of Minoan pottery but also resembles the spouted jars previously mentioned from Kafer Djarra, Tombs 51 and 74, and a footed goblet with painted decoration of spirals and triangles, which does not seem to fit within the usual MB I repertoire (Guigues 1939: pls. XIIb, IXf and Xa, respectively).

Majdalouna: The last tomb group from the Sidon area at Majdalouna (Chehab 1940: 37-53) also seems to span the period from MB I to the Late Bronze Age. Although few of the vessels can be assigned to MB I, these include several stepped-rim juglets which are either late MB I or early MB II, some with painted concentric circles, jugs with flat bases and either flat or pinched rims, bowls with rounded carination, a handleless store jar with painted concentric circles, similar in shape to the flat-based type, and the simple angular carinated bowls.

A treasure group which was smuggled out of Lebanon but was presumably excavated at some coastal site is comparable, although on a lesser scale, to the finds from the Royal Tombs at Byblos (Chehab 1937: 7-21). In addition to several Egyptian pieces in gold and other metals, including a pectoral with the name of Amenemhet III, the finds included two vases in gold (Nos. 33 and 34) which exhibit sharply carinated forms and are thus comparable to the pottery of this period, alabaster and faience vessels, including a spouted pitcher (No. 35), and gold pins with ribbed heads.

Sin el-Fil: A tomb on the Lebanese coast at Sin el-Fil near the Nahr Beyrouth (Chehab 1939: 803-10) contained a range of MB I and early MB II objects. The MB I pottery consisted of a collarette-rim juglet in light pink clay of early MB I date (Chehab 1939: fig. 4b), a juglet, also in pink beige clay, with a stepped rim, flat base, and six horizontal bands in red on the shoulder and a metope pattern of seven groups of vertical lines (Chehab 1939: fig. 7a), another juglet with red horizontal bands on the body and vertical rays above the bands (Chehab 1939: fig. 7b), a juglet in pink clay with red bands on the neck and shoulder and groups of concentric circles on the body (Chehab 1939: fig. 8a), a flat-based store jar with groups of circles in red (Chehab 1939: fig. 8c), and open bowls with disc base and lugs on the rim (Chehab 1939: fig. 9). The bronze objects included two fenestrated duckbill axes, lance heads, and dagger blades with midrib (Chehab 1939: fig. 10); there were also pins in silver and bronze, a silver bracelet, a gold ring, and five scarabs. Parallels particularly for the painted decoration, the juglets, and the duckbill axes can be drawn with other sites in the Lebanon (as at Byblos) and with sites to the south (Megiddo and Aphek).

Amrith: A group of Middle Bronze Age tombs was excavated at Amrith, 7 km. south of Tartous (Dunand, Saliby, and Khirichian 1954: 189-98). In Tomb 7, which had four superposed levels of burials, the third level contained two skeletons, each with a narrow fenestrated (duckbill) axe behind the head, bronze pins, typical MB I carinated bowls, a collarette juglet with concentric circles painted on the body, and several other jugs with various types of painted decoration (Dunand, Saliby, and Khirichian 1954: 197, pl. III: 2 [apparently mislabelled as Tomb 4]). This tomb also contained in its lowest level a semicircular fenestrated axe, which Dunand commented upon as "confirmation absolue de l'antériorité de la hache fenestrée semi-circulaire sur la hache fenestrée étroite" (Dunand, Saliby, and Khirichian 1954: 197, n. 1). Tomb 8 contained another narrow fenestrated axe and a lance head with medial rib, while another group included several jugs, one with painted decoration of crosses between horizontal bands, and MB I carinated bowls (Dunand, Saliby, and Khirichian 1954: 196-98, pl. III: 4).

Tell Simiriyan: Soundings of small tells along the coast have given some additional indication, although sparse, of the habitations which must have accompanied these tomb sites. An investigation of Tell Simiriyan, near the village of Mantar, approximately 45 km. north of Tripoli, revealed some indication of an occupation level attributed to MB I, although the sounding was limited in area and the only architectural feature was a burned floor (Braidwood 1940: 183-214). The pottery from this floor was fairly uniform and included sherds of flat-based carinated bowls, sometimes with burnishing (Braidwood 1940: 211-12, fig. 19:11 and 12), as well as of larger bowls and store jars. Some of the sherds had painted decoration, usually consisting of horizontal lines in brownish black; a handle had stripes in red orange, while another sherd had a zigzag pattern (Braidwood 1940: fig. 18:1 and 7). Decoration of combing in straight and wavy lines and molded bands also occurred (Braidwood 1940: fig. 18:3 and 8), thus showing another typical MB I feature. A bronze statuette, apparently of a male god (Braidwood 1940: pl. XXVI) with parallels from other Syrian sites (Negbi 1976: 10-11), was found in this level.

Tell Sukas: Additional indication of MB I occupation is given by the sherds excavated in a sounding at Tell Sukas (Ehrich 1939: 72-83) located on the Syrian coast about 35 km. south of Ugarit. The MB I period is represented by small wheelmade carinated bowls with flat base, red-to-black surface and burnishing (Ehrich 1939: pl. XX: fig. XVIII). Painted decoration, usually in red or black, with motifs typical of MB I in Syria and Cilicia (Ehrich 1939: 80-82, pls. XXII-XXIII) consists of oblique and vertical straight or wavy lines, triangles, sometimes with cross-hatching, and radiating stripes at the base of the necks of jars. An interesting piece is a juglet neck with pinched rim and horizontal stripes in red-to-black on a buff ground (1.P7.1). While this piece resembles the Cypriote White Painted wares (compare with the two juglet fragments from Kafer Djarra, Guigues 1938: fig. 48), the trefoil rim would seem to be a local Syrian feature (Ehrich 1939: 82; cf. Åström 1957: 64) so that without the body of the juglet (and without indication of whether the piece is wheelmade or handmade), it is difficult to determine whether this piece is of Syrian or Cypriote manufacture. A burial excavated by Forrer on the nearby tell of Qal^cat er-Rus (Ehrich 1939: 54, and Forrer in Ehrich 1939: 120-21) contained several bronze objects, including two bracelets, a pin, a bead, and a torque with spiral ends, which have been compared with the contents of the "Montet Jar" and variously dated from EB IV through MB II (Schaeffer 1948: 40-41).

Kāmid el-Lōz: An inland site, Kāmid el-Lōz, located in the Biqa^c Valley (Hachmann 1969: 77-84), yielded a tomb group from a cemetery on the north slope of the mound which may be assigned to the MB I period. This tomb $ID_{15}14$ (Hachmann 1969: 82-83, pl. VII: lower, and pl. XVI), contained a large jug in red clay with pinched rim and round body (No. 1), an open bowl with four lug handles on the rim (No. 2), a bowl with rounded carination and a low disc base (No. 5), another juglet with pinched rim, disc base, and vertical burnishing (No. 6), a cylindrical juglet (No. 3), and a juglet with button-base (No. 4), which would seem to place this group in mid-to-late MB I. More recent excavations at this site have continued to reveal additional evidence of MB I occupation (personal communication, L. Marfoe).

Tell es-Salihiyyeh: At Tell es-Salihiyyeh, located approximately 15 km. east of Damascus, the lowest level (Level XII) belongs to the MB I period. The architecture included a series of walls, but these did not seem to form coherent building plans (von der Osten 1956: 36-39). The ceramic forms included several bowls with high rounded carination, some with incised lines around the neck and one with quatrefoil rim, and several juglets, some with pinched rims, flat bases, and black and red painted horizontal bands or with thick red slip and burnishing (von der Osten 1956: pls. 42-43). The pottery of this level was all wheelmade of well-fired, light brown, sand-tempered clay (von der Osten 1956: 45-50, 77-78). This site, along with the cemetery at Kāmid el-Lōz, indicates that there is probably a significant region of MB I occupation sites in inland Syria awaiting future archaeological investigation.

B. THE ORONTES RIVER VALLEY

Hama: The site of Hama, located along the river, is unusual among the sites considered here in that while it presents several stratified architectural levels belonging primarily to the MB I period, the MB II period is not extensively represented. Although a few sherds of Tell el-Yahudiyeh ware and some early MB II forms are present (for example, high carinated bowls from Level H 1, Fugmann 1958: 104, fig. 127:2D211 and 214), one would be tempted to conclude that the fully developed MB II is missing.[73] The MB I period, meanwhile, is represented by five architectural levels in some areas of the mound, which are characterized by the presence of cylindrical silos in which much of the pottery was found.

The pottery types, although reflecting regionalized characteristics, also include various MB I features: small bowls of both the rounded type and the type with simple carination, generally with flat or low disc base; a variation of the carinated bowl with externally rounded rim and pointed carination; bowls with rounded carination and combed decoration, usually on the upper half of the vessel; and flat open bowls with disc, ring, or rounded base. Of the more interesting forms present, we should note a "Ḫabur"-type goblet, similar to examples from Aphek and Megiddo, the later carinated goblet with low ring base comparable to examples from Byblos, and a juglet with pinched rim (restored), painted decoration, a flat base reminiscent of EB IV forms, and painted decoration of horizontal and vertical lines and hatched triangles. The most prevalent type of decoration is that of combing in horizontal straight or zigzag lines, which tends to occur either on larger bowls of the type with pointed carination or on rounded cooking pots similar to a type known at Megiddo in MB II.[74]

The tomb material (Fugmann 1958: pl. X) presents several interesting forms and parallels with the coastal area, and the greater proportion of painted decoration may indicate a dichotomy between domestic and funerary pottery. While several of the bowl forms previously mentioned are repeated here, additional forms include: flat-based store jars (5B660, 5B397, 5B398, 5A996, 5A983), handleless bottles with gutter rim and burnishing (5B683, 5B185, 5B382), a juglet with stepped rim and ring base (5B167), several jugs or pitchers with foliated rims (5B370, 5B369, 5B507), and a pitcher, also with foliated rim and red painted horizontal and vertical lines (5B901). Ingholt mentions a vase with black painted zigzag lines, a fragment with black vertical lines and triangular motifs, a pitcher with trefoil rim and sieve which has vertical red lines painted within bands of horizontal lines, and another pitcher with a spout, brown slip, and vertical burnishing and four horizontal bands painted in red on the body (Ingholt 1940: 56, pl. XVII:3 and 5). One of the tomb groups (G VI) had a semicircular fenestrated axe, a torque, several pins, and lance heads, while Grave I contained two fenestrated duckbill axes and two pins, one with decorated head.

Mishrife (Qatna): The site of Mishrife, located 18 km. northeast of Homs on a tributary of the Orontes River, has been identified with the town of Qatna which is frequently mentioned in the Mari letters. These letters suggest that Qatna played an important role in the exchange of goods between Mesopotamia and the coastal areas. This interchange is perhaps indicated by the presence of a temple dedicated to a Mesopotamian deity, Nin-Egal, which should be dated to the Middle Bronze Age (probably MB II). Relations with Egypt are also attested by the Egyptian objects—especially the sphinx of It, daughter of Amenemhet II—which are comparable to the Egyptian objects found at coastal sites such as Byblos. The finds attributable to the MB I period are, however, relatively sparse, but again this may be the result of limited excavation, and the picture of the MB I occupation in the Orontes area can be filled out by the investigation of many smaller sites in this area.

The main group of MB I material from Qatna itself was found in Tomb I which included the following vessel types: the "eye" jug (with or without the painted eye) with pinched slanted rim, flat base, and usually painted decoration of lines, cross-hatched triangles, and zigzags; handleless bottles, some examples with an extra ridge below the rim and often also with painted decoration of horizontal bands or with burnishing; flat-based store jars, a "Ḫabur"-type goblet, and simple carinated bowls and open bowls on flat or low disc bases.[75] The decorative motifs consist of concentric circles, triangles with cross-hatching, radiating lines forming a collar beneath the neck, horizontal zigzags, and designs arranged in registers between lines; these may be painted in black, violet, brown, or red. The only metal objects were two lance points with midrib. This tomb therefore contains a homogeneous assemblage of typical MB I funerary pottery.

Additional MB I material was excavated in a sondage beneath the "Coupole de Loth" and included two jars with lines of horizontal straight and wavy combing, fragments of two bowls with a cross motif painted on the interior in red, part of a carinated bowl with a red burnished finish, and a fragment of a bowl with a cross in metope motif painted in maroon on a yellow ground.[76] Finally, the group from Tomb IV should also be mentioned since, although its pottery belongs primarily to EB IV, it contains vessels which relate to MB I forms, such as a carinated bowl and a spouted holemouth jar, as well as an abundance of combed decoration (Schaeffer 1948: fig. 99).

Dnebi; *Selimye*; *Osmaniye*; *Tell ᶜAs*: Several tombs in the vicinity of Qatna and of Hama shed additional light on the MB I period of the Orontes Valley. The pottery in the tombs from Dnebi, 16 km. northeast of Qatna, is also placed in the EB IV period, but, like the material from Tomb I at Qatna, it seems to herald some MB I forms. The juglets from Dnebi Tomb 3 are similar to MB I juglets except that they occur with the flat, squared-off base typical of the preceding period. A jar with gutter-rim profile relates to MB I types, while the carinated bowl with narrow base recalls the bowls from Ugarit.[77] The Selimiye tomb presents a comparable group of jugs with both painted and combed decoration but with EB IV form, and carinated jars (du Mesnil du Buisson 1930: pls. XXXI and XXXII). The tomb at Osmaniye, in the vicinity of Dnebi, should probably be placed in MB I, since it contains the usual carinated bowls, jars, including one with a stepped rim, and a rounded flask with the handle on the shoulder (du Mesnil du Buisson 1930: pls. XXXI-XXXIV).

The series of tombs from the necropolis at Tell ᶜAs located to the north of Hama probably spans the EB IV and MB I (du Mesnil du Buisson 1932: pls. XXXIX and XL). Tomb I contained flat-based, handleless store jars, several goblets which merge with the simple rounded cups of MB I, and the carinated bowls with narrow base similar to the type at Dnebi and Ugarit (*supra*, n. 77). Tomb II has a similar range of Syrian-type goblets, store jars, and a carinated bowl, as well as a higher proportion of combed decoration. Tombs III and IV add spouted jars and a bowl with rounded carination similar to the type from the later MB I.

Khan Sheikhoun; *Tell Masin*: The tell material from the nearby site of Khan Sheikhoun (du Mesnil du Buisson 1932: pl. XXXVI) included a painted Syrian goblet, a carinated bowl with gutter rim, and jars with horizontal lines in red, very similar to the examples from the "Coupole de Loth" sondage at Qatna (du Mesnil du Buisson 1930: fig. 3; compare a jar from Aphek, Ory 1937: 113:44). Soundings from Tell Masin, also located near Hama (du Mesnil du Buisson 1935b: pls. XLIX and L) revealed a comparable group of carinated bowls, bowls with narrow base, Syrian goblets with painted decoration, jugs with pinched rims, and spouted holemouth jars. All of these tombs in this region therefore supplement our corpus of pottery and give some indication of a transitional cultural development from the EB IV to MB I pottery forms.

Yabrud: Another necropolis located near the site of Yabrud (Assaf 1967: 55-68) in the Anti-Lebanon and south of Qatna presents a similar assemblage of pottery. The cist graves included multiple burials, some of them spanning a considerable period (such as Grave 4 with both a Mitannian and an Old Babylonian cylinder seal). The pottery included the following types (Assaf 1967: pls. II and III), several of which parallel the types previously mentioned at Hama: spouted jars with painted horizontal bands, bowls with rounded carination and painted and combed bands, a juglet with stepped-rim profile and another with gutter rim and painted decoration, large open bowls, bowls with pointed carination, and a flat-based storage jar. There is a fairly large amount of painted decoration of straight or wavy, horizontal or vertical lines in dark or reddish brown paint. The metal objects (Assaf 1967: pl. I) included a duckbill fenestrated axe, lance heads with marked midrib, a dagger blade, and several pins with ribbed heads. Sounding of the tell indicated occupation of the 3rd millennium during the EB IV period (including the ubiquitous painted Syrian goblets). The transformation of the area into a cemetery at the beginning of MB I was therefore interpreted by Assaf as an indication of the arrival of a new people who destroyed the previous settlement.

Tell et-Tin: The site of Tell et-Tin (Gautier 1895: 441-64), which is situated on an island in the lake of Homs, which forms part of the Orontes River system, consisted of several funerary chambers with multiple burials, many in slab-lined cists. The inventory from these tombs is homogeneously representative of MB I, including a juglet and jars with stepped rim, bowls with both sharp and rounded carination, and an open bowl with lugs on the rim. The pottery was all wheelmade but had no painted decoration except for some traces of black lozenges on the upper part of some vessels. The metal finds included a fenestrated duckbill axe, dagger blades, and lance heads with marked midrib, and a pin with ribbed head.

Tell Mardikh (*Ebla*): Tell Mardikh, also in the Orontes Valley and now identified with the ancient city of Ebla, was extensively occupied during the 3rd and early 2nd millennia B.C. Period III has been equated with Hama Stratum H and included a foritified acropolis with a palace and several temples around its base (Davico *et al.* 1965: 118-20; Matthiae 1971: 57-58). The town was composed of a lower city of private houses, temples, and a sanctuary surrounded by earthen rampart fortifications with four city gates. The development of a Syrian artistic style of the early 2nd millennium is well represented by the limestone basins sculpted with frieze scenes (Matthiae 1975a: 342-49). The dating of these structures, however, is very unclear. The excavation reports only generally assign these to the "period of the Amorite dynasties," that is, between 2000 and 1600 B.C. (or the Middle Bronze Age). Matthiae attempts to date the rampart more specifically to ca. 1900 B.C. (Matthiae 1975a: 342, n. 12) but does not give any clear stratigraphic evidence (see Dever 1976: 30, n. 87 for doubts concerning the dating of the fortifications). Only a few ceramic vessels from the first three seasons have been published and can be presented as evidence of MB I occupation. These include the typical carinated bowl, bowls with thick rims and pointed carination, simple bowls and cups, often with combed decoration, and a jar with painted band decoration (Davico *et al.* 1967: figs. 11-17; Castellino *et al.* 1966: 90, pl. LXXXIX; also Matthiae 1977: 114-59, especially, 146-59, figs. 33-34). Two tombs, excavated beneath Building Q, contained Egyptian inscriptional material, gold jewelry, and large groups of pottery, including carinated bowls and a jug with a painted ibex representation and twisted handle which belongs to the Syro-Cilician painted style (Matthiae 1980a: 8-17; 1980b: 11-20, fig. 13). All of the fragments of this Syro-Cilician style were found in one tomb, the "Tomb of the Princess," which is dated between 1825 and 1750/1700 B.C. The other tomb, the "Tomb of the Lord of the Goats," is dated later in the MB II period (Matthiae 1980b: 19).

ᶜAmuq: *Çatal Hüyük*, *Tell Taᶜyinat*, *Tell al-Judeideh*: The survey and soundings of sites in the ᶜAmuq Plain have shown that Phases K and L can be assigned to the MB I period. Remains of these phases were excavated at the sites of Çatal Hüyük, Tell al-Judeideh, and Tell Taᶜyinat, but these were not sufficient to give a clear indication of the architecture or habitation areas. The Phase K pottery is best typified by the flat-based carinated bowl (Swift 1958: fig. 1, similar in type to the narrow-based bowls of Ugarit, Schaeffer 1949: fig. 102:20) with painted patterns of oblique strokes or latticed triangles between horizontal bands in red-to-brown paint. There is not much painted decoration, however, while combed decoration and applied rope bands are also represented. Phase L continues the same trends of Phase K—similar decorated patterns but with a larger proportion of paint, a tendency to "elaboration in the details of form," and frequent double or triple handles. The small bowls, jars, and pitchers occur with a burnished yellow finish and sometimes geometric and animal designs in lustrous paints. The shapes represented include an "eye" pitcher with pinched rim and painted motifs of metopes, hatched triangles, and animals (Swift 1958: fig. 2), an open bowl, a carinated jar, and another pitcher fragment with a row of painted birds (Swift 1958: 15-17). These phases should fit well within the MB I period and are comparable to the early Middle Bronze Age strata of the other Syrian sites and those of such Cilician sites as Tarsus and Mersin.

Atçana (*Alalakh*): The corresponding levels at the site of Alalakh, Levels XVI-VIII, are marked by a continuity in both pottery forms and decorative motifs (Woolley 1955: 340-42). These levels are now all equated with the MB I period (Swift 1958: 58) and so this continuity is no longer surprising. The most distinctive element of these levels is the painted pottery which tends to occur on only two vessel types: Type 23 (Woolley 1955: pl. CX), a small bowl with rounded or sharp carination and a flat or low ring base, and its variant Type 119 (pl. CXX), which has a pedestal foot, and Type 70 (pl. CXV), which is the jug with pinched, slanted rim and flat or ring base. Both these forms are familiar from sites such as Hama and Ugarit, although the pedestal-footed bowl is an innovation typical of the Syro-Cilician region.

The decorative motifs are primarily limited to a metope arrangement between horizontal bands with the spaces sometimes filled by geometric designs or animals and, of course, the eyes painted on the rims of the "eye" pitchers. Additional ceramic types represented at Alalakh (Woolley 1955: 304-13) include MB I forms such as the carinated bowls with long neck decorated with combing (Type 100, Woolley 1955: pl. CXVIII, comparable to bowls from Hama H), open bowls usually on flat or low ring bases (Types 3 and 5, pl. CIX), additional variations of the usual carinated bowl (Types 7b, 21, and 24, pls. CIX and CX), a simple rounded bowl with horizontal projection on the rim and painted decoration including the cross motif on the base (Type 34, pl. CXI), and a jug with horizontal rim and flat base (Type 57, pl. CXIV). Some of the variations present here, in particular, certain painted motifs, show that Alalakh belongs to the cultural spheres of both the Orontes region and Cilicia. The only metal objects found in these levels which relate to comparable assemblages are the pins with either curled or bulbous head, the latter sometimes decorated with ribbing (Woolley 1955: 280, pl. LXXIII:P.1-P.18).

Alalakh is also a site which can be tied to Mesopotamian chronology since the Level VII palace contained tablets belonging to Iarimlim of Iamḫad (for a discussion of the kings represented in the Level VII texts, see Naʾaman 1976: 129-43; 1979: 103-13). The fact that we may roughly equate the beginning of Level VII (and therefore perhaps the end of MB I, as it is evident here) with Iarimlim may provide an approximate relative chronological guide for the placement of the MB I period.

III.4. Transjordan

Evidence for the presence of MB I occupation in Transjordan is currently meager, but this is probably more a result of limited archeological exploration than a lack of such occupation. While the relatively small amount of early MB I material in the eastern Galilee and Jordan River Valley may caution one not to expect extensive MB I occupation in Transjordan, there is at least some indication now that such occupation did exist, as shown by a recent survey of the East Jordan Valley which identified several sites with MB I pottery (Ibrahim, Sauer, and Yassine 1976: 54, fig. 18).

A. PELLA

The site of Pella, on the eastern side of the Jordan Valley and opposite Beth-shan, has evidence of strata of the MB I period in Plots F and T beneath the West Church in Area I (Smith 1973: 159 and 197-98). The pottery is characterized by a "thinness of ware, excellence of design and . . . variety of repertoire" and includes incurving bowl rims, flat bases, and red painted or slipped finish, sometimes with pattern burnishing (Smith 1973: 197, pls. 27 and 88A). While this pottery may not belong to the earliest MB I, the presence of some distinctive features, such as the thickened bowl rims with triangular section (for example, Smith

1973: pl. 27:496 and 982, pl. 88A:982), may indicate a mid-MB I date.

B. AMMAN TOMB

The contents of a tomb group from Amman, although mostly dated to the later Middle Bronze Age, included one painted jug which may belong in MB I (Harding 1953: 14, fig. 8, no. 89); the decoration consisted of red painted, horizontal, straight and wavy lines on a white-slip ground and was compared by Harding with pottery from Tell Beit Mirsim G.

C. FOᶜARA

An unpublished tomb at Foᶜara, north of Irbid, apparently included several flat-based store jars, some of which had painted horizontal bands (Williams 1975: 1035; the store jars are compared with those of Megiddo, Loud 1948: pls. 12:20 and 22 and 13: 1-2). This group would therefore belong in the early phase of MB I. Additional MB I sites in Transjordan have been identified but are unpublished (Williams 1975: 1035); it is apparent that future research in Transjordan will reveal much new material for the study of the MB I period.

III.5 The Egyptian Delta Region

While the identification and presence of Levantine culture in the Egyptian Delta have been a subject of much controversy since Petrie's excavations at Tell el-Yahudiyeh, such discussion has usually centered around the MB II or "Hyksos" culture, as often characterized by Tell el-Yahudiyeh ware. Only recently, however, primarily as a result of the Austrian excavations at the site of Tell ed-Dabᶜa in the eastern Delta region, has this controversy begun to include manifestations of a culture comparable to the MB I period in the Levant.[78] These finds may indicate that MB I pottery occurs with Egyptian inscriptional evidence in the Delta. This would be significant not only as an indication of the possible extent of the spread of such MB I pottery but also as a possible chronological determinant. An examination of this material is therefore necessary in order to complete our review of the MB I period.

Level G of Tell ed-Dabᶜa, which was built over the burnt layer marking the end of Level H, represented a new organization of the town plan and was apparently characterized by Levantine pottery, especially double-handled jugs (Bietak 1968: 89; 1970: 18-20). This level also included two burials: the first, Grave 4 in Quadrant A/II-1/12, contained only a scarab which Bietak assigned to Dynasty 13 (Bietak 1970: 19, fig. 1). The second grave (A/II-n/12, number 4) contained as grave gifts only a necklace of faience beads and a kohl-pot. In the fill near this grave, however, was found pottery which Bietak described as mostly of MB I type. However, amongst this pottery (and, in fact, the only piece specifically mentioned from this group) was the bottom of a black polished, incrusted Tell el-Yahudiyeh jug (Bietak 1970: pl. XIXc) which would not fit a classic definition of the MB I period. Level G also contained additional fragments of Tell el-Yahudiyeh ware as well as some sherds of red polished vessels and an ovoid, red polished juglet with double handle attached to a neck ridge (Bietak 1970: pl. XXIIa). The ovoid shape of this juglet, however, is much closer to that of the late MB I/MB II juglets than to that of the early MB I collarette juglets which have a rounder form.[79] It is clear, therefore, that despite assertions that Level G pottery belongs to the MB I period of the Levant, it is comparable, at the very earliest, to that of the end of MB I, and so the scarab from the grave in Level G cannot be used to provide a date for MB I.

Several artifacts (Bietak 1970: 23-24, 35-37; Williams 1975: 61-67) of Level F (dated by a scarab of Sebekhotep, Bietak 1970: 24) are also characteristic of MB II. The metal objects, including veined daggers (Bietak 1968: 92, 109, fig. 9:810; 1970: pl. XVIIa) which could be placed in either late MB I or MB II, and a chisel-axe (Bietak 1970: pl. XVIIb) which is definitely of MB II type (note the extensions above and below the socket; see also Chapter VI), should be mentioned. It is clear, therefore, that while the Tell ed-Dabᶜa material seems to represent an influx of Levantine characteristics into the Delta region, this material cannot be specifically equated with the MB I period in the Levant nor can it be used to date MB I. It would seem that the intermediaries between the Egyptian Delta and the Levant itself are yet to be found and, although sea travel was a possibility, the Negev and Sinai may still hold much evidence for this southward extension of the Levantine Middle Bronze Age culture.

The conclusions concerning the Levant in the MB I period which can be deduced from this analysis may now be summarized. The MB I period consisted of several architectural phases at

Table 6. MB I Sites of the Levant by Phase

Site	Early	Middle	Late
Megiddo	Phases 1-2	Phase 3	Phase 4
Aphek (Râs el ᶜAin)	prepalace	palace	postpalace
Tell Beit Mirsim		Str. G	Str. F
Tell el-ᶜAjjul	T. 1015	C.C. Groups 1-2 (unstratified tell material)	Groups 3-5
Lachish	← - T. 1513	T. 1504 (glacis fill) - - - →	T. 1552- - - - → - - - →
Tell el-Hesi			stray finds (Petrie and Bliss)
Tell en-Nagila			stray pottery-surface
Dhahrat el-Humraiya		Tombs (G. 21)	Tombs
Neby Rubin			Tomb
Beth-shemesh	T.2/Str. VI - - - →	- - - →	- - - →
Gezer	tombs in III 30 Str. XXI - - - →	- - - →	High Place Grotto Sep. Cave 15 I extramural Tomb 1 (lower)
Wadi et-Tin		? Tomb - - - →	- - - →
Khirbet Kufin		Tomb 3, Upper Chambers 3/4 Chambers 6/7 - - - →	- - - →
Moza		Tomb Group - - - →	- - - →
Gibeon	T. 58 (upper)	T. 31 (upper)	
Bethel			stray finds
ᶜAin es-Samiyeh/Sinjil		Tomb groups - - - →	- - - →
Jericho			Tomb K 3
Shechem		Temenos I (Str. XXII-XXI) - - - →	- - - →
Tell el-Farᶜah (N.)	Tomb 16 - - - → Tomb B	- - - → (Trench 692 ?) - - - →	Tombs AN and AD - - - →
Beth-shan		Tomb 92	
Kfar-Szold			Tomb
Ginosar		Tomb 1 - - - →	Tomb 4
Hazor			Tomb "pre-XVII" stratum
Tell Dan			burials beneath wall
Kedesh			stray finds
Turᶜan			burial
ᶜAffula			Burials 11-14; 19
Tel Zeror		Str. 21-19 (?) - - - →	- - - →
Tel Poleg	? - - - →	fortifications - - - →	- - - →
Barqai	Tomb. 2nd burial phase		
Mevorach		?-settlement - - - →	- - - →
Akko		?-settlement - - - →	- - - →
Nahariya	Temple precinct - - - →	- - - →	- - - →
Achzib		?-settlement - - - →	- - - →

Site	Early	Middle	Late
Sidon: Kafer Djarra, Lebe^{c}a, Ruweise, Majdalouna	Tombs ------------	------------------------	------------------------→
Beirut/Sin el Fil	Tomb		
Amrith	←----Tombs 4, 7, 8-------	------------------------	------→
Byblos	Offering deposits ------- (“Montet Jar”)	------------------------ 3rd private tomb	------------------------→ Royal Tombs 1-11
Ugarit	tomb and occupational debris	------------------------	------------------------→
Tell Simiriyan	?-occupational debris -------	------------------------	------------------------→
Tell Sukas	?-occupational debris		
Kāmid el-Lōz		Tomb ID$_{15}$14---------	------------------------→
Tell es-Salihiyyeh		?----Level XII ----------	------------------------→
Hama	Str. H 1-5; graves -------	------------------------	------------------------→
Qatna	Tomb 1	scattered occupational debris	------------------------→
Osmaniye	←----Tomb		
Dnebi	←----Tomb 3		
Selimiye	←----Tomb		
Tell ^{c}As	←----Tombs I-IV		
Khan Sheikhoun	←--tell material----------	------------------------	→
Tell Masin	←--tell material		
Yabrud	Tombs ------------------	------------------------	------------------------→
Tell et-Tin		Tomb	
Tell Mardikh	Period III (palace, temples, fortifications)	------------------------	------------------------→
Tell al-Judeideh	Phase K	Phase L -----------------	------------------------→
Tell Ta^{c}yinat	Phase K	Phase L -----------------	------------------------→
Alalakh	Levels XVI-VIII ----------	------------------------	------------------------→
Pella		settlement (?) ----------	------------------------→
Fo^{c}ara	tomb		

certain sites, such as Megiddo, Aphek, Tel Poleg, Hama, and probably Alalakh, and therefore a sufficient span of time must be allowed for the duration of MB I to account for these phases. At the same time, it is also clear that at several sites the MB I period seems much shorter and that at such sites primarily only the later phases are indicated, as, for example, at Hazor and Tel Dan. Along with these architectural phases, corresponding phases in the ceramic sequence may be discerned which allow for a chronological subdivision of the period and for the placement of certain developments within this scheme. As examples, we can conclude that the flat-based, handleless store jars appear earliest in the sequence; the painted wares begin early in the sequence but continue to increase in number through MB I; Anatolian-related elements occur in the middle phase of MB I and also increase in late MB I and into MB II; imported Cypriote vessels only make their appearance in the last phase of MB I. This ceramic phasing also allows the assignment of certain sites to a particular phase (table 6). Further implications for the relative and absolute chronologies of this period are specifically indicated by certain site material, as at Byblos and Alalakh, suggesting that the traditional dates should be raised.

A second factor which must be accounted for in an analysis of this period is the degree of dichotomy between funerary-related material and material from habitation areas. This is well demonstrated by the contrasting repertoires present at such sites as Megiddo, Aphek, Ginosar, Hama, and Qatna, and is significant since much of the available MB I pottery is from tombs. Two features seem particularly associated with tomb groups: first, the flat-based storage jars which may have been used as containers at least for child burials (Loud 1948: figs. 294, 297, 298, and 300); second, the painted juglets, which may have been more highly valued and therefore considered as worthy burial gifts. Since these two vessel types will be shown (in the next chapter) to be indicative of relations with the ceramics of Anatolia and Mesopotamia, this dichotomy can cause misrepresentation in our understanding of the distribution of foreign features in the Levantine ceramic repertoire.

The third element in this analysis is that of regionalism. Evidence for the MB I period seems most extensive at coastal sites and in areas with direct access to the coast in the southern Levant but appears both on the coast and inland in the northern Levant. At the same time, it is possible to discern some characteristics which are transitional between the EB IV and the MB I periods in the pottery of the tomb groups in inland Syria (as at Qatna Tomb IV and Dnebi Tomb 3) and at Ugarit and Byblos (for example, the "Montet Jar"). It is also seen that only a more limited distribution of MB I culture is indicated in the region of the Upper Galilee, the Biqa^{c} Valley and the Jordan River Valley, while the main distribution of MB I sites in the southern Levant may correspond to the coastal route and areas with easy access to the coast, including such sites as Megiddo and Aphek. This pattern seems to contradict the textual material and will be studied more fully in Chapters VIII and IX. This distribution and emphasis on coastal access may, however, be the key to an understanding of the MB I culture—its chronology, its character, and its origin.

NOTES

[1]Thompson attempted to point out various internal contradictions in the two Kenyon articles (Kenyon 1958: 51*-60*; 1969: 25-60) but then failed to utilize a reliable method for reordering the Megiddo loci. The field work of Dunayevsky and Kempinski showed that all of the Megiddo temples ceased to exist at the end of the EB III period (Dunayevsky and Kempinski 1973: 162-75) since the temples predate Pavement 4009 which is clearly of EB IV date. For a discussion of this area in the MB II period, see Epstein 1965: 204-21. In both articles (by Thompson and by Dunayevsky and Kempinski), however, the authors continue to assume that all structures and loci shown on one figure plan in the Megiddo publication are contemporary. This assumption is unacceptable without some consideration for pits and cuttings which can put later structures at the same absolute level as earlier ones; furthermore, unless two walls are connected, they should not necessarily be considered as contemporary. In order to attempt to straighten out this confusion, it is necessary to disregard the assignments to strata as given in the publication and to accept only a chronological ordering which does not depend on any of these assumptions. It is interesting that, although it is necessary to disagree with the methodology of Dunayevsky and Kempinski, it is possible to agree with their conclusion that there are probably three phases of MB I settlement at Megiddo (Dunayevsky and Kempinski 1973: 180). Williams, on the other hand, who did not utilize the field work of Dunayevsky and Kempinski, pointed out some additional weaknesses of Kenyon's reconstruction—primarily that she did not allow for the isometric projections of architectural features on the published plans. She therefore considered more tomb groups as sealed than really were. Williams, who rightly criticized the published plans on the basis of the original field plans (Williams 1975: 907-11), based his own theories primarily on a typological phasing of the Megiddo and Byblos pottery (*infra).*

In the following discussion, as much use as possible has been made of the original field plans of the Megiddo excavations, which include additional elevation levels omitted from the publication and do not have the confusing isometric projection of the walls shown on the publication plans. Reference is therefore made to both the publication plans and the original plans, as appropriate. I would like to thank the staff of the Oriental Institute and especially Ms. R. Burbank, Archivist, for providing for my use of the original Megiddo plans and for granting permission for me to use these unpublished plans in the drawing of fig. 9. I would also like to thank Dr. S. Gitin (Director, Albright Institute of Archaeological Research, Jerusalem) for advice concerning the methodology used here and the results presented below.

[2]Collarette juglet: Loud 1948: pl. 7:18, T. 3171, pl. 10:21, T. 3143, and pl. 10:17, T. 5181; bowl: Loud 1948: pl. 14:17; store jar: Loud 1948: pls. 12:20 and 12:22, T. 5181, and pl. 12:16, T. 3143, the last without painted bands.

[3]Tomb 3162 juglets: Loud 1948: pls. 10:13, 12:12, 12:14, and 14:7; the painted juglet: Loud 1948: pl. 11:9.

[4]A few vessels seem closer to those of the two later phases, for example, the juglet type from T. 4088 (Loud 1948: pl. 19:21) also appeared in T. 3125 (Phase 3); the one-handled jars of T. 4095 (Loud 1948: pls. 20:19 and 20:20) seem comparable to those of T. 5142 (Loud 1948: pls. 23:7 and 23:8).

[5]Of the pottery in T. 234, the cylindrical jug with flattened base (Guy 1938: pl. 26:6) is similar to the Phase 4 jugs from T. 5242 and T. 5088 (Loud 1948: pls. 23:17 and pl. 17:9, respectively). The one-handled jug (Guy 1938: pl. 26:9) recalls a jug from T. 5142 (Loud 1948: pl. 23:7) and the low ring base of the bowl (Guy 1938: pl. 26:5) would also tend to link this tomb group with Phase 4.

[6]It is also of interest to note the presence of several less typical vessels, apparently in MB II context, which may relate to northern or other foreign pottery forms. These would include: from T. 24, a jug with pinched rim, a mug with trefoil rim, and a basket-handled teapot with strainer spout (Guy 1938: pl. 23:15, 20, and 22, respectively); from T. 42, a loop-handled teapot with painted line decoration (Guy 1938: pl. 24:3), and, from T. 49, a tall teapot with beaked spout and another trefoil-rimmed mug (Guy 1938: pl. 25:6 and 9, respectively).

[7]The flat-based store jars: Loud 1948: pl. 12:21, =T. 5130 and pl. 13:5, E=T. 5147; juglet with painted circles: Loud 1948: pl. 19:33, =T. 4010. For a discussion of the circle motif, see Beck 1975: 76-82. The bowl with S-curved profile: Loud 1948: pl. 19:13, =T. 5103; "holemouth" jar: Loud 1948: pl. 13:11, T. E=T. 2152; for the Aphek kraters, see Beck 1975: 48-50, fig. 2:9; the pinched-rim pitchers: Loud 1948: pl. 11:12, N=T. 3143, two examples, and pl. 20:5, N=T. 3126. The first of these belongs early in the Megiddo sequence because of its similarity to a jug from T. 5180, Phase 2 (Loud 1948: pl. 11:13), while the latter probably belongs late in MB I.

[8]I would like to thank Dr. Beck for showing to me and discussing the pottery from the Aphek excavations.

[9]Simple rounded bowls: Beck 1975: figs. 1:11, 2:2; Loud 1948: pls. 14:24, 9:7, and 9:8 from T. 3143, T. 5175, and T. 5167, respectively; open bowls with ridge or knobs: Beck 1975: figs. 1:12-13, 2:6; Loud 1948: pl. 9:2-3, T. 5167 and pl. 15:12, T. 2152; bowls with inverted rim: Loud 1948: pl. 14:17 from T. 5181 and T. 3148, and pl. 9:4 from T. 3171.

[10]Kraters from Megiddo: Loud 1948: pl. 13:11, T. E=T. 2152, and pl. 21:4, 3119, which is placed by Amiran in MB II (Amiran 1969: 103 and pl. 32:9). Wheelmade cooking pots from Aphek: Beck 1975: figs. 1:1, 2:12-13; handmade cooking pots: Beck 1975: figs. 1:2, 2:15-16; Loud 1948: pls. 7:10-12 (4023), 9:19 (S=5161), 15:19 (W=T. 5185), 30:5 (=T. 2147).

[11]Beck compares this decoration to that on a Megiddo jar (Loud 1948: pl. 16:10) which, however, has no certain context. The Megiddo jar is to be associated with T. 5114 but was not found in this tomb, as Beck implies (1975: 52), while the other contents, especially the pitcher (Loud 1948: pl. 16:2) would argue for a later MB I date. The form of the store jar might also seem late MB I since it has a relatively narrow base, a feature indicative of late MB I at both sites, while no other store jar of early MB I at Megiddo has handles.

[12]Externally thickened rims: Beck 1975: figs. 3:5, 1:17-18; Loud 1948: pl. 12:16, 21, 22 and pl. 13:3; "moulded" rims: Beck 1975: figs. 5:11, 14:4; also Ory 1937: 119, Nos. 103-104; Loud 1948: pls. 12:17, 8:9, and 13:2.

[13]Loud 1948: pls. 7:18, 10:21, and 10:16, T. 3171, T. 3143, and T. 2152, respectively. Beck also compares the form to that of a juglet from T. 5171 (Loud 1948: pl. 10:18) which, although similar in the presence of a neck ridge, is quite different in its button base, which is generally considered a later feature. Based on this and other features of the pottery from this group, this tomb has been placed later in Phase 3.

[14]Some examples of this type at Megiddo include: Loud 1948: pls. 11:2, 25:12, and 16:2.

[15]Carinated bowl: Beck 1975: fig. 12:9, Loud 1948: pls. 14:33, 15:2, 19:3; open bowl: Beck 1975: fig. 11:3 and 8; Loud 1948: pls. 29:21 and 23, 19:11, 21:18; bowls with ring base: Beck 1975: figs. 11:7, 12:2, 13:7; Loud 1948: pl. 29:21 and 23.

[16]It does seem to appear in tomb groups which are probably to be placed early in MB II (Loud 1948: pl. 28:12, T. 2145, and pl. 28:10, T. 3137). The appearance of this type at the end of MB I and the beginning of MB II perhaps marks it as a forerunner of the typical MB II multiple-carinated types.

[17]Piriform juglet: Beck 1975: fig. 12:4; Loud 1948: pl. 24:4, 13, 14, 16, 17, 20, and 21; juglet with pinched rim: Beck 1975: fig. 12:13; Loud 1948: pl. 20:1; dipper juglet: Beck 1975: fig. 12:7 and 8; Loud 1948: pls. 20:9, 12:7; biconical jug: Beck 1975: fig. 12:5; Loud 1948: pls. 11:5, 24:9; cylindrical jug: Beck 1975: fig. 12:12; Loud 1948: pls. 17:9, 23:17; juglet with stepped rim: Beck 1975: fig. 11:4; Loud 1948: pl. 17:6.

[18]Pointed juglets: Ory 1937: 119:107, 113:48, 49: juglet with button base: Ory 1937: 109:12; bowls with low base: Ory 1937: 197:1-2A; two-handled bowls: Iliffe 1936: 122:21; Ory 1937: 111:35; bowl with cross band: Ory 1937: 107:2B; red-slipped bottle: Iliffe 1936: 125:74; handleless jar: Ory 1937: 113:44; juglets with trefoil rim: Ory 1937: 117:79 and 120:109; juglets with painted bands: Ory 1937: 117:80 and 82.

[19]Bowls with flat or disc bases: Albright 1932: pl. 41:3; 1933: pl. 4:1-2; bowls with high ring bases: Albright 1933: pl. 4:12; 1932: pl. 41:4; bowl with high rounded carination: Albright 1933: pl. 4:11, to be compared with Beck 1975: fig. 12:2; red-cross bowl: Albright 1933: pl. 5:5; "teapot": Albright 1933: pl. 5:1; juglet with pinched rim: Albright 1932: pl. 6:30; cooking pots: Albright 1932: pls. 41:6, 7:1-10.

[20]Painted pottery from Aphek: Ory 1937: 116-18, Nos. 77, 89, and 90; Cypriote sherd from Tell Beit Mirsim: Albright 1933: 74, n. 11, pl. 22:7.

[21]Albright 1938b: 344; Petrie 1933: 7. Albright's suggestion was based on the tomb's stratigraphic position beneath the MB II Tomb 303A; the material of Tomb 303B, however, also seems late and includes a pointed dipper juglet and a Tell el-Yahudiyeh vase.

[22]Trefoil-rimmed jug: Petrie 1931: pl. XLVIII:57H5; jar: Petrie 1933: pl. XXXIII:32A11 (QS1012), comparable to a jar from Aphek, Ory 1937: 113:44; teapots: Schaeffer 1948: figs. 122:11, 124:A.

[23]The other groups continue the carinated bowls, most of those in Group 3 still with red slip and/or burnish, with increasingly higher disc (Tufnell 1962: fig. 11:31) and then ring bases (Tufnell 1962: fig. 12:39 and 40; fig. 13:46, 47, 49, and 50). Several Tell el-Yahudiyeh juglets with punctate design are also present (Tufnell 1962: figs. 12:36 and 41, 13:52). The dipper juglets generally have more pointed bases (Tufnell 1962: figs. 11:29, 34b; 12:43-45; 13:48, 55, 56). The double-handled bowl from Group 3 (Tufnell 1962: fig. 11:22) is compared by Tufnell to a bowl from Tell Beit Mirsim Stratum E (Albright 1933: pl. 10:6). The double-handled jar from Group 4 (Tufnell 1962: fig. 12:37) may also be compared to two similar vessels with painted bands from Megiddo which are probably to be assigned to the very end of MB I (Phase 4) or to the beginning of MB II (Loud 1948: pl. 21:2, T. 2146; pl. 27:2, T. 2138).

[24]Bowls with low disc base: Tufnell 1958: fig. 3:194-96; store jar base: Tufnell 1958: fig. 3:166; cooking pots: Tufnell 1958: figs. 3:176; 4:219-21; sherds with painted decoration: Tufnell 1958: fig. 3:125, 133, compared to Albright 1933: pl. 4:13, 15, 16; juglet with red painted bands: Tufnell 1958: fig. 3:157; White Painted IV sherd: Tufnell 1958: fig. 3:174.

[25]Tomb 1552: Tufnell 1958: 272, pl. 50:8 (comparable to postpalace phase Aphek examples, especially Beck 1975: fig. 11:1 and 6); pl. 50:19-22, 27, and 28; Tomb 1504: Tufnell 1958: 255, pls. 69:550; 86:995, and 82:931; Tomb 1513: Tufnell 1958: 256-58, pls. 69:552 and 553; 59:135-37; 78:803 and 804.

[26]Petrie 1891: 41-42, pls. V:35, 50; VI:55-58, 99, 79, 90; Bliss 1894: 40-42, pl. 3:88-90.

[27]In one of the latter was found a bull-shaped rhyton with wheelmade hollow body, solid legs, an opening on the back, and a red slipped and burnished exterior (Amiran and Eitan 1965: 121, fig. 9). This vessel recalls the later Hittite pair of bulls from Boğazköy (Bittel 1970: pl. 15b), but it may also be related to the contemporary animal rhyta from the *kārum* Kaniš of the Assyrian Colony period.

[28]The carinated bowls (Ory 1948: 88, figs. 41-42) found in Graves 63 and 45, the piriform juglets (Ory 1948: 88, figs. 38-39) from Grave 63 and the bowl with hooked projections from Grave 65 (Ory 1948: fig. 31) which may be compared with several similar although not identical bowls from Megiddo (Loud 1948: pl. 30:1, T. 3087, Stratum XII; pl. 38:10, T. 3081, Stratum XI, and pl. 45:18, S=T. 3046, Stratum X) would seem to be indications of an MB II, albeit perhaps early, date.

[29]Several of the jar rim profiles (Ory 1948: fig. 3) may be compared with examples from Aphek: Type 3c (occurring on jars from Graves 18, 20, and 29) resembles the profile of two jars from Aphek Area B (Beck 1975: figs. 15:9, 16:7); Type 3e (a jar from Grave 29) recalls a type from the Aphek prepalace phase (Beck 1975: fig. 3:5) which continues at least into the palace phase (Beck 1975: fig. 7:12); Type 3f (Graves 18, 20, 38, 41, and 54) resembles another Aphek example from the same locus (Beck 1975: fig. 7:7); Type 3i (Graves 29 and 53) recalls an Aphek type of the palace phase (Beck 1975: fig. 5:11) which continues into the postpalace phase (Beck 1975: fig. 13:17); and, finally, Type 3j may be compared with examples of the Aphek palace phase (Beck 1975: figs. 5:3, 7:2). A store jar type, which occurs fairly frequently (Ory 1948: fig. 26, from Graves 44, 47, 49, 50) and which appears to be a later type because of its short neck and elongated form, is also paralleled at Aphek in the postpalace phase (Beck 1975: fig. 12:6, but note the different rim forms) while the two-handled types (Ory 1948: figs. 30 and 34) are paralleled by a postpalace phase Aphek example (Beck 1975: fig. 15:9) and a Megiddo Phase 3 example (Loud 1948: pl. 21:1, T. 3109, but again with differing rim profiles).

[30]There is also a one-handled mug with trefoil rim and a deep red slip from Grave 63, therefore probably to be dated to MB II (Ory 1948: 88, pl. XXXII:26) but providing a fairly distinctive example of a shape showing northern influence.

[31]A smaller tomb group from Ness Ziona (Ory 1926: 10) seems to belong to MB II (the pointed dipper juglet and the piriform juglet) but may be of some interest for the shaft-hole axe with notches both above and below the shaft hole, spear head, and dagger with slight midrib found with the group. This material, along with other pottery from the area of Tel Aviv, including a cemetery and the site of Yavneh Yam (Kaplan 1969a: 121), has been classified by Williams as MB IIIA (Williams 1975: 1062-64 and 1081) and by Dever as possibly MB IIA or B (Dever 1976: 25, nn. 42 and 43). These, however, represent such a marginal transition phase of MB I/II that their inclusion here did not seem warranted.

[32]This group (Mackenzie 1912-13: 42-46, pl. XVII) includes a juglet with pinched rim and small flat base (No. 14), simple open bowls (Nos. 9 and 11), carinated bowls on low base (Nos. 4 and 8), a two-handled store jar (No. 13), and an open bowl with cross bands in lustrous red-brown paint (No. 10).

[33]Bowls: Grant and Wright 1938: pl. XXIV:19 and 20; the Cypriote sherd: Grant and Wright 1938: pl. XXIV:8; polychrome sherds: Grant and Wright 1938: pl. XXIV:1-7, 9-11.

[34]Macalister 1912b: pls. LXI-LXIII. This tomb group includes store jars with small rounded base (Nos. 18 and 21), open bowls with low disc base (Nos. 15, 16, 19, 28-30), juglets with button base (Nos. 32, 35, 43, 49), and some carinated bowls (Nos. 37, 39, 45, 47, 48) but none of typical MB I type; the Cypriote juglet: No. 51; the red-cross bowl: No. 16.

[35]Macalister 1912b: pl. XXII:8, 9, and 19; pl. XXIII:13 and 15. These deposits include a Tell el-Yahudiyeh juglet (pl. XXIII:16), store jars (pls. XX:1 and XXII:4), and a pointed juglet (pl. XX:2) of MB II date; of MB I date are bowls on low bases (pls. XXII:1 and XXIII:8).

[36]As especially shown by the carinated bowls with high bases (Vincent 1947: fig. 6:10 and 12), the trumpet vases (Vincent 1947: fig. 6:1-4), and the piriform juglets, sometimes with button base (Vincent 1947: fig. 5:2, 4, 6). Attributable to MB I are the dipper juglets with flat base (Vincent 1947: fig. 5:1 and 15), the simple carinated bowls on low base (Vincent 1947: fig. 6:11 and 17), the carinated bowl with flaring neck, comparable to Aphek postpalace phase examples (Vincent 1947: fig. 6:6), carinated bowls with S-curve profiles and low base (Vincent 1947: fig. 6:23-25), and perhaps, the smaller of the two store jars (Vincent 1947: fig. 4:2) which still retains a relatively long neck.

[37]Handleless jar: Vincent 1947: fig. 4:4; handled jar: Vincent 1947: fig. 5:A; cross-painted bowl: Vincent 1947: fig. 6:18; pitcher with spout: Vincent 1947: pl. V:6 (since it is broken and there is no drawing, it is difficult to be certain of the exact form); flask: Vincent 1947: fig. 4:3.

[38]These include carinated bowls with S-curve profile, simple carinated bowls, open bowls, some with concave bases and one (Smith 1962: No. 25) with two handles and four hooks

projecting from bars on the rim and decorated with slip and radial burnish, and a deep bowl (No. 28) with a parallel from Megiddo (Loud 1948: pl. 28:2 from S=T. 3084); store jars similar to that from Chamber 3/4; a variety of jug types: Nos. 8 and 10 with flat bases and ovoid bodies, Nos. 11 and 12 with pointed bases (the latter with piriform body and the former with shaved body); a small squat juglet (No. 16) with slip and burnishing, and a flask (No. 15) with flattened base.

[39]Dever (1976: 24, n. 34) considers these to be MB I types, while Oren (1971: 114) puts the chisel-axe in MB II (and therefore also this tomb). For discussion of these metal types, see Chapter VI.

[40]Toombs and Wright 1961: 21-22, 28-29; 1963, 6, 11, 17-18, 25; Wright *et al.* 1965: 15-16, 26-28; and Wright 1965: 110-12, 121-22. See also Dever 1976: 24-25, n. 38.

[41]Carinated bowls with flat or disc bases (Kenyon 1965: fig. 93:5), some with S-curved profiles (Kenyon 1965: fig. 93:6-8); large one-handled jugs with flat or slightly rounded bases (Kenyon 1965: fig. 93:11, 14), a large, rounded, handleless store jar (Kenyon 1965: fig. 93:15) and piriform juglets, one with a button base and both with stepped-rim profiles (Kenyon 1965: fig. 93:16-17).

[42]The reviewers of the Jericho volumes (Lapp 1961: 70; Wright 1966: 149) have suggested that some of the material from tombs assigned to Group I may also belong to late MB I. As Kenyon herself illustrates with one tomb, B 48 (Kenyon 1965: 206-26), not all the tombs necessarily represent a homogeneous group of material, especially since some of the tombs were reused for many successive burials. This tomb (B 48) in particular may indicate some overlap from the MB I period (Kenyon 1965: fig. 95:1-6, 9, 11-13, 19; fig. 98:9; fig. 99:2; also Kenyon 1960: fig. 112:1-7, 10, 11; fig. 115:1-5 from Tombs A 1 and J 3, respectively). An attempt, however, to perform a fine sorting of all this material on purely typological grounds and with no tell or internal stratigraphy to provide guidelines would seem pointless.

Additional vessels of MB II date should be mentioned. These include a piriform juglet with painted spiral decoration (Kenyon 1960: fig. 142:6), a trefoil mug with single handle from Tomb A 1 (Kenyon 1960: fig. 112:17), and another trefoil mug covered with a yellowish slip (Garstang 1932: pl. 32:8 from Tomb 9 which may include some MB I material such as the carinated bowls on flat base, pl. 36:3, 6 and 7).

[43]Epstein 1974: fig. 5:3, with several parallels from Megiddo of both Phase 3 (T. 3147, Loud 1948: pl. 10:1) and Phase 4 (Loud 1948: pl. 10:2-3, T. 3155; and pl. 10:11 and 8, T. 5178 and T. 5186, respectively.

[44]Epstein 1974: fig. 6:3, compare with an example from Megiddo, Loud 1948: pl. 11:12, T. 3157, Phase 4.

[45]I would like to thank the excavator, Emmanuel Eisenberg of the Rockefeller Museum, for the opportunity to see and discuss with him the pottery from this tomb.

[46]Burial 3: a dipper juglet and a round deep bowl with inverted rim, Sukenik 1948: pl. XIV:1-2; Burials 11-14: juglet with candlestick rim and several bowls, one with a bar below the rim, Sukenik 1948: pl. XIV:3, 6-9; Burial 19: piriform juglets, open bowls on disc or low ring bases, carinated bowls, simple rounded cups, cooking pot fragments, and an ostrich egg shell, Sukenik 1948: pl. XV.

[47]The MB I pottery includes (possibly) a carinated bowl on flat base with an orange-slipped and burnished exterior, Stratum 19 (Ohata 1966: pl. VI:1), a red-slipped and burnished piriform juglet, also Stratum 19 (Ohata 1967: pl. XLVI:1 and pl. IX:1), and fragments of straight-sided cooking pots with a band of molded decoration beneath the rim (Ohata 1970: 64, pl. XIV:1 and 2)

[48]The pottery types represented include the following: simple bowls (Oren 1975: fig. 1:3, 10, 15, 17, 19-26), carinated bowls (Oren 1975: fig. 2:28-30, No. 29 with wheel combing), goblets (Oren 1975: fig. 2:31-35), flat-based jugs (Oren 1975: fig. 2:41-43), cooking pots or holemouth jars, some with wheel combing on the exterior and one with a pattern of cross-hatching on the rim (Oren 1975: fig. 3:54). The goblets are compared by Oren to those of the preceding Syrian Caliciform culture. Note that all of these vessel types from Achzib are usually decorated with an orange-to-red slip and burnishing.

[49]Loud 1948: pl. 11:20, T. 3168, but, in shape, it is closer to pl. 12:3, T. 5275. Other typical MB I shapes represented include: simple rounded and carinated bowls, often with gutter rim (Ben-Dor 1950: figs. 28-35), holemouth jars (compare the rim profiles of Ben-Dor 1950: fig. 23 with Beck 1975: fig. 2:7-9), jars with everted rims (Ben-Dor 1950: fig. 21a-d).

[50]See Tufnell 1969: 5-10; Tufnell and Ward 1966: 165-241; and Dever 1976: 10-11, for bibliography and history of the role of the Byblos material in the development of the Middle Bronze Age archaeology of the Levant.

[51]Silver teapots: Montet 1929: No. 746, pl. CXI, from Tomb I, and No. 747, pl. CXII, from Tomb II; ceramic teapots: Tufnell 1969: No. 52 and No. 805, Montet 1928: 201; 1929, pl. CXIX; Schaeffer 1948: fig. 64A; No. 805 apparently omitted from Tufnell's republication of the pottery.

[52]Montet 1929: pl. CXIII: No. 754 in gold, Tomb II, and No. 775 in bronze, pl. CXIV, Tomb II.

[53]For example, Megiddo: Loud 1948: pl. 11:12, T. 3157; pl. 11:10, T. 4110. The more typical MB I juglet with pinched rim shows different proportions and a flat base which, in terms of the internal development of Levantine ceramics, is a less developed form of the same vessel; more examples which are closer to both the Byblos and Anatolian examples appear in MB II, such as a vessel from Megiddo, Loud 1948: pl. 25:8, T. 2145.

[54]Beth-shemesh: Grant 1929: No. 239, Tomb 2, also with ring at the base of the neck; Aphek: Amiran 1969: 106, photo 107.

[55]Tell el-Yahudiyeh juglets: Montet 1929: pls. CXLVI and CXLVIII: Nos. 914-17; fenestrated duckbill axes: Montet 1928: 247; 1929, pl. CXLIX: Nos. 940-41; Oren 1971: 118; animal-headed juglet: Schaeffer 1948, fig. 65m, Montet 1929: pl. CXLV: No. 929; bowl: Montet 1929: pl. CXLVII: No. 937; juglets: Montet 1929: pl. CXLVII: Nos. 931-32; mug with wheel-combing: Montet 1929, pl. CXLVII: No. 933; biconical mug: Montet 1929: pl. CXLVI: No. 934, which Oren (1971: 118) compares with an example from Aphek (Ory 1937: pl. XXX:17).

[56]It also occurs at Megiddo on the upper portion of a vessel (either a store jar or a krater, Loud 1948: pl. 13:11) which also uses rope decoration and is without provenience. See Chapter IV.1 and 2 for further discussion of this painted style.

[57]The controversy includes such questions as: Were the foundation deposits buried at a single time before the construction of the overlying building, or are they collections of offerings left in the temples over a period of time and then buried in order to clear out the overcrowded temples, or even as a way of protecting the temples' accumulated wealth in time of danger? See Negbi and Moskowitz 1966: 21-26; Schaeffer 1948:

50-62; Dunand 1958: 948-51; Montet 1928: 127-39; and Williams 1975: 848-50.

[58]Dunand 1954: 380; 1950: pl. LXXIV: No. 10645 from deposit σ, as well as apparently ceremonial examples, such as one executed in silver from a deposit in the "Temple aux obélisques": Dunand 1958: 732, No. 14840; for more discussion of this, see Oren 1973: 117-18.

[59]Dunand 1954: 190, fig. 193: No. 8359; Dunand 1950: pl. LXVI: No. 9686 and pl. XCII: No. 15835; Dunand 1958: 946, fig. 1060: No. 17691 and 1002, fig. 1109: No. 18355; and an example without handles: Dunand 1958: 852: No. 16694; Dunand 1950: pl. CXXXI. Compare with Loud 1948: pl. 21:1, T. 3109, Megiddo Phase 3; Beck 1975: fig. 1:3, Aphek prepalace phase.

[60]A technique which recalls the decoration on store jars from Tell Beit Mirsim, Albright 1933: fig. 4:13, 15, 16.

[61]Dunand 1958: 809; 1950, pl. CXXVIII: No. 15889; bronze juglet: Dunand 1958: 815, fig. 929: No. 15964.

[62]Goblet: Dunand 1958: 805, 803, fig. 919: No. 15836, compared with Tufnell 1969: fig. 4:46-47; juglets: Dunand 1958: 1002, fig. 1109: No. 18350 (with burnishing) and Dunand 1954: 401, fig. 406: No. 10882 (with painted decoration); biconical mugs: Dunand 1958: 946, 939, fig. 1054: No. 17692, and 1045, 1044, fig. 1153: No. 18926; collarette juglet: Dunand 1939: 275-76, fig. 236: No. 3928, with parallels from Aphek and other sites which would indicate an early MB I date; Minoan pottery sherds: Dunand 1939: 193, fig. 178; Schaeffer 1948: 65-66.

[63]This point is crucial in an attempt to date the MB I period. First Albright, then Kenyon, and now Williams have argued that the Byblos Royal Tombs represent the earliest manifestation of MB I culture in the Levant. Williams takes this argument the furthest in suggesting that Byblos and its immediate region (and a few isolated southern sites, such as Tell el-ᶜAjjul) are also the *only* manifestations of early Middle Bronze Age culture (his MB IIA and B). The earliest Middle Bronze Age culture which he believes to appear elsewhere in the Levant is his MB IIC-MB IIIA1. He therefore implies: (1) that he can isolate a ceramic phase at Byblos which has no parallels elsewhere in the Levant; (2) that, by inference, he denies the existence of a pre-Tell el-Yahudiyeh ware ceramic phase in the rest of the Levant; and (3) that the Byblos deposits (with the exception of the "Montet Jar") represent an isolated painted style—his MB IIA2 (Williams 1975, 840-902). It is necessary here to reemphasize that the detailed analyses of Tufnell and Dever show that certain groups of the Byblos material do have parallels and are contemporary with the Middle Bronze Age culture at other Levantine sites, *but* that those groups for which an approximate date can be suggested (the "Montet Jar" and the Royal Tombs, the latter if accepted as sealed groups) indicate an earlier dating for the MB I period than that proposed by Albright.

[64]For example, Schaeffer (1938: 247) attributed the material from Caves XXXVI and LV to the end of the Middle Bronze Age, that is, U.M. 3, but later (1948: 16) placed at least Cave XXXVI, Level J, between 1900-1750 B.C., thus implying contemporaneity with Dynasty 12.

[65]It would thus be possible to argue, as at Byblos, that MB II material makes its debut in Syria by the 18th century B.C. While this may be correct, it is not possible to base such an argument on the Ras Shamra material, since the poor stratigraphy of the site and the lack of stratified material invalidate the attempt to draw chronological conclusions from this material. Perhaps it is also this confusion which led Åström (1957: 261-64) to the opposite conclusion, that is, by eliminating a Level 3, Åström wanted to lower the date of Level 2 because of the inclusion within that level of MB II material.

[66]Schaeffer 1938: 199-204, 247; 1939: 55-60; 1948: 15-16; North 1973: 136-37; juglets on ring base: Schaeffer 1938: fig. 6:B and F, the former is burnished black ware; bichrome juglets: Schaeffer 1938: fig. 6:D and E; Kamares ware sherds: Schaeffer 1939: figs. 43-44; juglet with stepped rim: Schaeffer 1939: 54, fig. 41.

[67]Schaeffer 1938: 224, 231; fig. 26:P, Y, and Za, Zb, respectively. Schaeffer compares a bichrome juglet (Z), also from Cave LV, with one from Tomb XXXVI, and uses this as an argument for an early date, but both would still seem to fall outside the MB I group. For Cave LV in general, see Schaeffer 1938: 222-24, fig. 26; 1948: 19, pl. VIII.

[68]Collarette juglet: Schaeffer 1949: fig. 130:12; painted stepped-rim juglet: Schaeffer 1949: fig. 130:4, and undecorated examples: Schaeffer 1931: pls. IX:3 and X:1; other painted juglets: Schaeffer 1949: fig. 130:1, 3, 6, 7, 9, 10, 11, 14, 15-17; fig. 131:11; Schaeffer 1932: 19, pl. XII:1; jug with cutaway spout: Schaeffer 1949: fig. 131:16, very similar to the typical Syrian "eye" pitchers but without the painted eye; two plain juglets: Schaeffer 1949: fig. 102:1 and 4; krater: Schaeffer 1949: fig. 99:28, which is assigned to the U.M. I or EB IV period. There is no description of the technique of manufacture of this vessel and so it is difficult to establish its date on that basis. Its form seems more MB I than earlier, especially the flat base and carinated body; its decoration seems equivalent to that of the "Montet Jar," and it should perhaps therefore be placed early in the MB I period. Carinated bowls: Schaeffer 1949: fig. 100:1; fig. 105:15, fig. 107:5, and possibly fig. 101:9, 12 and fig. 102:7, which seem a variant of the flaring carinated bowl of late MB I, these with combed or incised lines around the neck. Bowls with narrow base: Schaeffer 1949: fig. 102:6 and 20; fig. 101:21, fig. 100:4, probably the fragment shown in fig. 99:24. Pitchers with beaked spouts: Schaeffer 1949: fig. 102:19 and A, found with a painted juglet of the type shown in fig. 100:16; and fig. 103:B, left. Cypriote juglets: Schaeffer 1949: fig. 131, probably all except Nos. 1, 11, and 16; Middle Minoan pottery: Schaeffer 1949: fig. 109. Metal objects: Schaeffer 1949: fig. 105:1-6 and 11-13; duckbill axes: Schaeffer 1932: pl. XIII:4 and possibly Schaeffer 1933: 111, without photo; Schaeffer 1948: fig. 49:7-8; dagger blades: Schaeffer 1932: pl. XIII:5-6; 1933: 111; 1948: fig. 45:C-G, N-Q.

[69]Tomb 8: mug: Guigues 1937: fig. 23d, compare with an example from Megiddo, Loud 1948: pl. 11:6 of Phase 3; jug with horizontal rim: Guigues 1937: fig. 23b; globular jug: Guigues 1937: fig. 23a, compare with Loud 1948: pl. 10:11, Phase 4. Although the tripod jar is often considered MB II, its occurrence in the tomb at Turᶜan may indicate an MB I origin for this type. Tomb 14: Guigues 1937: figs. 28a, 28f, and 29j; for the last, compare with examples from Megiddo, Loud 1948: pl. 20:28, and from Hazor, Yadin 1975: 271.

[70]Guigues 1938: figs. 46 and 47; compare with Megiddo examples of Phases 3 and 4, Loud 1948: pls. 10:1, 19:23, and 10:11.

[71]Although the spouted vessels are most common in the Levant in the EB IV period, for example, at Til Barsib and Megiddo, this vessel can be compared with a spouted bowl with

an almost identical holemouth rim from Tell Beit Mirsim G (Amiran 1969: pl. 29:4). Such jars are also found in mixed EB IV and MB I contexts in tomb groups in the Orontes Valley region (*infra*).

[72]Compare with a pinched-rim juglet from the third "tombeau de particuliers" at Byblos, Montet 1929: pl. CXLV: No. 929.

[73]This can be explained, following Schaeffer (1948: 110; also North 1973: 134), by a gap between the end of MB I and the beginning of the Late Bronze Age (between 1750 and 1550 B.C., in his dating). Fugmann, however, presents the view that Stratum H lasted from ca. 1900-1550 B.C. and Stratum G begins without a break following this, primarily because the old wall foundations of G seemed reused in H. While there also seems to be continuity in some of the pottery forms, one can still argue that the typical Levantine MB II is not present here, as also seems to be the case at Tell Mardikh. A third possibility is that the MB II structures were destroyed by later construction, since Fugmann (1958: 95) mentions that much of Level H 1 was disturbed by structures of the Hellenistic period. Finally, it is possible that forms which would be considered MB I, as defined in terms of the southern Levant, may continue later in the north and are contemporary with MB II in the south.

[74]Simple bowls: Fugmann 1958: fig. 109:3C75, 126, 366, 3B310; fig. 117:3B278, 2C973; fig. 120:M180; fig. 124:2C909 and 901; also Ingholt 1940: 51-52; bowl with pointed carination: Fugmann 1958: fig. 109:3B721, 3C505, and 3C130; bowls with rounded carination: Fugmann 1958: fig. 110:3A900, 3A889, 3A898, 3B935, 3B941; open bowls: Fugmann 1958: fig. 127:4B178, 4C306; fig. 139:5B851; goblet: Fugmann 1958: fig. 109:3B988 and 312; goblet with ring base: Fugmann 1958: fig. 110:3A797, compare with Tufnell 1969: fig. 4:46-47; juglet with painted decoration: Fugmann 1958: fig. 109:3H197; combing: Ingholt 1940: 50-51; Fugmann 1958: fig. 109:3K162, 3C551; fig. 117:3A858, 2D218; fig. 139:5A85; fig. 110:3D582.

[75]du Mesnil du Buisson 1927: 14-19: "eye" jugs: figs. 47 and 49; pls. VIII:1-2; XI; XIII:1; bottles: figs. 46 and 48; pl. IX:1 and pl. XII:1; flat-based store jars: pl. IX: fig. 70B, C, D; goblets: figs. 53 and 54; bowls: pl. X; pl. XII:2.

[76]du Mesnil du Buisson 1930: 153, fig. 3; 1935a: 66-67, figs. 15-16; du Mesnil du Buisson 1927: 294-95, pl. LXXIX:43-44, 45, and 48.

[77]du Mesnil du Buisson 1930: juglets: pl. XXXI, compare especially No. 25, a pinched-rim jug, which is nearly identical in form, but without the painted decoration, to No. 61 from Qatna Tomb I; jar: pl. XXXII:24; carinated bowl: pl. XXXIV:35, compare with bowls from Ugarit, Schaeffer 1949: figs. 100:4 and 102:20.

[78]Recent survey and excavation in the area of the Wadi Tumilat have also discovered tombs with pottery of MB I type, including red-slipped and burnished wares (reported by J. S. Holladay, Jr., at the annual meeting of the Society of Biblical Literature; November 19, 1978; see also MacDonald 1980: 49-58). Several vessels of Levantine type (either imports or inspired by imports) found in Egypt were discussed by Merrillees (1973: 51-59), but none are from secure stratigraphic contexts.

[79]Compare, for example, two juglets from Megiddo, both with double handle attached to a neck ridge. The juglet illustrated in Loud 1948: pl. 10:20 (here fig. 18:3) from T. 3144, which is assigned stratigraphically to Phase 4, is much closer in body shape to the Tell ed-Dabᶜa juglet than is Loud 1948: pl. 10:21 (here fig. 11:2) from T. 3143, assigned stratigraphically to Phase 1/2.

Chapter IV
The Painted Wares

While it is difficult and perhaps misleading to discuss painted wares and monochrome wares separately, painted decoration occurs on such a limited variety of forms in the Levant at the beginning of the 2nd millennium B.C. that this division should cause little confusion, despite some overlap in the consideration of certain shapes. The types of painted pottery which occur at this time have generally been classified under the following terms: "Ḫabur" ware, Syro-Cilician painted ware, and imported Cypriote pottery. While the third category presents relatively little amibiguity, the first two have sometimes been considered as related (Seton Williams 1953: 57), while other analyses ignore any possible relationship. As we shall see, the first category—that of "Ḫabur" ware—may be inappropriate when discussing the ceramics of the Levant and Anatolia.

IV.1. The "Ḫabur" Ware

This class of pottery was first defined by Mallowan who found it in relative abundance during his excavations at Chagar Bazar (Mallowan 1936: 12; 1937a, 102-4). It was at first thought to begin ca. 2000 B.C., but later was changed to date ca. 1800 B.C. on the basis of tablets belonging to Iasmaḫ-Adad which were found in the same level (Gadd 1940: 22-24; Mallowan 1947: 82-84). This ware was described by Mallowan (1937a, 102-4) as consisting "largely of vases intended to carry liquids"—that is, store jars with wide mouth, high neck, flat base, and a more or less globular body. Other vessel types which are now recognized as occurring in this ware include open and carinated bowls and various types of beakers and goblets (Kantor 1958: 22). The vessels, at least in the Ḫabur region itself, are always wheelmade and, although the clay fabric may vary, it tends to be buff or greenish in color. The paint is matt red or reddish brown or black, while the designs usually consist of simple geometric elements placed on the upper part of the vessel; these include bands, triangles (sometimes with crosshatching), dots, zigzags, short strokes on the rim, and, at some sites, a few naturalistic motifs such as trees or silhouetted animals (Tell Billa, Speiser 1933: 256, pl. LIX:5). Because of the profusion of this ware in the Ḫabur Valley region, Mallowan dubbed it "Ḫabur Ware," although he did not intend to imply that the Ḫabur Valley was its source of origin (Mallowan 1937a: 103).

DISTRIBUTION

Two main vessel types which are considered to fall within the range of Ḫabur ware occur at sites in the Levant. One type is the store jar, which generally occurs in the earlier phases of MB I. The second type—the goblet—is found, to a more limited extent, in mid-to-late MB I contexts, although it develops into an MB II type with ring base, as at Byblos (Tufnell 1969: fig. 4:46-47). This goblet shape will be discussed in Chapter V.1. The Levantine sites where the store jar has been found include the following (fig. 19):

Megiddo: T. 5181, Loud 1948: pl. 12:22 and pl. 13:1; T. 5149, Loud 1948: pl. 8:8; T. 3143, Loud 1948: pl. 12:16, Phase 1/2; T. 5118, Loud 1948: pl. 12:16, Phase 3 (?); T. 3138, Loud 1948: pl. 12:17; T. 5156, Loud 1948: pl. 13:4; T. 5167, Loud 1948: pl. 8:9; T. 5185, Loud 1948: pl. 13:2 and 9, all of Phase 2; Loud 1948: pl. 12:21, =T. 5130; pl. 13:5, E=T. 5147 (with a pattern of concentric circles in red and black paint); Guy 1938: pl. 29:9, T. 911A1 and pl. 35:5, T. 912B.

Lachish: Tomb 1513, Group 4, Main Deposit, Tufnell 1958: 257, pl. 78:803 and 804.

Beth-shemesh: Tomb 2, Grant 1929: 155, No. 134.

Gezer: Cave III 30, Macalister 1912a: 298, fig. 158:3.

Aphek: Prepalace phase: Beck 1975: fig. 3:7-10 (with painted decoration of straight, zigzag, and crossed bands), fig. 14:4; Tomb 7: Iliffe 1936: 123:23, 24, 29, and 51; Ory 1937: 116:73-76.

Gibeon: Tomb 58, Pritchard 1963: fig. 64:9-11.

Barqai: Second burial phase, Gophna and Sussman 1969: fig. 4:12.

Tell el-Far^{c}ah (N.): Tomb 16, de Vaux 1955: 545, fig. 2:10 (painted), Tomb B, de Vaux and Steve 1948: 571, fig. 11:1.

and Steve 1948: 571, fig. 11:1.

Kafer Djarra: Tomb 14, Guigues 1937: fig. 28f (with painted horizontal bands); Tomb 8, Guigues 1937: fig. 22; Tomb 62, Guigues 1938: fig. 59 (with concentric circles, similar to the Megiddo jar).

Majdalouna: Chehab 1940: fig. 6d (also with concentric circles).

Sin el-Fil: Chehab 1939: fig. 8c (with groups of circles painted in red).

Hama: Fugmann 1958: pl. X: Grave III, 5A983, 5B613, 5D25; Grave VI, 5B397, 5B398 (all with painted and combed decoration).

Yabrud: Assaf 1967: pl. II:1 (with a raised band).

Qatna: Tomb I, du Mesnil du Buisson 1927: 28, fig. 70:B, C, D, pl. IX; from beneath the Temple of Nin-Egal, du Mesnil du Buisson 1935a:118, fig. 38 (with painted strokes on the rim and a row of triangles).

All these vessels, like those described by Mallowan, are wheelmade. The examples from the Levant, however, differ in that, with the exception of the jar from Megiddo and those from Majdalouna, Sin el-Fil, and Tomb 62 at Kafer Djarra, the painted motifs are limited to plain horizontal bands, while many of the vessels are unpainted.

In tracing further the distribution of these vessels to the north and west, one encounters them in Cilicia and southern Anatolia (fig. 19:10-11), where the shapes and painted motifs are virtually the same; the only local variation is the addition of handles on some of the jars. Jars from Tarsus have greater variety in painted motifs, including hatched and crosshatched triangles, lattices, and the crosshatched butterfly pattern, and are therefore closer to the examples from the Ḫabur region. An undecorated store jar with handles was found at Mersin, while examples of Ḫabur store jars have been reported at other sites in Cilicia and even the Konya Plain where sherds were found with simple patterns of parallel bands in bright red paint, and two examples had a zigzag and a tree motif.[1] The Cilician examples are not entirely wheelmade; the three jars from Tarsus all have turned necks and rims, while the bodies are handmade. Several examples were also found on Cyprus in Tomb 7 at Paleoskoutella, including two undecorated jars and one with two registers of crosshatched triangles in reddish brown matt paint (Åström 1957: 129, fig. XL:8 and 9, the latter painted).

In turning to the east (see fig. 5 for location of sites), a few vessels have been noted from sites along the upper Euphrates River and in the Balikh River Valley, as in the Carchemish region, where painted "Ḫabur" ware was reported from Sultantepe and Aşaği Yarmica (Prag 1970: 63, n. 8; 76). At Tell Rifa^{c}at a fragmentary example with black painted straight and wavy horizontal lines was found (Seton Williams 1961: pl. XL:15). At Tell Jidle a fragment of a "Ḫabur" vessel painted with red stripes was found in Level 4, and several examples of the more delicate late "Ḫabur" ware were found in Level 3 (Mallowan 1946: 119-20). A sherd was also found at Tall Sahlan on the Nahr al-Turkman, a tributary of the Balikh (Mallowan 1946: 138). Great quantities of the ware are not in evidence until one reaches the Ḫabur region itself where it was found at several sites which Mallowan surveyed, especially at Chagar Bazar. It was also found, although in more limited quantity, at both Tell Brak[2] and Tell Fakhariyah (Kantor 1958: 22). Whether this apparent discontinuity in the distribution of the ware in northern Mesopotamia may be the result of lack of sufficient excavation, a gap at sites in this area at the beginning of the 2nd millennium B.C. (*infra*), political factors, or an indication of a secondary influence from the east cannot here be determined.

In the region of the middle Euphrates, "Ḫabur" ware store jars with painted decoration were found at Mari (Parrot 1938: 308-10, fig. 1) where they were considered to be imports. A large number of these store jars was excavated at the cemetery site of Baghouz located 8 km. south of Tell Hariri (Mari) also along the Euphrates River (du Mesnil du Buisson 1948: pl. III; Engberg 1942: 17-23). Although no clear chronological correlation is given for the cemetery with the site of Mari, the presence of numerous fenestrated duckbill axes, as well as ribbed lance heads (du Mesnil du Buisson 1948: pls. LX-LXI), clearly indicates that this cemetery is part of the same cultural horizon as the MB I period in the Levant. The store jars are wheelmade of greyish brown clay with a buff-colored surface. The major decorative pattern is that of grooving or combing on the neck, sometimes with paint strokes (not shown on the drawings, du Mesnil du Buisson 1948: LXVIII-LXXII; Enberg 1942: 20, n. 1). The bases of the jars range from flat to rounded and some are even tapered, thus paralleling the diversity of the Levantine examples. Small bronze perforated cones were found inside the jars, presumably as part of a drinking device (Engberg 1942: 21). A similar device is described by Mallowan from Chagar Bazar (Mallowan 1937a: 99, pl. XIVc); some of these examples showed traces of a reed, thus providing a parallel for scenes on cylinder seals in which people are shown sipping from jars through straws (Frankfort 1939: 77-78, 238, pls. XVa, XLd and f). The sieves would apparently have prevented the dregs from passing into the reed straws. The presence of these jars in great quantity in the Mari region and particularly their apparent use for wine storage and drinking provide interesting links to the literary evidence, which may help in establishing a date and place of origin for these vessels.

Farther to the east, similar painted pottery was found at the sites of Tell Billa and Tepe Gawra. Stratum 4 of Tell Billa (Speiser 1933: 255-57, 270-73) represents a break in the ceramic repertoire of the preceding period at that site, particularly in terms of the use of painted and incised decoration. The decoration in red, brown, and black paint consists primarily of geometric patterns combined with some naturalistic motifs. The incised decorations are simpler and include double-rope moldings, combed bands, and hatched triangles (Speiser 1933: pl. LIX:1 and 4, from Tombs 48 and 61; here fig. 19:9).

"Ḫabur" ware vessels occur at Tepe Gawra in Strata VI-IV, including plain and incised decorated storage jars and a goblet with horizontal painted bands (Speiser 1935: pl. LXIX:134, 135; pl. LXXI:161; pl. LXXIII:194; here fig. 19:8). Farther to the south along the Tigris River, a few of these storage vessels were found at Assur (Hrouda 1957: pl. 9:1, 2, 4, 5), although these were outnumbered by examples of the later "Ḫabur" ware. Similar vessels were also found at the nearby site of Tell Aqrah (Hrouda 1957: 26, pl. 10:2). Finally, similar vessels were found at sites in northwestern Iran, as best exemplified by an example from Dinkha Tepe (Hamlin 1971: pl. I:36; 1974: 125-53).

DATING

The date of this ware, as mentioned above, was originally established by Mallowan on the basis of texts found with "Ḫabur" ware pottery in the earliest phase of Level I of Chagar Bazar. The majority of these texts refer to Iasmaḫ-Adad as ruler of the region. Much of the pottery of the first two seasons of excavation was found in graves dug into the floor of Level I. Mallowan, using Smith's middle chronology, dated the ware at ca. 1800 B.C. and wrote: "It is highly improbable that the Khabur pottery associated with these tablets were the earliest known examples of that ware" (Mallowan 1947: 82-83). It has since been accepted, perhaps because of the lack of typical "Ḫabur" ware jars at Alalakh prior to Level VII, that the Syro-Cilician painted ware was under the influence of the "Ḫabur" ware and therefore any painted pottery showing resemblances to "Ḫabur" ware must be dated later than 1800 B.C. (Welker 1948: 205-6).

This assumption may also be a result of the confusion of the early "Ḫabur" ware with the later type, whose shape and decorative motifs, which are more naturalistic, begin to merge with the characteristics of the so-called Mitannian or Nuzi ware (Kantor 1958: 22). This later ware does have parallels in the Levant, but these are with late MB II or early LB I pottery (Speiser 1933: 272-73). It should be emphasized that the early "Ḫabur" ware, described by Mallowan from the first phase of Chagar Bazar Level I (and not to be confused with Prag's "early Ḫabur ware" which is placed in the 3rd millennium B.C. at the site of Harran, Prag 1970: 71, 75, 79-81), should correlate with the Syro-Cilician painted wares which mark the beginning of the Middle Bronze Age at Tarsus, Mersin, Alalakh, and other sites in the Levant. Kramer (Hamlin 1971: 61-144) defined a distinct assemblage of pottery which included vessels similar to Mallowan's classification of "Ḫabur" ware at the site of Dinkha Tepe in northwestern Iran and then traced its appearance in northern Mesopotamia. She recognized that this "Ḫabur" ware does not occur in the Levant or Anatolia at the beginning of the 2nd millennium B.C., so that those painted wares should be considered separately. After this, the problem becomes semantic in terms of the definition of what "Ḫabur" ware is. However, some relationship among these store jars and, to a lesser extent, the painted carinated bowls, which appear from the Levant throughout northern Mesopotamia in the first quarter of the 2nd millennium B.C., should be acknowledged and, if possible, explained. Hrouda (1957: 26-27), as well, had recognized the necessity of analyzing the painted styles in terms of technique and motifs and the contemporaneity of the two styles.

Mallowan's date of 1800 B.C. is also open to question. First, he describes the tablets found in Room 106 as "resting on potsherds which had evidently once served as trays" (Mallowan 1947: 82). These sherds, some of which were of early "Ḫabur" ware with painted red stripes, were surely the remnants of previously used and broken vessels, thus implying that this ware, at Chagar Bazar, must date at least a "pot generation" earlier. A second difficulty with Mallowan's dating is that while tombs may be dug through a contemporary floor level, he describes the tombs in which the "Ḫabur" jars were first found (Graves 1, 2, and 3, Mallowan 1936: 55) as located beneath the *foundations* of Level I.[3] It seems unlikely that tombs would be tunnelled in under existing wall foundations, thus weakening the structure, so that we may suggest that these tombs should predate the earliest structures of Level I and thus also Iasmaḫ-Adad. How early these tombs should date and whether there is a gap at other sites in northern Mesopotamia for the beginning of the 2nd millennium B.C. cannot be answered here.[4]

As was already shown in Chapter III, the appearance of both "Ḫabur" ware store jars and "Ḫabur"-type decoration marks the beginning of the MB I period in the Levant. Not only is this shown by the stratigraphic evidence at Megiddo and Aphek, but also by the presence of vessels which are clearly transitional between the EB IV and the MB I periods which are of "Ḫabur" ware type. These include the "Montet Jar" from Byblos, the cooking pot with hatched triangles from the end of "Ugarit moyen" 1 (Schaeffer 1949: 99:28), and the jars from Tarsus partially handmade and wheelmade and assigned to a level which should be placed at the beginning of the Middle Bronze Age (that is, at the 8 m. level, Goldman 1956: 164).[5]

In order to fit the sequence of Levant phases into the generational slots established in Mesopotamia by the textual evidence, we must rely on a correlation of the end of the MB I period with the Alalakh VII palace which is assigned to Iarimlim. Since Iarimlim was approximately contemporary with Išme-Dagan and Iasmaḫ-Adad, we see that the "Ḫabur" store jars appear in quantity at Chagar Bazar, just before the end of the MB I period in the Levant. Since it has been shown that the MB I period must have lasted for some considerable length of time and that the "Ḫabur" store jars mark the beginning of MB I, the Levantine examples of this ware must be given chronological priority over the ware as it is so far known to appear in northern Mesopotamia.[6] That it may have been present there at an earlier date and is only missing at those sites excavated in northern Mesopotamia is perhaps shown by its presence in quantity at the Baghouz cemetery, which probably corresponds more closely to the Levant MB I than do the northern Mesopotamian sites, which seem to postdate the MB I period. A *terminus ante quem* for the appearance of "Ḫabur" ware can therefore be set by the date for the beginning of the MB I period in the Levant, without needing to depend on the date set by Mallowan for its appearance in the Ḫabur Valley.

ORIGIN

In naming this pottery "Ḫabur" ware, Mallowan did not intend to imply that the ware was "invented" in this region (Mallowan 1937a: 103-4). He did suggest, however, that the ware originated in western Iran where there was an unbroken tradition of painted pottery, although he acknowledged that the style must have died out there fairly quickly and only continued in the Ḫabur region itself. He failed, however, to recognize another region with a continuous painted pottery tradition, namely that of Syro-Cilicia.[7] The painted pottery styles in this area, although undergoing changes between the end of the Early Bronze Age and the beginning of the Middle Bronze Age, show some elements of continuity, namely the occurrence, though sparse, of basic geometric patterns on EB III Tarsus pottery[8] and in the ᶜAmuq Phase J (Braidwood and Braidwood 1960: 442-46, figs. 342-44)[9] and Hama Level I. Particularly in northern Syria, this phase is characterized by the painted Syrian goblet. Painted decoration also occurs on vessels in the tomb groups in the Orontes Valley region which are transitional between EB IV and MB I. These groups include vessels from beneath the "Butte de l'Église" at Qatna, Tomb I from Osmaniye, and the tombs at Tell ᶜAs, Selimiye, and Dnebi. To these may be added vessels from the hypogeum at Tell Ahmar and the graves excavated near Carchemish.[10] Mallowan suggested a date of post-2000 B.C. for the painted vessels from Hamman, and, by implication, for those from Tell Ahmar as well, so that these could be considered as contemporaries, rather than as predecessors, of the "Ḫabur" ware at Chagar Bazar (Mallowan 1937b: 337). Their forms, however, would still seem to argue for an EB IV placement. Only faint echoes of a painted style reached the southern Levant in this period. This influence can be seen in the regionalized group of painted, spouted vessels from Megiddo (Guy 1938: pl. 11:28-33, Tomb 877A2) which, nonetheless, do not relate to the MB I painted styles of northern Syria (cf. the spouted vessels from Yabrud, Assaf 1967: pl. III:23-24).

The striking similarity of geometric motifs and method of execution, including the use of the wheel, of both the "Ḫabur" ware and the Syro-Cilician painted ware leads to the conclusion that they are, in fact, the same style. The initial discovery of this style at a site where the store jar shape was dominant led archaeologists to divide this ware into two separate painted styles—a division which was, in fact, based only on a dichotomy in vessel shapes. The "Ḫabur" ware consisted primarily of storage jars; the Syro-Cilician ware primarily of carinated bowls and pinched-rim juglets. The fact that storage jars decorated in the same manner were later found at Tarsus (*supra*) and that carinated bowls were found in northern Mesopotamia[11] did not alter this interpretation.

Perhaps one reason for the relative scarcity of the storage jars in the Levant is that they were in use only during the beginning of the MB I period. At some sites, such as Aphek, this type of jar was never used exclusively, even in the earliest phase of MB I, while by the end of MB I a store jar with handles, shortened neck, and long tapering body had begun its evolution toward the "Canaanite jar." This type of jar which, because of its pointed base, could not stand independently, became the vessel which was widely imitated and in which commodities were shipped throughout the Aegean during the later 2nd millennium B.C. (Grace 1956: 80-109; Parr 1973: 176-77). Once the "Ḫabur" ware style and shape appeared in northern Mesopotamia, however, it remained virtually unchanged for centuries (Mallowan 1937a: 102) and continued there much later than in the Levant, although the jar with pointed base also appeared in Mesopotamia (Parr 1973: 178-79). This vessel shape seems appropriate both for transport and storage of liquids (note its frequent description as such, as well as the evidence from Baghouz and Chagar Bazar that it was used in connection with wine). One may therefore suggest that these were the vessels in which wine, olive oil, and honey, mentioned in the admittedly later Mari texts as being imported from western Asia into northern Mesopotamia, may have been transported.

One might also hypothesize that the absence of these particular store jars at Alalakh XVI-VIII was based on the political relationships revealed by the texts (cf. Kramer 1977: 104-5). If one assumes that these jars were the hallmarks of the trade in wine, oil, and honey between western Asia and Mesopotamia during the reigns of Šamši-Adad and Iasmaḫ-Adad, then their absence may be an archaeological witness to a lack of trade between these areas, since Aleppo (of which Alalakh was a vassal) was an ally of Zimrilim whom Šamši-Adad had ousted from Mari. Unfortunately, it is not possible to test this hypothesis further at the site of Aleppo itself, since this 2nd-millennium B.C. capital has not been excavated (Sauvaget 1939: 59-65), nor were any such jars found in a survey of the Aleppo region (Maxwell-Hyslop *et al.* 1942: 27; now also Matthers and others 1978: 138-42). The presence of this ware is, however, attested for Alalakh Level VII and later, which would correspond to the reestablishment of Zimrilim at Mari (Woolley 1955: pl. LXXXVII:a, Level V).

In suggesting that the "Ḫabur" ware jars belong to the Syro-Cilician painted style, an objection could be raised that there seems to be a chronological discontinuity in that these vessels were popular in the Levant at the beginning of MB I, but do not appear at Chagar Bazar until near the end of MB I. Three factors may help to explain this: (1) the vessels from Chagar Bazar may in fact date somewhat earlier than Mallowan had concluded; (2) the evidence from Baghouz shows that the dating of the vessels in Mesopotamia may correspond more closely to the MB I period than was previously thought; and (3) although the "Ḫabur" ware store jars did not continue in use into late MB I in the Levant, other vessel types, such as the goblets and carinated bowls and, more importantly, the Syro-Cilician painted style itself, did continue throughout MB I and into the MB II period.

The conclusions concerning "Ḫabur" ware may therefore be summarized as follows. First, the limited repertoire of decorative motifs and vessel shapes which characterize the "Ḫabur" ware of the

Levant should be recognized as distinct from the entire ceramic assemblage defined by Kramer (Hamlin 1971: 134-37), although cognates of this Levantine pottery probably appear in the assemblage in northern Mesopotamia and perhaps even in northwestern Iran. Second, this style originated at the beginning of the Middle Bronze Age in the Levant and in Cilicia representing a new technique which, nonetheless, shows some relationship to the late Early Bronze Age styles of northern Syria and Cilicia. Third, this style ultimately attained a distribution throughout southern Anatolia, Cyprus, the Levant, and Mesopotamia at least as far east as the Tigris River Valley and as far south as Baghouz and Assur. Fourth, since this style clearly belongs to the larger group of Syro-Cilician painted pottery, the term "Ḫabur" ware should not be used in considering vessels from the Levant. This term should only be used to describe those vessels from northern Mesopotamia where the style took on individual characteristics and where it remained relatively unchanged, while the style continued to develop in the Levant, and the typical storage jar dropped out of use before even the end of MB I. Fifth, the store jar, in particular, may have been used in the export of such liquids as wine and olive oil from the Levant to Mesopotamia, as documented in Mesopotamian texts; this was the mechanism by which the vessel type was introduced into that region. Sixth, the store jars from the southern Levant display a variation or simplification of the painted style. The only motif which occurs in the southern Levant is that of simple horizontal bands, usually straight, although sometimes wavy or with hatching, the only exception being a store jar from Megiddo with a design of concentric circles. This predilection for simplified design may indicate that painted decoration was not native or popular in this region but was a style imported from northern Syria. This characteristic, which may be considered a form of regionalism or "conservatism," will reappear as we consider other branches of this Syro-Cilician painted style.

IV.2. Syro-Cilician Painted Pottery

This group of painted pottery was first clearly defined by Seton Williams (1953: 56-68; Hrouda 1957: 27-31), although some of the examples and characteristics of this style had previously been discussed by Welker (1948: 205-6). The ware described by Seton Williams occurs primarily in the following vessel types: carinated bowls (both with and without pedestals), jugs, basket-handled jugs (or bowls) with or without a spout, cups, and amphorae. This last group has already been considered in the previous section concerning store jars. The main characteristic of this ware, according to Seton Williams, is the reddish brown-to-black decoration, usually in lustrous paint, consisting of simple geometric motifs of triangles, hatching, stippling, and crosses in metopes (also called the double-axe or butterfly motif) which tend to be arranged in horizontal registers concentrating on the upper half of the vessel. Naturalistic motifs are relatively rare and usually occur only on jugs. The designs are applied on a light ground, sometimes a cream, buff, or light brown slipped surface. Although Seton Williams writes that these vessels are usually handmade, there are also wheelmade examples.

The vessels which she used as examples of this ware are all from Cilicia and northern Syria (plus the jug from Ayia Paraskevi), but, when we consider the offshoots of these particular vessel shapes with this same painted style, this "ware" or "style" is shown to have had a distribution throughout the Levant and some major regional variants. First the jugs and juglets will be considered, followed by the carinated bowls and, finally, an additional group—the open bowls with painted crosses or diameters on the interior.

The first and most distinctive type of jug to fall into this class is that of the "eye" jug—a jug with pinched and usually slanting rim and an eye on either side of the rim at the pinch. Frequently, there are also lines painted above the eye and below, the latter often corresponding to a ridge or bulge in the neck, all of which increase the anthropomorphic aspect of the vessel. The number of vessels corresponding to this exact description is relatively small and includes the following (many of which are also illustrated by Seton Williams 1953: fig. 2:9 and fig. 3; here fig. 20):

Tarsus: Goldman 1956: 173-74, pl. 295:860 and 859 (also pl. 369), with painted eye moved to the metope, pl. 370:857.

Mersin: Level XI, Garstang 1953: 210, fig. 143: 2-5.

ᶜAmuq: Phase L, Swift 1958: fig. 1:2.

Alalakh: Primarily Levels XIV and XII-XI, Woolley 1955: pls. LXXXIV, LXXXVa-b, XCI, XCII, CXV: Type 70 (note that Seton Williams 1953: 60-61, attributes this vessel type to Level VII, thereby dating its appearance at Alalakh too low; Woolley 1955, 308-9).

Ugarit: "Ugarit moyen" 2, Schaeffer 1949: fig. 131:16 (but missing the painted eye); 1978: 208-9, figs. 4:4 and 4A.

Qatna: Tomb I, du Mesnil du Buisson 1927: fig. 47, pl. VIII (it is difficult to see the design clearly on some of the photographs but see also Schaeffer 1948: fig. 100:2, 11, 23; note especially No. 11, with squared-off base, which recalls the typical EB IV vessel shape).

Tell Rifaᶜat: Survey, Type 58, Matthers and others 1978: 142.

This vessel type also appears, apparently as an import, at other sites in central and southern Anatolia, including Maltepe in the Calycadnus Valley and Tömükkale near Elvanli (Mellaart 1958: 324, fig. 61) and at Kültepe where sherds of such jugs were found in Level IV.[12] While such vessels may be considered imports, a juglet type which clearly relates to these Cilician examples but which differs in size (smaller), proportions (the neck is longer), and shape (the body is biconical instead of rounded) may perhaps be a local product in imitation of the Cilician imports. These juglets retain the typical linear patterns on the body, the painted eye at the pinch, and the painted rim and handle (Hrozný 1927: pl. IV:2; Ankara Museum Kt o/k 58, 54-19-64, Level II). Since the imported jugs and at least one example of the juglet are assigned to Levels IV-II, it can be inferred that this aspect of Cilician influence reached central Anatolia in the earlier phase of the *kārum*'s existence, and that the *kārum* IV-II levels would therefore be synchronous with the beginning of the Cilician Middle Bronze Age (although it has also been suggested that the Cilician pottery in *kārum* Level IV should be considered as intrusive, so that Cilician influence would be restricted only to the *kārum* II period).

Additional jug or juglet types should be considered as regional variations, and variants of the "eye" jugs can also be identified. Many jugs from the north Syro-Cilician area itself relate to this type but lack the eye and sometimes the pinched rim, otherwise retaining the same body shape and painted style. Within this group are also included jugs which did not have the rim preserved and therefore cannot be securely placed in the "eye" jug category. Many of these jugs retain the ridged neck or at least have a ridge marked on the neck in paint and/or the handle attachment still at the neck. They have a round body, long, cylindrical neck, and a flat disc or low ring base. Examples include the following (here figs. 21:1-7):

Ugarit: Schaeffer 1949: fig. 108:22 and fig. 131: 17 (which shows the influence of the Cypriote White Painted III-IV Pendent Line style but also has a ridged neck and foliated rim).

Tarsus: Goldman 1956: 174, pl. 295:856, 865, and 866.

Mersin: Level XI, Garstang 1953: fig. 143:7 and fig. 148:7, 9, and 10.

Qatna: Tomb I, du Mesnil du Buisson 1927: pl. XI:1, fig. 49.

Hama: Grave II, Fugmann 1958: pl. X:5B901 (and others described by Ingholt 1940: 56).

Mardikh: "Tomb of the Princess," Matthiae 1980a: 12-15 (jug with ibex representation in a metope scheme); 1980b: 13, fig. 13.

Yabrud: Assaf 1967: pl. III:9 (although less closely related).

Lebeᶜa: Tomb 1, Guigues 1937: 38, fig. 3a.

Kafer Djarra: Tomb 8, Guigues 1937: 63, fig. 23b; Tomb 66, Guigues 1938: 45, fig. 69.

Aphek: Iliffe 1936: 123:No. 50; Ory 1937: pl. XXV: 77, 89, 90.

Gezer: Cave III 30, Macalister 1912a: 298, fig. 158:7.

Tell el-ᶜAjjul: Petrie 1931: pl. XLVIII:57H5.

A jug with painted animal motifs was found in a Middle Cypriote tomb at Ayia Paraskevi and was considered by Åström to be an import from Syria or Cilicia (Åström 1957: 130, 232; here fig. 21:10). The spread of this style should be considered as concentrated in the early and especially middle phases of MB I. Two unpublished jugs in the Gaziantep Museum, one with pinched rim and both with simple metope patterns in reddish brown paint, perhaps demonstrate the furthest distribution east of this particular form.

Another juglet which should, however, be considered as a primarily southern Levantine type is the dipper juglet, which is much smaller than the

Syro-Cilician jug and tends to develop from a flat base into a pointed base by the end of the MB I period. The dipper juglet was therefore a local product which followed the general evolution of local pottery of the southern Levant, but it also shows a clear relationship to (or influence from) northern Syria in the use of a pinched rim and painted decoration. The painted motifs, however, are primarily limited to horizontal bands, usually on the upper part of the vessels, with strokes sometimes painted on the rim and/or handle of the vessels and, more rarely, vertical strokes hanging from the lowest horizontal band on the neck forming a collar at the base of the neck. These southern examples therefore represent a dissolution of the original painted style of northern Syria and Cilicia, as did also the store jars which usually had only horizontal painted bands in contrast to the much richer northern repertoire of motifs.

Vessels of this type appear as far north as Ugarit and Kafer Djarra, while a related group of small juglets comes from Tarsus, including one which is painted with cross-hatched triangles. The examples of this group from some sites, such as Megiddo, are quite numerous and so the following list of examples should not necessarily be considered as complete (see fig. 21:8-9):

Ugarit: Schaeffer 1949: fig. 106:11; fig. 100:13-16 and 18; fig. 99:18, 19, 22.
Tarsus: Goldman 1956: 173-74, pl. 369:858.
Kafer Djarra: Tomb 66, Guigues 1938: 46, pl. IV:h.
Megiddo: Loud 1948: pl. 11:13, T. 5180; pl. 11:18, T. 5183; pl. 11:19, T. 5130; pl. 11:20, T. 3168; pl. 11:21, T. 3150; pl. 11:22, T. 3147, T. 4046, and T. 5074; pl. 16:4, E=5093; pl. 16:5, T. 5268; pl. 20:6, T. 3141; pl. 20:7, T. 2151; pl. 7:19, T. 5167; Guy 1938: pl. 31:18, 19, and 21 from T. 911D and pl. 29:2-5 from T. 911A1 (from all phases but with a concentration from Phase 3).
Barqai: Gophna and Sussman 1969: fig. 4:1 and 3 (early MB I).
Aphek: Ory 1937: 117, Nos. 80 and 82.
Gezer: Macalister 1912a: 298, fig. 158:6, Cave III 30.
Nahariya: Dothan 1956: fig. 8.
Lachish: Tufnell 1958: 55, No. 157 (only rim and and neck preserved).
Ginosar: Tomb 4, Epstein 1974: fig. 14:4 (a late example with button base).

Finally, another specialized group of juglets which is almost as distinctive as the "eye" jugs is the group of painted collarette juglets. The collarette juglet appears in both painted and unpainted examples as a mark of the earliest phase of MB I and then evolves into the stepped-rim juglet, an indicator of the end of MB I. The form of both the painted and unpainted types follows an internal development which matches the general trends of Levantine pottery to more ovoid and piriform-shaped bodies and to either higher, usually ring, bases or button bases. Thus we can see that there are two streams of influence which merge to produce the characteristics of the Levantine sequence: the local elements, which determine primarily the shapes and their development; and elements of foreign influence, in this case manifested in the painted style, which are usually a veneer and seem only to be conforming to the popular trends of a particular period.

The collarette juglets are distinguished by the neck ridge to which the handle is attached (perhaps related to this feature on the "eye" jugs and other pinched-rim juglets), a flat base, and rounded body which sometimes tapers toward the base. On the basis of the occurrence of the larger group of unpainted collarette juglets, this type is assigned to the early phase of MB I. The painted decoration is limited to either concentric circles or spirals generally bordered, at least on the top, by horizontal lines. The handle and rim may also be decorated, while the Aphek jug has a collar of vertical lines at the base of the neck. The motif of concentric circles links these juglets to the store jars with the same motif from Megiddo (Loud 1948: pl. 13:5), Kafer Djarra, Tomb 62 (Guigues 1938: fig. 59), Majdalouna (Chehab 1940: fig. 6d), and Sin el-Fil (Chehab 1939: fig. 8c). The juglets of this group are found at these sites (here fig. 22):

Ugarit: Schaeffer 1949: fig. 100:20; 1978: 208-9, fig. 4:3.
Aphek: Beck 1975: fig. 14:8, from Tomb 43 (with a cross in the center of the spiral).
Megiddo: Loud 1948: pl. 19:33, =T. 4010.
Byblos: Dunand 1939: 275, fig. 236:No. 3928.
Lebeᶜa: Tomb 3, Guigues 1937: 40-41, fig. 6.
Kfar Szold: Epstein 1974: fig. 1:5.
Nahariya: Ben-Dor 1950: fig. 16:No. 325.

The later MB I version of this juglet, the stepped-rim juglet, also occurs in both painted and, more frequently, unpainted examples. The decorative motifs are virtually unchanged from those of the collarette juglet—concentric circles or spirals on the body framed by horizontal lines above and below. There is less of a tendency to decorate the handle, neck, and rim. Some juglets show the introduction of naturalistic motifs, especially silhouetted animals and trees which parallel the more extensive repertoires of northern Syria and northern Mesopotamia and which preface MB II and Late Bronze Age painted styles. The group of painted stepped-rim juglets (fig. 22) consists primarily of those examples found at Ginosar in Tomb 4 (Epstein 1974: fig. 14:1-3, 5, and probably 9). Another stepped-rim juglet from Tomb 1 at this site (Epstein 1974: fig. 5:10) has a cross in metope motif, which is most typical of the group of carinated bowls and does not occur elsewhere in the southern Levant. Additional examples of the painted stepped-rim juglet are known from Ugarit (Schaeffer 1949: fig. 100:26), Tomb 66 at Kafer Djarra (Guigues 1938: pl. III, one with concentric circles and another with a herringbone pattern), and Majdalouna (Chehab 1940: fig. 3f) with a button base and concentric circles. The continuity of this motif on first the collarette juglet and then on its descendant, the stepped-rim juglet, is a further illustration of the relative conservatism of the southern Levant.

The other vessel types characteristic of the Syro-Cilician painted ware have a more limited distribution than do the jugs and juglets and generally do not reach the southern Levant. The small carinated bowls on flat base, with which the bowls on a pedestal may be grouped, are the hallmark of the beginning of the Middle Bronze Age at such sites as Tarsus, Mersin, and Alalakh. This vessel type also occurs, although unpainted, at several additional sites, including Hama and Ugarit, and is to be linked to the carinated bowls which occur throughout the Levant in MB I and which will be considered in the next chapter. The decoration of these bowls is usually limited to the rim and the part of the body above the carination. The motifs are primarily linear: horizontal and vertical lines sometimes arranged in a metopal scheme with the opening perhaps filled with a cross design (the butterfly or double-axe motif), stippling, triangles (sometimes with cross-hatching), and diagonal lines. An occasional stylized tree and other variations may also occur. These bowls appear at the following sites (here fig. 23:1-11, 15):

Mersin: Level XI, Garstang 1953: fig. 143:1; fig. 144 and fig. 148:1, 2, 4, 6.

Alalakh: Woolley 1955: pl. XCI, Level XII; pl. XCII, Level XII; pl. CX: Type 23 (although this type occurs throughout Levels XVI-VIII, the painted examples may be concentrated in Level XII).

ᶜAmuq: Phase K, Swift 1958: 206, fig. 1.

Tarsus: Goldman 1956: 165, 167-70; pl. 287.

Cilicia: Seton Williams 1953: fig. 2:8 and fig. 4:7, 6, and 9; see map, fig. 1 (sites of Boz, Alapunar, Cebra).

Qatna: Sondage beneath the "Coupole de Loth," du Mesnil du Buisson 1927: 295, pl.LXXIX:No. 45.

This type also appears at Kültepe in Level II where it is again considered to be a Cilician import (T. Özgüç 1950: 199, pl. LX:328, pl. LXXIX:616, restored with a high ring base). Although its distribution to the south is limited, this type has been identified in northern Mesopotamia, as at the following sites (here fig. 23:19-23):

Sakcegözü: Cave site, Waechter *et al.* 1951: pl. I:18 (placed in the 2nd millennium B.C.).

Chagar Bazar: Level I, Mallowan 1936: fig.17: 14; 1937a: fig. 16:8, fig. 22:2, fig. 23:1.

Tell Billa: Stratum 4, Speiser 1933: pl. LVI:5, pl. LIX:2 and 3.

Tell Rifa ᶜat: Type 58, Matthers and others 1978: 142, fig. 10:58.

Tepe Gawra: Stratum V, Speiser 1935: pl. LXXI: 157 (a small jar with decoration of hatched triangles and resembling the bowls with high rounded carination of Ugarit and Hama).

Nineveh: A bowl with the butterfly motif was found here and considered to be an import (Thompson and Hamilton 1932: pl. LIV:5, J.9.B); sherds with cross-hatched triangles (Thompson and Mallowan 1933: pl. LVIII:1, 12).

Nippur: Type 24, McCown and Haines 1967: 78, pl. 88:18 and 23—bowls with high rounded carination, decorated with vertical lines and crosses in a metope pattern (this type has a range in date of the Isin-Larsa to Old Babylonian periods).

Tell Taya: Reade 1968: 257, pl. LXXXVII:26 (Level IV)—bowl with pointed carination and high ring base has a band of cross-hatched triangles between the rim and the carination.

Examples of deep rounded bowls with similar decoration (here fig. 23:17-18) are also known, for example, at Alalakh (Woolley 1955: pl. XCII: Level XIIb and c), and, possibly related, the bowl from Ugarit (Schaeffer 1949: fig. 99:28) and one from Mersin (Seton Williams 1953: fig. 2:12). The distribution of this type is too limited, however, to be of further interest here.

The remaining vessel type to be considered also has a fairly limited distribution. The basket-handled bowls or jugs with spout (or "teapots") are primarily known from Tarsus (Goldman 1956: 175-76, pls. 297 and 370:868, 871, 872, 874, and 875, with side-spout); a fragment with a spout was found at Mersin (Garstang 1953: fig. 145:18), and a very similar vessel but with bichrome decoration occurs at Kültepe in Level Ia (T. Özgüç 1959: 48, 102, fig. 56, pl. XXVIII:3). An unpublished spouted pot with side loop handle from the Gaziantep region is also painted with linear decoration relating to this style.

The group of open bowls with cross bands (or diameters) painted on the interior of the vessel is fairly small, but nonetheless significant, since this distinctive decorative motif provides one of the clearest synchronisms between the Levant and Anatolia. The sites and contexts in which these bowls have been found in the Levant may be listed (here fig. 24):

Tell Beit Mirsim: Stratum F, Albright 1933: pl. 5:5.

Wadi et-Tin: Vincent 1947: 279, fig. 6:18.

Gezer: Tomb No. 1, Macalister 1912b: pl. LXI: 16.

Tel Poleg: Gophna 1973: 116, fig. 5:4.

Aphek: Ory 1937: 107:2B; sherds also reported from the third season of excavations at Aphek (Beck 1975: 80, n. 7).

Dhahrat el-Humraiya: Grave 21, Ory 1948: 83, fig. 22.

Tell el-Far^cah (N.): Tomb W, Mallet 1973: pl. 23:3.

Beth-shemesh: The "High Place Grotto Sepulchre," Mackenzie 1912-1913: pl. XVII: 10.

Hazor: The Water Tunnel burial group, Yadin 1975: 270-71.

Qatna: From beneath the "Coupole de Loth," du Mesnil du Buisson 1927: 294-95, pl. LXXIX:43-44.

While several of these contexts are not closed groups of MB I pottery (such as Gezer Tomb 1 and the "High Place Grotto Sepulchre" at Beth-shemesh), a sufficient number of these examples can be considered as coming from secure MB I contexts to define the appearance of this motif during MB I, although not at the beginning of the period.[13] The motif of the cross also occurs on other vessel types at several sites: at Alalakh where it is painted on the bottom of the base of bowls (Woolley 1955: pl. XCI:ATP/47/119, Level XIIb, and pl. CXI:34), at Aphek, where it occurs on a collarette juglet (Beck 1975: fig. 14:8), and at Byblos (Dunand 1937: pl. LVII:No. 2000). The motif is incised on the four knobs of deep rounded bowls at Aphek (Beck 1975: 64-65, fig. 10:4) and at Ugarit (Schaeffer 1949: fig. 101:19) and may be paralleled by cross-incised knobs from Karahöyük-Konya (Alp 1968: 279-80, pl. 250:760-62).

The motif of the cross bands painted on the bowl interior is more frequent in Cilicia and Anatolia. It occurs at Tarsus (Goldman 1956: 165, pls. 289:813, 290:811 and 812, 291:820-22) where it had first appeared near the end of EB III and is one of the few characteristics of that period to continue into the Middle Bronze Age, as well as at Mersin in Level XIb (Garstang 1953: 211), which is the very beginning of the Middle Bronze Age at that site. Examples of the cross-painted bowls are found at Troy where it appeared sporadically in the IVc settlement (Blegen 1951: 193, A 37-37.1126), but became the "hallmark par excellence" of the Fifth Settlement (Blegen 1951: 250-51, pl. 240:32.69, pl. 244:8, and pl. 246) where it occurs on both rounded open bowls and on bowls with carinated shoulders and a single handle (Blegen 1951: pl. 238:A 16, 18, 19, and 21). As with the examples from Tarsus and the Levant, these bowls may have the exterior and/or the rim red-slipped and burnished.

This motif appears near the end of the Early Bronze Age in central Anatolia, on both two-handled cups and bowls.[14] All of the Anatolian examples appear, when stratigraphically datable, as indicators of the end of EB III and the transition to the Middle Bronze Age, thus providing a clear trail across Anatolia linking Cilicia with the northwest at Troy. The motif appears on Cyprus but in local Cypriote wares and in later contexts—either at the end of the Middle Cypriote period or later (Gjerstad *et al.* 1934: pl. CVIII:6-8, in White

Painted IV Ware and pl. CX:8, Red-on-Red Ware).

The red-cross bowls are used to correlate the stratigraphic sequences of Troy and Tarsus with each other as well as with the sequence of central Anatolia. Thus it seems necessary to allow for some overlap of the Tarsus EB IIIb period with the Troy V settlement,[15] although Troy V is still primarily equivalent to the beginning of the Cilician Middle Bronze Age.

The fact that this motif was not popular in the Levant until the middle of the MB I period has several implications. First, this type continued through the Middle Bronze Age in Cilicia; conversely, the fact that the motif appears in the Levant on the open rounded bowl, rather than the bowl with tripodal, curled feet which was popular at Tarsus in EB III, may show that the motif was common to these regions during the Middle Bronze Age. Second, the early phase of MB I might be considered a relatively short phase so as to allow less of a gap between the occurrences of the motif.[16] Third, this motif reached the Levant at a different time than did the store jar, although they both may have been introduced from the Cilician region.[17] This time-differential could perhaps be explained by the difference between diffusion of a vessel type where the vessel itself may have travelled (that is, the store jar) in contrast to the diffusion of a decorative motif which would depend on the spread of styles and the travel of individuals who brought the style. This is therefore another argument for equating Levantine MB I with the beginning of the Middle Bronze Age in Cilicia and thus also for dating the former relatively early in the 2nd millennium B.C.

The questions of the dating and particularly of the origin of this Syro-Cilician painted style are complex. That the immediate center of distribution in the Levant in the Middle Bronze Age was northern Syria and especially Cilicia seems clear on the basis of the large quantity of vessels and variation of motifs and vessel shapes which were found at such sites as Tarsus, Mersin, and Alalakh, and on mounds surveyed in the Cilician plain. On the basis of her survey, Seton Williams wrote: "In the plain itself the ware was distributed among the mounds marking the trade routes. These sites are situated on roads leading to the Cilician gates on one side and the Bahçe on the other" (Seton Williams 1953: 59). The distribution of this ware therefore points to the routes to central Anatolia, and particularly to the *kārum* Kaniš, and, at the same time, southwards towards the ᶜAmuq plain via an overland route.

Seton Williams also suggested a relationship between the Syro-Cilician painted ware and the central Anatolian Cappadocian Ware which dates from the beginning of the *kārum* Kaniš. Such a relationship, however, should not be considered as more than generic and only shows that there is a fairly long and continuous painted pottery tradition in central Anatolia from at least the late 3rd millennium B.C. through the Middle Bronze Age. There are, however, three major differences between the two painted styles. The Cappadocian style tends to be bichrome or even polychrome, while the Syro-Cilician is monochrome, with the only variation in color on a single vessel probably the result of firing (that is, a paint color may range from red to brown). Second, while both styles consist primarily of geometric motifs, the Syro-Cilician is limited to certain parts of the vessel and does not attempt to fill all the available space, whereas the arrangement of the Cappadocian style motifs seems to show a *horror vacui*. Finally, the Cappadocian ware tends to have an apricot-to-reddish surface which increases the colorfulness of the style, while the Syro-Cilician tends to have a light, cream or buff background. It would also seem difficult to argue for a direct relationship between the two styles when their respective geographical ranges do not overlap except in terms of imports. Whether there is an ultimate common source of inspiration for both painted styles in northwestern Iran, as both Mallowan and Seton Williams argued, is beyond the scope of this study, unless one also sought a separate source from northwestern Iran for the "Ḫabur" ware which occurs in the Ḫabur region. The relative synchronic occurrence of this Syro-Cilician style, its homogeneity and its concentration in an area which has a tradition of painted pottery would seem to make this search for external sources unnecessary.

The appearance of the Syro-Cilician painted style and its associated forms seems synonymous with the introduction of the Middle Bronze Age throughout the Levant and in southern Anatolia. Because of a lack of sufficiently detailed stratification at the sites in the center of the style's distribution, it is impossible to determine whether all the aspects of this style appeared at the same time or whether there was a sequence of development. The red-cross bowls, however, seem to take precedence since they appear first in the EB IIIb period at Tarsus.

The different manifestations of this style did, however, spread through the southern Levant in different "waves": first, the store jars which are probably to be associated with trade, particularly that of liquids, such as wine, olive oil, and honey; then the different types of juglets followed in mid-to-late MB I and continued into MB II, thereby perhaps reflecting some differences in the mechanisms by which this style was spread. The appearances of this distinctive style should also provide an approximately contemporary ceramic horizon, the only exception perhaps being an allowance for cultural lag in the southern Levant. Finally, the distribution of this style and its different associated forms demonstrates a remarkably widespread homogeneity which, however, varies in conforming to the local traditions of the different areas in which this style appears. This variation emphasizes the regional diversity of the southern Levant and northern Mesopotamia.

IV.3. The Cypriote Pottery

The number of Cypriote vessels and sherds appearing in MB I in the Levant is relatively small. Those examples which can be phased within MB I either on the basis of stratigraphy or by typological comparison can all be assigned to the latest phase of MB I and may therefore help to define the end of this period. Two major criteria may be used for determining whether a vessel is a Cypriote product or a local imitation. First is the method of manufacture, since all Cypriote pottery of the early 2nd millennium B.C. (as far as we know, *infra,* n. 19) was handmade, while mainland products tend to be wheelmade. A related feature is that on Cypriote juglets the handle at the lower attachment is thrust through the vessel wall. The second criterion is the usually distinctive type of decoration, which is generally more useful since many publications do not indicate the method of manufacture. This sometimes fails, however, when dealing with sherd material. The following list presents the vessels and sherds attributed to a Cypriote origin, their context and their type, according to Åström's classification system (Åström 1957: 27-30, 64-65, 108).

White Painted III-IV, Pendent Line Style (here fig. 25:1-10):

Megiddo: Juglet Type IA1a (probable, rim not preserved), Locus 5048, Phase 4 (Loud 1948: pl. 26:16); Juglet Type IA1a, T. 3128, Phase 4 (Loud 1948: pl. 26: 13).

Lachish: Juglet, Type IA1a, Tomb 129 (Tufnell 1958: pl. 79:813).

Dhahrat el-Humraiya: Juglet, similar to Type IA1, but wider neck and pinched rim (local imitation?), Grave 2/3 (Ory 1948: fig. 4); Juglet, similar to Type IA1, but wider neck and pinched rim (local imitation?), Grave 2/3 (Ory 1948: fig. 5); Juglet, Type IA1a, Grave 12 (Ory 1948: fig. 13); Juglet, Type IA2a, Grave 18 (Ory 1948: fig. 15); Juglet, Type IA3c (?—handle and rim partially preserved), Grave 34 (Ory 1948: pl. XXXII:24); Juglet, Type IA1a, Graves 37 and 55 (Ory 1948: pl. XXXII:6); Juglet, Type IA1a, Grave 38 (Ory 1948: pl. XXXII:8).

Ginosar: Juglet, Type IA1a, Tomb 4 (Epstein 1974: fig. 15:9), may be a late example because of the broad wavy line (Åström 1957: 30).

Beth-shemesh: Juglet sherd, Stratum VI (Grant and Wright 1938: pl. XXIV:8); Juglet, Type IA3a, Tomb 3 (Amiran 1969: pl. 37:10).

Gezer: Juglet sherd (Macalister 1912b: pl. CXL: 18).

Qraye: Juglet, Type IA1a (Guigues 1939: p. XIIb).

Majdalouna: Juglet, Type IA2a (Chehab 1940: fig. 3e).

Ugarit: Juglet, Type IA2b, "Ugarit moyen" 2 (Schaeffer 1949: fig. 131:3); Juglet, Type IA2a, U.M. 2/beginning U.M. 3, Tomb LXXXV (Schaeffer 1949: fig. 131:6); Juglet, Type IA2a, U.M. 2/beginning U.M. 3, Tomb LXXXV (Schaeffer 1949: fig. 131:8); Juglet, Type IA2a, U.M. 2 (Schaeffer 1949: fig. 131:9).

Gaziantep Region: Two juglets (Gaziantep Museum), Pendent Line Style or closely related (decoration conforms to that described by Åström 1957: 29-30, but lacks the vertical wavy line).

White Painted IV-VI, Cross Line Style (here fig. 25: 11-18):

Lachish: Juglet sherd from fill of MB II glacis (Tufnell 1958: 55, fig. 3:174) attribution uncertain.

Tell Beit Mirsim: Juglet sherd, Strata G-F (Albright 1933: 74, n. 11, pl. 22:7) early, according to Åström (1957: 218).

Dhahrat el-Humraiya: Juglet, Type IA3c, Grave 13 (Ory 1948: 81, fig. 14).

Gezer: Juglet, Type IA1b, Tomb 1 (Macalister 1912b: pl. LXII:51), of early style, according to Åström (1957: 218).

Ugarit: Mug, U.M. 2 (Schaeffer 1949: fig. 131: 2); Juglet, Type IA4b, U.M. 2 (Schaeffer 1949: fig. 131:4), early type; Juglet, Type IA4a, U.M. 2 (Schaeffer 1949: fig. 131:7 = fig. 100:27); Juglet, Type IA1a, U.M. 2/beginning U.M. 3 (Schaeffer 1949: fig. 131:12); Juglet, Type IA2a, U.M. 2 (Schaeffer 1949: fig. 131:5), an early version (Åström 1957: 218); Zoomorphic Vase, U.M. 2 (Schaeffer 1949: fig. 106:10); Juglet, Type IA3d, Cave LV (Schaeffer 1938: fig. 26Y); Juglet, Type IA3a, Cave LV (Schaeffer 1938: fig. 26:Za).

Red-on-Black Ware:

Megiddo: Juglet, Type VIE1b, T. 5134, Phase 4 (Loud 1948: pl. 26:14); for shape, compare with Åström 1957: pl. XXXIV:8; according to the style of decoration, this juglet should be placed relatively early in the series (Åström 1957: 117, 227).

Of Uncertain Style:

Ugarit: Sherds, U.M. 2 (Schaeffer 1949: fig. 102: 15-16), incised knob-lug bowls, Class XIIIF3-3a.

Tell Sukas: Juglet sherd (Ehrich 1939: pl. XXIII: 1.P7.1), possible local imitation.

Gezer: Sherd (Macalister 1912b: pl. CXL:9) neck fragment with horizontal painted bands.

Kafer Djarra: Two juglet sherds, Tomb 57 (Guigues 1938: fig. 48), possible local imitations.

Fragments of juglets of White Painted III-IV Pendent Line and Cross Line Styles, of Framed Caduceus style, and probably the composite ware from Akko (Dothan 1976a: 12; 1976b: 9, figs. 8-12).

As would be expected, the distribution of these Cypriote vessels tends to be concentrated in the coastal areas as well as at those sites with direct access to the coast, such as Megiddo and Dhahrat el-Humraiya. The exceptions to this are Tell Beit Mirsim, Ginosar, and Lachish, but the number of vessels at these sites is small. This distribution among coastal sites seems to be fairly even, especially since some of the large number of vessels from Ugarit may belong in the MB II period, when the amount of imported Cypriote pottery increases.[18] The furthest eastern influence of the Cypriote styles may be seen in the two juglets from the Gaziantep region.

Åström had divided Cyprus into stylistic areas for the production of Middle Cypriote pottery, with the eastern area, centering around Kalopsidha, identified as having "a general linear tradition of decoration, exemplified by the cross line style" (Frankel 1974: 27) and its antecedent, the Pendent Line Style. Early examples of the Red-on-Black Style are also supposed to have had their place of origin in eastern Cyprus (Åström 1957: 276). The neutron activation analysis of Cypriote vessels from Akko, which shows that their composition is very similar to that of White Painted and Red Slip vessels excavated at Kalopsidha (Perlman 1976: 15; Dothan 1976b: 9), gives a neat confirmation of this site as the probable point of origin for much of the imported Cypriote pottery. The location of Kalopsidha near the east coast of Cyprus also makes it the logical source of exports to the Levant.

Almost all of the vessels are juglets and belong either to the White Painted III-IV Pendent Line Style or to the White Painted IV-VI Cross Line Style, with one juglet of Red-on-Black ware from Megiddo. The Pendent Line Style begins in the Middle Cypriote II period; the Cross Line Style belongs primarily to the Middle Cypriote III period, although it may also begin in late MC II (Åström 1957: 197-99), while the Red-on-Black Style begins in MC I-II and reaches its apogee in MC III. All of the examples of the Cross Line Style from the mainland occur in what may be mixed MB I and MB II contexts; therefore, while its earliest occurrence in Cyprus is uncertain, so too is its earliest appearance on the mainland.

Åström, by using the low Mesopotamian chronology, the confused stratigraphies of Ugarit and Megiddo, and the low dating for the Middle Minoan I and II on Crete, arrives at correspondingly low dates for the Middle Cypriote period: MC I = 1800-1750 B.C.; MC II = 1750-1700 B.C.; MC III = 1700-1600 B.C. Using such a chronological scheme, it would be impossible to end the MB I period in the Levant before ca. 1700 B.C. in order to allow for the contemporaneity of the MC II White Painted III-IV Pendent Line Style with the last phase of MB I.

More recent studies, however, have pointed out the need to raise the dating of the Middle Cypriote period. Frankel, on the basis of the trend to raise the dates for Middle Minoan I and II and the need to lengthen the MC III period, suggested that MC I should begin at about 1900 B.C. This, presumably, would also raise the beginning of MC II by about a century, that is to 1850 B.C. (Frankel 1974: 24-25). While Merrillees does not go along with such a high dating, he still proposes that the beginning of MC I should fall at about 1850 B.C. (Merrillees 1974: 59). These revisions, therefore, make it possible to place the end of MB I in the Levant in the first half of the 18th century B.C., while still overlapping with the MC II period. While juglets of both the Cross Line and the Pendent Line Styles have been found in Egypt, their contexts do not help to achieve an absolute date for the appearance of these styles (Merrillees 1968: 145-46).

There is some indication that local imitations of the Cypriote White Painted juglets were produced on the mainland, if one can judge by the criterion of wheelmade production.[19] Such examples occur primarily in the Cross Line Style and in MB II contexts, such as at Megiddo (Loud 1948: pl. 26:15, from T. 3086, T. 3111, and T. 5068; the first two examples are wheelmade and the third is handmade; at least the first two tombs belong to MB II). Cross Line Style juglets also show Syrian influence in the presence of pinched rims on examples found both on the mainland and Cyprus.[20] This tendency to imitate Syrian juglets is even more obvious in the White Painted V Ware juglets (and some of White Painted IV Ware) which often have both a pinched rim and a painted "eye" below the rim on either side of the mouth (Åström 1957: 77, fig. XVI:15). These juglets have also been excavated at Ugarit, primarily in U.M. 2 and/or beginning of U.M. 3 contexts and should be assigned to the MB II period (Schaeffer 1949: fig. 130:18-21; 1938: fig. 6E; here fig. 25:19). Several of these juglets, as well as examples from Cyprus, even have the "eye" moved to the shoulder of the vessel (Åström 1957: fig. XVI:14).

In addition to the problems of their dating and source, these vessels raise the question of purpose—Why were they exported to the mainland? They were presumably part of some exchange system and are usually assumed to have been part of the trade in copper (Dothan 1976a: 12), although the existence of such trade during the Middle Cypriote period has recently been questioned (Merrillees 1974: 51, 63-64). Even if one accepts the existence of this trade during the Middle Bronze Age, these juglets could not have been used as receptacles for transporting copper. The juglets were therefore either exported for their own intrinsic value or as containers for some suitable liquid (such as perfume) or unguent, although the fact that Cyprus was a source of such commodities is not at all clear. The reason for the export of these juglets will therefore have to remain a mystery.

NOTES

[1]Tarsus: Goldman 1956: 176-77, No. 879, figs. 298 and 373; No. 887, fig. 374 and No. 888, fig. 374. Mersin: Garstang 1953: 224:No. 5, fig. 145. Cilicia: Seton Williams 1954: 131-33. Konya Plain: Mellaart 1958: 324, pl. V:62 and 63. An example of the "late Ḫabur" ware, of which examples are also known from Chagar Bazar (Mallowan 1937a: pl. XIX:1-3), was found at the *kārum* Kaniš, Level Ib (T. Özgüç 1951: 547). Considering the absence of this type of "late Ḫabur" ware in Cilicia, it is likely that this vessel was imported directly from Mesopotamia. This pottery, however, should not be confused with that being discussed here, since it differs both in painted decoration and in form—the latter resembling the goblets with pointed base which may have developed into the still later "Nuzi" ware shape.

[2]Chagar Bazar: Mallowan 1936: fig. 14 (note No. 13 which resembles the goblet shape); figs. 16 and 17:11; Mallowan 1937a: figs. 21-23. Tell Brak: Mallowan 1947: 78, pl. LXIV.

[3]This fact is also shown in the section drawing (Mallowan 1936: fig. 2). Dever (1976: 36, n. 109) had already questioned whether these tombs were dug from the Level I floors.

[4]Gaps in occupation from approximately 2000 B.C. to 1800 B.C., or even later, are implied at Tell Jidle (Mallowan 1946: 119, 133-35); possibly Tell Chuera, where finds of the EB IV period equivalent to Hama J (Moortgat 1965: 49, fig. 35) and of the Nuzi ware period, Levels IV/V (Moortgat 1962: 17-22) were found, but there is nothing so far in the publication which can be placed in between; Harran, where only an erosion level, Phase 5, represents the entire span of the late 3rd millennium B.C.

to the Islamic period, in contradiction to the textual evidence (Prag 1970: 72-73); and possibly Tepe Gawra (Speiser 1935: 182). Although some early 2nd-millennium B.C. pottery was identified at the site of Tell Hadidi, the occurrence of painted pottery was reported as "extremely rare" (Dornemann 1979: 132, 139).

[5]While levels of absolute depth cannot be accepted as a stratigraphic indicator, this is our only clue as to a subdivision of the Middle Bronze Age at Tarsus, which is otherwise undifferentiated.

[6]Other writers have also implied for various reasons that the "Ḫabur" ware found in the Levant might predate the examples from Chagar Bazar (see Dever 1976: 36, n. 106). Kramer arrived at a date of ca. 1850/1800-1750 B.C., corresponding to the reigns of Šamši-Adad and Zimrilim (Hamlin 1971: 253).

[7]Mellaart (1971b: 692), however, sees the painted pottery styles of the early Middle Bronze Age as intrusive and attributes their introduction to the arrival of a new ethnic element.

[8]Goldman 1956: 148, 151, fig. 272:Nos. 560, 562, 565, 592; fig. 273:Nos. 445 and 448; fig. 275:No. 596.

[9]Note also such painted juglets with pinched rims as those from ᶜAmuq phase I (Braidwood and Braidwood 1960: 415, figs. 317:5 and 318:4). If its stratigraphic placement is correct, the juglet fragment of fig. 317:5 may be considered an early forerunner of the painted "eye" juglet of the Syro-Cilician painted style (*infra*).

[10]Qatna: Schaeffer 1948: fig. 102; Osmaniye: du Mesnil du Buisson 1930: pl. XXXIII:10; Tell ᶜAs: Schaeffer 1948: figs. 104:12 (Tomb II) and 105:10; Selimiye: du Mesnil du Buisson 1930: pl. XXXI; Dnebi: du Mesnil du Buisson 1930: pl. XXXII:28, 36; pl. XXXIII:10, 12, 27; Tell Ahmar: Thureau-Dangin and Dunand 1936: figs. 29, 31, and 32, the EB IV character of which has been previously recognized, Dever 1976: 32, n. 92; Hamman graves (near Carchemish): Woolley 1914: 89-90, pl. XXII:1 and 2.

[11]Compare Mallowan 1937a: figs. 16:8, 22:2, 23:1, and especially Speiser 1933: pl. LVIII:1, 3, and 5 and pl. LIX:2 to Alalakh Type 23, Woolley 1955: pl. CX.

[12]T. Özgüç 1950: 198-99, pl. LX:327, restored as a jug of this type, pl. LXXIX:617 and a neck fragment with the painted eye, pl. LX:341a.

[13]The motif apparently continues into MB II or perhaps even later, as shown by examples at Megiddo (Guy 1938: pl. 25:13, Tomb 233) and Barqai (Gophna and Sussman 1969: fig. 6:10, third burial phase). It also occurs on bowls of EB III-IV date (Dever 1975b:27, n. 37, fig. 5:27), although the shape of the bowl is quite different.

[14]Two-handled cups: Alişar Ib (von der Osten 1937a: 158, fig. 164:1-2). Bowls: Polatli, Phase II, Level 11 (Lloyd and Gökçe 1951: 46, 52, 57, fig. 13:12); Bitik and Karaoğlan (unpublished); in western Anatolia at Kusura (Lamb 1938: 237, fig. 14:13, Level B) and Beycesultan VII and VI (Lloyd and Mellaart 1962: 236, fig. P.64:23 and 26; 238, fig. P.65:2-3, all Level VIA; see map X, 257, for distribution of red-cross bowls throughout Anatolia); in the Konya Plain (Mellaart 1958: 322) at Seyeti Han Hüyük and Zincirli Hüyük (fig. 2), in the Calycadnus Valley (at Maltepe, fig. 3) and west of the Konya Plain (at Ortakaraviran, fig. 1, Kizilviran and Hüyüklü), near Akşehir and at other sites.

[15]Mellaart, while acknowledging the correlation, does not allow any overlap (Mellaart 1957: 71). For summaries of different positions on the synchronisms of the Trojan and Cilician sequences, see Mellaart 1971a: 395-99, 403-5; 1971b: 690-703; Mellink 1965: 115-17; Easton 1976: 158-65; Yakar 1979: 51-67. It is not really possible to enter here into this controversy which is primarily a problem of Anatolian EB II/III archaeology and so is peripheral to our consideration of the Levantine Middle Bronze Age.

[16]It is also possible to argue that, since there are so few examples of this type in the Levant, one cannot be rigid about defining its phasing. Nonetheless, such examples as those from Tel Poleg and Aphek could belong to the early phase of MB I. The appearance of this motif in EB III-IV contexts in the southern Levant (Dever 1975b: 27, n. 37; also, for example, on an unpublished sherd of a platter-bowl found in EB III context in the 1979 excavation at Tell el-Hesi) might indicate a priority for the motif in the Levant, especially if intermediary appearances of later EB IV and early MB I date were to be found. Such continuity might then indicate (1) that the motif was introduced into Cilicia from the Levant, and (2) that there is an element of continuity from EB IV to MB I within the Levant. However, several problems remain before such conclusions can be accepted, primarily involving the correlation of the Levantine and Cilician stratigraphic sequences and the significance of the appearance of such a simple motif as that being considered here.

[17]The place of origin of the motif has also been a subject of discussion. Mellaart (1957: 65) suggested that it was introduced into Troy from the east, but this question of where the motif occurred first, at Troy or at Tarsus, depends largely on the question of Early Bronze II and III synchronisms. It is possible that the motif arrived in central Anatolia from Tarsus since one of its earliest appearances there, at Alişar, is on a two-handled cup which relates to Tarsus EB III types. In arguing for a Cilician origin for the motif, one could again point to the greater abundance and variety of painted ornament in this region. Its restriction, however, to only the site of Tarsus during EB III also seems to create an anomaly. Lastly, one could again suggest that the motif may have an even longer history in the Levant than in Cilicia (*supra*, n. 16).

[18]For example, all the Cypriote vessels from the recent excavations at Tel Mevorach were from the MB II strata (Stern and Saltz 1978: 139).

[19]Such a criterion has, however, been brought into doubt by the realization that the Late Bronze Age Bichrome ware, which is wheelmade, was probably produced on Cyprus (Perlman, Asaro, and Artzy 1973: 446-61), thus demonstrating the introduction of the potter's wheel to Cyprus at an earlier date than had previously been suggested.

[20]Mainland: at Tell Sukas, Ehrich 1939: pl. XXIII:1.P7.1, and at Kafer Djarra, Tomb 57, Guigues 1938: fig. 48 (the place of manufacture of which is uncertain). Examples from Ugarit of uncertain classification include: Schaeffer 1949: figs. 107:28, 105:37, and 104:27. Cyprus: Åström 1957: 64-65, Types IA2a and b; IA5 and IB1a, fig. IX:13.

Chapter V
The Monochrome Pottery

This chapter will consider the technique of manufacture and forms of certain ceramic types from the Levant, Mesopotamia and Anatolia in order to demonstrate that certain elements in the ceramic assemblage of these regions, and not just the better known painted wares, were interrelated. That such connections were to be sought has previously been recognized, but the first exclusive treatment of this subject was an article by Amiran in which she presented a brief analysis of the correlations between the ceramics of the Levantine MB I and those of the Anatolian Assyrian Colony period (Amiran 1968: 59-62). In regarding both these groups as signifying breaks with the preceding ceramic traditions of their respective regions, Amiran pointed out similarities in technique (primarily the use of the fast wheel and the highly burnished slip finishes) as well as in specific forms. She also sought a common source of origin or at least inspiration in Mesopotamia, using the pottery of Mari and the Baghouz cemetery to exemplify the Mesopotamian repertoire. She wrote (1968:61):

> These two ceramic cultures, the Karum-Kanish IV-I and the MB IIA-B, have to have a common origin, which would count [*sic*] for all these phenomena. Such an origin has logically to be sought in the area of Upper Mesopotamia, which, as we know, produced the human element for the trading-centers in Anatolia. It so happens that the same area seems to have produced the ethnic element (incursions or invasions?) which brought about the transformation of Canaan during the same period, the 20th-19th centuries, B.C.

The link which Amiran implies between an ethnic group and a specific cultural or ceramic assemblage may be questioned (see Chapter IX). With this in mind, a comparison of the ceramics of these regions which had extensive interconnections will be presented in this chapter.

This subject was further considered by Kaplan (1969b: 8-13), who presented a comparison of those pottery types which he classified as MB IIA from the Nahariya temple precinct and from his own excavations at Jaffa with forms from Mesopotamia, specifically from the excavations of sites in the Diyala region. This study was perhaps somewhat superficial in its limitation to only these sites and in the simplicity of certain forms used as examples. It nonetheless presented a comparison of specific pottery types to substantiate a hypothesis of a relationship between Mesopotamian and Levantine ceramics, although it ignored the Anatolian material. Dever also emphasized the need to place the Levantine ceramic repertoire (and, indeed, its entire cultural assemblage) within the larger contexts of Mesopotamia and Anatolia (Dever 1976: 33-34, nn. 97-99),[1] but he offered little additional substantiation.

This discussion will examine several pottery types which appear in the Levant, Mesopotamia, and/or Anatolia at the time corresponding to the MB I period.[2] As already shown in Chapter II, this time period includes the Assyrian Colony period in Anatolia, the Old Assyrian period in northern Mesopotamia, and the Isin-Larsa and beginning of the Old Babylonian periods in southern Mesopotamia. The comparisons which will be discussed here, at the risk of creating a circular argument, should further substantiate the relationship between these regions. Specific forms which demonstrate these interrelationships will be discussed, but, again, no claim of total inclusiveness is made, since the available material is too diverse, and the limitations of the primary data are too great. Yet even from the limited examples presented, it is possible to show an overlap or even, to some extent, sharing of the ceramic characteristics of these regions.

V.1. Ceramic Forms

Specific examples of ceramic types which are known from the Levantine ceramic repertoire as presented in Chapter III and which also appear in either Mesopotamia or Anatolia will be discussed individually. Certain technical aspects as well as general conclusions concerning localized production, chronology, and interconnections will be considered later.

A. THE "GRAIN MEASURE" CUP OR GOBLET

This vessel type was first recognized by Mallowan (1946: 148-50) as distinctive of the early 2nd millennium B.C. at the sites which he investigated in the Ḫabur drainage area, including Chagar Bazar, Tell Brak, and Tell Jidle. He suggested that, on the basis of the convenience and similarity of the cylindrical shape to vessels used in contemporary western Asia and northern Africa, this form was used as a grain measure and possibly also as a liquid measure. He noted that the vessels tended to occur in approximately two sizes—one about 10 cm. in height and the larger about 20 cm. Based even on the examples known to Mallowan and confirmed by subsequent finds, there is a considerable amount of variation in types of decoration used, the specific shape of the vessel, the presence or absence of a handle, the size, and the fabrics. It is still valid, however, to consider all of these variants as representatives of a single type and perhaps to see in their distribution from Iran to the Levant and Anatolia during the first half of the 2nd millennium B.C. some unifying concept in the function of this form—whether as a standard measure or not. If Mallowan's interpretation of the function of this vessel is correct, it would be possible to suggest that this widespread distribution reflects some need for a standardization in measures which may correlate with a trade system which dealt in honey, oil, wine, and perhaps grains and sesame and which would therefore have required some unification of systems of weights and measures.[3]

The appearance of this vessel type in the Levant has already been discussed in Chapter III where it was noted that this vessel (sometimes referred to as a "Ḫabur" ware goblet because of the implied Mesopotamian connections) first occurs in the southern Levant in the middle phase of MB I, as exemplified by its introduction in Phase 3 of the Megiddo MB I sequence. It appears in Phase 3, both in the handleless goblet form and in the closely related mug form with a single handle. These types are also represented at Megiddo in Phase 4. Examples of this vessel type from the Levant include the following (here fig. 26:1-13):

Megiddo: Locus 5054, Loud 1948: pl. 18:6; T. 5275, Loud 1948: pl. 11:6 and 8 (both with red-slipped and burnished finish; mug form with single handle); Locus 5034, Loud 1948: pl. 17:11—Phase 3; Locus 5043, Loud 1948: pl. 26:18; T. 5104, Loud 1948: pl. 17:10 (with red and black painted horizontal bands)—Phase 4.

Aphek: Ory 1937: 108:No. 5, and 119:No. 101 (with red slip and vertical burnish); Iliffe 1936: 125:No. 76.

Gezer: Tomb No. 1, Macalister 1912b: pl. LXI: No. 34.

Tell el-ᶜAjjul: Petrie 1932: pl. XXIX:31V7 (0C990) and 31V8 (0C1000).

Byblos: Royal Tombs, Tufnell 1969: 14, fig. 4: No. 46 (Tomb II) and No. 47 (Tomb III), with thick red slip and burnish.
Offering Deposits: Dunand 1958: 803, fig. 919, and 1950: pl. XCII: No. 15836, with horizontal, straight and zigzag, red painted bands; Dunand 1958: 809, and 1950: pl. CXXVIII:No. 15889, used as the container for a deposit; Dunand 1937: pl. CLXIII:No. 3581.

Kafer Djarra: Tomb 8, Guigues 1937: fig. 23d.

Hama: Fugmann 1958: fig. 109:3B988, and fig. 110:3A797.

Qatna: Tomb I, du Mesnil du Buisson 1927: figs. 53 and 54.

Alalakh: Woolley 1955: 327, pl. CXVII, Type 94a and b, Levels VII-II.[4]

Several examples of this goblet type are known from Anatolia. One such vessel of bronze and with a handle was a tomb gift of the *kārum* Kaniš Ib period (T. Özgüç 1959: 55, 109, fig. 60; here fig. 26:14). Although Özgüç implies that examples in clay were found in the houses, he does not illustrate any.[5] Two fragmentary vessels from the 10T level at Alişar (von der Osten 1937b: pl. IV: c186 and c2478; here fig. 30:15), and a goblet from Tarsus (Goldman 1956: 172, fig. 294, No. 832) belong to this general type. Another example was found at Alaca Hüyük, Level III (the Old Hittite period, Koşay and Akok 1966: pl. 102:M57), thus showing the continuity of this form into later periods, as is also evident from the Mesopotamian material.

The examples of this vessel known from Mesopotamian sites are numerous and may be listed as follows (here fig. 27):

Chagar Bazar: Level I, Mallowan 1936: fig. 14: 13; 1937a: fig. 19:3.

Tell Brak: Mallowan 1947: pl. 73:5 (found with post-Ur III occupation) and pl. 73:7 (with burnishing and ribbed decoration; found with a group of Sargonic vases and therefore perhaps the earliest known example of this type).

Tell Jidle: Level 3, Mallowan 1946: fig. 10:13 (with incised, horizontal, straight and wavy lines) and fig. 11:11.

Tepe Gawra: Stratum IV, dated to the 19th century B.C. by Kramer (Hamlin 1971: 153), Speiser 1935: pl. LXXIII:Nos. 190 and 194 (No. 194 with painted horizontal bands).

Tell Billa: Stratum 4, Speiser 1933: pl. LVII: No. 2.

Mari: Parrot 1959: fig. 88:889.

Baghouz: du Mesnil du Buisson 1948: pl. LXXVII:Shape K:z137, 257, 102, 126, 251, 261, 161, 132, 178; Shape L1:Z12; all except the last decorated with horizontal ribs at the point of smallest diameter.

Assur: Haller 1954: 104, pl. l:aw, ax, and ay (all from Burial 21)—Old Assyrian period.

Telloh: de Genouillac 1936: pl. 80:1 (left) of metal, probably of Ur III date; pl. 33: No. 996 (of pottery) of either Ur III or Larsa period.

Larsa: Parrot 1968: fig. 15, elongated cylindrical goblets of the Larsa period.

Nuzi: Starr 1937: pls. 62S and T, 63A; Starr 1939:27 (transitional between the Ga.Sur and Nuzi periods).

Kish: de Genouillac 1925: pl. 56:1 (period of the First Babylonian Dynasty; considered here as a drinking vessel); de Genouillac 1924: pls. 50:132; 51:38; 54:123; and 58:122.

Bismya: Banks 1905-6: 141, No. 9.

Diyala Region: Delougaz 1952: pl. 153:B.236. 200a and c; B.237.200, B.246.200a-b, B.236.300 and B.237.100 (of Larsa to Old Babylonian date from Asmar, Ishchali, and Khafajeh).

Nippur: McCown and Haines 1967: pl. 95:5-7, Type 38 (TBII-I; TA XII-X, Isin-Larsa and Old Babylonian periods).

Abu Hatab: Heinrich 1931: fig. 41:F2806 and fig. 62:F2860 and 2859.

Susa: de la Füye 1934: 228, fig. 75:1, 11, and 16.

Provenance unknown: British Museum 134884 (1966-12-10,1) presumably from the area of Susa; Sollberger 1968: 30-33 (dated by inscription to Atta-Hušu, contemporary of Sumu-abum of Babylon, ca. 1894-1881 B.C.).

Dinkha Tepe: Jar Types 12 and 13, Hamlin 1971: 77, pl. 1:12-13.

Godin Tepe: Young 1969: 289, Ill. 8:12 (Stratum III).

Tepe Giyan: Contenau and Ghirshman 1935: pl. 21:3 (Burial 65) Level III; pl. 22 (Burial 69) Level II, and pl. 23:3 (Burial 75) Level II, a painted example with complex design.

The question of origin for this vessel type is difficult to resolve, primarily because many of the above-mentioned examples from Mesopotamia are not well dated, for example, the vessels from Telloh, Larsa, Kish, Bismya, and Abu Hatab. However, the vessel from Tell Brak which may date to the Sargonic period suggests that this shape appears in Mesopotamia by the late 3rd millennium B.C. Additional vessels which may relate to this type are also published. One vessel from Susa (de la Füye 1934: fig. 76:1) is dated to the 23rd century B.C. and, like the Tell Brak example, is distinguished by horizontal ribbing. Examples from the Royal Cemetery at Ur (Woolley 1934: pl. 251:12 and 14a) should also be dated to the Sargonic period. Alternatively, this vessel type may be derived from the "Syrian goblet" which occurs throughout most of northern Syria during the EB IV period and which also appears in the southern Levant, Cilicia, and possibly other areas.[6] Whatever the exact origin of this type, its distribution demonstrates that this goblet form had a long history in Syria and Mesopotamia, but only in the beginning of the 2nd millennium B.C. does its distribution area broaden to include the fringes, such as the southern Levant, Iran, and Anatolia. This vessel type also continued in use until approximately the mid 2nd millennium B.C. as shown by several examples from Nuzi (dating to the Nuzi period, Starr 1937: pls. 73H and L, 74A, 75K, 76C, D, J-M), Chagar Bazar (late Level I, Mallowan 1947: pl. 81:6-7), Tell Brak, Levels 1-3 (Mallowan 1947: pl. 67:19 and 21), and Fakhariyah (Kantor 1958: pl. 38:114).

Several examples of this goblet type are dated to the first quarter of the 2nd millennium B.C. One of the most interesting examples is probably the bronze goblet in the British Museum (Sollberger 1968: 30-33) bearing an inscription which explains that the goblet was presented to Atta-Hušu, the ruler of Susa, by a servant (translated as an assistant scribe). Atta-Hušu is dated to the time of Sumu-abum of Babylon, thus providing a firm date in the early 19th century B.C. (according to the middle chronology) for the spread of this type as far as Elam. The word *gunagi*, used to describe the vessel, does not have a clear translation which could help to elucidate the vessel's function. It is interesting, however, that such an object was considered worthy to be a royal gift, while the two other published examples of metal (the goblets from Kültepe and Telloh) were funerary gifts.

B. STORAGE JARS

Several types of storage jars were in use throughout the Levant, Anatolia and Mesopotamia during the first quarter of the 2nd millennium B.C., and it is here that the combination of regionalism in styles and a degree of cosmopolitanism becomes evident. The storage vessel which is most characteristic of the early MB I in the Levant was the handleless jar with flat base, globular body and high neck which was extensively discussed in Chapter IV.1. It needs only to be restated here that this vessel often appears in an undecorated form as well with a distribution covering the Levant and Mesopotamia, but not Anatolia. Some examples known from the Levant were found at the following sites (fig. 28:1-7):

Gibeon: Tomb 58, Pritchard 1963: fig. 64:9 and 10.
Lachish: Tufnell 1958: pl. 78:804, T. 1513.
Tell el-Far^{c}ah (N.): Tomb B, de Vaux and Steve 1948: 571, fig. 11:1.
Gezer: Cave III 30, Macalister 1912a: 298, fig. 158:3.
Beth-shemesh: Tomb 2, Grant 1929: 155, No. 134.
Barqai: Gophna and Sussman 1969: fig. 4: No. 12.
Megiddo: Phase 1/2, Loud 1948: pl. 12:16, T. 3143; pl. 12:17, T. 3138; pl. 13:4, T. 5156 (with ridges).
Yabrud: Assaf 1967: pl. II:1.

This unpainted jar, sometimes decorated only with a ridge at the juncture of neck and body, also occurs at Mesopotamian sites, matching and even exceeding the distribution of the painted version (fig. 28:8-12):

Chagar Bazar: Mallowan 1936: figs. 14:5 and 14:10.
Baghouz: du Mesnil du Buisson 1948: pl. LXVIII: Types A and A1.
Tell Billa: Speiser 1933: pl. LVIII:9 (Stratum 4, Tomb 42).
Tepe Gawra: Speiser 1935: pl. LXIX:135 and 137 (Stratum VI).
Diyala region: Delougaz 1952: pl. 158:B.545.220c and B.545.240c; pl. 187:C.655.240 (of the Early to Late Larsa period from Tell Asmar)—a more flat-based version.
Assur: Haller 1954: pl. 1aa (Old Assyrian period).
Dinkha Tepe: Hamlin 1971: pl. 1:11.

The implication of a dichotomy between the painted and unpainted versions is only incidental since these variants undoubtedly served the same function. The wide distribution of this type further emphasizes the utility of this shape for the storage and perhaps transport of liquids, as was discussed in Chapter IV.1.

The second major type of storage vessel employed in the Levant during MB I became dominant in the middle and late phases of this period and should probably be viewed as the precursor of the later Middle and Late Bronze Age "Canaanite jar" with long body tapering to a point, handles, and short constricted neck. Apparently only one example of this jar has been found outside of the region of the Levant in a context which may be contemporary with the period under consideration. This example was found at Tarsus in the Middle Bronze Age level (Goldman 1956: 176, fig. 298:No. 880), but, because of the lack of subdivision of the Middle Bronze stratum at this site, it is not possible to judge in which part of the Middle Bronze Age the vessel belongs (although both its shape and its association with Cypriote Red-on-Black fragments suggest a later date).[7]

Another type of store jar used in central Anatolia during the Assyrian Colony period is a very elongated, graceful form with two or four usually horizontally-placed handles, sometimes a ridge along the neck, and a small ring base. Several examples of this type were found in both the earlier and later grave groups at Osmankayasi (Fischer 1963: 134, pl. 66:Nos. 607-10), and one was found at Alaca Hüyük, Level IV (Koşay and Akok 1947: 157, fig. 5, Al c367; 1966: pl. 110:e246). This type has several analogues from Mesopotamia where the type never has handles and the ridges around the neck are more emphasized; the body shapes, however, are extremely similar.[8] At least one example of this type was found in the Levant at Jaffa, although apparently in an MB II context (Kaplan 1969b: 10, fig. 9H). Examples of this jar in Mesopotamia therefore range from the late 3rd millennium through the first quarter of the 2nd millennium B.C., while occurring in Anatolia during the Assyrian Colony period and, judging from the single example so far published, slightly later in the Levant.

The similarity and implied relationship between these storage vessels from Anatolia and Mesopotamia (*supra*, n. 7) are not surprising when one considers the extensive trade system between these areas and even the resident Assyrian population in central Anatolia. The links of some of the Anatolian forms to late 3rd millennium Mesopotamia may serve as another indication that trade relations between Mesopotamia and central Anatolia may have originated during the Sargonic period and may confirm indications for such connections in the textual evidence (*supra*, Chapter II.1).

C. BOWLS

Several types of bowls are represented in the ceramic repertoire of the Levant. Primarily the material from Megiddo will be used to illustrate the bowls of the Levant in this section, since it is not necessary to duplicate examples, except where different types are represented at other sites.

(1) Simple carinated bowl (fig. 29:1): The most typical forms of these bowls are well represented by a series from Megiddo (Loud 1948: pl. 14:26-28, 31, 33-35, 37-39), and these continue through the different phases of the MB I. There are few direct parallels for this type outside of the Levant, but a series from Level I of Chagar Bazar (Mallowan 1937a: fig. 16:1-3, here fig. 30:4-6) presents the same forms as seen in the Levant. It is of interest to note the two metal bowls from the "Montet Jar" at Byblos (Tufnell and Ward 1966: fig. 9:207 and 209; here fig. 30:2-3) which also belong in this group.

(2) A variant of the typical MB I carinated bowl (here fig. 29:7-11), which is more open, tends to have a relatively small base and has the carination placed fairly high, is represented at several sites in the Levant (although in smaller quantity): for example, at Megiddo (Loud 1948: pl. 21:9, T. 3109 and T. 3107; pl. 15:9, T. 4110), Alalakh (Woolley 1955: pl. CIX:Types 7a and b, and pl. CX:Type 24), Yabrud (Assaf 1967: pl. II:2-3), and Hama (Fugmann 1958: fig. 110:3K155, 3K156, 3H916). It thus seems to have a distribution which is concentrated in the north. Outside of the Levant, this type is represented in Anatolia and Mesopotamia by the following examples (here fig. 29:12-19):[9]

Tarsus: Goldman 1956: fig. 368:767-69.
Alaca Hüyük: Level IV, Koşay and Akok 1966: pl. 109:e267 and k158.
Alişar: von der Osten 1937b: fig. 168:c1096 and d2829.
Osmankayasi: Younger grave group, Bittel *et al.* 1958: pl. XXIII:3 and fig. 5:17.
Nuzi: Starr 1937: pl. 62R and W (transitional period between Ga.Sur and Nuzi).
Assur: Haller 1954: pl. 2:n-q (Old Assyrian period.
Tell al-Rimah: Oates 1970: pl. IX:3 (with painted rim).
Telloh: de Genouillac 1936: pl. 33:1110.
Chagar Bazar: Level I, Mallowan 1936: fig. 17:14.

(3) The carinated bowl which occurs on a ring base or low pedestal foot was previously discussed in Chapter IV.2 with the Syro-Cilician painted ware with which this form is most often associated. As with so-called "Ḫabur" storage jars, however, the pedestalled bowl also occurs in unpainted examples over a larger distribution area outside of the Levant or Syro-Cilicia. As already mentioned, these bowls appear in painted examples at Mersin, Alalakh, in the ᶜAmuq, at Tarsus, at several surveyed sites in the Cilician plain, and at Qatna (see Chapter IV.2) and in unpainted examples at Ugarit (Schaeffer 1948: fig. 47K-M) and Hama (Fugmann 1958: fig. 109:3C466).

From outside the Levant, painted examples have been cited from Kültepe Level II (T. Özgüç 1950: pl. LX:328, the only central Anatolian example which is considered to have been an import from Cilicia) and from Mesopotamia: the Sakcegözü cave site, Chagar Bazar, Tell Billa, Tepe Gawra, and Nineveh. Additional unpainted examples from the area of Mesopotamia may also be cited, as for example:

Chagar Bazar: Mallowan 1937a: fig. 17:4.
Tell Jidle: Level 3, Mallowan 1946: fig. 11:4.
Baghouz: Type S.1, du Mesnil du Buisson 1948: pl. LXXIX.
Mari: Parrot 1959: 127, fig. 89.
Diyala region: Delougaz 1952: pl. 170:C.142.310 (Tell Asmar, Early Larsa period; here fig. 29:20).

(4) Another group of bowls, often occurring with painted decoration in the Mesopotamian examples, relates to the common late MB I bowl with high rounded carination (here fig. 30:1-13) as best exemplified by vessels from Aphek (Beck 1974: fig. 11:1, 2, 6; fig. 12:1-2). Several unpainted examples, but also one with painted horizontal bands, were found in Tomb 1 at Ginosar (Epstein 1974: fig. 7:4-13), and these may be compared with Mesopotamian examples from Nippur (McCown and Haines 1967: pl. 88:18, 20, 22, 23, Type 24) where the motifs recall those of the Syro-Cilician painted ware including a metopal system with double-axe and cross motifs; Tell Taya (Reade 1968: 264, pl. LXXXVII:26, Level IV); Chagar Bazar, Level I (Mallowan 1936: fig. 17:1-3; here fig. 30:14-15); and, in unpainted forms, at the Baghouz cemetery (du Mesnil du Buisson 1948: pl. LXXIX:Type R).[10]

(5) The last group is characterized by the open bowl with a bar or other projection just below the rim (here fig. 30:16-23). Several examples of this type are known from Megiddo, Aphek, and ᶜAin es-Samiyeh.[11] The bowl with lug or rolled projection seems to occur only at Baghouz in Mesopotamia (du Mesnil du Buisson 1948: pl. LXXX:Type U and pl. LXXIX:z269), but in Anatolia it also occurs at Kültepe (Level II, Emre 1963: fig. 10: Kt n/k3) and Acemhüyük (Emre 1966: fig. 26). The bowl with folded rim forming a bar beneath the rim exterior has several additional parallels at the following Mesopotamian sites:

Assur: Haller 1954: pl. 2f, h, and k (the Old Assyrian period).
Baghouz: du Mesnil du Buisson 1948: pl. LXXX: Type V (especially z108).
Nippur: McCown and Haines 1967: pl. 82:18-19, Types 8A and 8B (Ur III to Isin-Larsa periods).
Diyala region: Delougaz 1952: pl. 150:B.151.210 (Asmar, Larsa period).
Ur: Royal Cemetery, Woolley 1934: pl. 252:Types 26 and 27 (Sargonic).
Abu Hatab: Heinrich 1931: fig. 64:F2867.
Susa: de Morgan 1900: 115, figs. 192, 194.

While some of the comparisons utilized in this discussion of bowls may vary in exactness and several of the types delineated may merge into each other or overlap, it does seem clear that there is a basic similarity in both the individual elements used and in the overall forms produced.

D. JUGS/PITCHERS

This vessel type, conspicuous for its absence at Mesopotamian sites, is characteristic of MB I in both Anatolia and the Levant. Three variants will be discussed here which differ primarily in their rim form, which can be either straight, pinched or foliated, or slanting to form a rising spout.

The juglet with horizontal rim is present in all phases of MB I and is exemplified by several vessels from Megiddo (see figs. 10:4, 11:9-10).[12] There is a tendency for such juglets, especially in the early and middle MB I phases, to be decorated with red slip and burnishing. This type is paralleled in Anatolia at the following sites (also Fischer 1963: fig. 7, 47-50; here fig. 31:1-6):

Alaca Hüyük: Koşay and Akok 1966: pls. 12 and 110:f2 and f37, Level IV; Koşay 1951: pl. XLV: figs. 1 and 3; pl. XLVIII: figs. 2-4; Koşay 1944: pl. XXVII: Al/a154, 151, 156.
Alişar: von der Osten 1937b: pl. V:b1678.
Kültepe: Level II: T. Özgüç 1950: 174-75,pl. XXXVIII:No. 159; Level Ib: T. Özgüç and N. Özgüç 1953: 159, pl. XXV: Nos. 117-20.
Osmankayasi: Bittel *et al.* 158: fig. 4:5, 9, 10 and 12; fig. 5:4; fig. 8:3, 8.
Gordion: Cemetery, Mellink 1956: P. 319, 13e, 27a, and P. 511, pls. 13f, 27b.
Acemhüyük: Emre 1966: 105, figs. 16-17.

The juglet with pinched or foliated rim is even more ubiquitous in both regions. The earlier discovery of this type in great numbers at both Ugarit and Megiddo at first led to the suggestion that the Anatolian examples showed influence from the Levant. The Özgüçs suggested that the frequency of this type at Kültepe in particular was a result of its role as a trading center and its contact with northern Syria (T. Özgüç and N. Özgüç 1953: 158-59). Considering the large numbers of such juglets from both areas, however, it is certain that these were produced locally. The continuity shown in this type from the 3rd to the 2nd millennium B.C. in Anatolia tends to favor the supposition that the form originated in Anatolia. If there was a relationship between the Anatolian and the Levantine juglets, then presumably this form spread from Anatolia to the Levant. This type continues in the Levant into MB II, at which time its association with the Anatolian examples is even clearer (Loud 1948: pl. 25:8, T. 2145; here fig. 31:13).

These pinched-rim juglets may again be typified by examples from Megiddo, but they are also found at other Levantine sites (see figs. 31:7-12; 32:1-9, 18):

Megiddo: Loud 1948: pl. 11:13, T. 5180; pl. 11:21, T. 3150; pl. 7:16, T. 3151; pl. 11:11, T. 5171; pl. 11:12, T. 3157; pl. 25:14, T. 5259; pl. 25:6, T. 5137; pl. 11:10, T. 4110; pl. 20:4, with button at handle and rim attachment, T. 4112.
Barqai: Gophna and Sussman 1969: fig 4:1 and 3.
Gezer: Cave III 30, Macalister 1912a: 298, fig. 158:1, and Tomb No. 1, Macalister 1912b: pl. LXIII:No. 68.
Lachish: Tufnell 1958: pl. 86:995.
Tell el-Far^cah (N.): Tomb 16, de Vaux 1955: fig. 2:4-7.
Byblos: Tufnell 1969: fig. 5:No. 50.

This type is represented in Mesopotamia only at the site of Mari, where Parrot assumed that because of the large numbers of extant examples the type must have been locally produced, despite its unusual form for the Mesopotamian ceramic repertoire (Parrot 1959: 142-43). Jugs with and without handle and with pinched rim are represented in addition to the jug with horizontal rim (Parrot 1959: 114-18, figs. 83 and 84:905; here fig. 32:19). It is of course not surprising that Mari should display such western-oriented elements, considering the evidence for extensive contacts with the west presented by the Mari archives.

The Anatolian examples of this type are also numerous (see Fischer 1963: 46-47, fig. 6:9-14; here fig. 32:10-17, 20):

Tarsus: Goldman 1956: fig. 369:Nos. 848, 849, and 852.
Kültepe: T. Özgüç 1959: pl. XXXVIII:2-3; Emre 1963: fig. 10:Kt e/k74 and Kt m/k69, Level II.
Alişar: von der Osten 1937b: pl. IV:d2660, d2957, and 3154; pl. V:b1426, c 2735, and b1081; also c2738 and e1960 (Ankara Museum).
Alaca Hüyük: Koşay and Akok 1966: pl. 109:k157, Level IV.
Acemhüyük: Emre 1966: 103-5, figs. 14-15.

The third type of jug—that with rising spout—is most popular in Anatolia. Levantine examples are known from Megiddo, primarily from Phases 3 and 4, while fragments from Wadi et-Tin and Aphek and two spouts from Nahariya may also represent this type. Probably related are the "teapots" from Byblos, in both clay and metal, which have separate side-spouts, sometimes attached by a bridge to the rim, and the examples from Tell el-^cAjjul.[13] The type is exemplified in Anatolia at the following sites (here fig. 33:11-13):

Alişar: von der Osten 1937b: pl. V:b1671.
Alaca Hüyük: Koşay and Akok 1966: pls. 20 and 109:e150, Level IV.
Boğazköy: Fischer 1963: 119-20, pl. 22:271, pl. 25:291, 288, and 290, from the Lower City, Level 4; also 117, pl. 21:Nos. 232-35, from M/18, equivalent to Büyükkale Level IVd.
Kültepe: T. Özgüç 1950: pl. XXXVI:149a, 150-52, Level II; 1959: pl. XXXVII:1.
Gordion: Mellink 1956: P.373, pls. 13a, 26e; P.296, pls. 13c, 26d.

The Byblos and Tell el-^cAjjul spouted teapots may also be paralleled by the following Anatolian examples from Alişar (von der Osten 1937b: pl. VI:c1748), Alaca (Koşay and Akok 1966: pls. 12 and 109:k100, Level IV), and Boğazköy (Fischer 1963: 122, pl. 31:341-43).

The similarity of some of these Levantine jugs to the Anatolian examples is so great that Schaeffer had even suggested that examples found at Ugarit (Schaeffer 1948: fig. 52A and B) were actual imports from Anatolia. It is difficult to evaluate this hypothesis on stylistic criteria alone, but neutron activation or other analyses of the clay used might offer interesting results if it were shown that such vessels (in addition to store jars) were transported between these regions.

The similarity of this group of vessels is further emphasized by the use of a red slip with high burnish, giving an appearance which can only be appreciated when the vessel itself is seen. Although the relatively large numbers of vessels presented here seem to preclude the necessity of explaining these similarities through the mechanism of trade, one might still wish to suggest that some of these may have been direct imports, such as possibly the pitchers from Ugarit. Only careful analyses of the clay of these vessels, however, could provide substantiation for such a suggestion. There seems to be a concentration of such vessels in the Levant at the sites of Megiddo and Ugarit, but this may be a consequence of the extensive publication of these large sites or their roles as transit trade centers.

Because of the continuity shown in Anatolia during the 3rd millennium B.C. when such types as the "Schnabelkanne" were also very popular, it seems likely that the concept of these vessels was most at home in Anatolia and that the Levantine examples are the product of the transmittance of this concept from Anatolia to the Levant at the beginning of the Middle Bronze Age. The grace and elegance of these vessels from both Anatolia and the Levant represent a considerable aesthetic achievement. It is this aesthetic and artistic quality, evident both in form and in finish, which is also transmitted and which provides points of similarity in these cultural spheres which transcend simple comparison of specific forms and types.

E. JARS/BOTTLES

This distinctive type of vessel which has not generally been recognized as typical of MB I in the Levant occurs at several sites in MB I contexts (here fig. 34):

Aphek: Iliffe 1936: 125:No. 74, pl. LXVII.
Beth-shemesh: Tomb 2, Grant 1929: 129, 153, No. 239.
Dhahrat el-Humraiya: Ory 1948: 83, fig. 21, Grave 21.
Wadi et-Tin: Vincent 1947: 276, fig. 4:4.
ᶜAin es-Samiyeh: Dever 1975: fig. 3:5.
Byblos: Tufnell 1969: fig. 5:No. 51.
Qatna: "Coupole de Loth," du Mesnil du Buisson 1935a: 67, fig. 16:4.
Alalakh: Woolley 1955: pl. CXXII, Type 137.

As with the pitchers, these bottles have a slipped and highly burnished finish. The squatness of the body varies; some examples have ribbing either around the juncture of neck and body or beneath the rim. Despite these variations, however, these bottles form a distinctive group of MB I pottery.

This type is paralleled by a few examples from Mesopotamia, such as at Baghouz (du Mesnil du Buisson 1948: pl. LXXVII, Type H1:z260), Mari (Parrot 1959: 126, fig. 88:874), and Chagar Bazar (Mallowan 1937a: fig. 15:13, early Level 1, Grave 151).[14] Despite the limited distribution of this specific form, it emphasizes the western orientation of these particular sites, Mari and Baghouz, as already shown above in the discussion of jugs, as well as Chagar Bazar, as implied by the concentration of painted store jars there—which may also correlate with what is known of these sites from the textual evidence.

F. MUGS

Two types of mug shapes will be briefly considered here as demonstrating, in addition to the jugs, a link between the ceramics of Anatolia and the Levant. The first mug type, which is considered to be characteristic of the MB I repertoire (Oren 1971: 118), has a rather limited distribution in the Levant since it occurs at only two sites. This mug has a very simple biconical form, flat base, and loop handle (here fig. 35:1-4) and occurs at Aphek (Grave 4, Ory 1937: 118, No. 88) and at Byblos in the third "tombeau de particulier" (Montet 1929: pl. CXLVI:No. 934) as well as in offering deposits (Dunand 1958: 939, fig. 1054:No. 17692, and 1044, fig. 1153:No. 18926).

It finds almost exact parallels (here fig 35:5-12) in an example from Kültepe, Level II (Emre 1963: fig. 10:Kt h/k129) and another from Alişar (von der Osten 1937b: pl. IV:e26). The frequency of this general type in Anatolia is shown by several examples from Boğazköy dating to the *kārum* Kaniš Ib period (Fischer 1963: 137, pl. 82:Nos. 675, 680, and 681) and additional examples from Kültepe and Alişar (Fischer 1963: 64, fig. 13:Nos. 2-4), from Acemhüyük (Emre 1966: figs. 62-65), and from Tarsus (Goldman 1956: fig. 369:No. 837).

The second type of mug is distinguished by a trefoil or quatrefoil rim (here fig. 35:13-19) which is more characteristic of the *kārum* Kaniš Ib period than the *kārum* Kaniš II period in Anatolia (see Emre 1963: fig. 11 Kt e/k97), where it is typified by examples from Alişar (von der Osten 1937b: pl. IV:b1674), Kültepe (T. Özgüç and N. Özgüç 1953, pl. XXIV:107-16), and Acemhüyük (Emre 1966: figs. 12-13). In the Levant the earliest example comes from T. 3109 at Megiddo, which is placed in Phase 3 (Loud 1948: pl. 20:17, if correctly restored), but is even better represented by a vessel from Jericho which should be placed in MB II (Garstang 1932: pl. 32:8) and by MB II examples from Megiddo (Loud 1948: pl. 25:3, T. 4099; pl. 25:4, T. 3122; and pl. 25:5, T. 4107) and Ginosar, Tomb 4 (Epstein 1974: fig. 15:2). Although this small number of vessels is perhaps meager evidence, the appearance of this type primarily in MB II in the Levant and the *kārum* Ib period in central Anatolia may help to support a correlation of these two periods. Such a correlation may later permit a chronological link between archaeological phases and historical events to be established.[15]

V.2. Technique

Information concerning technical aspects of these ceramic styles is relatively sparse compared to illustrations of this material which permit lengthy comparisons based on form. Three elements in the manufacture of pottery—fabric, the use of the wheel, and types of decoration—will be considered here in as much detail as the published information allows.

The definition of fabrics used in the manufacture of clay vessels is not generally agreed upon by either archaeologists or scientists. The result is that, except for a few studies of quantitative analyses of clay composition, it is virtually impossible to compare fabrics used at different sites or to identify a single fabric as distinctive of a particular style or vessel shape. The only study concerned with this region which has considered the occurrence of a specific pottery style and the use of fabrics is that of C. Kramer (Hamlin 1971) concerning Ḫabur ware. Although she correlates the Ḫabur ware style with a specific fabric at the site of Dinkha Tepe, she acknowledges that this painted style occurs in different fabrics at different sites and, even at Chagar Bazar, it does not seem to be associated with a single fabric. A specific fabric, a gray ware, occurs throughout northern Mesopotamia and northern Syria, but this seems to postdate the period under consideration here. At least as far as Ḫabur ware is concerned, there is apparently no single associated fabric and, therefore, the majority of vessels belonging to this style should be considered as locally produced.

Only in a few cases, where distinctive styles would seem to warrant such an explanation, does the suggestion of exchange of specific vessels seem justified. Such examples may include the Syro-Cilician painted vessels from Kültepe and the red-slipped and burnished beak-spouted pitchers at Ugarit. In the case of the widespread type of the flat-based, handleless store jar, the similarity may also be a result of the movement of the jars when used as containers for traded commodities, a function which is substantiated by the textual evidence which records the shipment of *karpatu*-vessels in fairly large quantitites between cities. However, in the case of other vessel types, for example, jugs (with the probable exception of the imported Cypriote juglets) and bowls, it would seem more advantageous to seek other explanations for such similarities.

The use of the pottery wheel in the manufacture of vessels cannot always be determined with accuracy. However, the presence of wheel marks on the exterior and/or interior surfaces or of other indicators such as a string-cut base generally indicates the use of the wheel during at least some stage of the manufacturing process. In Anatolia, the wheel seems to have been in use during the 3rd millennium B.C., although not all vessels then were necessarily wheelmade. The major innovation at the beginning of the Middle Bronze Age, at least on the basis of the description of pottery from Tarsus, seems to have been the use of the fast wheel. This permitted the manufacture of the small carinated bowls, often with string-cut base, which are so typical of the Middle Bronze Age at Tarsus and elsewhere in Anatolia and the Levant. The thin walls and sharp profiles of these vessels are the result of a facility of use of the fast wheel and give these vessels a metallic appearance.

There is less information available concerning the use of the wheel in Mesopotamia, although it is attested from approximately the second half of the 4th millennium B.C. (Porada 1965: 147, 153). Both wheelmade and handmade vessels continued contemporaneously, presumably even into the 2nd millennium B.C. (Delougaz 1952: 114). A similar refinement of forms, the appearance of the Ḫabur ware style whose vessels are nearly always wheelmade, and the large numbers of other types of wheelmade vessels attest to the extensive use of the wheel in Mesopotamia at this time. The ceramic repertoire of Mesopotamia, however, may be distinguished from those of Anatolia and the Levant in that it displays a considerable degree of uniformity from the late 3rd millennium through the beginning of the 2nd millennium B.C.[16]

In the Levant the potter's wheel had also been in use during the 3rd millennium B.C., but the majority of the pottery of EV IV was either handmade or partially handmade and wheelmade. Only one group of pottery (Amiran's Group C), which is primarily known from Megiddo, includes vessels which were entirely wheelmade and thus provides some continuity of method into MB I (Amiran 1969: 90). However, as both Amiran and Dever have implied,[17] the pottery of the MB I period represents an almost complete break with the pottery of the immediately preceding period, although also presenting certain elements of continuity (perhaps coincidental) in form, technique, and decoration with earlier pottery of the EB II and III periods in the Levant. The appearance of the MB I culture, as seen in its pottery repertoire, represents a dramatic change from what preceded (Amiran 1968: 59; Dever 1976: 5) and an advanced technological and aesthetic standard which culminated quickly within the MB I period and then, in certain respects, soon declined during MB II (Dever 1976: 36, n. 113).

The third element to be considered is that of decoration. The painted styles will not be considered here since they were so extensively treated in the preceding chapter. Two other main types of decoration were used in Levantine pottery. The most distinctive of these was probably the use of a slip, usually some shade of red, to cover the vessel which was then burnished to a high lustrous finish. This treatment was also characteristic of Anatolian pottery of the Assyrian Colony period and had been previously used in both Anatolia and the Levant, particularly during the mid 3rd millennium B.C. It was therefore not a new technique in either region, but its nearly simultaneous reappearance in combination with the forms distinctive of the use of the wheel emphasizes the metallic aspect of these ceramic groups. Slip, which was not necessarily red, and burnishing were also used, although to a more limited extent, in Mesopotamia (McCown and Haines 1967: 78).

The other type of ornament was linear decoration consisting of incisions, ribbing, or grooving. Such lines were often used to emphasize the shoulders, carination, or narrow points of a vessel and was perhaps more popular in Mesopotamia than in either the Levant or Anatolia, as exemplified by the assemblages from Assur and Baghouz. In the Levant, a combed effect, which may have been the wheel marks on the exterior of the vessel, was often used as a type of decoration and is particularly apparent in the publication of the Aphek ceramics (Beck 1975). Whether this is related to the combing which was popular during the EB IV period is unclear. The use of lugs, bosses, and other types of plastic attachments seems to have been primarily restricted to Anatolia where it had also been popular in earlier periods.

In concluding this chapter it is perhaps necessary to recall the differences between the ceramic assemblages of the three areas considered here. First, there are entire groups of vessel types which are distinctive of each region. Levantine examples include the handmade pierced-rim cooking pot, the juglet with candlestick rim and its successor, the juglet with stepped rim. While it is not surprising that cooking pots should be localized types, the regionalism of these particular juglets is more remarkable.

Second, certain pottery elements are also regionalized, such as the use of handles. Handles are ubiquitous in Anatolia, rare in Mesopotamia, but occur on certain forms in the Levant and not on others. This distinction is even clearer when one recalls the similarity of certain shapes which occur in both Anatolia and Mesopotamia, but which consistently differ by region in the presence or absence of handles. It is such factors which argue for local production of the majority of these repertoires, because they show that local traditions modified foreign influence. What meager evidence there is concerning fabrics would support the likelihood of local manufacture, while regional predilections for certain decorative styles are also evident and again reemphasize the localized appearance of these assemblages.

Despite these differences, however, there is still a considerable degree of similarity among these assemblages over relatively large geographical distances. Many forms are shared by two or three of the regions, while the distinctive slip and burnish finish occurs in both Anatolia and the Levant. Only in a few cases has it been possible to attempt to identify a place of origin by finding examples which clearly predate those of other areas. Perhaps the apparent continuity in the Mesopotamian ceramic repertoire would allow this region to take precedence, and the similarity of forms from Anatolia and the Levant should be attributed to a mutual ancestry in Mesopotamian ceramics (as Amiran [1968: 61-62] tentatively suggested). However, the fact that certain features appear only in the Levant and Anatolia would indicate that this is not the entire explanation.

There are several possible ways in which these ceramic similarities may have developed. One is export and import; this has been proposed in regard to the store jars which may have been used as transport containers for the commodities which the texts record as exchanged between specific locations. A second possibility may have been the need for a unified system, perhaps involving measures, and this has been tentatively used to explain the appearance of the goblet or "grain measure" from Iran to Anatolia and the Levant. This function would also have been a by-product of the trade system which would have required that traded commodities be weighed or measured in standard units common to all the regions participating in this trade system.

A third mechanism might be the exchange of the vessels for their own intrinsic value. This could be used to explain similarities in such vessel types as the pitchers or jugs. There is, however, no direct archaeological confirmation of this suggestion based on analyses of the vessels themselves and only indirect confirmation based on the possibility that individuals may have carried pottery with them when they travelled. A fourth mechanism would be the travel of the styles, perhaps helped by the transport of a few examples, through the movements of individuals (traders, diplomats, artisans, all documented in the texts as travelling over great distances and residing in foreign cities for considerable lengths of time). Perhaps the only argument against this is that in the *kārum* at Kültepe where the residential quarter of foreign Assyrian merchants was identified through texts, there seemed to be no distinctions in artifactual evidence from the quarter in which the local Anatolians lived. This fourth mechanism, however, probably did play some role in the spread of ideas and concepts—as well as of specific artifacts—throughout these regions which were obviously in close contact with each other.

The fifth factor involves the concept that reactions to similar stimuli, especially among interrelated cultural spheres, will produce similar results, at least in the artifactual evidence. This notion may best be illustrated by the appearance in both Anatolia and the Levant of a ceramic assemblage which in form and finish seems to reflect the popularity of metallic vessels. This appearance of a metallic-influenced ceramic assemblage in both these regions may parallel technological innovations in both the use of the potter's wheel and in bronze production and metal objects—which is particularly evident in the southern Levant during MB I (as will be seen in the next chapter). This emphasis on the use or simulation of metallic vessels may be a manifestation of the effects of an approximately contemporary cultural or, more specifically, technological change in all these areas. Such a change could have been the result of an opening of communications between these areas and, in effect, the same or similar reaction to the same or similar cultural processes. It is perhaps the similarity of these processes which produced similarities in the material cultures of these regions at about the same time and resulted in similar ideal types or concepts being prevalent throughout these regions, rather than simply the diffusion of specific types or forms occurring as isolated phenomena. This technological change in the Levantine culture of the MB I period is perhaps best documented in the metal artifacts, which form the subject of the next chapter.

NOTES

[1]Dever also pointed out a basic similarity which appears in much of the pottery which will be discussed here. "That there is a connection [between Mesopotamian and Palestinian ceramics] . . . is shown by the fact that *metallic* forms are astonishingly close from Ur all the way around the Fertile Crescent, beginning in Early Dynastic II or III" (Dever 1976: 34, n. 98).

[2]The task of this study is complicated by several aspects of the publications of the relevant material, particularly that of Mesopotamia. First, there are few published syntheses of the ceramics of either Anatolia (although see Fischer 1963) or Mesopotamia during the 2nd millennium B.C. The second difficulty, particularly with the Mesopotamian material, is that many of the excavations were undertaken in the late 19th and early 20th centuries, so that there is a significant lack of stratigraphic excavation, subdivision by levels and historical periods, and correlation with other sites. Furthermore, perhaps because of the wealth of extant textual evidence from Mesopotamia in this period, there seems generally to have been less emphasis on publication of ceramic material and on the use of ceramics as a chronological criterion. The nature of many of the site publications is therefore responsible for some of the generalities which will be evident in the following analysis.

[3]See, for example, Veenhof's discussion (Veenhof 1972: 54-68) based on the textual evidence of the use of standard weights and measures in Assur and Kaniš involving the tin trade and the complications which resulted when the weights in the two cities did not exactly correlate. Kramer considered the two jar types 12 and 13 from Dinkha Tepe to "represent two opposite ends in a functionally graded size range of a single type" (Hamlin 1971: 77), thus further supporting the functional identity of this type, despite some variation in specific form.

[4]Unpublished examples of this vessel are mentioned by Mallowan (1946: 150) as having been found in the ᶜAmuq region. Whether Mallowan was referring to the vessels found at Alalakh is not clear.

[5]Kramer (Hamlin 1971: 188) refers to additional examples from Kültepe but without mentioning specific examples.

[6]Dnebi: Schaeffer 1948: fig. 106:8 and 13, Tomb 1; fig. 106:9,

Tomb III; Tell Masin: du Mesnil du Buisson 1935b: pls. XLIX:3, L:41 and 56; Tarsus: Goldman 1956: 182, fig. 293:947; Ugarit: Schaeffer 1949: fig. 101:35.

[7]From the differing patterns of distribution of these two storage jar types, one might suggest that their different forms were suited to different means of transport. Since travel between Mesopotamia and the Levant, although partially along rivers, would have involved primarily overland transport, one might conclude that the flat-based version was more practical for donkey or cart use, but that the pointed version was more easily stored in a ship. Such a hypothesis, however, would need to be studied in the context of later periods, when the pointed jar was more popular, in order to determine whether the different distribution is a function of time, fashion or utility.

The type of storage jar common in central Anatolia during the Assyrian Colony period differed markedly from the Levantine types. Yet it is possible to suggest that the Anatolian jars share some similarity with their Mesopotamian counterparts—with the major exception that virtually all the Anatolian storage jars have either two or four handles, while no Mesopotamian jar has handles. The more common type of Anatolian storage jar has a rounded, almost pointed base, oval body, constricted neck, and flaring rim. It has either two or four handles, one pair sometimes placed horizontally. Some examples are painted with geometric designs (generally only on the upper portion of the vessel), while others may have incised lines, ridges, or bosses. Sometimes the same shape may have a small ring base instead of the pointed bottom. Some examples of this type are known from:

Alişar Hüyük: von der Osten 1937b: pl. VII:d2309, d2310, c2377, and b2546.
Alaca Hüyük: Koşay and Akok 1966: pls. 18 and 108:j205 and f10; pl. 108:g256, Level IV.
Kültepe: Level II, Emre 1963: fig. 13: Kt j/k27, and T. Özgüç 1950: pl. LXXIV:No. 551.

This vessel type may be compared with several examples from Mesopotamian sites which date to the Larsa period or earlier, including:

Nuzi: Starr 1937: pl. 52F and G (see Starr 1937: 517 where this type is assigned to the transitional level between the Ga.Sur and Nuzi periods).
Diyala region: Delougaz 1952: pl. 143:A.545.360, Asmar, Gutium-Ur III period; pl. 177:C.507.570, Asmar, Larsa period.
Telloh: de Genouillac 1936: pl. 30:3769, 2242, 3346, and pl. 33:988 (all dated to the Ur III-Larsa periods).
Ur: Royal Cemetery, Woolley 1934: pl. 253:44a and b, 45 (Sargonic).
Tepe Gawra: Speiser 1935: pl. LXIX:130 (Stratum VI).
Tell Taya: Reade 1968: pl. LXXXV:15 (Level VII).

[8]Examples from Mesopotamian sites, although not common, include the following:

Telloh: de Genouillac 1936: pl. 28:3755 and pl. 29:614 (Ur III-Larsa).
Diyala region: Delougaz 1952: pl. 189:C.777.340 (Asmar, Late Akkadian period).
Nippur: McCown and Haines 1967: pl. 85:1-2 (Akkadian to Isin-Larsa periods).
Tell Brak: Mallowan 1947: pl. LXV:12 (Sargonic).
Ur: Royal Cemetery, Woolley 1934: pl. 255:Types 75 and 76 (Sargonic).

[9]This type may also be related to what seems to be an exaggerated form which is characteristic of the Larsa period and continues into the Kassite period in Mesopotamia, occurring at Larsa (Parrot 1968: fig. 14), Telloh (de Genouillac 1936: pl. 30:4101), and in the Diyala region (Delougaz 1952: pl. 148: B.061.210, Larsa period, Tell Asmar).

[10]A vessel with painted bands which may be related to this group or perhaps, more likely, to the EB IV goblet was found at Tell al-Rimah and tentatively dated to the early 19th century B.C. (Oates 1970: pl. IX:2).

[11]Megiddo: Loud 1948: pl. 15:12, T. 3147 and T. 2152; pl. 14:12, T. 5178 and T. 5183; pl. 9:3, T. 5167; pl. 15:15, T. 3162; Aphek: Beck 1975: fig. 4:17; ᶜAin es-Samiyeh: Dever 1975a; fig. 3:4 (here fig. 30:16-20).

[12]Loud 1948: pl. 11:17, T. 5181 and T. 5179; pl. 12:6, T. 3148; pl. 17:21, T. 5097; pl. 12:3, T. 3148 and T. 5275.

[13]Megiddo: Loud 1948: pl. 25:12, T. 5106; pl. 16:2, T. 5114; pl. 11:2, T. 5121; pl. 17:14, T. 5090; pl. 17:15, T. 5252; Wadi et-Tin: Vincent 1947: pl. V:6; Aphek: Beck 1975: 68, fig. 10:3; Nahariya: Ben-Dor 1950: fig. 25; Byblos: Tufnell 1969: fig. 5:52; Schaeffer 1948: fig. 63:0 and P (Nos. 746 and 747), and fig. 64A; Tell el-ᶜAjjul: Schaeffer 1948: fig. 122:11 (here fig. 33:1-10).

[14]Grave 151 is considered to be one of the earliest graves of Level 1. Note that the other contents of this grave included two simple carinated bowls (Mallowan 1937a: fig. 16:2-3) and a toggle pin with fluted ball head and ribbed shank (fig. 12:9) which is closely paralleled at Tell et-Tin.

[15]One additional type of vessel should be considered, primarily because of its distinctiveness. Several of the Iranian sites (Tepe Giyan: Contenau and Ghirshman 1935: pl. 29:2, Burial 99, Level III; Godin Tepe: Young 1969: 289, Ill. 8:No. 11; Dinkha Tepe, Hamlin 1971: pl. I:4) have small tripodic goblets, often with painted horizontal-banded decoration. Although various types of tripodic bowls appear in the Levantine MB I and MB II sequences, an unusual example with some similarity to the Iranian examples occurred at Megiddo, Phase 3 (Loud 1948: pl. 15:11, T. 3147, with red slip and burnish (here fig. 13:10), while three examples which are even closer to the Iranian vessels are known from Anatolia at Kültepe, Level II (Emre 1963: fig. 10:Kt n/k30 with incised horizontal ribbing), Alaca Hüyük (with reddish brown slip and vertical handle rising above the rim to which it is attached—unpublished, No. e223, Ankara Museum), and Tarsus (Hamlin 1971: 144, perhaps Goldman 1956: 178, No. 898, fig. 372). The goblet shape of some of these examples is similar to that of the "grain measure," so this vessel could represent another variation of that basic form. The question of whether more examples are still to be found in the great geographical lacuna, giving a distribution comparable to that of the goblet "grain measure," or whether these examples are merely unrelated coincidence cannot now be answered.

[16]Hansen, primarily on the basis of the pottery from Nippur, wrote: ". . . there are some forty different pottery types covering the period from the Third Dynasty of Ur to the end of the First Dynasty of Babylon. These pottery types present a continually evolving series; there are no sharp breaks until the end of the

First Dynasty of Babylon. The fact that there is no sharp break in the pottery sequence implies that it is difficult to define this time range from the Ur III through the Old Babylonian Period in precise cultural phases on the basis of pottery . . ." (Hansen 1965: 210). This continuity may be reflected in the similarity of certain Anatolian storage jars to late 3rd millennium Mesopotamian types and in the occurrence of similar pottery forms in Mesopotamia at apparently earlier periods than in Anatolia and the Levant.

[17]In commenting on the more extensive and versatile use of the potter's wheel from the beginning of the MB I period, Amiran (1969: 90) wrote: "The widespread use of the potter's wheel is mainly responsible for the technical advances in pottery making and for the greater refinement of forms . . . in MB II A, pottery making attains new artistic and technical levels. The wheel gives the potter a greater mastery of his craft and enables him, for instance, to shape rims and bases with greater delicacy and precision." Dever (1976: 7-8) described the pottery of MB I as follows:

> The pottery of MB IIA is exceptionally well made on a fast wheel, evidence of which is seen in the numerous fine wheel-marks which are often left visible. The delicate and graceful forms, many of them carinated, are those which only a past mastery of wheel technique makes possible, and most of them now appear for the first time in the history of the country. The clays are well levigated and fired, and many of the wares on the smaller vessels are metallic and almost eggshell thin; even body sherds on the large storejars are so well finished that they are a delight to handle. Attention to detail is evident in the finishing of rims, handle attachments, and even the underside of the bases. . . . Bowls, juglets, and all classes of jugs and pitchers are usually covered with a heavy dark red or purplish-red slip, even on the base; and the burnishing is so skillfully done that the best examples almost appear to be glazed.

Chapter VI
The Metal Artifacts

The quantity and range of extant metal artifacts from the first quarter of the 2nd millennium B.C. in the Levant is much smaller than the number and variety of pottery vessels known from this period. In addition, it is often more difficult to place these metal objects within secure stratigraphic contexts, perhaps because frequently they are found in graves or are present in isolated hoards. Despite these drawbacks, metal objects can often be useful chronological indicators because of their distinctive forms, once specific types are established for certain time periods.

The metal implements which have been identified in the Levant from the MB I period are relatively limited and, with the exception of the toggle pins, tend to be weapons. Four weapon types found in a tomb at Beth-shan were discussed by Oren (1971: 109-39) in terms of their chronological placement and foreign relationships. It is possible to add to his discussion additional weaponry types which are also associated with the MB I period and other examples which expand the geographical area in which these types have been found.

A study of the metal objects can help in our consideration of the relations between the Levant and the contiguous regions in three ways: (1) particularly in considering bronzes, a study of the sources of the necessary raw materials which are not locally available (such as tin) may indicate the trade routes involved in the procurement of these materials; (2) the use of a relatively specialized technology, such as the alloying of metals and casting of objects, as well as specific advances in forms, may indicate the travel both of ideas and perhaps of itinerant workers; (3) the presence of isolated examples of specific metal types indicates the trade of the finished product.

In addition to the archaeological evidence, the textual sources (previously discussed in Chapter II) provide information concerning the first two points outlined above. For a consideration of both the technology of production and the sources of raw materials, it is necessary to know the elemental compositions of the objects under consideration; unfortunately, this information is not always given in excavation reports, and so only generalized conclusions drawn from those examples where metallurgical analyses were performed can be given. First, the distribution of specific types will be considered, followed by discussions of the technology and sources of the raw materials used.

VI.1. Distribution of Artifact Types

A. AXES

Oren (1971: 111-14) established the duckbill fenestrated axe as distinctive of the MB I period throughout the Levant, while eliminating other forms of axes from this period. Dever, however, pointed out that an early form of the chisel-axe (which Oren had considered to occur only in the MB II period) with a notch for the attachment of the blade to the handle also appeared during MB I (Dever 1976: 26, n. 51). This conclusion is now supported by the occurrence of both duckbill axes and notched chisel-axes in the same deposit (as at Kafer Djarra, Tomb 57, and at ᶜAin es-Samiyeh) and, even more clearly, by the association of the notched chisel-axe with pottery of MB I type (as at Gibeon, Tomb 31; Megiddo, Tomb 3168; Ginosar, Tomb 1; and Khirbet Kufin, Tomb 3, Chambers 3-4, upper stratum). The contemporary appearance of these two axe types marks a transition from the crescentic axe series, which was most typical of the 3rd millennium B.C. and of which the duckbill axe is the last and most fully developed manifestation, to the chisel-axes which continued to develop into more complex forms in the later MB II period. These two concurrent types will now be considered separately.

(1) The "Duckbill" Fenestrated Axe: This axe ype (Maxwell-Hyslop's Type B.4) developed from the semi-circular crescentic axe which is typical of the EB IV period in the Levant. This development is clearly demonstrated at the sites of Ugarit and

Byblos where both types, as well as intermediary examples, were found, along with molds which attest to the local manufacture of these products (Oren 1971: 111-13; Maxwell-Hyslop 1949: 119; here fig. 36):

Beth-shan: Tomb 92, Oren 1971: fig. 2:4.
ᶜAin es-Samiyeh: Dever 1975a: fig. 1:4.
Esh-Shejara (Galilee): Schumacher 1889: fig. 15 (from caves in the area of Nazareth/ ᶜAffula).
Safed: Tomb (Israel Dept. of Antiquities Collection—Oren 1971: 115).
Tel Dan: Biran 1973: 111, pl. 27B.
Ashkelon(?): British Museum, No. 1913,523,73, Maxwell-Hyslop 1949: 121, pl. 37:7 (listed by Oren 1971: 129, as Reg. No. 1913.5-23.73).
Yabrud: Tomb 4, Assaf 1967: pl. I:1.
Byblos: Dunand 1954: 380; 1950: pl. LXXIV:No. 10645, "dépôt σ"; Dunand 1958: 732, No. 14840; 1950: pl. CXXVII; Montet 1929: pl. CXLIX:Nos. 940 and 941, third "tombeau de particulier."
Ugarit: Schaeffer 1932: pl. XIII:4, burial of Level II; Schaeffer 1948: fig. 49:7-8 (U.M. 2); Schaeffer 1949: fig. 18:13 and 17 (U.M. 2) and 29 (U.M. 1); fig. 25:G, F, I (U.M., miniatures).
Kafer Djarra: Tomb 57, Guigues 1938: fig. 51a.
Lebeᶜa: Tomb 1, Guigues 1937: fig. 4a.
Sin el-Fil: Chehab 1939: fig. 10a.
Amrith: Dunand, Saliby, and Khirichian 1954: 197-98, pl. III:2 (two examples from Tomb 7 and one example from Tomb 8).
Yauron: Unpublished axe from southern Lebanon (southern Biqaᶜ), said to be in the Toledo Museum of Art (Williams 1975: 993).
Hama: Fugmann 1958: pl. X:5A813 and 5A812 (G I).
Beirut: British Museum, No. W.G. 844, Greenwell 1902: 13-14, fig. 15.
Tell et-Tin: Gautier 1895: 457-58, fig. 10 (in the Lyons Museum, similar to the Tell et-Tin examples).
Kadesh (Orontes): Petrie 1917: pl. VI:169.
Baghouz: du Mesnil du Buisson 1948: pl. LX: z123,143, 95, 305, 102.
Mari: Parrot 1959: 85, pl. XXXIII:994 (written on plate as 999), a miniature or votive; additional examples (miniatures) said to be in the Toledo Museum of Art (Williams 1975: 866, n. 5).
Kültepe: T. Özgüç 1959: 109-10, fig. 64 (an intermediary type between the crescentic and duckbill types).
Izmir region: Przeworski 1939: pl. XXI:5.
Karaköy: Oxford, Ashmolean Museum, No. 1913.428 (Maxwell-Hyslop 1949: 121).
Cyprus: (provenance unknown) Oxford, Ashmolean Museum, No. 1927.1276 and 1927.1277 (Maxwell-Hyslop 1949: 121).
Provenance unknown: Axe purchased in Jerusalem, Birmingham 1977: 115-17, fig. 1: A2; Fogg Art Museum (Cambridge, Mass.), No. 1968.110.

The distribution of the duckbill axe is concentrated in the area of northern Syria and especially along the coast. Several examples also occur in the south and one might assume that these were locally produced, although, as we shall see, they were not as popular there as was the notched chisel-axe. Three examples have been reported from Anatolia where it should be considered an import.[1] The example from Kültepe seems intermediary between the crescentic and duckbill types, thus showing that it should be placed early in the series and that it may have been imported from northern Syria where similar examples were found, especially at Ugarit (Schaeffer 1948: fig. 56). The large number of duckbill axes from the Baghouz cemetery near Mari seems to argue for local production in northern Mesopotamia, although it is unfortunate that no examples have so far been excavated at other sites in this area.

The duckbill axe may also be depicted in a wall painting in the tomb of the nomarch Khnumhotep III at Beni Hasan dated to the 6th year of the reign of Senusert II, or 1890 B.C. (Newberry 1893: 69, pl. XXX, third register, center and detail; pl. XXXI, lower register, first figure from left, Tomb No. 3, main chamber, north wall). The axe is carried by a warrior who is part of a procession of foreigners (usually interpreted as Asiatics). While the outline of the axe corresponds to that of a duckbill axe, the two "eyes" are not clearly depicted in the original published drawing. Most writers accept that this illustration represents the typical duckbill axe (Oren 1971: 113, and 136, although Williams does not, 1975: 860), and, if so, this would provide a chronological indication for the absolute dating of the MB I period (see Chapter VII).

(2) The Notched Chisel-Axe: This type of axe (Maxwell-Hyslop 1949: 116, Type 24), as mentioned above, should probably be considered the most typical form of axe occurring in the southern Levant in MB I. It has a thin blade which was attached to a handle by a thong looped through the notch (here fig. 37):

Megiddo: Tomb 911D (M2818), Guy 1938: pl. 122:1, fig. 173:1; Tomb 911D (M2816), Guy 1938: pl. 122:2, fig. 173:2; Tomb 912D (M2966), Guy 1938: pl. 133:4; Tomb 911A1 (M2693), Guy 1938: pl. 118:3; Tomb 3168 (Megiddo Phase 3), Loud 1948: pl. 182:1.
Tell el-ᶜAjjul: Tomb 1015, Tufnell 1962: fig. 4:1c.
Moza: Cave No. 2, Sussmann 1966: fig. 3:2.
Khirbet Kufin: Tomb 3, Chambers 3-4, upper stratum, Smith 1962: pl. XIII:6 and 7.
Gibeon: Tomb 31 (B306), Pritchard 1963: fig. 34:4.
Ginosar: Tomb 1, Epstein 1974: fig. 7:15.
ᶜAin es-Samiyeh: Dever 1975a: fig. 1:7.
Kafer Malik (near Sinjil): British Museum, No. W.G. 876 (Maxwell-Hyslop 1949: pl. XXXV:24); British Museum, No. W.G. 875 (Maxwell-Hyslop 1949: 116).
Kafer Djarra: Tomb 57, Guigues 1938: fig. 51c and d; Tomb 66, Guigues 1938: fig. 70; Tomb 74, Guigues 1938: fig. 95d and e.
Provenance unknown: axe purchased in Jerusalem, Birmingham 1977: 115, fig. 1:A1.

So far as is known, no examples of this axe type have been found in northern Syria,[2] Mesopotamia or Anatolia, thus demonstrating an independent local development of this type. From several of the examples which were found in closed context, it would seem possible to assign the notched chisel-axe to the middle and late phases of MB I—for example, the Gibeon axe, which occurred with a handled store jar, and the axe from Megiddo, Tomb 3168, which is assigned to Phase 3 of MB I at Megiddo.

B. SPEARHEADS

A distinctive type of spearhead first appears during the EB IV period and becomes the standard type throughout the Middle Bronze Age in the Levant. This spearhead has a socketed shaft for attachment and thus differs from the other EB IV type which has a narrow tang for this purpose. The MB I type is perhaps best distinguished from later examples by its tapering form which narrows to a pointed tip and by its narrow midrib, whereas the later type is blunted at the tip (Guy 1938: fig. 170). The MB I spearheads often vary in terms of the proportions of the haft and head lengths. This variation, however, does not seem to have either chronological or geographic implications, since varying types are sometimes found together, but may reflect a difference in function (Oren 1971: 115).

The process of manufacture was described by Guy (1938: 163-64) on the basis of the Megiddo examples. He suggested that the entire spearhead was made by the hammering into shape of a single piece of metal, as indicated by the tube of the hollowed haft which continues into the head.[3] Bands encircling the haft were sometimes used to secure the attachment. This technique seems to vary markedly from that used in the earlier examples of socketed spearheads; in at least the Megiddo Early Bronze example (Guy 1938: 163, fig. 170:1), the haft was formed simply by bending together the edges of the metal piece and would therefore seem weaker than the Middle Bronze Age examples. The MB I spearheads should therefore be considered as representing a technological advance in method of production which resulted in a much stronger implement (here fig. 38).

Megiddo: T. 911D (M2813), Guy 1938: pl. 122:7, fig. 170:3; T. 911D (M2819), Guy 1938: pl. 122:5, fig. 170:4; T. 912B (M3042), Guy 1938: pl. 125:12; T. 912D (M2957), Guy 1938: pl. 133:7; T. 911A1 (M2761), Guy 1938: pl. 118:6; T. 911A1 (M2762), Guy 1938: pl. 118:7; T. 911A1 (M2772), Guy 1938: pl. 118:8; T. 911C (M2696), Guy 1938: pl. 120:13 (copper); N=3106 (b1006), Loud 1948: pl. 173:9; W=T. 3157 (b1049), Loud 1948: pl. 173:5; E=5061 (d265), Loud 1948: pl. 173:6.
Aphek: Grave 4, Ory 1937: 120, No. 2, pl. 32: B7; Grave 2, Ory 1937: 120, No. 4, pl. 32:B5.
Barqai: Second burial phase, Gophna and Sussman 1969: fig. 4:13 and 14 (No. 14 possibly an arrowhead).
Tell el-ᶜAjjul: T. 1417 (Courtyard Cemetery Group 2) No. 1170, Tufnell 1962:

fig. 10:18; T. 1015, Tufnell 1962: fig. 4: 1b; T. 303B, Tufnell 1962: fig. 4:5b.

Kfar Szold: Epstein 1974: fig. 4:10.

Ginosar: Tomb 1, Epstein 1974: fig. 7:14; Tomb 4, Epstein 1974: fig. 18:1.

Nahariya: Temple precinct, Dothan 1956: pl. 4:D.

Beth-shan: Tomb 92, Oren 1971: fig. 2:2.

ᶜAin es-Samiyeh: Dever 1975a: fig. 1:2-3.

Sinjil: Dever 1975a: fig. 3:2-3.

Safed: Tomb (Israel Dept. of Antiquities Collec tion), Oren 1971: 115.

Byblos: third "tombeau de particulier," Montet 1929: pl. CXLIX:No. 942.

Ugarit: Burials of Level II, Schaeffer 1932: pl. XIII:1-2; Schaeffer 1949: fig. 18: 9-10; fig. 25B.

Yabrud: Tomb 4, Assaf 1967: pl. I:4-5.

Sin el-Fil: Chehab 1939: fig. 10b:No. 26.

Amrith: Dunand, Saliby, and Khirichian 1954: 198, Tomb 8.

Lebeᶜa: Guigues 1937: fig. 4c.

Kafer Djarra: Tomb 33, Guigues 1938: fig. 41; Tomb 57, Guigues 1938: fig. 51b; Tomb 66, Guigues 1938: fig. 70 (two examples); Tomb 74, Guigues 1938: fig. 95c.

Tell et-Tim: Gautier 1895: fig. 9.

Qatna: Tomb I, du Mesnil du Buisson 1927: pl. XIII: Γ and Δ

Hama: G VI, Fugmann 1958: pl. X:5B420:2 and 4.

Tell Mardikh: de Maigret 1976: 31-41 (also Matthiae 1977: pl. 97); two examples found near the Middle Bronze Age fortifications, both with cuneiform inscriptions: TM.71.M.841: TE-*ir-še* dub . sar: "Te-irše, the scribe"; TM.71.M.842: ⌜*a*?⌝-*li-šu* IGI.DU/UŠ: "Ališu, the leader."

Chagar Bazar: Level 1, Mallowan 1937a: fig. 13:10-13 (copper); Mallowan 1947: pl. LV:10 and 16 (No. 10 found with a shaft-hole axe of later Middle Bronze Age type, therefore probably to be dated later).

Mari: Parrot 1959: 85, pl. XXXIII:1316.

Baghouz: du Mesnil du Buisson 1948: pl. LXI.

Alişar: Level II, von der Osten 1937b: fig. 291:d2447.

Kültepe: Level II, T. Özgüç 1959: fig. 67; Level Ib, T. Özgüç 1959: figs. 66, 68, and 73.

These spearheads appear throughout the Levant as well as in northern Mesopotamia, where the small number of relevant excavated sites is compensated for by the large number of spearheads found, especially at Baghouz. Examples of the spearhead are sufficiently numerous throughout a relatively large geographical area to permit the assumption that these were locally produced. The simultaneous introduction of a new technique of manufacture which resulted in a stronger and more advanced type of weapon may, however, be attributed to the transmission of such technological advances throughout this region. The great similarity in form throughout this area may also argue in favor of this suggestion.

C. ARROWHEADS

The relatively small number of examples of this category of weapon may be due to a confusion with the spearheads just discussed. These two types of weapons are generally similar in form, but the arrowhead is usually a smaller version, thus making it a subjective decision into which category a specific example should be placed. Some of the examples classified here as arrowheads have a somewhat different form; instead of a marked break between the head and the shaft, these two parts merge into each other producing a thin haft and a leaf-shaped head. This difference in form should indicate some corresponding difference in method of manufacture since the sharpness of the juncture between haft and head in the spearhead was caused by cutting the metal piece. The arrowheads seem to have been formed by hammering out a thin metal piece and then rolling one end into a tip to form the haft. The distribution of arrowheads, although more restricted, is nonetheless comparable to that of the spearheads—as one would expect from the general similarity of form.

Beth-shan: Tomb 92, Oren 1971: fig. 2:3.

Yabrud: Tomb 4, Assaf 1967: pl. I:6-8.

Megiddo: T. 2138 (a1113), Loud 1948: pl. 174:2 (probably MB II); =5077 (d204), Loud 1948: pl. 174:1.

Ugarit: Schaeffer 1948: fig. 56:5 and 7.

Chagar Bazar: Level I, Mallowan 1937a: fig. 13:14.

Alişar: Level II, von der Osten 1937b: fig. 291: d2255.

Mersin: Levels XI-IX, Garstang 1953: 233, fig. 149:18 (bronze) and 19 (Level IX).

D. DAGGERS

Two basic types of daggers occur in the Levant. The more primitive type has a flat blade with two or three rivet holes and either a tang or a rounded butt. This type corresponds to Maxwell-Hyslop's Types 20-23, depending on the shape of the tang or the butt (Maxwell-Hyslop 1946: 22-25). The following examples may be classified in one of four groups, depending on whether they have a well-shaped tang, a sloping tang, a rounded butt, or a concave butt. The examples of this type usually have a blunt tip and no ribbing.

Sloping tang (here fig. 39:1-4):

Megiddo: T. 912D (M2959), Guy 1938: pl. 133:6; T. 2135 (a1119), Loud 1948: pl. 178:10 (probably MB II).
Byblos: Third "tombeau de particulier," Schaeffer 1948: fig. 65 (943 and 945; Montet 1929: pl. CXLIX).
Ugarit: Burials of Level II, Schaeffer 1932: pl. XIII:6; Schaeffer 1948: fig. 45:N-Q.
Boğazköy: Level 8a, Northwest slope (Inv. Nr400/s), Schirmer 1969: 59, pl. 46:No. 247.

Well-shaped tang (here fig. 39:7):

Moza: Cave No. 2, Sussman 1966: fig. 3:1.
Yabrud: Tomb 4, Assaf 1967: pl. I:2.
Tarsus: Room O (Middle Bronze Age), Goldman 1956: 292, fig. 428:No. 103.
Mersin: Level XI, Garstang 1953: 233, fig. 149: 23.

Rounded butt (here fig. 39:8):

Megiddo: Tomb 911D (M2817), Guy 1938: pl. 122:8, fig. 171:5; Tomb 911A1 (M2773), Guy 1938: pl. 118:9.
Wadi et-Tin: Vincent 1947: pl. VII, right.
Alişar: Level II, von der Osten 1937b: fig. 287: d2480.
Kültepe: Level Ib, T. Özgüç 1959: fig. 72.

Concave butt:

Beth-shemesh: Tomb 3, Grant 1929: 123:4 (second from right).
Kafer Djarra: Tomb 74, Guigues 1938: fig. 95a.
Alişar: Level II, von der Osten 1937b: fig. 287: d2111.
Alaca Hüyük: Level IV, Koşay and Akok 1966: pl. 47:h192.

The other major type of dagger—that with two to five ribs or veins (also called the "blood rilled" dagger)—corresponds to Maxwell-Hyslop's Type 25. It is technically more advanced, being cast in a closed mold, and has a pointed tip, leaf-shaped blade with multiple longitudinal ribs, and a short tang with two or three rivets (Maxwell-Hyslop 1946: 26; Dever 1976: 26, n. 51; Guy 1938: 164). This type continues into later MB II (and even the Late Bronze Age), when it is often considered as characteristic, and was originally classified as "Hyksos." Numerous examples from secure contexts, however, show the beginning of this type in MB I, with some of the examples (such as that from Beth-shan) perhaps being typologically earlier because of fewer ribs (here fig. 40).[4] Examples of the veined dagger found in the Levant include the following:

Megiddo: Tomb 911D (M2814), Guy 1938: pl. 122:9, fig. 171:6; Tomb 911A1 (M2694), Guy 1938: pl. 118:5; W=5087 (d295), Loud 1948: pl. 178:3.
Gibeon: Tomb 31 (B305), Pritchard 1963: fig. 34:2.
Tell el-^{c}Ajjul: T. 1417 (Courtyard Cemetery Group 2), Tufnell 1962: fig. 10:17; T. 1015, Tufnell 1962: fig. 4:1a; T. 303C, Tufnell 1962: fig. 4:5a.
Beth-shan: Tomb 92, Oren 1971: fig. 2:1.
Wadi et-Tin: Vincent 1947: pl. VII, left.
Tell el-Far^{c}ah (N.): Tomb AD, de Vaux 1962: 244, fig. 4:1.
^{c}Ain es-Samiyeh: Dever 1975a: fig. 1:1.
Sinjil: Dever 1975a: fig. 3:1.
Gezer: T. 226, Tufnell 1962: fig. 4:7d, fig. 4:7a.
Safed: Tomb (Israel Dept. of Antiquities Collec tion) Oren 1971: 116.
Khirbet Kufin: Tomb 3, Chambers 3-4, upper stratum, Smith 1962: pl. XIII:5.
Tell et-Tin: Gautier 1895: fig. 9 (center).
Lebe^{c}a: Guigues 1937: fig. 4d and e.
Kafer Djarra: Tomb 57, Guigues 1938: fig. 52.
Sin el-Fil: Chehab 1939: 807, fig. 10c:No. 27.
Hama: G VI, Fugmann 1958: pl. X:No. 7; Level H 4, Fugmann 1958: fig. 117.
Provenance unknown: Tufnell 1962: fig. 4:4 (bought in Lebanon; now in the Royal Ontario Museum in Toronto; analyzed as copper).

The contrast in the distribution of these two main types of daggers presents an interesting picture. The simpler, flat dagger is related to examples of the preceding period (for example, daggers of the U.M. 1 period at Ugarit which are distinguished by the crescentic handle, Schaeffer 1949: fig. 18:23-25 and fig. 19:3-4). This type probably developed from the dagger which was typical of northern Syria and southern Anatolia at the end of the 3rd millennium B.C. and which had round sloping shoulders, tapering tang, and a triangular rivet system (Stronach 1957: Type 6, 100-1, fig. 2:21-23). Stronach suggested that this flat dagger type was introduced first into Cilicia and later into central Anatolia from northern Syria where it continued as late as Late Bronze I at Tarsus. In the early 2nd millennium B.C., this type has a fairly even distribution throughout the Levant, with examples also from Anatolia and northern Mesopotamia, if one accepts the daggers from Baghouz and Chagar Bazar as variants of this type (*supra*, n. 4).

The blood-rilled dagger, however, has a greater concentration in the southern Levant with only two examples, one each from Hama and Tell et-Tin, representing the area of Syria. As in the case of the development and distribution of the notched chisel-axes, it would seem that not only is there an element of regionalism in the development of certain types, but that it is in the southern Levant that the innovations were first introduced.[5]

E. TOGGLE PINS

Toggle pins will be briefly considered here, since they are often mentioned in the literature as indicative of connections over large geographical distances.[6] Several groups of toggle pins have been excavated at various sites throughout the Levant. The earliest date to the EB IV period, appearing at such sites as Ugarit and Byblos, and later examples continue through at least the later Middle Bronze periods. The toggle pins are distinguished by an eyelet pierced through the upper part of the shank, a head which may vary in shape (flat, bulbous, or rounded) and is sometimes decorated with fluting, and a pattern sometimes incised on the upper shank between the eyelet and the head. Some of the groups of such pins were found at the following sites:

Megiddo: Guy 1938: 168-70, fig. 174; Loud 1948: pls. 219-20, Nos. 10-15, 18-29.
Dhahrat el-Humraiya: Ory 1948: Grave 12, pl. XXXIII:22.
Moza: Sussman 1966: fig. 3:3.
Nahariya: Dothan 1956: pl. 3:E.
Tell el-Far^cah (N.): de Vaux 1962: Tombs AN and AD, 244, fig. 4:2-3.
Wadi et-Tin: Vincent 1947: pl. VII, center.
Tell el-^cAjjul: Tufnell 1962: 18, fig. 5.
Ugarit: Burials of Level II, Schaeffer 1932: pl. XIII:3; Schaeffer 1949: fig. 105b and g-i.
Byblos: Schaeffer 1948: figs. 66-67; Dunand 1937: pls. CII-CV.
Hama: Fugmann 1958: pl. X:G I:5A820 and 5A821; G III:5A883; G VI:5B420:6, 10, 13, and G X: 6A359.
Tell et-Tin: Gautier 1895: fig. 9, right.
Tell Mardikh: Matthiae 1980b: 14, "Tomb of the Princess."
Alalakh: Woolley 1955: pl. LXXIII:P.1-P.7.
Mersin: Garstang 1953: fig. 149:6 and 14 (bronze), and 13 (copper).
Kültepe: T. Özgüç 1959: figs. 75 and 76.
Chagar Bazar: Mallowan 1936: 28, fig. 8:11, Grave 3; Mallowan 1937a: 98, fig. 12:9; Mallowan 1947: 166-68, pl. XXXI:3-4.

The first extensive study of toggle pins was that of Henschel-Simon who divided them into types which she illustrated with examples from the Palestine Archaeological Museum. She proposed that the pins found in the Levant in the early 2nd millennium B.C. (her "pre-Hyksos" group) were descended from 3rd millennium examples from Mesopotamia and particularly from Tepe Gawra, Stratum VI, while she denied a close relationship with examples from the Caucasus region. Finally, she suggested that the pins of a closely related group (Henschel-Simon 1937: 186, fig. 7)—with examples from Byblos, Hamman, Lapithos, Troy, and Megiddo—may have had a common center of production whence they were exported to these various sites. Since the time of this study, however, new groups of pins have been found throughout the Levant, as well as in northern Mesopotamia and Anatolia, and it would no longer seem feasible to try to support the theory of a single manufacturing center.

Schaeffer showed in his study of "les porteurs de torques" (Schaeffer 1949: 49-120) that toggle pins were introduced into the Levant at the beginning of the EB IV period (U.M. 1) along with a distinctive assemblage of metal artifacts. Such pins were found in contexts of this date throughout northern Syria, including sites along the coast and in the Orontes River Valley, at: Ugarit (Schaeffer

1949: fig. 22), Byblos (the "Montet Jar," Tufnell and Ward 1966: fig. 10), Qatna Tomb IV (Schaeffer 1948: fig. 99), Tell ᶜAs (Schaeffer 1948: fig. 104-5), and Hamman near Carchemish (Schaeffer 1948: fig. 79). The toggle pins thus constitute a group which shows continuity from the EB IV period into the Middle Bronze Age. Schaeffer suggested that the highly skilled metal workers, with whom he associated his "torque-bearers," came from the highlands of southern Anatolia and northern Syria and moved into the Syrian coastal region in search of new copper and tin sources after the resources of the mountainous areas had been depleted. Although it is not possible either to prove or to disprove Schaeffer's theory of origin, the toggle pin was evidently in use throughout a relatively large geographical area from at least the beginning of the 2nd millennium B.C. Its appearance was probably associated with the use of specific garment types so that its spread might be associated with a combination of practicality[7] and fashion.

While a more extensive study of the typology of these pins is not practical here, it may be relevant to note that Ward and Tufnell suggested a correlation between the length, the relative amount of tin, and the chronology of the pins. They have stated that the later pins seem to be shorter, while the shorter pins contain a higher proportion of tin (for example, a pin of 20.5 cm. had less than 3% tin, while a pin of 13.8 cm. had over 18%). While such conclusions are tentative because of the small number of analyzed examples,[8] it might be possible to conclude that the later pins had a higher proportion of tin because of improvements in the technology of bronze alloying and production (*infra*, Chapter VI.3).

In summary, then, one can conclude that the toggle pins, with some variation in decoration and form, were used throughout the Levant and northern Mesopotamia, as well as in Anatolia to a lesser extent, from approximately the mid or late 3rd millennium through the 2nd millennium B.C. Their distribution, however, is probably related to practicality and fashion, while their local manufacture is attested by the finding of molds at different sites (see, for example, Henschel-Simon 1937: 174-75, pl. LXX, for a mold from Beth-shemesh).

VI.2. Sources of Copper and Tin

Two methods are available for determining the sources of the copper and tin used in antiquity: first, the textual evidence in combination with modern geological information of known sources; and, second, compositional analysis of artifacts to determine trace elements which might identify a specific source. While some work has been done on this latter method (Muhly 1973: 339-42), none of these results has been accepted with respect to the sources which might have been available in western Asia during this period, so that only the former method will be discussed here.

There are several potential copper sources in the eastern Mediterranean and western Asia which may have been exploited during the early 2nd millennium B.C. Cyprus is generally considered to have been the major source of copper in the eastern Mediterranean, but its role in the early 2nd millennium metals trade depends primarily on the assumption that Cyprus is the Alašiya mentioned in the Mari texts as a source of copper.[9] Anatolia is known to have been exploiting its copper sources, such as that at Ergani Maden, from possibly as early as the Neolithic, and this region may have supplied the copper for the objects from Shanidar, Cayönü Tepesi, and even Ali Kosh, dated between the 9th to 7th millennia B.C. (Muhly 1973: 200-1; 1976: 83-84; Heltzer 1978: 107-8). An active internal Anatolian trade is documented in the Old Assyrian "Cappadocian" texts (see Chapter II.1), although copper does not seem to have been exported to Mesopotamia.

Palestine also has copper sources in the Arabah region, and there is archaeological evidence that these sources were worked during the Chalcolithic period as well as in EB IV (Rothenberg 1962: especially 60-61; Muhly 1976: 88). Copper objects, most notably the Nahal Mishmar hoard, and the evidence for metallurgical activity at Tell Abu Matar during the Chalcolithic period (perhaps late 4th millennium B.C.) may also attest to the use of the Negev copper sources at that time (Muhly 1976: 88). Although there is no definitive information on the use of these sources in the Middle Bronze Age, since the export of tin from Mesopotamia to the southern Levant via Syria is documented in the Mari texts but no comparable trade in copper is mentioned, it may be hypothesized that the Arabah mines were being worked during the Middle Bronze Age as well. Syria has no proven copper sources, and so it is assumed to have imported copper from Cyprus, Anatolia, or possibly even Mesopotamia, although there is no specific documentation (except for the mention of copper from Alašiya).

Mesopotamia also has no copper sources of its own and therefore must have imported all of its copper supplies. The major attested source for Mesopotamian copper is the trade from the Persian Gulf region which flourished from the mid-3rd millennium B.C. to some time in the first half of the 2nd millennium B.C. (Muhly 1973: 220-32). This Persian Gulf trade was sufficient to make any copper trade with Anatolia unprofitable, since the price of Anatolian copper apparently could not compete with the price of copper imported from the Persian Gulf region (Muhly 1973: 206-8).

The sources of tin are more limited and, as such, have been the subject of much controversy. Confusion over the identification of the Akkadian word for tin and the translation of *annaku* as either tin or lead has made the attempt to analyze ancient texts concerning sources of tin difficult.[10] Even if a translation of *annaku* as tin is accepted, the problem of its source still remains. According to the texts, *annaku* was imported into Mesopotamia from the east, either from the northeast via Shemshara and Assur, or from the southeast, possibly via Elam. Muhly has cited evidence for some tin sources located in the Shahr-i Sokhta area of Dasht-e Lut found by the Geological Survey of Iran (Muhly 1976: 98), a location which would have suited the southeast direction for Mesopotamian imports (cf. Heltzer 1978: 108-11; North 1975: 489-90).

There is also now some evidence for tin sources in central Asia, although the possibility that these were used in the 3rd or early 2nd millennium B.C. is not certain since tin-bronze technology is not attested there at such an early time.[11] As Crawford points out, a route from Bukhara to Mesopotamia would have coincided with a trade route for lapis lazuli from Badakhshan (Herrmann 1968: 21-27) which then correlates with a tendency in Mesopotamian myths to associate the sources of tin, carnelian, and lapis lazuli (Crawford 1974: 243). The lapis and tin might have been imported into Mesopotamia either via a short route—from the northeast via such sites as Yanik Tepe, Haftavan, Geoy Tepe, and Tepe Gawra into Assyria—or a longer route from the southeast possibly via such sites as Shahr-i Sokhta and Tepe Yahya, then overland to Susa and Ešnunna or by sea to southern Mesopotamia. It seems probable that there was some alternation in the selection of the northern or southern route in different periods (see Herrmann 1968: 53; Crawford 1974: 243-44; Muhly 1973: 337-38). The reasons for these variations may have depended upon complex and changing political relationships —a factor already discussed in relation to the Mari texts and the Larsa to Emar itinerary (Chapter II.2) and one which may have been a determinant in trade and other cultural patterns (Muhly 1973: 294-95).

Whatever the original source of the tin imported into Mesopotamia, it is clear from the textual evidence that tin was then exported from Mesopotamia to Syria, as shown in the Mari texts which mention Aleppo, Qatna, Hazor, and Laiš as tin recipients. Tin was also exported from Mesopotamia to Anatolia, although there may also be some evidence for tin sources in Anatolia. It is not known, however, whether these were exploited in antiquity. It has also been suggested that alluvial tin in Anatolia could have been entirely depleted in antiquity so that there is now no modern evidence for these sources (Muhly 1973: 256-57). Yet such an argument *ex silentio* cannot be accepted, particularly when the extant texts only document the export of tin from Mesopotamia to Anatolia.

VI.3. Technology of Bronze Production

With respect to the technology involved in the production of metal objects in the Levant at this time, there is even less information available. The question of technology primarily centers around the production of bronze—that is, the alloying of copper and tin.[12] The manufacture of bronze, which has the advantage of allowing the use of a closed mold which can produce more complex and developed forms and of producing a harder metal at a lower melting point, was known in Mesopotamia, Anatolia, and Syria before the beginning of the MB I period in the Levant. While bronze was produced in Mesopotamia and Anatolia from at least the 3rd millennium B.C., bronze technology only seems to have been introduced into Syria at the beginning of the EB IV period (equivalent to the U.M. 1 period at Ugarit, Schaeffer 1949: 55).[13] The only region into which this technology was introduced at the beginning of MB I was therefore the southern Levant.

In considering the spread of bronze technology, especially into areas for which there is no contemporary textual evidence, the crucial factor is quantitative analyses of the composition of artifacts. Several such groups of artifacts have been analyzed and published, but it is still doubtful whether generalized conclusions can be drawn from this evidence. While some publications may describe a particular object as either bronze or copper (and, in such cases, the identification has been mentioned in the above listings of the relevant objects), these descriptions cannot be accepted as technical identifications unless some indication is given of how the conclusion was derived.

Six groups of objects have been analyzed:[14] (1) a group of metal objects from Ugarit and Byblos (specifically, the "Montet Jar") which are assigned to the U.M. 1 period; (2) a group of Middle Bronze Age objects from the tombs at Megiddo, most of which may be typologically assigned to the MB I period; (3) the analyses of a group of duckbill axes published by Oren (1971: 128-34); (4) analyses published by Moorey and Schweizer (1972: 190) of which only two analyses of duckbill axes are relevant here; (5) the "duckbill" axe from ᶜAin es-Samiyeh; and (6) the two axes purchased in Jerusalem and published by J. Birmingham (1977: 117-18).

Most of these objects have a significant tin content (*supra*, n. 13) and therefore presumably represent the deliberate alloying of copper and tin, sometimes also with other metals, such as lead and arsenic.[15] The analyses of all objects earlier than MB I show that only copper and possibly arsenical bronzes (Moorey and Schweizer 1972: 193) were used prior to MB I in the southern Levant (although see *supra*, n. 13), and therefore bronze makes its appearance at the beginning of MB I (although not entirely replacing copper and arsenical bronzes, Moorey and Schweizer 1972: 193).

It is generally assumed that bronze technology was introduced into the southern Levant from Syria (Oren 1971: 128-31), but whether the original source for Syrian bronze production was Anatolia or Mesopotamia is not clear. The use of tin-bronze in Mesopotamia is indicated as early as ca. 2750-2600 B.C. (Moorey and Schweizer 1972: 194) and in the Troad even earlier, by the late 4th millennium B.C. (Muhly 1976: 100). The clear indication that tin was used in Syria during the EB IV period shows that the tin trade between Mesopotamia and northern Syria documented in the Mari texts must also have existed during the late 3rd millennium and very early in the 2nd millennium B.C.. The fact that this trade is not mentioned in the Old Assyrian texts may show that even in the pre-Mari period the trade was operated from central or southern Mesopotamia. The lacunae in the textual material for the early 2nd millennium B.C. may thus be inferred, and one might hypothesize that texts from a site such as Ebla may eventually produce the relevant texts of this period.

The conclusions regarding the use of specific metal artifactual types may be summarized as follows:

(1) While the northern Levant shows considerable continuity, particularly in bronze production from the preceding period into MB I, the southern Levant underwent a change from primarily copper to bronze technology which was introduced from the region of Syria.

(2) There is a fair degree of uniformity both in the types of weapons which would be represented in the repertoire of the typical MB I warrior (Smith 1962: 19-21 and Oren 1971: 131-35 for discussion of MB I warrior graves) and in many of the specific forms of weapons throughout the Levant, northern Mesopotamia, and, to a lesser degree, Anatolia, Such a distribution may reflect the spread of ideas along the metals trade routes, as shown in the discussion of the sources of the copper and tin used in this period. Although there is some evidence from the Mari texts for the travel of artisans, it is not necessary to explain this uniformity through itinerant metalworkers; yet the mobility of people, including traders, diplomats, and perhaps ordinary citizens, along the trade routes of this period would have given ample opportunity for the diffusion of ideas and would account for the cosmopolitan atmosphere evident in the metal artifacts.

(3) As Dever (1976: 26, n. 51) has proposed, most of the categories of weapons continued from the EB IV period to MB I, but their specific types changed. In two cases, those of the daggers and the axes, an older type showing continuity from the 3rd millennium B.C. is replaced by a new type which becomes the typical form of the later Middle Bronze Age.

(4) The extent of originality of the Syrian metal industry may be somewhat exaggerated in current literature. While the Syrian coastal region did witness the modification of standard weapon types in MB I, the basic types were, in fact, of 3rd millennium Mesopotamian origin. Only the socketed spearhead may have developed along the Syrian coast in the U.M. 1 or 2 periods. Despite the large quantity of metal objects found at Ugarit and Byblos, the problem of whether tin and especially copper sources were utilized by the north

Syrian area remains an important unresolved element in our understanding of trade and cultural relationships in this period.

(5) On the other hand, the development of the notched chisel-axe and the rilled dagger in the southern Levant indicates the existence of a strong and inventive local school of metalworking in the southern Levant as well as perhaps the exploitation of the copper sources in the Wadi Arabah region. This would imply a more active and creative local metal industry than is usually credited to the southern Levant.[16]

(6) Changes in the routes by which tin reached Mesopotamia may reflect shifts in political alliances between the Mesopotamian kingdoms. In addition, the use of tin in Syria during the EB IV period shows that the tin route must have extended to the Syrian coast from at least that time, while the introduction of tin-bronze into the southern Levant would seem to show an extension of the trade and perhaps associated political relationships into the southern Levant in MB I.

This presents a more complex picture than is often presented of the cultural development of the southern Levant in the MB I—a region which is usually considered a backwater and a less developed provincial satellite of Syria. A shift in cultural development and creativity in the Levant at the beginning of MB I may relate to changing political relationships between the Levant and the kingdoms of Mesopotamia—shifting relationships which will be more fully considered in Chapters VIII and IX.

NOTES

[1]The typical Anatolian axe of this period is a flat type with projecting lugs at the attachment of the handle and blade, a flaring cutting edge and tapered butt. This type occurs throughout Anatolia, for example, at Tarsus (Goldman 1956: fig. 424:19), Alaca Hüyük (Koşay and Akok 1966: pl. 47:l60), Alişar (von der Osten 1937b: fig. 286:c1741, c1648, c1093), and Mersin (Garstang 1953: 211, fig. 129, Level IX). Another type of axe also appears at several sites. It is very simple, with the butt end smaller and blunt and the blade end curved. It occurs, for example, at Alişar Hüyük, Level II (von der Osten 1937b: 261, fig. 286:d2452, d2033, and d2974) and at Hama, Level H 5 (Fugmann 1958: fig. 109:3A175). The form of this axe, however, would seem so simple and logical that it could have evolved independently in several areas and should therefore not be used as an indication of contact.

[2]Deshayes (1960: 185-86) mentions an axe of this type from Hama but neither illustrates it nor gives a reference for it.

[3]Guy (1938: 164) described the process as follows: "A lump of metal was first beaten out and trimmed to shape, allowing for folds. Cuts were made at the junction of haft and head. A round rod with tapered end was then employed to keep the haft-hollow uniform while it was being formed. With this still in place the head was fashioned by folding and hammering, it being solid except for the tapered extension of the hollowed haft."

[4]Two additional examples, which probably belong to this category but are difficult to classify because they are not well preserved, were found at Aphek (Ory 1937: 120: No. 3, pl. 32:B.6, Grave 5) and Yabrud (Assaf 1967: pl. I:3, Tomb 4). In northern Mesopotamia, the dagger type is distinctive although perhaps related to the first type. It is also a flat blade, some examples having a broad central flange. The shoulders are well marked, and the rectangular tang has two or three rivets (here fig. 39:5, 6, 9-11):

Baghouz: du Mesnil du Buisson 1948: pl. LX (Z305, Z193, and Z95).

Chagar Bazar: Grave 167 (A522), Mallowan 1937a: fig. 13:4; Grave 143 (A521), Mallowan 1937a: fig. 13:5 (both of copper).

Tell et-Tin: Gautier 1895: fig. 9 (left).

Mersin (?): Garstang 1953: 233, fig. 149:22 (Level X).

[5]One last dagger type found in the Levant also needs to be discussed. Although Dever wrote that the dagger with slotted blade and curled tang occurs in the Levant "sporadically" (Dever 1976: 8), only one example seems to be known. This example, from Megiddo (Locus 5061, Loud 1948: pl. 178:5), is most closely related to another dagger type which was prevalent in northern Syria and southern Anatolia near the end of the 3rd millennium B.C. It is perhaps closest in shape to an example from Tell al-Judeideh in the ʿAmuq (Stronach 1957: 107-10, fig. 6, where this type is called a spearhead), but similar daggers also appear in the early 2nd millennium B.C. in Anatolia, as at Boğazköy (Schirmer 1969: 58-59, No. 246, pl. 46, from the Northwest Slope, later *kārum* period) and Alaca Hüyük (Koşay and Akok 1966: pl. 47:h194). This isolated example from the southern Levant would seem to be an anomaly, and one might therefore suggest that it is an import from either north Syria or Anatolia, or that it does not belong in the MB I period since it was not found in a datable context.

[6]Other types of metal objects which present potentially interesting problems, such as metal plaques and figurines depicting presumably divine pairs and triads, have been found at Ugarit (Schaeffer 1949: 73-106), Chagar Bazar (Mallowan 1937a: 100), Kültepe (T. Özgüç 1959: 105-7), and Acemhüyük (N. Özgüç 1966: 51-52). Although such objects have been excavated at sites throughout the Levant, these categories of artifacts would require an entirely new line of inquiry (including artistic and religious standards) which is not directly within the province of this study. See Negbi's discussion of both metal plaques and figurines of deities (Negbi 1976: 120-32).

[7]Note, for example, that it did not occur in Egypt, where, because of a hotter climate, it is likely that different garments

were worn than in the Levant and northern Mesopotamia (see Tufnell and Ward 1966: 220).

[8]Of the pins found in the Courtyard Cemetery at Tell el-ʿAjjul, the longest (Tufnell 1962: 16, fig. 5:1, Tomb 1409) is also considered the earliest (from Group 1), but the other pins from this site do not fall into a similar sequence.

[9]While this identification has generally been accepted (see, for example, Muhly 1973: 209), two points have recently been raised against it: first, the analysis of clay samples from texts supposedly from Alašiya in the Amarna archives does not seem to agree with that of the clay from the island of Cyprus (Artzy, Perlman, and Asaro 1976: 171-82); second, Merrillees has pointed out the lack of evidence for the exploitation of Cypriote copper mines in the early 2nd millennium B.C. and for the export of copper at that time (Merrillees 1974: 51, 63-64).

[10]Both Lewys translated *annaku* as lead and suggested that it was exported from Assur to Anatolia where it was desilvered or used in the desilvering of copper ores (J. Lewy 1958: 91-93, n. 11. H. Lewy 1971a: 724-25). Subsequently, however, several writers proposed, and it was generally accepted, that *annaku* should be translated as tin, primarily because it seemed more logical that tin should have been exported from Assur to Anatolia (Landsberger 1965: 285-93; Laessøe 1959b: 83-84, 94; Leemans 1968: 201-14; and Muhly 1973: 244).

The major difficulty with this translation, however, remained—that while the texts document the import of *annaku* into Mesopotamia from the region of Iran, no definitive sources of tin in this region had been proven (Muhly 1973: 260-61). This situation led Dayton to reopen the entire question of the sources of tin which were utilized in the eastern Mediterranean region during the 3rd and 2nd millennia B.C., and, as a corollary to this, he had to reject the translation of *annaku* as tin (Dayton 1971: 49-70; 1973: 123-25).

While it is difficult to summarize Dayton's theory (see Muhly and Wertime 1973: 111-22, for a critique), he seems to propose, since he was not able to cite any proven tin sources in the Caucasus or Iran and because the C-14 calibrations date European artifacts of the 3rd millennium B.C. earlier than previously thought, that the eastern Mediterranean region and Mesopotamia imported its tin from central Europe and may even have learned its tin-bronze technology there. In addition to the weaknesses of Dayton's argument—such as his late date for the beginning of tin-bronze technology in Anatolia and the lack of textual evidence for the importation of tin from Europe via Anatolia into Mesopotamia—two lines of reasoning may be applied to this controversy.

First is an analysis of the textual evidence for a translation of *annaku* as tin which proves several important facts concerning the nature of *annaku*. We know, for example, that it was used to make weapons, as shown by a text from Shemshara (Laessøe 1959b), and that it was used in combination with copper. A "Cappadocian" text (CCT 1, 37b, 13) reads: 4 MA.NA URUDU *u* 1/2 MA.NA AN.NA *nappāḫum ilqi*: "the smith received 4 minas of copper and half a mina of tin" (*CAD*, vol. I, pt. II, 128)—therefore in the ratio of 8:1 (copper:tin). Muhly quotes a series of texts from the pre-Sargonic, Ur III, Old Babylonian, and Neo-Assyrian periods which show that copper was mixed with *annaku* in a ratio of 6:1 or 7:1 to produce bronze (Muhly 1973: 243-44). The translation of *annaku* as tin is therefore supported. A possible translation of *annaku* as a tin-rich copper or bronze ingot would also fit this evidence, although then the proportions might seem less likely. Muhly and Wertime, however, have refuted this on the basis of the types of words used to describe *annaku* (Muhly and Wertime 1973: 116-17). Eaton and McKerrell (1976: 182) suggested that *annaku* could refer to either a tin-rich or arsenic-rich copper alloy.

[11]The central Asian tin sources are summarized by Crawford (1974: 242-44) as follows: (1) A tin source near the rich copper-bearing ores of the Caucasus in southern Ossetia is mentioned by Sulimirsky (which Crawford doubts because of lack of geologic substantiation). (2) A tin source near the site of Metsamor in the northwestern corner of the Ararat Plain (Mkrtiachan 1967: 76-78). Recent excavations at this site have reported evidence for the working of copper (from the nearby mines at Kagyzvan) and cassiterite, which may have come from alluvial deposits at the foot of Mt. Aragats. This site apparently had blast and smelting furnaces, sedimentation pits, and "workshops," while spectroscopic and chemical analyses of slag found there had high copper and tin contents. The dating of these structures, however, seems to be at the end of the 2nd millennium B.C., and so the possibility of the exploitation of these tin sources any earlier is somewhat doubtful, although there is earlier occupation at the site. (3) The use of arsenical copper is attested in Azerbaijan during the 3rd millennium B.C. and also the presence of tin-bronzes in the second half of the 3rd millennium B.C. and the first half of the 2nd millennium B.C., as shown by the analyses of a series of dagger blades from Uzuntepe, Eshektepe, and Stepanavan which had tin contents of 10.08% to 12.60% (Selimkhanov 1962: 69-75). Selimkhanov also refers to rich sources of arsenic in the Caucasus, although without specific documentation (Selimkhanov 1962: 76). (4) A source is mentioned in the region of Bukhara (Masson and Sariainidi 1972: 124-28, although without specific substantiation) which might have been used in the production of the bronze artifacts from Zaman-baba which may date to this period.

[12]Other alloys—primarily that of copper and arsenic to form arsenical bronze—although occurring in the Aegean region, were not a factor in Levantine metallurgy in this period (Branigan 1968: 47; although see *infra* for the existence of some leaded tin-bronzes). Arsenical bronzes occurred in Anatolia and Mesopotamia during the 3rd millennium B.C. but gave way to tin-bronzes by the beginning of the 2nd millennium B.C. or earlier (Muhly 1976: 89; Buchholz 1967: 215, 224; cf. Eaton and McKerrell 1976: 169-91). Some of the Levantine copper objects of the 4th to 3rd millennium B.C. may have been composed of arsenical bronze, as indicated by Moorey and Schweizer 1972: 192.

[13]See Buchholz (1967: 248-51) who lists objects from Ugarit of up to 10.99% tin from the EB II and III periods, as well as an EB nail fragment from Gezer with 7.73% tin (No. 358). Moorey and Schweizer (1972: 193) mention a dagger blade from Jericho Tomb G 83a of the EB IV period (1958.628) which had 11.9% tin and 15% tin in the two samples analyzed. Objects of EB IV date which they analyzed from the Carchemish region (Moorey and Schweizer 1972: 190) had the following tin contents: a dagger blade from Kara Kuzak (1913.24) had 15.5% Sn; a twisted torque from Amarna (1935.28) had 8.5% Sn. The definition of bronze production, however, is neither simple nor universally accepted. It is usually identified with the deliberate alloying of tin and copper, as opposed to the accidental alloying which may have preceded recognition of tin as a distinct metal. The method by which this technology was developed lies outside the scope of this study, since it predates the Middle

Bronze Age. The criterion used to determine whether an alloy was accidental or deliberate is usually the proportion of tin to copper. Although modern bronzes usually contain approximately 10% tin, the exact composition of ancient bronzes varied more; it has even been suggested that any amount over 1% tin may have represented deliberate alloying (Branigan 1968: 46). Sumerian and Old Babylonian texts seem to suggest that a copper:tin ratio of 6:1 or 7:1 was considered the ideal (Muhly 1973: 243-44; *supra*, n. 10).

[14]In addition, two daggers (one from Tell el-ᶜAjjul Tomb 1417 and the other bought in Lebanon and now in the Royal Ontario Museum in Toronto) contained, respectively, 1.0% and 0.01% tin and should therefore be considered as made of impure copper (Tufnell 1962: 17).

[15]The duckbill axes which were analyzed showed the following compositions: the axe from Beth-shan, Tomb 92, had 8.4% tin and 82.4% copper (Oren 1971: 128); two axes from the Ashmolean Museum (Oren 1971: 128) were analyzed as leaded tin-bronzes (No. 1927-1276: Cu—76.8%, Sn—9.1%, Pb—13.9%; No. 1913-428: Cu—85.1%, Sn—8.4%, Pb—6.3%; this axe was analyzed, Moorey and Schweizer 1972: 190, as having 7.5% Sn); a third axe from the Ashmolean Museum (No. 1927-1277) was a tin-bronze (Cu—90.8%, Sn—7.3%); the axe from Ashkelon had 82.79% copper and 7.23% tin (Oren 1971: 129). An "eye" axe in the Burrell Collection in Glasgow (no provenance) had 4.9% tin content (Moorey and Schweizer 1972: 190). The ᶜAin es-Samiyeh axe (Dever 1975a: 30-31) had 14.77% tin and 0.49% arsenic "for hardening." The purchased "duckbill" axe had a "medium percentage" of tin and a "strong trace" of arsenic (Birmingham 1977: 118). The chisel-axe also had a "medium percentage" of tin and lead (Birmingham 1977: 118). The amounts of tin reported from the Ugarit and Byblos objects (see Schaeffer 1945: 92-95; Schaeffer 1949: 64-66; Buchholz 1967: 248-51) range from 2.84% to 18.21%, with only one piece having a negligible amount. This shows that the alloying of copper and tin appeared in the northern Levant by the EB IV period. The tin content in a group of objects from Megiddo (Guy 1938: 161; Buchholz 1967: 254) varied from 1.19% to 10.78%, with one object having only .80% tin classified as copper.

[16]See, for example, the statement of Muhly that "there is very little evidence for any native Palestinian metal industry. . . . The major bronze industry of the Middle Bronze Age was of Syrian origin. . . ." (Muhly 1973: 216).

Chapter VII
Chronology

The preceding chapters have presented the material culture of the Levantine MB I period with its correlations to the contiguous regions of Mesopotamia and Anatolia and have also discussed the extant textual material. These should now permit the placement of Levantine MB I within the relative and absolute chronological schemes of western Asia in the early 2nd millennium B.C. The determination of the chronological position of a specific cultural assemblage relies on the sequential ordering of discrete groups of artifacts based on their stratigraphic position at a specific site. Once such a sequence is established at a single site, it may be compared with those at other sites within the same cultural region, so that a complete sequence is then built, and isolated groups or incomplete sequences may be fitted into such a scheme. It is essential, however, that such a typological sequence be derived initially from a stratigraphic sequence. This method was applied to the material culture of MB I in the Levant in Chapter III, where a ceramic typology, based on the stratified evidence primarily from Aphek and Megiddo, was used to place isolated groups of material into the MB I ceramic phases.

Once such a sequence is established for a limited region, it can be used to determine the chronological placement of an assemblage within a broader spectrum by two methods: first, its relative placement and the relation of this sequence to those of neighboring regions; and, second, its absolute placement in terms of calendar years. Absolute dating is usually determined either by textual sources which give this specific information or by the use of independent scientific dating methods, primarily radiocarbon dating, which can give absolute dates within the margins of error inherent in the method (see Callaway and Weinstein 1977: 3-13, for a discussion of the problems in the use of radiocarbon dates, especially as applied to Early Bronze Age Palestine, and Michael and Ralph 1970: 109-20, for a discussion of Egyptian radiocarbon dates of the Middle Kingdom).

The attempt to determine a chronology for the Levant during MB I must begin with the realization that there is little internal evidence for an absolute date. There are apparently no radiocarbon dates for the MB I period and no extant textual evidence from securely stratified contexts in the Levant itself. Alternatively, one could try to determine absolute dates for the end of EB IV and beginning of MB II, in which case one must also consider the possibility of a gap separating MB I either from EB IV or MB II. Finally, absolute dates may be determined by means of synchronisms with regions which have independently established absolute chronologies. This last method requires examination both of the absolute dating of these other regions and of the synchronisms or relative chronology by which the Levant is linked to these other regions.

Since there are no available C-14 determinations for Levantine MB I,[1] one can attempt to use determinations of the preceding EB IV period which should still give an approximate range for the beginning of MB I. A series of dates from Hama, Level J, gave approximately 2450-2350 B.C. (5730 half-life, uncorrected, Watson 1965: 90; Albright 1965b: 53, where dates given were determined with the 5568 half-life). A series from Selenkahiye, also in Syria, gave a MASCA corrected range of 2610-2190 B.C. for Phase 5 (Lawn 1974: 224-25) which is equivalent to the end of Hama, Stratum J (van Loon 1969: 276-77). Two more recent determinations give MASCA corrected dates for Selenkahiye of 2413 B.C. (P-1795) and 2340 B.C. (P-1796) (van Loon 1979: 111).[2] Finally, the EB IV occupation at Bab edh-Dhra^c in Transjordan has been dated ca. 2300 to 2200/2150 B.C. (Rast and Schaub 1978: 2).

While not much of direct relevance for Levantine MB I can be drawn from these C-14 dates, they seem to indicate a general upward trend for the dating of the EB IV period and the earlier part of the Middle Bronze Age, or at least the choice of dates near the upper end of previously accepted chronological ranges. In order for the earlier adjustment of Early Bronze Age dates to affect the date of the beginning of MB I, it is also necessary to posit that there is no chronological gap between the end of EB IV and the beginning of MB I, despite the apparently marked changes in material culture between the two periods.[3]

Lacking sufficient evidence from radiocarbon dating, one must turn to contiguous regions which have a system of absolute chronology determined on other grounds. The dating of much of the Egyptian Middle Kingdom, based primarily on textual evidence, seems to be relatively well established (Hayes 1971: 464-531), but three distinct systems of Mesopotamian chronology (the high, middle, and low, separated from each other by approximately 60 years) are still prevalent (for summaries of this disagreement concerning Mesopotamian chronology, see Hamlin 1971: 247-51; Albright 1938c: 18-21; 1940a: 25-30; 1942: 28-33; Smith 1940; 1945: 18-23; Rowton 1970: 231-33; and Sachs 1970: 19-22; Mellaart 1979: 6-18, has recently advocated adoption of the high chronology which would then correlate better with calibrated C-14 dates, but see Yakar 1979: 65-67). The effect of this controversy on the chronology of the Levant in MB I primarily concerns the dating of Hammurabi of Babylon and, through synchronisms provided by contemporary texts, also Šamši-Adad I and the Assyrian colonies in Anatolia.

Albright, who was the main proponent of the "low chronology" within the context of Levantine archaeology, established a sequence of Byblite rulers for the 19th to 18th centuries B.C. (1965a: 42; 1973: 13) and argued that a synchronism between Zimrilim and Neferhotep, an Egyptian pharaoh of Dynasty 13, via a Byblos ruler proved the lower chronology. Both these men were apparently in contact with Yantin-ᶜammu of Byblos, whom Albright identified with Yantin or Entin, known from an inscription in Royal Tomb IV (Albright 1964: 38-44; 1965b: 55). Since Neferhotep is dated to ca. 1740-1730 B.C., Albright assumed that the lower dating for Zimrilim of 1714-1696 B.C. was necessary and that Yantin-ᶜammu ruled from at least 1740-1715 B.C. Kitchen demonstrated, however, that Zimrilim's rule was only partially contemporary with that of Hammurabi and this synchronism is therefore not necessarily a proof of the lower chronology, since Zimrilim could have been either an older or a younger contemporary of Yantin-ᶜammu. The reign of the latter could have spanned the reigns of both Neferhotep and Zimrilim, regardless of whether the middle or low dating is used for Zimrilim (therefore Yantin-ᶜammu either ruled from 1760-1740 B.C. or from 1740-1715 B.C., Kitchen 1967: 39-51; Mazar 1968: 74, n. 20; Williams 1975: 872-74; see table 7).[4]

Another argument which is sometimes used to support the low chronology is that the references to Hazor and Laiš in the letters of Zimrilim must refer to the fortified stages of these sites, that is, the MB II. Assuming Albright's low dating of his MB IIB as beginning in the late 18th century, it was therefore concluded that Zimrilim must be placed later. This argument need not be accepted as valid if one moves the dating of both the MB I and the Mesopotamian sequences earlier, as long as the synchronism between Zimrilim and the MB II period is maintained (Mazar 1968: 83; Yadin 1972: 107-8).[5]

The "traditional" date for MB I has generally been put at approximately the late 19th or early 18th century to the end of the 18th century. This has been based primarily on the views of Kenyon (1973: 87: second half 19th century to the early 18th century) and of Albright (who varied his exact dating at different times; for his latest arguments based on other Egyptian-Mesopotamian synchronisms, see Albright 1973: 12-18), which, until recently, were also supported by Yadin (1972: 108) and Williams (1975: 2045, table 75), although for differing reasons. All of these theories suggesting a relatively low dating for MB I, apart from arguments involving the "low chronology" for Mesopotamian history, are based primarily on two assumptions: (1) that Royal Tombs I and II at Byblos represent the beginning of the MB I ceramic sequence, and (2) that these tombs and all of their contents are dated to ca. 1800-1790 B.C. (Albright 1965b: 54-55; 1966: 26-29). A more recent trend, however, has been to raise the dating of MB I[6] (Mazar 1968: 70-80; Dever 1976; Oren 1971: Epstein 1974: 39; Yadin 1978: 20-22; for a summary of the different proposed dates for this period, see table 8).

The major points discussed in the preceding chapters which are relevant to this question of the dating of the MB I period may be summarized as follows:

The MB I period encompasses multiple architectural phases at several sites, for example, three at Aphek, three or four at Megiddo, and five at Hama. These architectural phases correspond to at least three ceramic phases which have been defined

Table 7. Kings of Byblos and their Synchronisms (adapted from Kitchen 1967: 53-54).

Egyptian Pharaohs	Middle Chron.	Byblos Rulers	Low Chron.	Mesopotamian Rulers
	ca. 2050	Ib-dadi (? years)	ca. 2000	Amar-Suen (III Ur Dyn.)
Amenemhet III 1842-1797	ca. 1820-1795	Abishemu I (25 yrs.)	ca. 1820-1795	
Amenemhet IV 1798-1789	1795-1780	Yapi-shemu-abi (15/25)	1795-1770	
Sehetepibre II or III 1776-1770	1780-1765	Yakin (-ilu) (15/35)	1770-1735	
Neferhotep I 1741-1730	1765-1735	Yatin(-ᶜammu) (30/25)	1735-1710	Zimrilim (1778-1760 or 1714-1696)
	1735-1720	Ilima-yapi(?) (15)	1710-1695	
	1720-1700	Abishemu II (20)	1695-1675	
	1700-1690	Yapaᶜ-shemu-abi (10)	1675-1665	
	1690-1670	ᶜEgel/ᶜEgliya (20)	1665-1645	
	ca. 1730	Ḥasrurum, son of Rum, tribal chieftain, contemporary of Sihathor ca. 1730		

typologically. The MB I period may therefore span more than the approximate century allotted to it by such writers as Kenyon and Albright, and it might be possible to suggest a minimum of 150 years in the southern Levant and perhaps even more in the northern Levant, where MB I probably began earlier.

Most of the pottery of the Royal Tombs at Byblos fits typologically near the end of the MB I period, while some of it may be even later, as Dever has suggested, although the lack of firm identification of which pottery came from which tomb eliminates the necessity of dating all the tombs to the end of the MB II period (see Tufnell 1969: 6). While one may question the validity of the assumption that all of the pottery from Royal Tombs I and II should be dated by the cartouches of Amenemhet III and IV found in these tombs, the only date which the tombs could provide would be an approximate date for the *end* of the MB I period, even if this assumption is accepted.

The offering deposits cannot be accepted as a homogeneous group of material, and so they lose most of their usefulness as a dating criterion. The "Montet Jar," however, on the basis of its form, technique and decoration, must be placed near the beginning of the MB I period or between EB IV and MB I. Such a vessel therefore argues against a gap between EB IV and MB I, at least in Syria (*supra*, n. 3) and, if one were to date it ca. 2000 B.C. (Tufnell and Ward 1966: 227, although disputed by Porada 1966: 254), it would suggest a date of ca. 2000 B.C. for the transition from EB IV to MB I in Syria.

Table 8. Proposed Dates for the MB I Period.

Albright (1942; 1964; 1965a and b; 1966)			1800	MB IIA		1700 MB IIB
Kenyon (1973)			1850/1800	MB I		MB II
Mazar (1968)	2000	MB IIA	1800	MB IIB		
Oren (1971)		1900 MB I			1750	MB II
Yadin (1972)			1850/1800	MB IIA	1750	MB IIB
Dever (1973; 1976)	2000/1950	MB IIA	1800	MB IIB		
Epstein (1974)	1950	MB IIA	1800/1780 trans. MB IIA-B			
Williams (1975)			1800 MB IIA1-2		1725	MB IIB1-IIC
Yadin (1978)	1950/1900	MB IIA		1780/1750	MB IIB	

The duckbill axe type may be dated to ca. 1890 B.C. by its possible depiction in the tomb of the nomarch Khnumhotep III at Beni Hasan, dated to the 6th year of Senusert II or 1890 B.C., where it is shown being carried by a group of Asiatics (Oren 1971: 113 and fig. 3; Newberry 1893: 69, pls. XXX-XXXI).

The scarabs found at Megiddo and studied by Tufnell (1973: 69-82) also help to some extent in establishing an absolute date for MB I. It is necessary, however, to recall that such evidence can only be used to provide a *terminus post quem* since scarabs are often found in later contexts, presumably having been saved as heirlooms. The fact that scarabs with motifs which begin during the First Intermediate Period and Dynasty 12 were found in MB II tombs cannot therefore be used as a dating criterion for MB I (cf. Weinstein 1975: 10-11). Several tombs which have been assigned to MB I (table 5) contained scarabs: Tombs 5274, 5106, 5259, 5137, 5090, 3109, and 3143. All of these tombs belong to Phase 4, except T. 3143 (Phase 1/2), 3109 (Phase 3), and 5090 (Phase 3/4). All of these scarabs have motifs which begin during the First Intermediate Period or the early part of Dynasty 12, and they therefore do not help in establishing a more precise date for these tomb groups. Only one scarab, from Tomb 5259 (Loud 1948: pl. 149:52), depicts a scene of human or mythical figures which could place this scarab after the beginning of Dynasty 13 (Tufnell 1973: 78), that is, after 1786 B.C.[7] While this evidence of the scarabs does not negate the proposed scheme of synchronisms, it is also not of much help in attempting to refine it further.

The appearance of the painted store jars belonging to the "Syro-Cilician" painted style at the beginning of the MB I period in the Levant allows this to be correlated with the beginning of the Middle Bronze Age in southern Anatolia, especially, for example, at Tarsus and Mersin. The earliest occurrence of these jars in northern Mesopotamia can only be determined as having been prior to the time of Šamši-Adad I on the basis of their discovery in tombs at Chagar Bazar which were sealed by walls and floors on which were lying tablets of Šamši-Adad's time. The gap at Chagar Bazar between Levels 2/3 and 1 prevents any closer determination of the dating of this pottery.

The probable identification of these store jars as the vessels used in the extensive trade between northern Mesopotamia and the Levant (and its possible identity with the *karpatu*-vessels mentioned in the Mari texts) makes its absence at Alalakh striking. The sudden introduction of the "later" Ḫabur ware (the goblets with band-painted decoration) in Alalakh VII may show that this level corresponds to the opening of closer relations between Alalakh (and presumably Aleppo) and northern Mesopotamia, perhaps to be correlated approximately with the restoration of Zimrilim to the throne at Mari.

The pottery of the middle MB I phase shows the first elements of central Anatolian influence, primarily in the tendency to pinched and beaked rims and spouts on jugs or pitchers. While these elements cannot be well-placed in the Anatolian ceramic sequence (other than to indicate that these features typify the Assyrian Colony period in general), the appearance of quatrefoil and trefoil mugs (which are specifically dated to *kārum* Kaniš Ib) only at the end of MB I and even more so in MB II shows that the late MB I and MB II periods should correspond at least in part to the *kārum* Kaniš Ib period in Anatolia.

The occurrence of the Anatolian-influenced red-cross bowls in the middle phase of MB I also shows that this phase should not be far removed from the end of the Anatolian Early Bronze Age and beginning of the Middle Bronze Age since this is when these bowls were most popular there (although one must recall the possible continuity of this motif from EB III Palestine, *supra*, n. 3). The general beginning of Anatolian elements during the middle phase of MB I (as opposed to limited Syro-Cilician influence in the early phase) should perhaps also correspond to some increase in the extent of contact between Anatolia and the Levant at that time.

The introduction of the "Ḫabur" goblet or grain measure in the middle phase of MB I may also indicate a greater amount of trade with northern Mesopotamia in this period, if one accepts the hypothesis that these types of vessels were part of a standard measure system. The only well-dated example of this vessel type is the one with the inscription of Atta-Hušu (Sollberger 1968: 30-33), a contemporary of Sumu-abum, founder of the Old Babylonian dynasty, but since there are later (and probably earlier) examples, this does not help much in dating this phase of MB I.

The appearance of Cypriote White Painted Pendent Line and Cross Line style jugs at the very end of MB I seems to correlate with the Middle Cypriote II period, which may now be dated ca. 1800 B.C.

While some of these factors are largely pertinent only to the question of relative chronology, others pertain to the question of absolute chronology. In terms of a relative sequence, the interconnections with the neighboring regions of Egypt, Cyprus, Anatolia, and northern Mesopotamia allow correlations for the different phases of MB I as expressed in table 9. The absolute dates which are used in this chart are based on the "middle chronology" for the First Dynasty of Babylon. The use of these dates is, to some extent, necessitated by the synchronisms with Egypt and Cyprus, while the use of the "low chronology" would stretch MB I for nearly 250-300 years and compress MB II into a span of only 150 years—a solution which, at least for the southern Levant, seems unacceptable. The features outlined primarily in Chapters IV-VI would not allow a chronological gap between MB I in the Levant and the Mari periods of Šamši-Adad and Zimrilim, thus also requiring the use of the "middle chronology" (for a chart of the phasing of all Levantine sites previously discussed, see table 6; only the most significant are repeated here). Additional evidence for the absolute dating of MB I is mostly circumstantial and cumulative and is based on several of the points previously summarized. The date of 2000/1950 B.C. for the beginning of MB I in the northern Levant would allow for a later introduction of MB I culture in the southern Levant (*supra*, n. 3).

Several factors give indications for the dating of the end of the MB I period. First is the association of the change from Alalakh VIII (which is equivalent to the end of the MB I period on ceramic criteria) to Alalakh VII with the return of Zimrilim to Mari. This probably occurred between 1780 and 1775 B.C. Second, the scarab from T. 5259 at Megiddo and other scarabs from Jericho and Tell

Table 9. Chronology of MB I in the Levant.

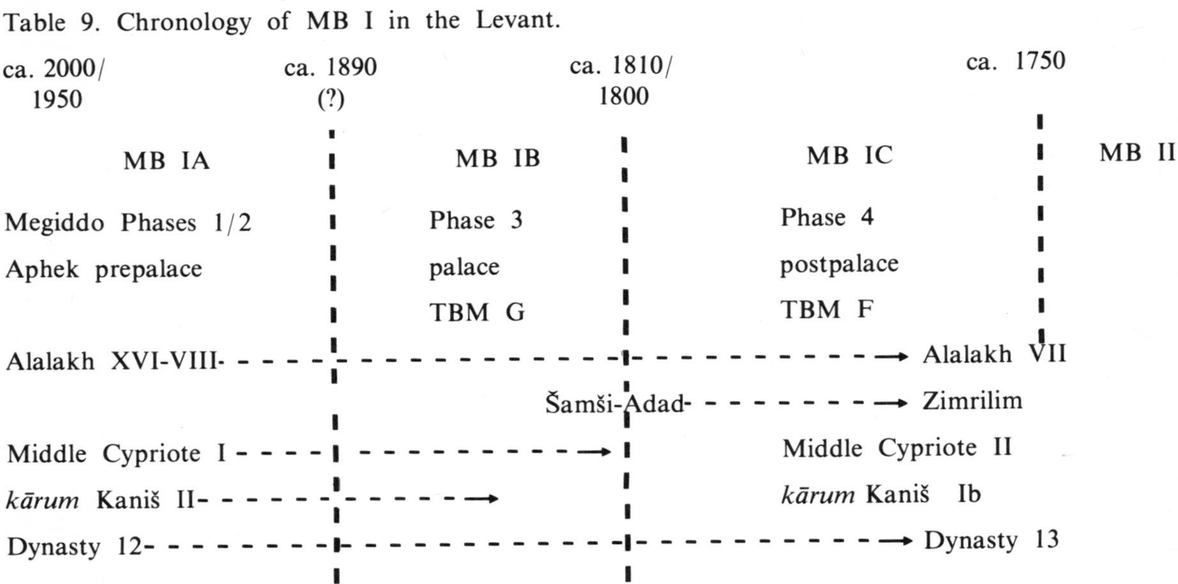

el-ᶜAjjul (Weinstein 1975: 10-11) may indicate some overlap of MB I with the Egyptian 13th Dynasty.

It is also possible to consider absolute dates for the early, middle, and late phases of MB I, which have previously been referred to and which may now be termed the "MB IA," "MB IB," and "MB IC" periods. The MB IC phase, which is associated with the introduction of Cypriote pottery into the Levant, could not begin any earlier than approximately 1810/1800 B.C. A date for the division between MB IA and MB IB is more difficult to estimate. The smaller quantity of MB IA material would seem to argue for a shorter duration, but the possible presence of two phases within MB IA at Megiddo cautions against underestimation of the duration of this period. A provisional date derived on more or less arbitrary grounds for the division between MB IA and MB IB may be suggested at ca. 1890 B.C.

This proposed dating of the MB I period and its ceramic phases in the Levant and their correlation with events in Mesopotamian history present the framework for a closer examination of the interaction between these regions during the first quarter of the 2nd millennium B.C. The next two chapters will attempt to examine some of the mechanisms which may have been involved in the cultural changes which occurred in the Levant during MB I, and the interaction between the trade system, the political relationships of the various kingdoms, and cultural developments in the Levant as shown in the textual and artifactual records. This chronological system allows the fitting together of these different factors and helps to demonstrate the interdependency of these regions during the beginning of the Middle Bronze Age.

NOTES

[1]Although there are no C-14 determinations for the Levant during MB I, there are some dates from Anatolia and Mesopotamia which are equivalent to MB I. Two samples of carbonized wood from Room 219 in the palace at Mari give uncorrected dates (based on the 5568 half-life) between 1870 and 1770 B.C. (Delibrias *et al.* 1971: 228) perhaps implying that the actual date may be even earlier, although one must still allow for the problems of interpretation of long-lived samples (Gif-722, Mari 4, Room 219, 3820 ± 120 B.P., 1870 B.C.; Gif-723, Mari 5, Room 219, 3720 ± 150 B.P., 1770 B.C.). A pair of dates from the Gedikli Hüyük Middle Bronze Age cremation cemetery are not as useful as they might be since there is no indication what phase of the Middle Bronze Age they represent (Vogel and Waterbolk 1972: 51, GrN-5580 and GrN-5581; dates of 3990 ± 40 B.P., 2040 B.C., and 3820 ± 40 B.P., 1870 B.C., respectively, based on the 5568 half-life, are given for "EB III-MBA"). A date from burnt

textiles from Alaca Hüyük Level 4 (the Assyrian Colony period) is 1794 B.C. (Stuckenrath and Ralph 1965: 191, P-824, 3744 ± 51 B.P., based on the 5568 half-life).

[2]The discovery of Egyptian vessel fragments with inscriptions of Chephren (Dynasty 4) and Pepi I (Dynasty 6) in Palace G of Tell Mardihk, Level IIB1 (Matthiae 1978: 540-43), has been used to establish an absolute date for the EB IV period at Tell Mardikh (probably equivalent to ʿAmuq Phases I and possibly J, and EB IIIb in the southern Levant). The uncertainty of stratigraphic correlations between Mardikh and other sites in the Levant and the likelihood that one or even both of these inscribed vessels may have been heirlooms make it difficult to apply this synchronism to the problem under consideration here. One may also note here the discovery of an Egyptian inscription on a scepter, possibly of a king of Dynasty 13, in the "Tomb of the Lord of the Goats" at Tell Mardikh. Both the reading of this inscription and the date of the tomb are too problematic to permit further use of this material in establishing an absolutely chronology (Matthiae 1980a: 16; 1980b: 17).

[3]Despite the fact that the position that there was no chronological gap between the end of EB IV and the beginning of MB I may seem contrary to a main thesis of this study (that is, the contrasts between these two periods), it is still possible to argue for such continuity. Continuity in certain metal and ceramic types may be used as illustrations. The strongest evidence comes from the duckbill axe and the simple dagger which continue from EB IV into MB I (the duckbill axe clearly being a development of the EB IV "eye" axe); it is only *during* MB I that these types are replaced by their typical Middle Bronze Age successors, the chisel-axe and the veined dagger. In ceramics, also, possible continuity has been sought in the single-spouted lamps (Amiran 1969: pls. 22:16, 24:14, 59:2-4) and perhaps the red-cross motif (*supra*, pp. 68-69), although these are perhaps tenuous. The situation in Syria, however, is clearer. At many sites, including Qatna, Tell ʿAs, Dnebi, Byblos, Khan Sheikhoun, Osmaniye, and Selimiye (Schaeffer 1948: figs. 99-106; *supra*, pp. 46-47), ceramic forms which are clearly transitional in decoration and manufacture have been identified, with perhaps the most notable example being the "Montet Jar." While this does not specifically influence the question of an absolute date, it is not possible to posit a gap in Syria, and this would probably support the hypothesis that MB I began earlier in Syria. The fact that some sites in the southern Levant were unoccupied briefly during the first phase of MB I and that EB IV culture continued longer at some sites, concurrent with the beginning of MB I culture, should also be considered. The distinction between use of terms like "EB IV" and "MB I" as cultural indicators and as chronological markers must here be maintained. It is also likely that MB I culture continued longer in Syria than in the southern Levant; this may perhaps explain the relatively weak indications for MB II culture in the north.

[4]A more recent advocacy of the "low chronology" is presented by Williams (1975: 1161-66). He asserts that the "low chronology" is proven by a synchronism between Alalakh VII and Egypt which places the end of Alalakh VII in the mid-16th century B.C. Since the destruction of Alalakh VII is generally equated with a campaign of Ḫattušiliš I and this must have preceded the destruction of Babylon by Ḫattušiliš's grandson, Muršiliš, Williams puts the end of the First Dynasty of Babylon at approximately 1530 B.C. Since use of a "higher chronology" for the dates of Hammurabi would give too long a time span (ca. 200 years) for the number of kings attested between Hammurabi of Aleppo and the destruction of the Alalakh VII archives, Williams then concludes that the "low chronology" must be used for the entire Old Babylonian period. Regardless of whether one might find fault with Williams's latter argument (for example, he equates Hammurabi of Babylon with Hammurabi of Aleppo chronologically, while it is generally assumed that the latter was a younger contemporary of the former, so that some reduction in the excessively long span of 200 years might be warranted), a careful perusal of his discussion of Alalakh reveals that he does not fully explain this synchronism between Alalakh VII and mid-16th century Egypt. Without this, it is difficult to evaluate Williams's argument. For a recent treatment of the sequence of rulers at Alalakh during Level VII and the conclusion that the "middle chronology" should be used for dating the destruction of Alalakh VII, see Naʾaman 1976: 129-43; 1979: 103-13.

[5]Even as a guide for relative chronology, the equation of Hazor MB II with the reign of Zimrilim can be questioned when one takes into consideration the relatively small area of the mound which was excavated and/or the possibility that the extensive MB II building projects may have eradicated architectural remains of the MB I period. The assumption that the Mari letters could only refer to a walled city is also problematic, since even a relatively small city (as viewed with the hindsight of knowing what the MB II city looked like) may have had external contacts. Yadin (1978: 21), in writing that it is very difficult to accept "this supposition [*i.e.*, that the Mari texts refer to MB I Hazor], since the tell proper is not different in size and importance from the other tells," forgets that one Mari text (*supra*, p. 11; *ARMT* VI, 23) is broken and probably mentioned at least one other site in the southern Levant. Yadin himself seems to have shifted from his earlier position of a preference for a relatively low date (1972: 107-8) to a higher date (1978: 20-22): ". . . there is practical unanimity that the main part of the period [the MB I] falls within the limits of the 12th Dynasty (ca. 1990-1780 B.C.E.). . . . the beginning of the phase should be dated to ca. 1950-1900 B.C.E. . . ." Although this dating is similar to the one proposed here (see table 9), it seems necessary to reiterate that, in view of the problems inherent in the nature of the evidence, it does not seem possible to use either the Execration Texts or the Egyptian statuettes found in Palestine (see Chapter II.3) in attempting to date the MB I period in the Levant.

[6]This trend parallels similar trends, especially in Minoan and Cypriote archaeology, to raise comparable dates. This is probably prompted to some extent at least by the need to calibrate previously accepted C-14 dates, which results in earlier dates. In the Levant this trend is even more relevantly obvious in the tendency to date EB IV earlier so that the end of EB IV is now considered to fall ca. 2000-1950 B.C. in most recent opinions. For a summary of proposed dates for EB IV, see Dever 1973: 38, fig. 1. This makes the suggestion by Williams to *begin* the Middle Bronze Age in the southern Levant at 1700 B.C. even more devastating in that he must, by corollary, propose either a lengthening of EB IV for as long as 600 years (see Dever's dates for beginning EB IV at 2300 B.C.) or a depopulation of the southern Levant for approximately 200-300 years, that is 2000/1900-1700 B.C. (Williams 1975: 2045, table 75—note that the Middle Bronze Age begins in the southern Levant in what he terms the "MB IIB1").

[7]Tufnell describes the scene depicted on this scarab as "perhaps a moment of myth or history in miniature" (Tufnell

1973: 78). The value of Tufnell's study for dating purposes is limited by her fitting of the scarab evidence into the sequences of tomb groups established for Jericho and Megiddo by Kenyon and Müller, rather than attempting to date the scarabs on independent grounds and then using them to test the stratigraphic sequences. Tufnell's placement of this scarab from Tomb 5259 early in Dynasty 13 is actually based on Kenyon's assignment of the tomb pottery to her MB IIB group (that is, relatively early in her MB II period). The argument that this scarab gives an early Dynasty 13 date for the tomb group would therefore be circular, since both assignments are ultimately based on ceramic analyses. Tufnell does, however, cite parallels for the Tomb 5259 scarab which lead her to conclude that it might be relatively early in date (Tufnell 1973: 78, n. 48)—which is independently corroborated by her conclusion that size can be used as a criterion for dating. Another scarab from Tomb 5090 (Loud 1948: pl. 149:5; Tufnell 1973: 71, No. 38) has an unusual motif which is paralleled by a plaque with the royal name of Senusert II (Tufnell 1973: 76). If this parallel can be used as a dating criterion, it would place the transition between Phases 3 and 4 after ca. 1890 B.C. This conclusion, however, could have been derived independently and still allows for much latitude. This discussion merely highlights the difficulties of attempting to use such evidence in formulating an absolute chronology.

Chapter VIII
Settlement and Urbanism

The patterns of settlement and the growth of urbanism in the Levant during MB I may be considered as a summation of several cultural subsystems, including economy, technology, environment, and political, social, and cognitive institutions. Preceding chapters of this work have attempted to elucidate certain aspects of these various subsystems. The development of ceramic and bronze technologies, which has implications for craft specialization, has been considered, while certain elements of trade and economy were studied from the textual sources. Information concerning the political and social institutions is very limited and is primarily based on study of the architectural and settlement organization of particular sites; as such, this information will be presented in the course of this chapter.

Since these various subsystems can combine to influence the development of a settlement pattern system, it is to be expected that a study of the latter can help to illuminate several aspects of the former. Trigger (1968: 70-71) wrote that "if we conceive of the settlement pattern as an outcome of the adjustments a society makes to a series of determinants that vary both in importance and in the kinds of demands they make on the society, we must consider not merely the range of factors affecting settlement patterns but also the manner in which different factors interact with another to influence a particular pattern. Factors vary in importance according to both the local situation and the temporal relationship that they have to one another." Information concerning the various subsystems and the organization of a society may be deduced from a study of the settlement pattern system, although it is not valid to adopt a deterministic view that a pattern or response can result from only one particular set of circumstances. Yet the study of the variables and the response (the settlement pattern) in the context of the Levant in MB I should permit a greater understanding of the cultural development of this region.

Settlement patterns may be studied in various ways and on different levels. Trigger has specifically defined three such "levels": "The first and most basic of these is the individual building or structure; the second, the manner in which these structures are arranged within single communities; and the third, the manner in which communities are distributed over the landscape" (Trigger 1968: 55). The variables previously mentioned as contributing to the formation of the settlement pattern system act in different ways on these three levels, and so different types of information may also be derived from the studies of these levels of settlement.

The first of these levels—the organization of the individual buildings or structures—can not be adequately studied for the MB I period because of an almost complete lack of publication of any relevant information from site excavations. Although site maps sometimes include plans of individual buildings, descriptions of the internal structure or architecture of such buildings are usually not given and, with the dubious exception of the Megiddo locus system (and the most recent excavations at Aphek), the pottery and other objects are generally not grouped by architectural findspots. This makes it impossible to draw conclusions concerning the functions of different areas within a structure on the basis of the relationship between societal and architectural organization. While certain buildings which have been assigned specific functions by individual site excavators will be discussed in terms of their role in the organization of an entire site, the organization within such structures will not be studied.

The second level, concerning the organization and relationship of buildings within a single site, involves the identification of private or domestic units and of public structures which would indicate some communal function and organization in the construction of the structures. Such public structures may include buildings which have been labelled "palaces" by the excavator, other types of communal buildings, and walls or fortifications surrounding a site. These are often interpreted by the archaeologist as implying some unified government control which sponsored such projects, while the presence of a city wall has been specifically correlated with a degree of urbanism.

The third level involves the distribution of sites over a particular landscape. It is also possible to subdivide this into two types of relationships: those which have been termed "man-land" or, in other words, relationships determined by the topography and geomorphology of a region; and those which are termed "man-man" or those which are based on the interactions between the humans resident at the different sites (see Johnson 1972: 769). Both of these types of relationships involve an ecological approach to the study of settlement patterns, but they also encompass other aspects of various subsystems (particularly the economy). It is this aspect about which there is the most information available and which will receive the fullest treatment in this chapter in an attempt to determine the relationship between the settlement pattern and the cultural development of this region.

The types of evidence available for this study are somewhat limited and therefore restrict its extent. As indicated above, the quality of individual excavations and the methods of publication limit our consideration of the first two levels of settlement pattern analysis. The tendency of excavators to determine the functions of particular structures and to apply subjective nomenclature—such as palace, fortress, and fortification—without substantive reasons based on the stratigraphic association of objects with architecture has tended to confuse the attempt to determine the functions of individual structures. Furthermore, the fact that most MB I sites were rebuilt on a larger scale in MB II (with Aphek as a possible exception) and that some of these were also important Iron Age sites (such as Megiddo, Hazor, and Dan) has restricted the modern horizontal clearance of structures of the MB I period, while at some sites the MB I structures were probably destroyed and rebuilt even in antiquity. Thus, at many of the most prominent sites,[1] only soundings or relatively restricted trenches have been dug to reveal the strata of the MB I period—a factor which is not conducive to an effective study of the sructures and organization of an entire site. Finally, there has been a lack of intensive site surveys (or at least of their publication) in the entire region of the Levant. Such surveys would be most helpful in the attempt to reconstruct the overall settlement pattern and the relationships between sites and betwen sites and topography.

Some information, although again with various limitations, can be culled from the textual sources. The Mari texts are not much help, since in this case it would not seem valid to extrapolate from the MB II period to the MB I period because of the differences in urban development between the two periods. The two group of Egyptian Execration Texts (see Chapter II.3), despite disagreements over their precise dating which limit their usefulness, are often placed in a period corresponding to Levantine MB I. Differences in the number of towns and the number of rulers mentioned in the earlier and later groups of texts have been used by some archaeologists to demonstrate corresponding changes in the settlement pattern systems which it is assumed are reflected in the texts (see, as examples, Albright 1941a: 18-19; Posener 1971: 548-56; 1940: 40; Albright 1928: 224-50; and Weinstein 1975: 13; *supra*, pp. 18-19).[2]

VIII.1. Intrasite Organization

To review the evidence for intrasite settlement organization, one may begin with a survey of domestic or private architecture—that is, structures for which some communal purpose has not been suggested. The stratum plans for the Megiddo publication reveal several such structures, primarily in Area BB, but, because of the difficulties involved in sorting out the MB I phases at Megiddo, it would seem premature to attempt a finer subdivision of the architectural phases than has already been presented in Chapter III.1. Some generalizations, however, can be drawn concerning structures at this site attributable to the MB I period.

Such structures often consist of several rooms which seem to be undifferentiated by categories of finds, and no evidence concerning functions of the rooms is given in the publication (Loud 1948: 84-87). It is therefore difficult to determine whether such structures are individual buildings composed of several rooms or whether they represent several buildings or houses sharing common walls (for this suggestion, see Eitan 1972: 23). Loud does mention that such a "block" or group of rooms in Stratum XIIIA was bounded by streets on three sides.

Although Loud (1948: 84-87) recognized that the earliest city wall of Stratum XIII (see *infra*) was not directly connected to the domestic structures, Eitan still inferred, from the organization of "blocks," some element of overall city planning in relation to the city wall (Eitan 1972: 23). The entire question of the existence of MB I city walls will, however, be discussed separately.

Albright excavated domestic structures at Tell Beit Mirsim in Strata G and F. The organization of these structures may also have been that of blocks of houses bounded by streets. One well-preserved house of Stratum G had a long hall with a row of bases presumably for pillars and three smaller rooms on the side. The house was constructed with a stone substructure and mudbrick superstructure; the thickness of the walls led Albright to suggest that there had been a second story, and he compared this building to that of a palace, apparently on the basis of its size (Albright 1938a: 20-23, pl. 56).

Although Albright admitted some difficulty in the isolation of a distinct Stratum F, which he considered to be thin and fragmentary (Albright 1933: 68), he was able to distinguish a change in the orientation of the structures between the two strata (Albright 1938a: 17). Eitan attributes this change to the construction of the city wall in Stratum F (which Albright had attributed to Stratum G) and interprets this as a preconceived overall city plan which began with the wall and then proceeded inward with blocks of houses in radially arranged trapezoids and with streets running parallel and radially to the wall (Eitan 1972: 23). While this interpretation depends on the acceptance of an MB I date for the wall, Tell Beit Mirsim may present an early Middle Bronze Age example of city-planning in the Levant.

At several sites, similar examples of the relationship between an outer city wall and houses may be present; unfortunately, all of these possible examples may be questioned. This arrangement includes the practice of constructing rooms or houses along the interior of a city wall in a casemate system (Parr 1968: 26-27). This type of plan is indicated for the site of Tel Poleg, although only a relatively small area has been excavated (Gophna 1973: fig. 2); for Megiddo, where the stratigraphic association of the walls and the rooms is open to serious question (especially in Area CC, discussed by Parr, where the remains are very fragmentary; Loud 1948: fig. 407); and for Byblos, where the structures are labelled Middle Bronze Age but again the excavation procedure precludes any firm statement concerning date and association.

The excavations and published plans of Hama reveal more information. Level H, which included five architectural phases, had mostly small houses in the central part of the mound; some houses were freestanding with three or four rooms, while others were in groups of attached structures (Fugmann 1958: figs. 107, 108, 116, 119, 123, 126, and 131). These houses, which were constructed in the usual technique of rows of mudbricks placed on a foundation of stones, were separated by streets. Both pottery and stone vessels were found in the rooms as well as other features such as ovens, sets of stairs, cisterns, wells, and conduits. The question of whether there was an overall plan for the site is difficult to answer because the excavated area is still small in comparison with the total size of the mound. The walls of the houses do not seem oriented in a single direction; some of the walls are curved, while the straight ones meet each other at varying angles. The different phases also show changes in orientation of the structures, so it would be unlikely that there was a uniform plan throughout the site or that the buildings were all placed in relationship to a major structure, such as a city wall.

Several sites of the MB I period also revealed walls and floors which are usually interpreted as belonging to domestic structures. Such sites include Aphek (the prepalace and postpalace phases), Tell Simiriyan, Pella, Tell el-Far^cah (N.), Alalakh, and the ^cAmuq sites, but these sites have either not been excavated over a sufficiently large area or the architectural remains were too scanty to allow any conclusions concerning their planning or functions.

Several types of communal or public structures have been identified at various MB I sites.[3] Structures which have been termed "palaces" have been identified at Tell Beit Mirsim and Aphek. The palace at Aphek, which Kochavi (1975: 25-27, fig. 6) assigned to the middle phase of MB I, has been described as a monumental building complex with three phases. The first phase was represented by a series of flat stones, interpreted as pillar bases and therefore assumed to indicate a roofed hall. The second phase included pebbled flooring and walls, while in the third phase the palace had two large courtyards paved with lime plaster and thick walls. Although some burials were found in the palace area, there were few objects in the palace which could be used to interpret the function of rooms within the complex. The differences in orientation, organization, and careful treatment of the architecture of this building permit the conclusion that this structure was not private; the interpretation of its exact function, however, must await the publication of later excavation seasons.

At the site of Alalakh a series of major buildings of Levels XII-VIII were excavated in the "stratification pit." Because of the nature of these buildings, which were "of quite unusual importance," and their placement beneath the Level VII palace of Iarimlim, Woolley concluded that these buildings also represented a successive series of palaces which, although continuously rebuilt on different plans, maintained the same orientation and position on a traditional site (Woolley 1955: 20). The Level XII palace with three phases consisted of a main room with subsidiary rooms and a colonnaded hall or porch (Woolley 1955: figs. 8 and 10). Private buildings, however, continued to exist in the area during the first two phases of this level. The change in the character of the buildings in this area (which prior to Level XII had been only private) led Woolley to suggest that "Level XII . . . seems to witness to a social change at Alalakh almost amounting to a revolution" (Woolley 1955: 17), while the continued isolation of the main building seemed to indicate the growing importance of the ruling family. Woolley wrote: "The rebuilding of the palace in an embellished form [in XIIA] must imply the greater prosperity of the ruling family, and a natural corollary of it was the sweeping away of the private buildings which had encroached upon and marred the dignity of its predecessor" (Woolley 1955: 23). The later palaces of Levels XI-VIII (Woolley 1955: 25-32, figs. 12, 14, and 17) continued as progressively more impressive structures, although those of Levels IX and VIII were not well preserved due to the construction of the Level VII palace.

It is difficult to evaluate Woolley's hypotheses concerning social change as reflected in the increasing size and isolation of this monumental building since no other domestic areas of these levels were excavated for the purpose of comparison. If, however, Woolley's interpretation is valid, then Alalakh provides us with an interesting illustration of the gradual growth of social stratification and concentration of power—features which may be correlated with an increase in urban characteristics—as reflected in the architectural development of a settlement.

Few structures from MB I sites have been identified as temples. There has been considerable disagreement concerning the dating of the temples (Loci 5269, 5192, and 4040) at Megiddo with their circular altar (Locus 4017) which, according to Loud, were originally constructed in Stratum XV (Loud 1948: 78-84). Although Loud concluded that the temples went out of use before the MB I period, he assumed that the area above Altar 4017 continued as a sacred area in Strata XIV and XIII. Kenyon concluded that only Temple 4040 continued through MB I and at least the beginning of MB II (Kenyon 1969: 40-42, thus changing her previous opinion according to which all the temples went out of use during her Intermediate EB-MB period, Kenyon 1958: 57*-58*). Dunayevsky and Kempinski (1973: 162-72), however, in their subsequent soundings, found a wall of Temple 4040 which was cut by the construction of Temples 5269 and 5192 and thus concluded that Temple 4040 was the earliest and that neither the temples nor Altar 4017 continued into the Middle Bronze Age.

Only one structure from the MB I sites of the southern Levant remains identified as a temple. The temple precinct at Nahariya, which continued with some rebuilding through the Middle Bronze Age and perhaps into the Late Bronze Age, seems to be isolated from any settlement.[4] Ben-Dor (1950: 4-16) excavated a long rectangular building with various additions and several phases represented by accumulated occupational debris. Dothan also defined several building phases—the earliest with a smaller square plan—and a roughly circular stone *bamah* to the south which may not belong to the earliest level of the first phase (Dothan 1956: 15-17). The identification of this building as a temple seems reasonable, since it is based on the finds which included figurines of silver, bronze, and clay, silver plaques of female deities, miniature vessels (or "model pots"), incense burners, and multiple vessels as well as more usual pottery types such as jars, juglets, bowls, and cooking vessels.

The implications of this single sacred precinct for the religious institutions of the MB I period are interesting. One could postulate that such a precinct may have been used by people from several settlements (or even by nomadic groups, as Ben-Dor suggested), although it is difficult to imagine that people from the entire southern Levant travelled to Nahariya. One could, however, propose other possibilities: that an insufficient area of other sites has been excavated to allow the conclusion that there were no temples at other sites; that the temples were not always sufficiently distinct from other building types to permit their easy identification at the excavated sites; or even that "religion" did not play such a dominant role in MB I life that temples at many individual sites were required. The solution to this problem remains one of the enigmas of MB I and must await further excavation at other sites of this period.

A series of superposed structures which Woolley termed temples was excavated at Alalakh, corresponding approximately to Levels XVI-VIII (Woolley 1955: 33-59). As with the palaces, these temples were located beneath the Level VII temple, thus emphasizing the continuity of tradition attached to a particular location, although the plans and rituals of the individual buildings were changed from level to level. The temples of Levels XVI-XIII maintained the same basic plans and apparently certain ritual aspects (as exemplified by the persistence of the block of brickwork which Woolley called a "mastaba"). Both the Level XII and XI temples underwent major alterations in their layout, which presumably reflect corresponding changes in the associated ritual. Woolley compared the Level XII plan to the typical Syrian or indigenous building type (an outer chamber and an inner one for the "Holy of Holies") and the Level XI temple to the "Breitraum" plan which is more typical of Mesopotamia. The later temples of Levels X-VIII were not well preserved because of rebuilding and the construction of the Level VII temple. The presence of this series of temples is another indication of the particular continuity and complexity of the settlement at Alalakh throughout this period.

Several temples have been identified at Tell Mardikh (Matthiae 1977: 129-38; 1975a: 342-46). Two of these, Temples N and B 1 (Matthiae 1977: figs. 27 and 28), are simple rectangular structures with the entrance on a short side (although Temple N is not completely preserved). A third, Temple D, has three rooms oriented on the long axis and a niche in the back wall in line with the entrance to these rooms (Matthiae 1975b: 50-51, plan 3). Along with the temples from Tell Mardikh,[5] the Alalakh evidence may imply that such structures remain to be found at other major sites of this period (such as Aphek), although there may have been major differences in the degree of urbanism and specialization between the sites of the northern and southern Levant, especially in the earlier phases of MB I. Matthiae furthermore suggests that the temples at Mardikh and Alalakh, along with Building II at Byblos, represent the development of a specific architectural style in Syria during the early part of the 2nd millennium B.C. (Matthiae 1975b: 56-61).

Another type of public structure was identified at Hama where Stratum H is characterized by the presence of cylindrical silos (Fugmann 1958: 89-93). Many fragments of vessels of typical Stratum H type were found in the silos, while the masonry corresponded to that of the Stratum H buildings. Fugmann concluded that the silos were a public establishment for some purpose such as the accumulation of provisions for the army. While proof for the involvement of an army is perhaps tenuous, it would seem possible that the silos were used for public storage of food supplies, as evidenced by the broken pottery vessels which could have been used as containers and/or for removing the supplies when wanted. It is of course also possible to suggest that the broken pottery indicates a reuse of these silos for trash.

The last type of public construction to be considered is that of walls and fortifications. The function of these walls, sometimes found in conjunction with plastered ramparts or glacis (although mostly of MB II date), has recently been extensively discussed in terms of their possible military purpose (Parr 1968: 18-45; Wright 1968: 1-17). The conclusion was that walls with ramparts initially served to consolidate the mound on which the settlement was located from weathering which could have undermined structures built along the edge of the mound. Such constructions first appeared in the Levant during the 3rd millennium B.C. and were then used whenever deemed necessary, depending apparently on the height and particular nature of the individual mounds. Any attempt to date these structures *a priori* on the assumption that they occurred only within a limited time span cannot be accepted.

The first site at which a city wall was assigned to the MB I period was Tell Beit Mirsim, Stratum G, with a reconstruction of that wall occurring in Stratum F (Albright 1938a: 17-20, pl. 49). Albright's interpretation was subsequently modified by Eitan who proposed that the city wall actually belonged only to Stratum F because of the general alignment of the Stratum G houses near the city wall (Eitan 1972: 21-22). Kenyon had also reached this conclusion based on the orientation of the houses (Kenyon 1973: 81), and she also assigned the wall to Stratum F.

Meanwhile, the excavations at Megiddo had revealed a sizeable city wall with gateway entrances and offset buttresses which was assigned to Stratum XIII in Area AA (Loud 1948: fig. 378) and Stratum XIIIA in Area BB (Loud 1948: fig. 397) and which thus provided a second example of an impressive MB I city wall. Kenyon, however, showed that the city wall in Area BB truncates and therefore must postdate the building immediately to the west of it (Kenyon 1969: 44) which seems to be associated with MB I tombs (Tombs 2151, 3146, and 3109). A more definite date for the wall is provided by the tomb found in Wall 3182 which contained a cooking bowl and distinctive button-based piriform juglet (Loud 1948: pls. 30:3 and 24:16), thus probably dating the wall to MB II. The question of the wall in Area AA is more difficult to resolve because it is not sealed by any ceramic material. Kenyon, in her concluding table, placed Phase AA (equivalent to her Phase K in Area BB) of Area AA (that is, Stratum XIII) in the beginning of MB II, and she concluded that, because the gate was associated with tombs of early MB II and one (Tomb 4112) of MB I, "the date of the gate and the associated structures inside is therefore probably early in MB II, or possibly MB I" (Kenyon 1969: 55).[6]

Recently, however, Yadin has redated both the Tell Beit Mirsim and the Megiddo city walls. Using a larger scale plan than the one published by Albright and the elevation markings for the house and wall foundations, Yadin argued that the Tell Beit Mirsim city wall also cuts off walls of Stratum F and that the elevations indicated for the house walls and for the foundation of the city wall show that the city wall is later and must therefore belong to Stratum E (Yadin 1973: 23-25). While his observations may seem valid, although not provable, from the plan which he reproduced,[7] Yadin then uses this to argue that there were no city walls in the MB I period at all (see also his earlier statement on this subject, Yadin 1972: 201-6). His conclusion that the city wall of Megiddo Stratum XIII, Area AA, must predate the entire Middle Bronze Age seems to be based on the fact that it is associated with a tomb of MB I date as well as with tombs of MB II date. Since he assumes that there cannot be walls during MB I, he concludes, by default, that the gate must be Early Bronze Age (see Yadin 1973: 25, n. 15; *supra*, n. 6). Yet, in fact, Kenyon is correct that the wall can be either MB I or early MB II in date since the structures of the Stratum XIII plan are only sealed by MB II material and there is no information concerning the date of material sealed in turn by the Stratum XIII structures, since the excavations did not continue beneath the Stratum XIII structures in this area. If one were to accept Parr's statement that the similarity in construction technique of the walls in BB and AA proves that they are contemporary, then one would have to conclude that the entire system dates to MB II (probably early MB II) rather than MB I, since the wall in Area BB seems to be MB II. Such a conclusion is, however, not necessarily definitive and so the possibility remains that the wall and gate of Stratum XIII in Area AA can be either MB I or early MB II in date.

The recent excavations at Aphek thus provide our clearest evidence for a city wall of MB I date. In Area B, Stratum V, an earlier MB I wall was excavated (Kochavi 1975: 30-33, figs. 10 and 12—Wall C 250). It was 2.5-3 m. wide and had two rows of stones in courses with rubble fill and an upper structure of sun-dried bricks with mortar. A buttress (No. 346) was also found of similar construction and bound to the outer face of the wall.[8] In Stratum B IV a new city wall (C 261, Kochavi 1975: figs. 8, 9, 11, and 12) was constructed, and its foundation laid in segments so as to compensate more effectively for the steep gradient of the mound. All of the pottery associated with the wall was clearly of MB I date, and Kochavi also suggested that the two walls found by Ory may correspond to these two phases of the MB I wall (Kochavi 1975: 39).[9]

Another MB I wall was identified at the site of Tel Poleg. MB I pottery, probably belonging to the middle and late phases, was found in rooms adjacent to the city wall in Area A. In a different area of the mound the excavations revealed more of this "fortress," including the west wall, a large tower, a gateway, and a glacis composed of crushed kurkar (Gophna 1973: wall with rooms: fig. 2; south and west walls: figs. 3-4, Level IV = MB I). The only illustrated pottery comes from the rooms, although the pottery from the southern and western walls is described as being similar. One may therefore assume that the fortifications were constructed in the middle phase of MB I, although the sketchy publication of the pottery and stratigraphy of this site still allows for many questions concerning the date of these structures (Yadin 1978: 5-6). The fortifications seem to have been constructed on bedrock, and their primary purpose may have been to provide protection along what was apparently an important road through the Plain of Sharon, as the excavator has suggested (Gophna 1964: 111). Another city wall has been found at the site of Tel Zeror and assigned to MB I, although its minimal publication precludes any further discussion.

Recent excavations at the site of Akko (Dothan and Raban 1980: 35-39) have led to the redating of the fortification system, including a *terre pisée* rampart and a city gate, to the MB I period. The discovery of MB I sherds not only in the construction fill but also on the floor of the gate guardroom led the excavators to believe that all three phases of construction of the "Sea Gate" belong in MB I. They conclude: "Against those scholars who argue that rampart fortifications (or, for that matter, any other fortifications) in Canaan were not built in the MB IIA period, this Sea Gate of Akko casts its weight in the affirmative" (Dothan and Raban 1980: 39).

It has thus been demonstrated that, while the dating of the walls at Tell Beit Mirsim and Megiddo is still uncertain, the MB I walls at Aphek and probably Tel Poleg and Akko show that such walls did exist in MB I and therefore such walls cannot be automatically assigned to the MB II period. The varying dates of the city walls and associated features and the analysis of the wall at Aphek tend to support the interpretation of these walls primarily as constructional features to consolidate the mound itself rather than exclusively as defensive military fortifications, although such a function is not entirely excluded, as at Tel Poleg. While a military function is thus not inherently implied, the presence of a city wall still represents a communal effort perhaps carried out under strong and unified leadership; this would have implications for our interpretation of the social structure of these MB I settlements. It is therefore possible to infer that these MB I settlements had a greater degree of political unity and leadership than had existed in the preceding EB IV period and that a sufficient level of social stratification and craft specialization existed to support such an organization.

In summary, the evidence of the second level of settlement analysis—that of individual structures at sites—would seem to indicate a certain amount of specialization in the types of buildings and centralization in power and labor needed to construct the more monumental buildings. The sites of the northern Levant, such as Alalakh, Tell Mardikh, Hama (although lacking a "palace" or "temple" structure), and presumably Byblos, present a striking contrast to those of the southern Levant. The northern sites seem to emphasize continuity in an urban tradition not shown at the southern sites and also a greater degree of centralization and specialization from the beginning of the MB I period. These features developed at the southern sites during the MB I period, but do not seem dominant until the MB II period when walls, temples, and other major complexes appear at many sites. Some of this contrast may be partially a result of the extent of excavations at the southern sites, but this is not the complete explanation. The successive appearance of the palace and walls at Aphek, the fortress at Tel Poleg and possibly one at Tel Zeror, the gate and rampart at Akko, and the walls of Tell Beit Mirsim and Megiddo show a progressive development toward a specialization and centralization of authority and a corresponding concentration of what may be termed urbanism through the MB I period, which, by early MB II, becomes comparable to the development and urbanism of the northern Levant.

VIII.2. Intersite Organization.

It is now possible to turn to the third level of settlement analysis, which conerns the distribution of sites over the landscape. It is in this last area of study of settlement patterns that principles from the discipline of geography have been applied to the interpretation of archaeological data.[10] The extent to, and manner in which, the principles of locational geography can be applied to prehistoric archaeology are, however, dependent on the type and development of the economy. The degree of interaction between the settlement pattern and the economic system may be used by the archaeologist to analyze determinants and to describe the development of both these systems.

One of the most useful principles is the "law of minimum effort," which was first presented by Lösch. "This concept suggests that natural events reach their goal by the shortest route. . . . However, we may argue . . . that the actual paths are likely to diverge from the optimum paths (in distance terms) for a wide range of rational and irrational reasons" (Haggett 1966: 32-33). Writing about an industrial society, Haggett takes this concept to refer primarily to a minimization of transport effort in terms of such problems as the procurement of natural resources or the shipment of goods to a market. This can also be applied to various types of preindustrial societies which utilized trade and market systems, as the textual evidence shows was the case in the Levant during MB I.

The application of this principle of minimization of effort will vary, however, when considering preindustrial societies which are not dependent on extensive and complex trade systems. In such a case, the most efficient distribution of settlements will not necessarily reflect maximum efficiency for intersite transport. Blouet pointed out the potential relevance of other types of economic factors: "The term efficient distribution [can be used] . . . in relation to agricultural exploitation of the land. Historically, settlement distributions have frequently had to respond to other major pressures besides the need to promote the efficient utilization of land. For instance, the need to provide for the defence of inhabitants has been a common addition, or, sometimes, paramount pressure. In short, the word efficient means efficient in relation to some function or group of functions" (Blouet 1972: 3-4).

In a primarily subsistence economy in which most of the settlements are self-sufficient, one would not expect to find in operation the principle of least effort in transport for marketing purposes; rather, the notions of optimal land for agricultural uses, the location of natural resources and a fresh water supply, and other factors, such as defense, would probably play a primary role. Johnson has called this latter approach a basically "man-land" relationship which "has been highly productive, especially when dealing with cultural systems of relatively low complexity. . . . when dealing with systems of greater complexity, man-man relationships take on increasing importance in the determination of the spatial distribution of activity loci and thus of settlement" (Johnson 1972: 769).

In contrast to "man-land" relationships, "man-man" relationships require the arrangement of settlements so as to minimize transport effort between settlements. According to Christaller's Central Place Theory, such an arrangement would optimally conform to that of hexagonal patterns with a hierarchy of settlements in which certain services, because of specialization, are only available at certain levels of the hierarchy. A detailed analysis of the settlement pattern of the Levant in MB I, utilizing the concepts of settlement hierarchy and catchment area models, is not possible since such an analysis requires intensive survey data which is not now available. The only relevant data[11] come from the Sharon Valley Archaeological Survey reported by Kochavi (1975: 38). This survey located three small MB I settlements contemporary with the major period of settlement at Aphek and within a radius of 7 km. east and south of Aphek. Kochavi concluded "that these sites represent the usual relationship of a city state and her dependent villages"—in other words, a hierarchy with Aphek functioning as a "central place" surrounded by sites of a lower order. It is likely that other major sites, such as Megiddo, played a similar role with dependent sites, but this hypothesis must await further survey data for substantiation.

The most important factor in the analysis of the distribution of MB I sites is that almost every site (for which excavations have proceeded beneath the MB I levels) is located on a mound which had previously been inhabited during the Early Bronze Age (with the apparent exception of Tel Poleg and some sites consisting solely of isolated tomb groups). Only some of these sites were settled during EB IV, while the others show a break between the EB III and the MB I periods. The analysis of settlement distribution must therefore involve two different considerations: (1) the selection of the original site within a particular region, a choice which was evidently made in the Early Bronze Age or even earlier; and (2) the selection of which sites were to be resettled in the different phases of the Middle Bronze Age, a choice made at that time and one which should be commensurate with the economic system prevalent during the Middle Bronze Age. This dichotomy in the two facets of the site selection process may be interpreted as representing the different economic systems implicit in the "man-land" and "man-man" relationships previously discussed. This study will attempt to elucidate the integration of these relationships and different economic systems and how this influenced MB I settlement distribution.

Studies of habitats and soil types in the southern Levant have shown that the major tells in their beginning stages during the Neolithic and Early Bronze Age tended to be located along river valleys, near adequate fresh water supplies, and within close proximity to at least two different soil types, although the sites themselves were located on soils with good drainage (Webley 1972: 169-71). Although sites tended to be located in more uniform habitats in the Middle Bronze Age and progressively into the Iron Age, this was probably caused by the fact that the ecologically advantageous positions were already occupied and so new settlements had to utilize less desirable locations. However, in MB I and even early MB II, the site selection process must have approximated that of the Early Bronze Age since it is primarily Early Bronze Age sites (although not necessarily all Early Bronze Age sites) which were reinhabited in the Middle Bronze Age. This tendency to duplicate the previous selection process was reinforced by the advantageous habitats of the Early Bronze Age sites as well as by the *a priori* existence of a raised mound (the result of earlier habitation) which would have given added security, if defense was also a consideration.

The similarity of the site selection process in the Early Bronze Age and in MB I renders this site description applicable to MB I sites as well: "The Proto-Urban and Early Bronze Age situations are closely tied to river valleys, and tell formation established the norm for future land use. In most cases the pattern is similar: all are sited on freely drained land with at least two soil types nearby and, in some cases, three or more. One of the series is usually a heavy wet deposit. A typical site occupies a valley flank on colluvial-alluvial or Terra Rossa materials, with alluvium and vertisols on the valley floor; towards the mountains are light limestone soils" (Webley 1972: 171-72).

Although a macroscopic view of the settlement pattern in Palestine from the Early Bronze Age through the Early Iron Age would lead to the conclusion that continuing population expansion led to the selection of less advantageous site locations (Webley 1972: 172), such a continuous, uninterrupted progression was not the case. The disruptions of the EB IV period in Palestine led to a very different type of settlement distribution in that period, with a concentration of sites in the northern Negev and in Transjordan (see Dever 1973: fig. 2) —a pattern which contrasts markedly with that of the preceding and subsequent distributions. The situation during MB I, especially during its early and middle phases, was one of fewer settled sites. The crucial question in the settlement distribution of the MB I period was therefore not where to locate a settlement—since this was largely predetermined by the Early Bronze Age site selection process—but which of the already existing tell formations should be selected for either continued occupation or resettlement. It is this selection process which reveals the influence of the "man-man" relationships and its integration with the MB I economic system.

A topographic map of the Levant (fig. 1; see also Chapter I.2 for a discussion of Levantine topography) shows that there are two north-south corridors through the Levant which are separated by a mountain range reaching an elevation of over 3000 m. in Syria and Lebanon (comprising the Lebanon and Amanus ranges) and over 500 m. in Palestine. These mountainous zones are cut by three main passes which allow east-west communications: the Orontes River Valley and the ᶜAmuq; the Litani River Valley which turns north and almost meets the southern continuation of the Orontes River system; and the Jezreel Valley which joins the Haifa and Beth-shan regions. Other smaller river and wadi valleys partially cut this central mountain area but have not served as effective means of east-west communications.

The eastern corridor follows the Great Rift Valley and includes the Orontes River Valley, the Biqaᶜ, the Litani River Valley, the Huleh and Galilee lakes, the Jordan River Valley, and the Dead Sea, with the last three features being below sea level. The western corridor consists primarily of the Mediterranean coastal plain which in the north and especially in Lebanon is very narrow, but broadens in the south to form the Plain of Sharon and the Philistine Plain. Although it is difficult to reconstruct the climate and land conditions of the Levant in antiquity, this coastal plain plus the Biqaᶜ Valley system and the Jezreel were probably well-suited for even primitive agricultural methods. The hill country in Palestine, which is less rugged than that in the north and which today supports typical Mediterranean olive and vine agriculture, was probably also capable of cultivation in antiquity. The availability of fresh water would have made the area of the Huleh suitable for settlement (see Webley 1972: 170-71, for discussion of Hazor's advantageous ecological habitat), while settlement in the Jordan River Valley was restricted to such sites as Jericho, where springs provided a reliable water supply.

A study of figs. 4 and 6-8 (see also table 6), representing occupied sites in the three phases of MB I, would seem to show a concentration of sites in specific regions: the coastal plain throughout the

Levant, the hill country of the southern Levant, the Orontes River system in the north and, only in the last phase of the MB I, the area of the Huleh. Both the ᶜAmuq Plain and the Jezreel Valley, as would be expected, contained two of the larger and most continuously inhabited sites—Alalakh and Megiddo, while Braidwood's survey has shown that several smaller sites in the ᶜAmuq were settled as well. The convergence of accessible transportation and communication routes and desirable agricultural land would seem to imply that a combination of both these factors would have determined the resulting settlement pattern. This is apparently accurate in that the placement of a settlement in either an inaccessible location or in a disadvantageous habitat did not occur as long as more desirable sites were still available.

It is nevertheless important to note that these two determinants did not necessarily operate equally. The striking feature of these maps is the lack of settlements in regions of high agricultural desirability, such as the Biqaᶜ and Litani valleys and the Huleh area during MB IA and MB IB. While this situation may be partially the result of the accidents of discovery and less intensive archaeological effort in these areas, this pattern may also be the result of other factors. It is therefore suggested that land usage patterns should not be considered as the major determinant in the choice of regions for settlement, but rather that communications and accessibility were the more dominant characteristics.

As has previously been discussed, continuity of settlement in the northern Levant contrasts with a discontinuity in the southern Levant. The same sites are occupied in the northern Levant throughout MB I (and were previously occupied in EB IV as well) with, as far as is now apparent, no new sites founded during the MB I period. The situation in the south is quite different. All of the settlements (that is, excluding tomb groups without associated occupational debris) of the MB IA phase are located either along the Mediterranean coastal plain or within easy reach of the coastal plain. This pattern persists in the MB IB phase, with only the possible addition of Shechem.[12] Only in MB IC are the Huleh and Galilee regions inhabited, implying perhaps that the most desirable sites in the coastal regions were already occupied. The sites in the Huleh and Galilee were still relatively accessible from the coast, however, and it is probable that their primary communication links were with the coast via the Jezreel Valley or the valleys just west of Akko and Nahariya[13] rather than to the north via the Biqaᶜ where the relative lack of MB I settlements would seem to preclude the extension of a communications network in this direction.[14]

Why were these transportation networks crucial to the development of MB I settlements and what purpose did they serve? In reviewing the salient characteristics of the MB I culture, two technological advances were defined: the introduction of bronze production into the southern Levant and the more proficient and sophisticated use of the fast pottery wheel which was responsible for the distinctive style of MB I ceramics. Both of these innovations were introduced from Mesopotamia and/or Anatolia through Syria into the southern Levant. Other characteristics such as urban agglomeration and social stratification had a continuous tradition in northern Syria and can be seen to have developed in the southern Levant during the course of MB I. The distribution of specific pottery styles, such as the variations of the Syro-Cilician painted ware and particularly the band-painted store jars, also shows a concentration along these routes, and particularly the coastal route between the northern and southern Levant.

The reason for the selection of this coastal route is more difficult to explain. The distribution of MB I sites in the southern Levant would perhaps seem to have been determined by the location of political centers in the northern Levant, particularly the centers which traded most extensively with both Anatolia and Mesopotamia. The trade routes linking both Mesopotamia and Anatolia with the Levant (as discussed in Chapters II.1 and 2) involved the sites of Aleppo, Ebla (Tell Mardikh), Ugarit, and Byblos. Alalakh, which was located within the state of Aleppo (Iamḫad), presumably would have shared in the trade of the capital city, although it was not specifically mentioned in the texts. Qatna, which was mentioned in the texts, only represented an offshoot of the main trade which passed first through Aleppo and then split towards Qatna or towards Ugarit. Only under unusual political conditions was the direct route between Qatna and Mari across the desert used (see Chapter II.2). Some direct connection between Qatna and the Tel Dan-Hazor region is indicated in the Mari texts of Zimrilim, so the relationship of settlement distribution and communication routes may have changed by that time.

The major sites of Ugarit and Byblos, which were emporia for trade and communications, would therefore have served as central places for the exchange of information from both Mesopotamia, as indicated by the texts, and Anatolia. Although the routes utilized in this exchange would have logically tended to follow a coastal orientation, this by no means implies that the MB I culture is a "coastal phenomenon" (as suggested by Kenyon 1966: 53-55; Williams 1975: 843), with a localized point of development specifically in the region of Byblos. On the contrary, in the northern Levant MB I culture developed at such inland sites as Alalakh, Hama, Qatna, the smaller sites in the Hama region, and presumably at Ebla, just as it developed at Ugarit and Byblos. These inland Syrian sites played a crucial role in the link between Mesopotamia and the Levant—a link which is tied to the dissemination of characteristic MB I elements and which was probably involved in the tin trade from Mesopotamia to the Levant. In the southern Levant, however, MB I culture does seem in its earlier phases to have belonged to the coastal plain region and only began to spread inland as an apparent population pressure forced the selection of favorable site locations in perhaps less favorable regions. It was only in MB II, however, that such sites as Jericho, located in even less favorable positions, were reoccupied.

The settlement distribution of the MB I period in the Levant was therefore determined by a combination of political and economic relationships—both of which were closely related to the trade network. Such relationships, which may fit Johnson's appellation of "man-man" relationships because they depend on the interaction between the residents of different sites (although these may also be determined by such features as topography), seem to have been a major determinant in the macroscopic settlement pattern of the MB I period. The importance of these economic determinants can also be interpreted as a function of the complexity of the economic system which existed in the Levant. It is evident that these settlements, rather than being economically self-sufficient, in fact depended on their relationships with other settlements and in this atmosphere of interdependence and exchange, as witnessed by the artifactual and textual evidence, the MB I culture was able to develop.

The analysis of the structures at individual sites revealed that a certain level of political unity, specialization of functions and social stratification, which had perhaps been disrupted during EB IV, redeveloped in the southern Levant during the course of MB I. These attributes, however, seem to have been part of a continuous urban development in the northern Levant, and it is possible to propose that their appearance in the southern Levant was at least partially the result of stimulus from the north. The evidence of the distribution of sites shows that, while ecological diversity and advantageous habitats led to the settlement of sites previously occupied during the Early Bronze Age, an economic system in which transportation efficiency was a major consideration was the primary determinant of the overall site distribution pattern. This consideration of efficiency for purposes of trade and communication not only permitted the exchange of such commodities as copper and tin between the northern and southern Levant, but also the exchange of technology (bronze production and the use of the fast wheel), fashion (ceramic styles), and religious and social institutions (such as social stratification and political unification). This permitted the development and culmination of the fully urban phase of the MB II period.

NOTES

[1]Some of the earlier excavated sites, such as Ugarit and Byblos, were not excavated and published in such a way as to permit the clear assignment of specific structures to a specific time period. This precludes all but the most general comments concerning their degree of urban development. This is especially unfortunate in the case of Byblos, where there seems to have been a fairly large Middle Bronze Age town complex.

[2]Posener suggested that the larger number of towns but smaller number of rulers mentioned in the later texts (as compared to that in the earlier texts) should reflect a growth of population or consolidation of the population into urbanized settlements with greater political unity showing a shift from a tribal or clan organization to a unified "city-state" structure. However, the lack of precision in the dating of the texts precludes any attempt to assign these developments, if such an interpretation were accepted, specifically to the EB IV-MB I period. Yet it can be shown that the MB I period does correspond to a phase of consolidation of sites with an initial decrease in the number of sites but with a corresponding increase in the size and complexity of these sites. The increase in the known number of such consolidated settlements at the end of MB I and into MB II may therefore reflect (although perhaps fortuitously, particularly since there are no comprehensive systematic surveys) such an interpretation of the Execration Texts.

[3]The excavations at Tell Mardikh have revealed a palace, fortifications and several temples of the early 2nd millennium B.C. The fortifications included four city gates, one of which, the southwest, is described as monumental, with an outer entrance, a courtyard with towers and bastions, and an inner complex

with two entryways. The lower city consisted of private houses with several temples, while the acropolis had a palace with a large courtyard, rooms, and a "cloister." According to the excavators, Ebla seems to have had a complex, unified city plan during this period. While such structures can be assigned to the early 2nd millennium and therefore Tell Mardikh added to our roster of MB I walled sites, the scanty published evidence of the architecture and especially its precise dating preclude further comment or analysis of this site. However, Tell Mardikh represents, as do such other Syrian sites as Hama, Byblos, and Ugarit, a continuous urban development from the Early Bronze Age through MB I without the disruption caused in the southern Levant during EB IV (Matthiae 1971: 57-60; 1975a: 342-46; 1977: 116-40; 1980b: 1-11). For a discussion of the architecture of Ebla during the late 3rd millennium—the EB III and EB IV periods—see Matthiae 1976: 94-100.

[4]It is possible that there is a nearby settlement which is now covered by the modern city of Nahariya, or, as Ben-Dor suggested, that the temple served a settlement at Achzib. He also suggests, however, that the temple may have been used by nomadic tribes in the region (Ben-Dor 1950: 40-41). This apparent lack of religious structures at MB I sites in the southern Levant is significant for the question of continuity of religious or ethnic groups from MB I through the Late Bronze Age, as has been proposed (see, for example, Kenyon 1966: 1-5 and 64). This also contrasts with the appearance in MB II and the Late Bronze Age of sacred precincts or "high places" at individual sites such as Gezer, Shechem, Hazor, and Byblos (the temples at the latter site probably dating to MB II).

[5]Several temples have also of course been excavated at Byblos. Their dating to a particular phase of the Middle Bronze Age is, however, somewhat problematic and so they have been omitted from this discussion. The "Syrian Temple" or Building II was compared by Matthiae (1975b: 53, plan 4) to the Alalakh Level XII temple and Temple D at Tell Mardikh and also considered contemporary with them.

[6]Yadin, however, apparently misunderstood Kenyon's conclusion and wrote: "Kenyon has shown that the gate is earlier than Tomb 4112, which clearly belongs to MBIIA. . . . The stratigraphic situation tends to indicate that the gate is earlier than the MBII period. In this case it could only belong to the EB system" (Yadin 1973: 25, n. 15; cf. Yadin 1978: 4). Tomb 4112 cannot be used to date the wall precisely (as Kenyon recognized) since there is no direct stratigraphic relationship between them; the tomb does not actually cut into or overlie the wall, so that one cannot conclude that the wall must be earlier than the tomb. A. Harif (1978: 27-29) disagrees with Kenyon's suggestion that the city wall in Area BB truncates and is therefore later than the building to the west. He prefers to date both this building and the city wall to MB I and finds parallels for the Megiddo wall in Egyptian constructions dated to Dynasty 12. J. Kaplan (1975: 3-17) accepted several Middle Bronze fortification systems of different types as MB I, including those at Tel Poleg and Yavneh-Yam, but he did not specifically date the Megiddo wall.

[7]Some of Yadin's arguments, however, are difficult to accept using either his or Albright's published plan. Incongruencies in the elevations of house walls which Albright assigned to the same stratum would cast doubt on Albright's stratigraphy, but this does not relate to the question of the city wall. Furthermore, as the example of Megiddo teaches us, one cannot use absolute elevations to interpret plans without a topographic map of the site. Only one wall mentioned by Yadin (his W3) seems to be cut by the city wall, if in fact it (W3) originally extended beyond the intersection with W2 (compare Yadin's plan with that of Albright 1938a: pl. 49). Walls W4, W9, and W10, which Yadin claims to have been cut by the city wall, either meet or stop short of the F wall which runs along the interior of the city wall east of the buttress, while W11, in fact, stops considerably short of the city wall. The situation of W12, W13, and W14 also seems not to be directly related to the city wall. The question involves the function of the wall which is flush to the city wall just east of the buttress. It should have been constructed after the city wall, but would this wall and others also flush to the city wall but further east have coexisted with the city wall, thus integrating the city wall into the domestic architecture of the site (as has previously been implied may have been the case at Tel Poleg and Megiddo)? One could also question the assignment of these "flush" walls to Stratum F. The confusion of the published plan and perhaps also some confusion in the clear separation of strata (which Albright himself admitted) do not permit a definitive answer regarding the dating of the Tell Beit Mirsim wall.

[8]Kochavi's comments (1975: 31) on the wall and buttress serve to elucidate the function of these constructions: "The small size of the buttress and its position on the steep slope suggests its purpose was more constructional than strategic. Attempts made in antiquity to stabilize the upper earth layers of the steep slope were detected in the form of plastered surfaces on top of the slope and radiating out from the base of the buttress. All measures taken were to no avail. . . ."

[9]Yadin (1978: 10-20) has seriously questioned Kochavi's dating of these walls to the MB I period. Although one may agree with Yadin that such an important site should be published in greater detail and that it is difficult to relate exactly the palace of Area A with the city wall of Area B, it does not seem necessary to doubt the assignment of this wall to MB I. As even Yadin stated (1978: 19-20), it does not seem possible to draw further conclusions concerning the Aphek wall without future excavation and more detailed publication. However, on the basis of the pottery from Stratum B Vd and c (Beck 1975: 78-79, fig. 15), it may be possible to suggest that this phase of the wall belongs to the middle phase of MB I rather than to the early phase (note the handled store jar of T. 350, Beck 1975: fig. 15:9 and Kochavi 1975: 31-32, and the pinched-rim jugs, also of T. 350, Beck 1975: fig. 15:6-8). Such a later dating for the wall might bring the existence of the wall into better alignment with the existence of the palace in Area A (see Yadin 1978: 12).

[10]The application of locational geography to archaeology was spurred by Haggett's work (1966) which presented a synthesis of these concepts which were, however, presented primarily within a framework of an industrial economy. The relevance of the use of locational geography in archaeology has been summarized by Renfrew who wrote: "The aims of geography and prehistory are closely and increasingly linked: both are essentially concerned with the distribution of human population, the use of natural resources, and the inter-relations of man with his environment" (Renfrew 1969: 74).

[11]Survey work in the region of Akko and Achzib is also providing interesting results concerning the placement of Middle Bronze Age towns particularly in relation to factors of defense and transportation; these results have only been briefly mentioned in publication (Prausnitz 1975b: 202-10).

[12]Since the Shechem MB I pottery is not published, no definitive conclusion concerning the initial phase of Middle Bronze Age occupation at the site can yet be drawn.

[13]This conclusion is also supported by the results of the survey in the Akko region which has identified several Middle Bronze Age sites along the approaches to the hill country, including Tel ʿAvdon and Tel Bira. The pottery from this survey is not published and so finer chronological assessment cannot be given (Prausnitz 1975b: 202).

[14]The so-called "Dream Book route," discussed in Chapter II.2, implies a direct Aleppo-Qatna-Hazor link, but, since this source dates from the later Middle Babylonian period, its testimony cannot be accepted as negating the archaeological evidence of the MB I period itself.

Chapter IX
Conclusion

It has been emphasized continuously throughout this study that the MB I period represents a major break (especially in the southern Levant) in terms of technology, trade, and social and political institutions from the preceding period. At the same time, the MB I period is the formative phase of the succeeding, fully urban MB II and MB III periods. The remaining question to be considered is that of how or why this transformation, which ushered in the Middle Bronze Age of the Levant, occurred. Two hypotheses which attempt to explain this change have been current in the literature and will be discussed here before a different analysis of the evidence is presented.

Both of these hypotheses involve a variation of the "Amorite hypothesis," which has also been used to explain the introduction of the EB IV culture into the southern Levant as a result of the advent of nomadic groups from Syria or western Mesopotamia who should be identified with the *amurru* (MAR.TU) of late 3rd millennium Mesopotamian texts.[1] Dever, on the basis of the similarities in the material culture of the southern Levant to that of Syria and Mesopotamia and the textual evidence (the Mari and Execration texts) which may be interpreted as supporting the movements of West Semitic peoples into Palestine, has attributed the appearance of the MB I culture to a second Amorite incursion. It is expedient to quote at length Dever's presentation of this theory so as to facilitate our later analysis of this view:

> The sudden appearance of a material culture as mature and sophisticated as that of Palestine in the MB IIA period demands explanation. This culture cannot have simply developed out of the local MB I culture which preceded it, for as we have seen the break between the two periods is one of the most abrupt and complete in the entire cultural sequence of the country. The *Vorlage* of MB IIA has been sought to the north since Albright's pioneering studies in the early 1930s demonstrated beyond doubt the links of the pottery of Tell Beit Mirsim G-F with that of sites in Syria and northern Mesopotamia. . . . the "Amorite" expansion in the early second millennium B.C. . . . brought large-scale incursions of West Semitic peoples from the aforementioned areas into Palestine . . . (Dever 1976: 9-10).
>
> Today the "Amorite" background of the MB IIA period is so widely accepted that the detailed ceramic comparisons we have offered only strengthen the consensus. One of the few objections offered to this view is the difficulty of explaining the nearly complete cultural break between MB I and MB IIA if *both* are to be attributed, as seems likely, to the "Amorites." But . . . while the earlier waves of "Amorites" came from a seminomadic culture on the fringes of Syria, by the late twentieth and nineteenth centuries B.C. succeeding waves of "Amorites" coming from the same areas had meanwhile been partly or wholly urbanized (Dever 1976: 15).

This scenario presupposes or implies several factors: (1) that the "Amorites," a group of people who are discerned in the Mesopotamian texts, can be assigned to one or more specific artifact assemblages whose appearance in the southern Levant is the result of population movements; (2) that there were significant population movements at the beginning of both the EB IV and the MB I periods and that, since there is no indication of destructions at the end of EB IV (Dever 1976: 15), there must have been an increase in the population of the southern Levant at the beginning of MB I; and (3) that the types of cultural changes, which have previously been defined as characteristic of the beginning of MB I, could have been and were introduced into a new region by the mechanism of population movements.

Kenyon's theory involves only one main population incursion—that of the Amorites at the beginning of the EB IV (her Intermediate EB-MB) period—although she still suggests some movements from the coast near Byblos, where the MB I culture which she calls "Canaanite" developed, to the rest of the Levant. Kenyon (1966: 58-61) has explained her theory in this way:

> Thus it would seem that this culture, of which the pottery is the evidence, developed in coastal Syria, in the region centred on Byblos. In Palestine and at Ras Shamra it was superimposed on the pre-existing culture without any development therefrom. It thus developed

> in a most important area of the land known to the Akkadians as Kinahna . . . ; the culture can therefore be called Canaanite. It is also reasonable to suggest that the pottery that developed at Qatna became characteristic of the Amorites of the second millennium B.C., owing something to shared influences in the initial stages, but thereafter diverging. . . . There is not yet enough evidence to say how the superimposition of the new culture upon the old took place in Palestine. As already stated, evidence of M.B.I is found only on a few sites. Unless this is an accident of excavation, it suggests a small-scale infiltration. The country-wide spread of which the distribution of M.B.II pottery is evidence may have taken place by expansion from a few original centres, or perhaps more likely by the adoption by the inhabitants of the more advanced culture they saw in their midst. The land of Canaan of the Books of Exodus and Joshua was thus established. What it is not possible to say is why the inhabitants of some towns still regarded themselves as Amorite some five hundred years later. It may be something to do with how they acquired the Canaanite culture, whether by absorption or by being captured.

A third theory, which is a variation of that of Kenyon, is presented by Williams (1975: 1237-40). Williams, following Kenyon, proposes that the Byblos region was the original center of the Middle Bronze Age culture which he terms "proto-Canaanite," and that the later spread of Middle Bronze Age culture should be attributed to the Hyksos.[2] All three of these theories therefore share the basic principle that the MB I culture was brought into Palestine from either the Syrian region in general or the Byblos area in particular by migrating peoples—either Amorites, Canaanites, or Hyksos.

It has previously been mentioned, in agreement with the theory of Dever, that the MB I culture developed out of the EB IV culture in the northern Levant where transitional ceramic forms, bronze technology, indications of urbanism, social stratification, and developed social institutions appear before the end of EB IV. At the same time, the discontinuity between the EB IV and MB I cultures of the southern Levant, where indications of a transitional phase are lacking, has also been emphasized. The conclusion that the MB I culture appeared in the southern Levant as the result of some stimulus from the north is unavoidable. The question therefore is, What was the nature of this stimulus? The three assumptions involved in Dever's theory, and to some extent implicit in Kenyon's theory as well, will be considered.

It is first of all necessary to remove linguistic and ethnic designations from the discussion of an archaeologically defined assemblage or culture. While groups of peoples who may be labelled as "Amorite," "Canaanite," or "Hyksos" may be defined on the basis of linguistic or onomastic evidence in contemporary texts, and some indications of their movements may also be given, it is invalid to attempt to apply such linguistic terms to assemblages which do not themselves include such evidence. The most obvious reason for this is simply that a material culture and an ethnic group are not necessarily totally coinciding sets. In cases where such evidence is available, including modern history, it is easy to see that the distribution of a material culture and that of an ethnic group are not necessarily identical. Furthermore, the term "ethnic group" is "an irrelevant theoretical construct" for archaeological purposes and "for most archaeological situations, markers of ethnic identity are probably not recognizable" (Hamlin 1971: 12; also Kramer 1977: 107-8). In this particular case, even the textual evidence is so confused that it is impossible to write of such groups as "Amorites" and "Canaanites" with any clear definition which would be acceptable to all philologists studying the Mesopotamian texts (see Thompson 1974: 67-143).

The second assumption is that there was a population movement from Syria into the southern Levant at the beginning of the MB I period which brought with it the characteristic culture. There is, however, no evidence for such a population movement at the *beginning* of the MB I period—there being no evidence for an increase in population at that time—which is a necessary corollary since there was apparently no destruction of EB IV sites. However, when the number of sites which show early MB I culture is compared to the number of sites with EB IV settlements (see, for example, Dever 1973: fig. 2), it is apparent that there was no increase in the number of sites from EB IV to the beginning of MB I. The proportion of settled EB IV and MB I sites, as now understood, is such that no population increase can be postulated.

It is apparent that the number of settled sites increases through the MB I period and especially at the beginning of MB II, but if one recalls that the MB I culture appeared fully developed at the beginning of MB I, then these later population increments cannot be related to the introduction of Syrian cultural elements in the south. In fact, some of the distinctive MB I cultural features which appear during the course of the MB I period, such as the notched chisel-axe and the veined dagger (see Chapter VI), probably developed in the southern Levant and then spread northwards, so that again one cannot attribute later MB I developments to stimulus from the north. An alternate explanation for the increase in number of later MB I sites will be suggested later in this chapter.

The third assumption of the "Amorite" hypothesis is that the distinctive features of MB I culture were brought from Syria to Palestine as the result of population movements. These features have already been extensively discussed elsewhere in this study, but they may be summarized as follows: bronze technology, which is associated with the production of certain metallic forms; specific ceramic styles, including the band-painted store jars, pinched-rim and painted juglets, and the distinctive monochrome burnished wares made on a fast pottery wheel; a sufficiently complex economic system to have supported a trade network, which brought tin and possibly other commodities from Mesopotamia and required the location of sites along routes favorable for communication with the Syrian trade centers; the beginnings of unified political authority and social stratification which are evidenced in the construction of the first public structures. These characteristics represent innovations in nearly all the subsystems in a cultural system (with the exception of innovations in subsistence technology, which have not been documented but may also have occurred). While it is possible for such cultural features to be brought into a new region as the result of population movements, this is by no means the only possible mechanism, and a different explanation for the introduction of these innovations will be suggested here.

The one element which all these innovations share is their link to the trade network. The beginnings of political unification and social stratification in the southern Levant may have been the result of exposure to, and competition with, the more developed settlements of the northern Levant. Other innovations, such as the development of a bronze technology, the required importation of tin and the presence of the band-painted store jars which seem to have been associated with overland trade, are also documented in relation to the trade network to Mesopotamia and Anatolia.

It is not intended to suggest that the opening of trade and communication between the southern Levant and the northern Levant, and thus also with Mesopotamia and Anatolia, was the single cause of the development of the Middle Bronze Age culture. Rather, this may be viewed as an initial change motivated by external factors, which then produced changes and innovations in other cultural subsystems. These changes, with a greater degree of craft specialization and technology, might also have fostered a population increase (particularly if improvements in the subsistence system also resulted), thus explaining the larger number of sites inhabited toward the end of MB I and beginning of MB II. Such an exchange network, involving both ideas and commodities, which has been amply documented throughout this study, may be a more efficient explanation for the initial cause of changes in Levantine culture at the beginning of MB I (which was characterized by innovations in technology and trade systems) than that of population movements.

The MB I period has thus been shown to be a period of changes and innovations in technology, trade, and communications, and cognitive institutions, including political unification, social stratification, and eventually the growth of urbanism. Our analysis of several aspects of the MB I culture and, in particular, its relationship with the contemporary cultures of Mesopotamia and Anatolia, allowed a fuller understanding of the nature and attributes of this period in the Levant. MB I was a longer period, with more complex internal and external relationships, than had previously been assumed. The innovations which characterized MB I led to the development of the city-states of the later MB II period and justify our analysis of MB I as a truly formative phase of the urbanized Middle Bronze Age culture of the Levant.

NOTES

[1]For a discussion of this theory, see Dever 1976: 5-6, with references, and also for such dissenting views as those of Lapp and Kochavi, who attribute the EB IV culture to non-Semitic invaders. For a critique of the philological evidence and the difficulty in attempting to combine linguistic and archaeological evidence, see Thompson 1974: 67-97.

[2]Williams denies the existence of any equivalent phase of MB I or even (his) MB IIA in Palestine and of a pre-Tell el-Yahudiyeh ware ceramic phase. As a consequence, the later expansion of the Middle Bronze Age culture into Palestine he attributes to the "Hyksos" who invaded the Egyptian Delta region in his MB IIC period, leaving pottery and weapons at

such sites as Tell ed-Dab^ca and led by the king of Hazor, either the son or grandson of the Ibni-Adad mentioned in the Mari texts.

The supposition of both Kenyon and Williams that the origin of the Middle Bronze Age culture should be sought in the Byblos region has already been discussed here and, more fully, by Dever (1976: 12). This view cannot be accepted because much of the Byblos pottery in fact represents a late MB I assemblage. Byblos itself, because of its extensive relationship with Egypt, should be considered as anomalous and atypical, and therefore cannot be utilized as an MB I type-site. The clearest transition from EB IV to MB I ceramic forms is shown in the repertoires of such inland Syrian sites as Osmaniye, Dnebi, Selimiye, Khan Sheikhoun, Qatna, Tell ᶜAs, and Tell Masin. One can easily recall, as examples, the pinched-rim jugs with flat bases which are similar to EB IV forms and the large proportion of incised decoration from some of these tomb groups to emphasize the transitional nature of this corpus (see also Chapter III, pp. 46-47; for examples, see the pottery of Dnebi, Tomb 3, du Mesnil du Buisson 1930: pl. XXXI).

ABBREVIATIONS

AAS	*Annales archéologiques arabes syriennes*
AASOR	Annual of the American Schools of Oriental Research
Acta O	*Acta Orientalia*
AfO	*Archiv für Orientforschung*
AJA	*American Journal of Archaeology*
AJSL	*American Journal of Semitic Languages and Literatures*
ARMT	*Archives Royales de Mari—Transcription et Traduction*
AS	*Anatolian Studies*
ᶜAtiqot	*ᶜAtiqot: Journal of the Israel Department of Antiquities*
BA	*Biblical Archaeologist*
BASOR	*Bulletin of the American Schools of Oriental Research*
BMB	*Bulletin du Musée de Beyrouth*
CAH	*Cambridge Ancient History*
CRAIBL	*Comptes rendus de l'Académie des inscriptions et belles lettres*
HUCA	*Annual of the Hebrew Union College*
IEJ	*Israel Exploration Journal*
ILN	*Illustrated London News*
JAOS	*Journal of the American Oriental Society*
JBL	*Journal of Biblical Literature*
JCS	*Journal of Cuneiform Studies*
JEA	*Journal of Egyptian Archaeology*
JESHO	*Journal of the Economic and Social History of the Orient*
JNES	*Journal of Near Eastern Studies*
JPOS	*Journal of the Palestine Oriental Society*
LAAA	*University of Liverpool, Annals of Archaeology and Anthropology*
MDAIK	*Mitteilungen des deutschen Archäologischen Instituts Abteilung Kairo*
MJ	*The Museum Journal* (University of Pennsylvania)
OIP	Oriental Institute Publications
PEFA	*Palestine Exploration Fund Annual*
PEFQ	*Palestine Exploration Fund Quarterly Statement*
PEQ	*Palestine Exploration Quarterly* (=*PEFQ* after 1936)
PMB	*Bulletin of the Palestine Museum*
PPS	*Proceedings of the Prehistoric Society*
QDAP	*Quarterly of the Department of Antiquities of Palestine*
RA	*Revue d'assyriologie et d'archéologie orientale*
RB	*Revue biblique*
RHA	*Revue hittite et asianique*
RSO	*Revista degli Studi Orientali*
SIMA	Studies in Mediterranean Archaeology
TAPS	*Transactions of the American Philosophical Society*
TTK Bell	*Türk Tarih Kurumu Belleten*
TTK Y	Türk Tarih Kurumu Yayinlarindan
WVDOG	*Wissenschaftliche Veröffentlichung der deutschen Orient-Gesellschaft*
ZDPV	*Zeitschrift des deutschen Palästina-Vereins*

BIBLIOGRAPHY

Aharoni, Yohanan.

1974 *The Land of the Bible: A Historical Geography*. London: Burns and Oates.

Albright, W. F.

1928 The Egyptian Empire in Asia in the Twenty-first Century B.C. *JPOS* 8: 223-56.

1932 *The Excavation of Tell Beit Mirsim in Palestine* I: *The Pottery of the First Three Campaigns*. AASOR 12. New Haven, Conn.: American Schools of Oriental Research.

1933 *The Excavation of Tell Beit Mirsim* IA: *The Bronze Age Pottery of the Fourth Campaign*. AASOR 13. New Haven, Conn.: American Schools of Oriental Research. 55-127.

1938a *The Excavation of Tell Beit Mirsim* II: *The Bronze Age*. AASOR 17. New Haven, Conn.: American Schools of Oriental Research.

1938b The Chronology of a South Palestinian City, Tell el-ᶜAjjul. *AJSL* 55: 337-59.

1938c A Revolution in the Chronology of Ancient Western Asia. *BASOR* 69: 18-21.

1940a New Light on the History of Western Asia in the Second Millennium B.C. *BASOR* 77: 20-32.

1940b New Light on the History of Western Asia in the Second Millennium B.C. (cont.) *BASOR* 78: 23-31.

1941a New Egyptian Data on Palestine in the Patriarchal Age. *BASOR* 81: 16-21.

1941b The Land of Damascus between 1850 and 1750 B.C. *BASOR* 83: 30-36.

1942 A Third Revision of the Early Chronology of Western Asia. *BASOR* 88: 28-33.

1964 The Eighteenth-Century Princes of Byblos and the Chronology of Middle Bronze. *BASOR* 176: 38-46.

1965a Further Light on the History of Middle-Bronze Byblos. *BASOR* 179: 38-43.

1965b Some Remarks on the Archaeological Chronology of Palestine before about 1500 B.C. In *Chronologies in Old World Archaeology*, ed. Robert W. Ehrich. Chicago: University of Chicago. 47-60.

1966 Remarks on the Chronology of Early Bronze IV-Middle Bronze IIA in Phoenicia and Syria-Palestine. *BASOR* 184: 26-35.

1973 The Historical Framework of Palestinian Archaeology between 2100 and 1600 B.C. (E.B. IV, M.B. I, M.B. IIA-B). *BASOR* 209: 12-18.

Allen, T. George.

1929 A Middle Kingdom Egyptian Contact with Asia Minor. In *Explorations in Central Anatolia, Season of 1926*, by H. H. von der Osten. OIP 5. Chicago: University of Chicago. 66-67.

Alp, Sedat.

1968 *Zylinder- und Stempelsiegel aus Karahöyük bei Konya*. TTK Y-V. Seri, Sayi 26. Ankara: Türk Tarih Kurumu Basimevi.

Amiran, Ruth.

1968 Similarities between the Pottery of the MB IIA Period and the Pottery of the Assyrian Colonies, and their Implications. *Anatolia* 12: 59-62.

1969 *Ancient Pottery of the Holy Land: from its beginnings in the Neolithic Period to the Iron Age*. Jerusalem: Massada.

Amiran, Ruth, and Eitan, A.

1965 A Canaanite-Hyksos City at Tell Nagila. *Archaeology* 18: 113-23.

Archi, Alfonso.

1979 The Epigraphic Evidence from Ebla and the Old Testament. *Biblica* 60: 556-66.

Archives Royales de Mari-Transcription et Traduction. (*ARMT*).

I. Correspondance de Šamši-Addu et de ses fils. Georges Dossin. 1950. Paris: Geuthner.

II. Lettres diverses. Charles-F. Jean. 1950. Paris: Geuthner.

V. Correspondance de Iasmaḫ-Addu. Georges Dossin. 1952. Paris: Geuthner.

VI. Correspondance de Baḫdi-Lim, préfet du palais de Mari. J. R. Kupper. 1954. Paris: Geuthner.

VII. Textes économiques et administratifs. Jean Bottéro. 1957. Paris: Geuthner.

VIII. Textes juridiques. Georges Boyer. 1958. Paris: Geuthner.

IX. Textes administratifs de la salle 5 du palais. Maurice Birot. 1960. Paris: Geuthner.

XII. Textes administratifs de la salle 5 du palais (2ème partie). Maurice Birot. 1964. Paris: Geuthner.

XIII. Textes divers. G. Dossin, J. Bottéro, M. Birot, Mme. M. Lurton Burke, J. R. Kupper, A. Finet. 1964. Paris: Geuthner.

XIV. Lettres de Yaqqim-Addu, Gouverneur de Sagarâtum. Maurice Birot. 1974. Paris: Geuthner.

XVIII. Mukannišum. L'administration et l'économie palatiales à Mari. O. Rouault. 1977. Paris: Geuthner.

XIX. Textes administratifs de l'époque des *šakkanaku*. Henri Limet. 1976. Paris: Geuthner.

Artzy, Michal; Perlman, I.; and Asaro, F.

1976 Alašiya of the Amarna Letters. *JNES* 35: 171-82.

Assaf, Ali Abou.

1967 Der Friedhof von Yabrud. *AAS* 17: 55-68.

Åström, Paul.

1957 *The Middle Cypriote Bronze Age*. Lund: Håkan Ohlssons Boktryckeri.

Balkan, Kemal.

1955 *Observations on the Chronological Problems of the Kārum Kaniš*. TTK Y-VII. Seri, Sayi 28. Ankara: Türk Tarih Kurumu Basımevi.

1957 *Letter of King Anum-Hirbi of Mama to King Warshama of Kanish*. TTK Y-VII. Seri, Sayi 31a. Ankara: Türk Tarih Kurumu Basımevi.

Banks, E. J.
1905-6 Terra-Cotta Vases from Bismya. *AJSL* 22: 139-43.

Beck, Pirhiya.
1975 The Pottery of the Middle Bronze Age IIA at Tel Aphek. *Tel Aviv* 2: 45-85.

Ben-Dor, I.
1950 A Middle Bronze-Age Temple at Nahariya. *QDAP* 14: 1-41.

Bietak, Manfred.
1968 Vorläufiger Bericht über die erste und zweite Kampagne der österreichischen Ausgrabungen auf Tell Ed-Dab^{c}a im Ostdelta Ägyptens (1966, 1967). *MDAIK* 23: 79-114.
1970 Vorläufiger Bericht über die dritte Kampagne der österreichischen Ausgrabungen auf Tell ed-Dab^{c}a im Ostdelta Ägyptens (1968). *MDAIK* 26: 15-41.

Biggs, Robert.
1980 The Ebla Tablets: An Interim Perspective. *BA* 43: 76-87.

Bilgiç, Emin.
1945-51 Die Ortsnamen der "kappadokischen" Urkunden im Rahmen der alten Sprachen Anatoliens. *AfO* 15: 1-37.

Biran, A.
1973 Tel Dan. *IEJ* 23: 110-12.
1975 Tel Dan. In *Encyclopedia of Archaeological Excavations in the Holy Land*, ed. Michael Avi-Yonah. Vol. I. Jerusalem: Israel Exploration Society and Massada. 313-21.

Birmingham, J.
1977 Spectrographic Analyses of Some Middle Bronze Age Metal Objects. *Levant* 9: 115-20.

Birot, Maurice.
1964 Les lettres de Iasîm-Sumû. *Syria* 41: 25-65.

Bittel, Kurt.
1970 *Hattusha: The Capital of the Hittites.* New York: Oxford University.

Bittel, Kurt, *et al.*
1958 *Die Hethitischen Grabfunde von Osmankayasi. WVDOG* 71. Berlin: Gebr. Mann.

Blegen, Carl, *et al.*
1951 *Troy: The Third, Fourth and Fifth Settlements.* Text and Plates. Vol. II. Princeton: Princeton University.

Bliss, Frederick Jones.
1894 *A Mound of Many Cities or Tell El Hesy Excavated.* London: Committee of the Palestine Exploration Fund.

Blouet, Brian W.
1972 Factors Influencing the Evolution of Settlement Patterns. In *Man, Settlement and Urbanism*, ed. P. J. Ucko, R. E. Tringham, and G. W. Dimbleby. London: Duckworth. 3-16.

Braidwood, Robert J.
1940 Report on Two Sondages on the Coast of Syria, South of Tartous. *Syria* 21: 183-221.

Braidwood, Robert J., and Braidwood, Linda S.
1960 *Excavations in the Plain of Antioch.* I. *The Earlier Assemblages, Phases A-J.* OIP 61. Chicago: University of Chicago.

Branigan, Keith.
1968 *Copper and Bronze Working in Early Bronze Age Crete.* SIMA XIX. Lund: P. Aström.

Buchanan, Briggs.
1969 The End of the Assyrian Colonies in Anatolia: The Evidence of the Seals. *JAOS* 89: 758-62.

Buchholz, Hans-Günter.
1967 Analysen prähistorischer Metallfunde aus Zypern und den Nachbarländern. *Berliner Jahrbuch* 7: 189-256.

Burke, Madeleine Lurton.
1964 Lettres de Numušda-Naḫrari et de trois autres correspondants à Idiniatum. *Syria* 41: 67-103.

Butzer, K. W.
1970 Physical Conditions in Eastern Europe, Western Asia and Egypt Before the Period of Agricultural and Urban Settlement. *CAH* 3rd ed. Vol. I, Pt. 1. London: Cambridge University. 35-69.

Callaway, Joseph A., and Weinstein, James M.
1977 Radiocarbon Dating of Palestine in the Early Bronze Age. *BASOR* 225: 1-16.

Castellino, G., *et al.*
1966 *Missione Archeologica Italiana in Siria. Rapporto preliminare della Campagna 1965 (Tell Mardikh).* Istituto di Studi del Vicino Oriente-Università. Serie Archeologica 10. Rome: Aziende Tipografiche Eredi Dott. G. Bardi.

Chehab, Maurice.
1937 Trésor d'orfèvrerie syro-égyptien. *BMB* 1: 7-21.
1939 Tombe phénicienne de Sin el Fil. *Mélanges syriens offerts à René Dussaud.* Tome II. Paris: Paul Geuthner. 803-10.
1940 Tombes phéniciennes, Majdalouna. *BMB* 4: 37-53.

Contenau, Georges.
1920 Mission archéologique à Sidon (1914). *Syria* 1: 108-54.
1924 Deuxième mission archéologique à Sidon (1920). *Syria* 5: 123-34.

Contenau, G., and Ghirshman, R.
1935 *Fouilles du Tépé-Giyan.* Musée du Louvre. Série archéologique. Tome III. Paris: Paul Geuthner.

Courtois, Jacques-Claude.
1973 La XXXIIIe campagne de fouilles à Ras Shamra en 1972, rapport préliminarie: C. Bronze Moyen et début du Bronze Récent I à l'extrémité orientale du tell. *Syria* 50: 293-97.
1974 Ugarit Grid, Strata, and Find-Localizations—A Re-assessment. *ZDPV* 90: 97-114.

Crawford, H. E. W.
1973 Mesopotamia's invisible exports in the third millennium B.C. *World Archaeology* 5: 232-41.
1974 The Problem of Tin in Mesopotamian Bronzes. *World Archaeology* 6: 242-47.

Crawford, Vaughn Emerson.
1954 *Sumerian Economic Texts from the First Dynasty of Isin.* Babylonian Inscriptions in the Collection of James B. Nies, Yale University, Vol. 9. New Haven: Yale University.

Dalley, Stephanie.
1977 Old Babylonian Trade in Textiles at Tell al Rimah. *Iraq* 39: 155-59.

Dalley, Stephanie, *et al.*
1976 *The Old Babylonian Tablets from Tell al Rimah.* Hertford: Stephen Austin.

Davico, A., *et al.*
1965 *Missione Archeologica Italiana in Siria. Rapporto*

preliminare della Campagne 1964. Centro di Studi Semitici, Università di Roma. Serie Archeologica 8. Rome: Aziende Tipografiche Eredi Dott. G. Bardi.
1967 *Missione Archeologica Italiana in Siria. Rapporto preliminare della Campagna 1966 (Tell Mardikh).* Istituto di Studi del Vicino Oriente, Università. Serie Archeologica 13. Rome: Aziende Tipografiche Eredi Dott. G. Bardi.

Dayton, J. E.
1971 The Problem of Tin in the Ancient World. *World Archaeology* 3: 49-70.
1973 The Problem of Tin in the Ancient World: a reply to Dr. Muhly and Dr. Wertime. *World Archaeology* 5: 123-25.

de Genouillac, Henri.
1924 *Premières recherches archéologiques à Kich, 1911-1912.* Vol. I. Paris: Édouard Champion.
1925 *Premières recherches archéologiques à Kich, 1911-1912.* Vol. II. Paris: Édouard Champion.
1936 *Fouilles de Telloh.* II: *Époques d'Ur IIIe Dynastie et de Larsa.* Mission archéologique du Musée du Louvre et du Ministère de l'instruction publique. Paris: Paul Geuthner.

de la Füye, Allotte, *et al.*
1934 *Mémoires de la mission archéologique de Perse.* Tome XXV. Mission en Susiane. Paris: Ernest Leroux.

de Maigret, Alessandro.
1976 Due punte di lancia iscritte da Tell Mardikh-Ebla. *RSO* 50: 31-41.

de Morgan, J., *et al.*
1900 *Mémoires, Délégation en Perse.* Tome I: *Fouilles à Suse en 1897-1898 et 1898-1899.* Paris: Ernest Le Roux.

de Vaux, R.
1955 Les fouilles de Tell el-Far^{c}ah, près Naplouse. *RB* 62: 541-89.
1962 Les fouilles de Tell el-Far^{c}ah: Rapport préliminaire sur les 7e, 8e, 9e campagnes, 1958-1960. *RB* 69: 212-53.

de Vaux, R., and Steve, A. M.
1948 La seconde campagne de fouilles à Tell el-Far^{c}ah, près Naplouse. *RB* 55: 544-80.

Delibrias, G.; Guillier, M. T.; and Labeyrie, J.
1971 Gif Natural Radiocarbon Measurements VI. *Radiocarbon* 13: 213-54.

Delougaz, Pinhas.
1952 *Pottery from the Diyala Region.* OIP 63. Chicago: University of Chicago.

Deshayes, Jean.
1960 *Les Outils de bronze, de l'Indus au Danube (IVe au IIe millénaire).* Institut français d'archéologie de Beyrouth, Bibliothèque archéologique et historique, Tome 71. Paris: Paul Geuthner.

Dever, William G.
1970 The "Middle Bronze I" Period in Syria and Palestine. In *Near Eastern Archaeology in the Twentieth Century*, ed. James A. Sanders. Garden City, N.Y.: Doubleday. 132-63.
1973 The EB IV-MB I Horizon in Transjordan and Southern Palestine. *BASOR* 210: 37-63.
1975a MB IIA Cemeteries at ^{c}Ain es-Sâmiyeh and Sinjil. *BASOR* 217: 23-36.
1975b A Middle Bronze I Cemetery at Khirbet el-Kirmil. *Eretz-Israel* 12: 18*-33*.
1976 The Beginning of the Middle Bronze Age in Syria-Palestine. In *Magnalia Dei: The Mighty Acts of God. Essays on the Bible and Archaeology in Memory of G. Ernest Wright*, ed. F. M. Cross, W. E. Lemke, and P. D. Miller, Jr., Garden City, N.Y.: Doubleday. 3-38.

Dever, William G.; Lance, H. Darrell; and Wright, G. Ernest.
1970 *Gezer I: Preliminary Report of the 1964-66 Seasons.* With a contribution by Aaron Shaffer. Annual of the Hebrew Union College Biblical and Archaeological School in Jerusalem. Jerusalem: Keter.

Dever, William, G., *et al.*
1971 Further Excavations at Gezer, 1967-1971. *BA* 34: 94-132.
1974 *Gezer II: Report of the 1967-70 Seasons in Fields I and II.* Annual of the Hebrew Union College/Nelson Glueck School of Biblical Archaeology. Jerusalem: Keter.

Dornemann, Rudolph H.
1979 Tell Hadidi: A Millennium of Bronze Age City Occupation. In *Archaeological Reports from the Tabqa Dam Project: Euphrates Valley, Syria*, ed. David Noel Freedman. AASOR 44. Cambridge, Mass.: American Schools of Oriental Research. 113-51.

Dossin, Georges.
1938 Les archives épistolaires du palais de Mari. *Syria* 19: 105-26.
1939a Les archives économiques du palais de Mari. *Syria* 20: 97-113.
1939b Une mention de Ḫattuša dans une lettre de Mari. *RHA* 35: 70-76.
1939c Iamḫad et Qatanum. *RA* 36: 46-54.
1955 L'inscription de fondation de Iaḫdun-Lim, roi de Mari. *Syria* 32: 1-28.
1970 La route de l'étain en Mesopotamie au temps de Zimri-Lim. *RA* 64: 97-106.

Dothan, Moshe.
1956 The Excavations at Nahariyah. *IEJ* 6: 14-25.
1975 ^{c}Akko, 1975. *IEJ* 25: 163-66.
1976a MB IIA Settlements on the Northern Coast of Israel and their Cypriote Connections. Paper read at Fourth Archaeological Conference in Israel. Jerusalem, March 17-18, 1976.
1976b Akko: Interim Excavation Report First Season, 1973/4. *BASOR* 224: 1-48.

Dothan, M., and Raban, A.
1980 The Sea Gate of Ancient Akko. *BA* 43: 35-39.

du Mesnil du Buisson, Le Comte Robert.
1927 Les ruines d'el Mishrifé au nord-est de Ḥomṣ (Émèse). *Syria* 8: 13-33; 277-301.
1930 Compte rendu de la quatrième campagne de fouilles à Mishrifé-Qatna. *Syria* 11: 146-63.
1932 Une campagne de fouilles à Khan Sheikhoun. *Syria* 13: 171-88.
1935a *Le site archéologique de Mishrifé-Qatna.* Paris: E. de Boccard.
1935b Sourān et Tell Maṣin. *Berytus* 2: 121-34.
1948 *Baghouz: L'Ancienne Corsôtê: Le tell archaique et*

la nécropole de l'âge du bronze. Leiden: E. J. Brill.

Dunand, Maurice.
1937 *Fouilles de Byblos, 1926-1932*. Tome Ier Atlas. Études et Documents d'Archéologie, Tome I. Paris: Paul Geuthner.
1939 *Fouilles de Byblos, 1926-1932*. Tome Ier Texte. Études et Documents d'Archéologie, Tome I. Paris: Paul Geuthner.
1950 *Fouilles de Byblos, 1933-1938*. Tome II. Atlas. Études et Documents d'Archéologie, Tome III. Paris: Adrien Maisonneuve.
1954 *Fouilles de Byblos, 1933-1938*. Tome II. Texte, pt. 1. Études et Documents d'Archéologie, Tome III. Paris: Adrien Maisonneuve.
1958 *Fouilles de Byblos, 1933-1938*. Tome II. Texte, pt. 2. Études et Documents d'Archéologie, Tome III. Paris: Adrien Maisonneuve.

Dunand, M.; Saliby, Nessib; and Khirichian, Agop.
1954 Les fouilles d'Amrith en 1954, rapport préliminaire. *AAS* 4: 189-204.

Dunayevsky, Immanuel, and Kempinski, Aharon.
1973 The Megiddo Temples. *ZDPV* 89: 161-87.

Dussaud, René.
1927 Nouveaux renseignements sur la Palestine et la Syria vers 2000 avant notre ère. *Syria* 8: 216-33.

Easton, D. F.
1976 Towards a Chronology for the Anatolian Early Bronze Age. *AS* 26: 145-73.

Eaton, E. R., and McKerrell, Hugh.
1976 Near Eastern Alloying and some Textual Evidence for the Use of Arsenical Bronzes. *World Archaeology* 8: 169-91.

Edzard, D. O., ed.
1976 *Reallexikon der Assyriologie und vorderasiatischen Archäologie*. Vol. 5. Berlin: Walter de Gruyter.

Ehrich, Ann M. H.
1939 *Early Pottery of the Jebeleh Region*. Memoirs of the American Philosophical Society. Vol. 13. Philadelphia.

Eitan, Avraham.
1969 Excavations at the Foot of Tel Rosh Ha[c]ayin. *[c]Atiqot* 5: 49-68 (Hebrew series).
1972 Tel Beit Mirsin G-F—The Middle Bronze IIA Settlement. *BASOR* 208: 19-24.

Emre, Kutlu.
1963 The Pottery of the Assyrian Colony Period according to the Building Levels of the Kaniş Karum. *Anatolia* 7: 87-99.
1966 The Pottery from Acemhöyük. *Anatolia* 10: 99-153.

Engberg, Robert M.
1942 Tombs of the Early Second Millennium from Bāghuz on the Middle Euphrates. *BASOR* 87: 17-23.

Epstein, Claire.
1965 An Interpretation of the Megiddo Sacred Area During Middle Bronze II. *IEJ* 15: 204-21.
1974 Middle Bronze Age Tombs at Kfar Szold and Ginosar. *[c]Atiqot* 7: 13-39 (Hebrew series).

Evans, Arthur.
1921 *The Palace of Minos: A Comparative Account of the Successive Stages of the Early Cretan Civilization as Illustrated by the Discoveries*. Vol. I: *The Neolithic and Early and Middle Minoan Ages*. London: Macmillan.

Fargo, Valerie M., and O'Connell, Kevin G.
1978 Five Seasons of Excavation at Tell el-Hesi (1970-1977). *BA* 41: 165-82.

Fischer, Franz.
1963 *Die Hethitische Keramik von Boğazköy*. *WVDOG* 75. Berlin: Gebr. Mann.

Frankel, D.
1974 Recent Developments in the Cypriot Middle Bronze Age. In *Australian Studies in Archaeology* No. 1. (1973), ed. J. Birmingham. Sydney: Southwood. 23-43.

Frankfort, H.
1939 *Cylinder Seals, a Documentary Essay on the Art and Religion of the Ancient Near East*. London: Macmillan.

Fugmann, E.
1958 *Hama: Fouilles et Recherches 1931-1938*. II,1: *L'architecture des périodes pré-hellenistiques*. Nationalmuseets Skrifter, Større Beretninger 4. Copenhagen: Nationalmuseet.

Gadd, C. J.
1937 Tablets from Chagar Bazar, 1936. *Iraq* 4: 178-85.
1940 Tablets from Chagar Bazar and Tell Brak, 1937-38. *Iraq* 7: 22-66.

Garelli, Paul.
1963 *Les Assyriens en Cappadoce*. Bibliothèque archéologique et historique de l'institut français d'archéologie d'Istanbul 19. Paris: Adrien Maisonneuve.

Garstang, John.
1932 Jericho: City and Necropolis. *LAAA* 19: 3-22; 35-54.
1933 Jericho: City and Necropolis. *LAAA* 20: 3-42.
1953 *Prehistoric Mersin: Yümük Tepe in Southern Turkey*. Oxford: Clarendon.

Gautier, J.-E.
1895 Note sur les fouilles entreprises dans la haute vallée de l'Oronte. *CRAIBL* 23, 4th series: 441-64.

Gjerstad, Einer, *et al.*
1934 *The Swedish Cyprus Expedition. Finds and Results of the Excavations in Cyprus. 1927-1931*. Vol. I: Plates. Stockholm: Swedish Cyprus Expedition.

Goetze, Albrecht.
1953 An Old Babylonian Itinerary. *JCS* 7: 51-72.
1964 Remarks on the Old Babylonian Itinerary. *JCS* 18: 114-19.

Goldman, Hetty.
1956 *Excavations at Gözlü Kule, Tarsus*. Vol. II: *From the Neolithic through the Bronze Age*. Princeton: Princeton University.

Gophna, Ram.
1964 Tel Poleg. *IEJ* 14: 109-11.
1965 Tel Poleg. *RB* 72: 552-53.
1973 The Middle Bronze Age II Fortifications at Tel Poleg. *Eretz-Israel* 11: 111-19 (Hebrew).

Gophna, Ram, and Sussman, Varda.
1969 A Middle Bronze Age Tomb at Barqai. *[c]Atiqot* 5: 1-13 (Hebrew series).

Grace, Virginia R.
1956 The Canaanite Jar. In *The Aegean and the Near East, Studies presented to Hetty Goldman*, ed.

Saul S. Weinberg. Locust Valley, New York: J. J. Augustin. 80-109.

Grant, Elihu.
1929 *Beth Shemesh.* Biblical and Kindred Studies. Haverford, Penna.

Grant, Elihu, and Wright, G. Ernest.
1938 *Ain Shems Excavations.* Part IV: *Pottery.* Biblical and Kindred Studies No. 7, Haverford College. Baltimore: J. H. Furst.
1939 *Ain Shems Excavations.* Part V: Text. Biblical and Kindred Studies No. 8, Haverford College. Baltimore: J. H. Furst.

Greenwell, William.
1902 On Some Rare Forms of Bronze Weapons and Implements. *Archaeologia* 58: 1-16.

Guigues, P. E.
1937 Lébéᶜa, Kafer-Ǧarra, Qrayé: Nécropoles de la région sidonienne. *BMB* I: 35-76.
1938 Lébéᶜa, Kafer-Ǧarra, Qrayé: Nécropoles de la region sidonienne (suite). *BMB* 2: 27-72.
1939 Lébéᶜa, Kafer-Ǧarra, Qrayé: Nécropoles de la région sidonienne (suite). *BMB* 3: 53-63.

Güterbock, H. G.
1964 Sargon of Akkad Mentioned by Ḫattušili I of Ḫatti. *JCS* 18: 1-6.

Guy, P. L. O.
1938 *Megiddo Tombs.* OIP 33. Chicago: University of Chicago.

Hachmann, R.
1969 Rapport préliminaire sur les fouilles au Tell Kāmid el-Lōz de 1966-1968. *BMB* 22: 49-84.

Haggett, Peter.
1966 *Locational Analysis in Human Geography.* New York: St. Martin's.

Haller, Arndt.
1954 *Die Gräber und Grüfte von Assur. WVDOG* 65. Berlin: Gebr. Mann.

Hallo, William W.
1964 The Road to Emar. *JCS* 18: 57-88.

Hamlin, Carol. (Kramer).
1971 *The Habur Ware Ceramic Assemblage of Northern Mesopotamia: An Analysis of Its Distribution.* Ph.D. Dissertation, University of Pennsylvania. Ann Arbor, Michigan: University Microfilms.
1974 The Early Second Millennium Ceramic Assemblage of Dinkha Tepe. *Iran* 12: 125-53.

Hansen, Donald P.
1965 The Relative Chronology of Mesopotamia Part II. The Pottery Sequence at Nippur from the Middle Uruk to the End of the Old Babylonian Period (3400-1600 B.C.). In *Chronologies in Old World Archaeology*, ed. Robert W. Ehrich. Chicago: University of Chicago. 201-13.

Harding, Lankester G.
1953 Four Tomb Groups from Jordan. *PEFA* 6: 14-26.

Harif, A.
1978 Middle Kingdom Architectural Elements in Middle Bronze Age Megiddo, *ZDPV* 94: 24-31.

Hayes, William C.
1971 The Middle Kingdom in Egypt: Internal History from the Rise of the Heracleopolitans to the Death of Ammenemes III. *CAH* 3rd ed. Vol. I, Pt. 2. London: Cambridge University. 464-531.

Heinrich, Ernst.
1931 *Fara: Ergebnisse der Ausgrabungen der Deutschen Orient-Gesellschaft in Fara und Abu Hatab 1902/03.* Staatliche Museen zu Berlin Vorderasiatische Abteilung. Berlin.

Heltzer, Michael.
1978 *Goods, Prices and the Organization of Trade in Ugarit.* Weisbaden: Dr. Ludwig Reichert.

Henschel-Simon, E.
1937 The "Toggle-Pins" in the Palestine Archaeological Museum. *QDAP* 6: 169-209.

Herrmann, Georgina.
1968 Lapis Lazuli: The Early Phases of its Trade. *Iraq* 30: 21-57.

Hrouda, Barthel.
1957 *Die bemalte Keramik des zweiten Jahrtausends in Nordmesopotamien und Nordsyrien.* Herausgegeben von der Abteilung Istanbul des Deutschen Archäologischen Instituts, Band 19. Berlin: Gebr. Mann.

Hrozný, Frédéric.
1927 Rapport préliminaire sur les fouilles tchécoslovaques du Kultépé (1925). *Syria* 8: 1-12.

Ibrahim, M.; Sauer, J.; and Yassine, K.
1976 The East Jordan Valley Survey, 1975. *BASOR* 222: 41-66.

Iliffe, J. H.
1936 Pottery from Rās el ᶜAin. *QDAP* 5: 113-26.

Ingholt, Harald.
1940 *Rapport préliminaire sur sept campagnes de fouilles à Hama en Syrie (1932-1938).* Copenhagen: Ejnar Munksgaard.
1957 The Danish Dokan Expedition. *Sumer* 13: 214-15.

Johnson, Gregory A.
1972 A Test of the Utility of Central Place Theory in Archaeology. In *Man, Settlement* and *Urbanism*, ed. P. J. Ucko, R. E. Tringham, and G. W. Dimbleby. London: Duckworth. 769-85.

Kantor, Helene J.
1958 The Pottery. In *Soundings at Tell Fakhariyah*, by C. W. McEwan *et al.* OIP 79. Chicago: University of Chicago. 21-41.

Kaplan, J.
1969a Yavneh-Yam. *IEJ* 19: 120-21.
1969b *Mesopotamian Elements in the Culture of the Middle Bronze Age II in Eretz-Israel.* Publication of the Museum of Antiquities of Tel Aviv-Jaffa, No. 3. Tel Aviv.
1975 Further Aspects of the Middle Bronze Age II Fortifications in Palestine. *ZDPV* 91: 1-17.

Kelso, James L.
1968 *The Excavation of Bethel (1934-1960).* AASOR 39. Cambridge, Mass.: American Schools of Oriental Research.

Kenyon, Kathleen M.
1958 Some Notes on the Early and Middle Bronze Age Strata of Megiddo. *Eretz-Israel* 5: 51*-60*.
1960 *Excavations at Jericho.* Vol. I: *The Tombs excavated in 1952-54.* British School of Archaeology in Jerusalem. London: Harrison.

1965 *Excavations at Jericho*. Vol. II: *The Tombs excavated in 1955-58*. British School of Archaeology in Jerusalem. London: Harrison.

1966 *Amorites and Canaanites*. The Schweich Lectures of the British Academy. London: Oxford University.

1969 The Middle and Late Bronze Age Strata at Megiddo. *Levant* 1: 25-60.

1971 Syria and Palestine c. 2160-1780 B.C.: The Archaeological Sites. *CAH* 3rd ed. Vol. I, Pt. 2. London: Cambridge University. 567-94.

1973 Palestine in the Middle Bronze Age. *CAH* 3rd ed. Vol. II, Pt. 1. London: Cambridge University. 77-116.

Kitchen, K. A.

1967 Byblos, Egypt and Mari in the Early Second Millennium B.C. *Orientalia* 36: 39-54.

Kochavi, M.

1975 The First Two Seasons of Excavations at Aphek-Antipatris. *Tel Aviv* 2: 17-42.

Kochavi, M., ed.

1972 *Judaea, Samaria and the Golan Archaeological Survey 1967-1968*. Jerusalem: Keter. (Hebrew).

Koşay, H. Z.

1944 *Ausgrabungen von Alaca Höyük*. TTK Y-V. Seri, Sayi 2a. Ankara: Türk Tarih Kurumu Basımevi.

1951 *Les Fouilles d'Alaca Höyük: Rapport préliminaire sur les travaux en 1937-1939*. TTK Y-V. Seri, Sayi 5. Ankara: Türk Tarih Kurumu Basımevi.

Koşay, H. Z., and Akok, Mahmut.

1947 The Pottery of Alaca Höyük. *AJA* 51: 152-57.

1966 *Alaca Höyük Kazisi*. TTK Y-V. Seri, Sayi, 6. Ankara: Türk Tarih Kurumu Basımevi.

Kramer, Carol.

1977 Pots and People. In *Mountains and Lowlands: Essays in the Archaeology of Greater Mesopotamia*, ed. Louis D. Levine and T. Cuyler Young, Jr., Bibliotheca Mesopotamica. Vol. 7. Malibu: Undena. 91-112.

Kupper, J.-R.

1964 Correspondance de Kibri-Dagan. *Syria* 41: 105-16.

1973 Northern Mesopotamia and Syria. *CAH* 3rd ed. Vol. II, Pt. 1. London: Cambridge University. 1-41.

Laessøe, Jørgen.

1957 An Old-Babylonian Archive Discovered at Tell Shemshara. *Sumer* 13: 216-18.

1959a *The Shemshāra Tablets. A Preliminary Report*. Arkaeologiskkunsthistoriske Meddelelser-Det Kongelige Danske Videnskabernes Selskab. Vol. 4, No. 3. Copenhagen: Ejnar Munksgaard.

1959b Akkadian Annakum: "Tin" or "Lead"? *Acta O* 24: 83-94.

1960 The Second Shemshāra Archive. *Sumer* 16: 12-19.

1965 IM 62100: A Letter from Tell Shemshara. *Studies in Honor of Benno Landsberger*. Assyriological Studies, No. 16. Chicago: University of Chicago. 189-96.

Lamb, Winifred.

1938 Excavations at Kusura near Afyon Karahisar: II. *Archaeologia* 87: 216-73.

Landsberger, Benno.

1965 Tin and Lead: The Adventures of Two Vocables. *JNES* 24: 285-96.

Landsberger, B., and Tadmor, H.

1964 Fragments of Clay Liver Models from Hazor. *IEJ* 14: 201-18.

Lapp, Paul W.

1961 Review of *Excavations at Jericho*. Vol. I. by K. M. Kenyon. *AJA* 65: 69-70.

Larsen, Mogens Trolle.

1967 *Old Assyrian Caravan Procedures*. Uitgaven van het Nederlands Historisch-Archaeologisch Institut te Istanbul 22. Leiden.

1976 *The Old Assyrian City-State and its Colonies. Mesopotamia*. Copenhagen Studies in Assyriology, Vol. 4. Copenhagen: Akademisk Forlag.

Lawn, Barbara.

1974 University of Pennsylvania Radiocarbon Dates XVII. *Radiocarbon* 16: 219-37.

Leemans, W. F.

1968 Old Babylonian Letters and Economic History: a review article with a digression on Foreign Trade. *JESHO* 11: 171-226.

Lewy, Hildegard.

1971a Anatolia in the Old Assyrian Period. *CAH* 3rd ed. Vol. I, Pt. 2. London: Cambridge University. 707-28.

1971b Assyria c. 2600-1816 B.C. *CAH* 3rd ed. Vol. I, Pt. 2. London: Cambridge University. 752-62.

Lewy, Julius.

1956 On Some Institutions of the Old Assyrian Empire. *HUCA* 27: 1-79.

1958 Some Aspects of Commercial Life in Assyria and Asia Minor in the Nineteenth Pre-Christian Century. *JAOS* 78: 89-101.

1961 Amurritica. *HUCA* 32: 31-74.

Lloyd, Seton, and Gökçe, Nuri.

1951 Excavations at Polatli. *AS* I: 21-75.

Lloyd, Seton, and Mellaart, James.

1962 *Beycesultan I*. British Institute of Archaeology at Ankara, Occasional Publications, No. 6. London: William Clowes.

Loud, Gordon.

1948 *Megiddo II: Seasons of 1935-39*. Text and Plates. OIP 62. Chicago: University of Chicago.

Macalister, R. A. Stewart.

1912a *The Excavation of Gezer, 1902-1905 and 1907-1909*. Vol. I. London: John Murray.

1912b *The Excavation of Gezer, 1902-1905 and 1907-1909*. Vol. III. London: John Murray.

MacDonald, Burton.

1980 Excavations at Tell el-Maskhuta. *BA* 43: 49-58.

Mackenzie, Duncan.

1912-13 *Excavations at Ain Shems (Beth-Shemesh). PEFA* 2: 42-46.

Malamat, Abraham.

1960 Hazor "The Head of All Those Kingdoms." *JBL* 79: 12-19.

1965 Campaigns to the Mediterranean by Iahdunlim and other Early Mesopotamian Rulers. *Studies in Honor of Benno Landsberger*. Assyriological Studies, No. 16. Chicago: University of Chicago. 365-73.

1970 Northern Canaan and the Mari Texts. In *Near Eastern Archaeology in the Twentieth Century. Essays in Honor of Nelson Glueck*. ed. James A.

Sanders. Garden City, N.Y.: Doubleday. 164-77.
1971 Syro-Palestinian Destinations in a Mari Tin Inventory. *IEJ* 21: 31-38.

Mallet, Joël.
1973 *Tell el-Far^cah (Région de Naplouse): L'installation du Moyen Bronze antérieur au rempart*. Cahiers de la Revue biblique. Paris: J. Gabalda.

Mallowan, M. E. L.
1936 The Excavations at Tall Chagar Bazar, and an Archaeological Survey of the Ḫabur Region, 1934-5. *Iraq* 3: 1-59.
1937a The Excavations at Tall Chagar Bazar and an Archaeological Survey of the Ḫabur Region. Second Campaign, 1936. *Iraq* 4: 91-154.
1937b The Syrian City of Til-Barsib, review of *Til-Barsib*, by F. Thureau-Dangin and M. Dunand. *Antiquity* 11: 328-39.
1946 Excavations in the Baliḫ Valley, 1938. *Iraq* 8: 111-59.
1947 Excavations at Brak and Chagar Bazar. *Iraq* 9: 1-259.

Masson, V. M., and Sariainidi, V. I.
1972 *Central Asia: Turkmenia before the Achaemenids*. Ancient Peoples and Places, Vol. 79. Trans. and ed. Ruth Tringham. London: Thames and Hudson.

Matthers, J. and others.
1978 Tel Rifa ^cat 1977: Preliminary Report of an Archaeological Survey. *Iraq* 40: 119-62.

Matthiae, Paolo.
1971 Tell Mardikh, Syria, Excavations of 1967 and 1968. *Archaeology* 24: 55-61.
1975a Ebla nel periodo delle dinastie amoree e della dinastia di Akkad: Scoperte archeologiche recenti a Tell Mardikh. *Orientalia* N.S. 44: 337-60.
1975b "Unité et développement du temple dans la Syrie du bronze moyen. In *Le Temple et le culte: Compte rendu de la vingtième rencontre assyriologique internationale*. Leiden: Nederlands Historisch-Archeologisch Instituut te Istanbul. 43-72.
1976 Ebla in the Late Early Syrian Period: The Royal Palace and the State Archives. *BA* 39: 94-113.
1977 *Ebla: Un impero ritrovato*. Torino: Giulio Einaudi.
1978 Tell Mardikh: Ancient Ebla. *AJA* 82: 540-43.
1980a Two Princely Tombs at Tell Mardikh-Ebla. *Archaeology* 33: 8-17.
1980b Fouilles à Tell Mardikh-Ebla, 1978: le bâtiment Q et la nécropole princière du Bronze Moyen II. *Akkadica* 17: 1-52.

Maxwell-Hyslop, Rachel.
1946 Daggers and Swords in Western Asia: A Study from Prehistoric Times to 600 B.C. *Iraq* 8: 1-65.
1949 Western Asiatic Shaft-Hole Axes. *Iraq* 11: 90-129.
1972 The Metals *Amūtu* and *Aši^ɔu* in the Kültepe Texts. *AS* 22: 159-62.

Maxwell-Hyslop, R., *et al.*
1942 An Archaeological Survey of the Plain of Jabbul, 1939. *PEQ*: 8-40.

Mayer, L. A.
1926 A Bronze Age Deposit from a Cave near Neby Rubin (Jaffa District). *PMB* 2: 2-7.

Mazar, B.
1968 The Middle Bronze Age in Palestine. *IEJ* 18: 65-97.

McCown, Donald E., and Haines, Richard C.
1967 *Nippur I. Temple of Enlil, Scribal Quarter, and Soundings*. OIP 78. Chicago: University of Chicago.

Mellaart, James.
1957 Anatolian Chronology in the Early and Middle Bronze Age. *AS* 7: 55-88.
1958 Second Millennium Pottery from the Konya Plain and Neighborhood. *TTK Bell* 22: 311-45.
1971a Anatolia c. 4000-2300 B.C. *CAH* 3rd ed. Vol. I, Pt. 2. London: Cambridge University. 363-410.
1971b Anatolia c. 2300-1750 B.C. *CAH* 3rd ed. Vol. I, Pt. 2. London: Cambridge University. 681-704.
1979 Egyptian and Near Eastern Chronology: a dilemma? *Antiquity* 53: 6-18.

Mellink, Machteld J.
1956 *A Hittite Cemetery at Gordion*. Museum Monographs. Philadelphia. University Museum, University of Pennsylvania.
1963 An Akkadian Illustration of a Campaign in Cilicia? *Anatolia* 7: 101-15.
1965 Anatolian Chronology. In *Chronologies in Old World Archaeology*, ed. Robert W. Ehrich. Chicago: University of Chicago. 101-31.

Merrillees, R. S.
1968 *The Cypriote Bronze Age Pottery Found in Egypt*. SIMA XVIII. Lund: P. Åström.
1973 Syrian Pottery from Middle Kingdom Egypt. *Australian Journal of Biblical Archaeology* 2: 51-59.
1974 Settlement, Sanctuary and Cemetery in Bronze Age Cyprus. In *Australian Studies in Archaeology* No. 1. (1973), ed. J. Birmingham. Sydney: Southwood. 44-57.

Michael, H. N., and Ralph, E. K.
1970 Correction factors applied to Egyptian radiocarbon dates from the era before Christ. In *Radiocarbon Variations and Absolute Chronology*. Proceedings of the Twelfth Nobel Symposium held at the Institute of Physics at Uppsala University. Stockholm: Almqvist and Wiksell. 109-20.

Mkrtiachan, Boris.
1967 The Mystery of Metsamor. *New Orient* 1967 (3): 76-78.

Montet, Pierre.
1928 *Byblos et L'Égypte*. Texte. Bibliothèque archéologique et historique. Tome 11. Paris: Paul Geuthner.
1929 *Byblos et L'Égypte*. Atlas. Bibliothèque archéologique et historique. Tome 11. Paris: Paul Geuthner.

Moorey, P. R. S., and Schweizer, F.
1972 Copper and Copper Alloys in Ancient Iraq, Syria and Palestine: Some New Analyses. *Archaeometry* 14: 177-98.

Moortgat, Anton.
1962 *Tell Chuēra in Nordost-Syrien*. Vorläufiger Bericht über die dritte Grabungskampagne 1960. Köln: Westdeutscher.
1965 *Tell Chuēra in Nordost-Syrien*. Bericht über die vierte Grabungskampagne 1963. Köln: Westdeutscher.

Muhly, James David.
1973 *Copper and Tin: The Distribution of Mineral Resources and the Nature of the Metals Trade in the Bronze Age. Transactions of the Connecticut*

Academy of Arts and Sciences, Vol. 43. Hamden, Conn.: Archon Books. 155-535.

1976 *Supplement to Copper and Tin. Transactions of the Connecticut Academy of Arts and Sciences*, Vol. 46. Hamden, Conn.: Archon Books. 77-136.

Muhly, J. D., and Wertime, T. A.

1973 Evidence for the sources and use of tin during the Bronze Age of the Near East: a reply to J. E. Dayton. *World Archaeology* 5: 111-22.

Munn-Rankin, J. M.

1956 Diplomacy in Western Asia in the Early Second Millennium B.C. *Iraq* 18: 68-110.

Naʾaman, Nadav.

1976 A New Look at the Chronology of Alalakh Level VII. *AS* 26: 129-43.

1979 The Chronology of Alalakh Level VII once again. *AS* 29: 103-13.

Negbi, Ora.

1976 *Canaanite Gods in Metal. An Archaeological Study of Ancient Syro-Palestinian Figurines*. Publications of the Institute of Archaeology, No. 4. Tel Aviv: Tel Aviv University.

Negbi, Ora, and Moskowitz, S.

1966 The "Foundation Deposits" or "Offering Deposits" of Byblos. *BASOR* 184: 21-26.

Newberry, Percy E.

1893 *Beni Hasan*. Part I. London: Kegan, Paul, Trübner.

North, Robert.

1973 Ugarit Grid, Strata, and Find-Localizations. *ZDPV* 89: 113-60.

1975 Tin, Gift-Mercantilism: Archaeological Varia. *Orientalia* N.S. 44: 489-91.

Oates, David.

1965 The Excavations at Tell al Rimah, 1964. *Iraq* 27: 62-80.

1968 The Excavations at Tell al Rimah, 1967. *Iraq* 30: 115-38.

1970 The Excavations at Tell al Rimah, 1968. *Iraq* 32: 1-26.

Ohata, Kiyoshi.

1966 *Tel Zeror I: preliminary report of the excavation, first season 1964*. Tokyo: Society for Near Eastern Studies in Japan.

1967 *Tel Zeror II: preliminary report of the excavation, second season 1965*. Tokyo: Society for Near Eastern Studies in Japan.

1970 *Tel Zeror III: report of the excavation, third season 1966*. Tokyo: Society for Near Eastern Studies in Japan.

Oppenheim, A. Leo.

1956 *The Interpretation of Dreams in the Ancient Near East: with a Translation of an Assyrian Dream-Book. TAPS* N. S. Vol. 46, Pt. 3. Philadelphia: The American Philosophical Society. Lancaster, Pa.: Lancaster. 179-373.

Oren, Eliezer D.

1971 A Middle Bronze Age I Warrior Tomb at Beth-Shan. *ZDPV* 87: 109-39.

1973 *The Northern Cemetery of Beth Shan*. Museum Monograph of the University Museum, University of Pennsylvania. Leiden: E. J. Brill.

1975 The Pottery from the Achzib Defence System, Area D: 1963 and 1964 Seasons. *IEJ* 25: 211-25.

Orlin, Louis.

1970 *Assyrian Colonies in Cappadocia*. The Hague: Mouton.

Orni, Efraim, and Efrat, Elisha.

1976 *Geography of Israel*. 3rd rev. ed. Jerusalem: Israel Universities.

Ory, J.

1926 Pottery of the Middle Bronze Age and Bronze Objects from Ness-Ziona, in the Wady Hanîn (near Jaffa). *PMB* 2: 10-11.

1936 Excavations at Rās el ʿAin. *QDAP* 5: 111-12.

1937 Excavations at Rās el ʿAin. II. *QDAP* 6: 99-120.

1948 A Bronze-Age Cemetery at Dhahrat el Humraiya. *QDAP* 13: 75-89.

Özgüç, Nimet.

1966 Excavations at Acemhöyük. *Anatolia* 10: 29-52.

1968 New Light on the Dating of the Levels of the Karum and of Acemhüyük near Aksaray. *AJA* 72: 318-20.

Özgüç, Tahsin.

1950 *Kültepe Kazisi Raporu, 1948*. TTK Y-V. Seri, Sayi 10. Ankara: Türk Tarih Kurumu Basımevi.

1951 New Finds in the "Karum" of Kanesh. *ILN* 219[2]: 544-47.

1959 *Kültepe-Kaniş: New Researches at the Center of the Assyrian Trade Colonies*. TTK Y-V. Seri, Sayi 19. Ankara: Türk Tarih Kurumu Basımevi.

Özgüç, Tahsin, and Özgüç, Nimet.

1953 *Kültepe Kazisi Raporu 1949*. TTK Y-V. Seri, Sayi 12. Ankara: Türk Tarih Kurumu Basımevi.

Page, Stephanie. (Dalley).

1968 The Tablets from Tell al-Rimah 1967: A Preliminary Report. *Iraq* 30: 87-97.

Parr, Peter, J.

1968 The Origin of the Rampart Fortifications of Middle Bronze Age Palestine and Syria. *ZDPV* 84: 18-45.

1973 The Origin of the Canaanite Jar. In *Archaeological Theory and Practice: Essays presented to Professor W. F. Grimes*, ed. D. E. Strong. London: Seminar. 173-81.

Parrot, André.

1938 Mari et Chagar Bazar. *Syria* 19: 308-10.

1959 *Mission archéologique de Mari*. Vol. II: *Le Palais. Documents et Monuments*. Institut français d'archéologie de Beyrouth. Bibliothèque archéologique et historique. Tome 70. Paris: Paul Geuthner.

1968 Les fouilles de Larsa: deuxième et troisième campagnes (1967). *Syria* 45: 205-39.

Perlman, I.

1976 Provenience of M. B. Cypriote White-Painted Ware from Tel Akko. Paper presented at the Fourth Archaeological Conference in Israel. Jerusalem, March 17-18, 1976.

Perlman, I.; Asaro, F.; and Artzy, M.

1973 The Origin of the "Palestinian" Bichrome Ware. *JAOS* 93: 446-61.

Petrie, W. M. Flinders.

1891 *Tell el Hesy (Lachish)*. London: Committee of the Palestine Exploration Fund.

1917 *Tools and Weapons*. London: British School of Archaeology in Egypt.

1931 *Ancient Gaza I: Tell El Ajjūl.* London: British School of Archaeology in Egypt and Bernard Quaritch.

1932 *Ancient Gaza II: Tell El Ajjūl.* London: British School of Archaeology in Egypt and Bernard Quaritch.

1933 *Ancient Gaza III: Tell El Ajjūl.* London: British School of Archaeology in Egypt and Bernard Quaritch.

1934 *Ancient Gaza IV: Tell El Ajjūl.* London: British School of Archaeology in Egypt and Bernard Quaritch.

Pettinato, G.

1975 Testi cuneiformi del 3. millennio in paleo-cananeo rinvenuti nella campagna 1974 a Tell Mardīkh = Ebla. *Orientalia* N.S. 44: 361-74.

1976 The Royal Archives of Tell Mardikh-Ebla. *BA* 39: 44-52.

Pettinato, G., and Matthiae, P.

1976 Aspetti amministrativi e topografici di Ebla nel III. millennio Av. Cr. *RSO* 50: 1-30.

Porada, Edith.

1965 The Relative Chronology of Mesopotamia. Part I. In *Chronologies in Old World Archaeology*, ed. Robert W. Ehrich. Chicago: University of Chicago. 133-200.

1966 Les Cylindres de la Jarre Montet. *Syria* 43: 243-58.

Porter, Bertha, and Moss, Rosalind L. B.

1951 *Topographical Bibliography of Ancient Egyptian Hieroglyphic Texts, Reliefs, and Paintings VII: Nubia, The Deserts, and Outside Egypt.* Oxford: Clarendon.

Posener, Georges.

1939 Nouveaux textes hiératiques de proscription. *Mélanges syriens offerts à Monsieur René Dussaud.* Vol. I. Paris: Geuthner. 313-17.

1940 *Princes et pays d'Asie et de Nubie: textes hiératiques sue des figurines d'envoûtement du moyen Empire.* Fondation égyptologique Reine Elisabeth, parc du cinquantenaire. Brussels: Etts Vromant.

1966 Les textes d'envoûtement de Mirgissa. *Syria* 43: 277-87.

1971 Syria and Palestine c. 2160-1780 B.C.: Relations with Egypt. *CAH* 3rd ed. Vol. I, Pt. 2. London: Cambridge University. 532-58.

Prag, Kay.

1970 The 1959 Deep Sounding at Harran in Turkey. *Levant* 2: 63-94.

Prausnitz, M. W.

1975a Accho, Plain of; Achzib. In *Encyclopedia of Archaeological Excavations in the Holy Land*, ed. Michael Avi-Yonah. Vol. I. Jerusalem: Israel Exploration Society and Massada. 23-30.

1975b The Planning of the Middle Bronze Age Town at Achzib and its Defences. *IEJ* 25: 202-10.

Pritchard, James B.

1963 *The Bronze Age Cemetery at Gibeon.* Museum Monographs. Philadelphia: The University Museum, University of Pennsylvania.

Przeworski, Stefan.

1939 *Die Metallindustrie anatoliens in der Zeit von 1500 bis 700 vor chr.* Internationales Archiv für Ethnographie, Band 36, Supplement. Leiden: E. J. Brill.

Rast, Walter E., and Schaub, R. Thomas.

1978 A Preliminary Report of Excavations at Bâb edh-Dhrâᶜ, 1975. In *Preliminary Excavation Reports: Bâb edh-Dhrâᶜ, Sardis, Meiron, Tell el-Hesi, Carthage (Punic)*, ed. David Noel Freedman. AASOR 43. Cambridge, Mass.: American Schools of Oriental Research. 1-32.

Reade, J. E.

1968 Tell Taya (1967): Summary Report. *Iraq* 30: 234-64.

Renfrew, Colin.

1969 Review of *Locational Analysis in Human Geography*, by P. Haggett. *Antiquity* 43: 74-75.

1972 *The Emergence of Civilisation: The Cyclades and the Aegean in the Third Millennium* B.C. London: Methuen.

Richard, Suzanne.

1978 *The End of the Early Bronze Age in Palestine-Transjordan: A Study of the Post-EB III Cultural Complex.* Ph.D. Dissertation, The Johns Hopkins University. Baltimore, Maryland.

Rothenberg, Benno.

1962 Ancient Copper Industries in the Western Arabah. *PEQ* 1962-63: 5-71.

Rowton, Michael B.

1970 Chronology II. Ancient Western Asia. *CAH* 3rd ed. Vol. I, Pt. 1. London: Cambridge University. 193-239.

Sachs, A.

1970 Absolute Dating from Mesopotamian Records. *Transactions of the Royal Society, London.* A. 269. 19-22.

Sasson, Jack M.

1966 A Sketch of North Syrian Economic Relations in the Middle Bronze Age. *JESHO* 9: 161-81.

1968 Instances of Mobility Among Mari Artisans. *BASOR* 190: 46-54.

Sauvaget, M.

1939 Le "Tell" d'Alep. *Mélanges syriens offerts à René Dussaud.* Paris: Paul Geuthner. 59-65.

Schaeffer, Claude, F. A.

1931 Les Fouilles de Minet-el-Beidha et de Ras-Shamra, deuxième campagne (printemps 1930). *Syria* 12: 1-14.

1932 Les fouilles de Minet-el-Beida et de Ras-Shamra, troisième campagne (printemps 1931). *Syria* 13: 1-27.

1933 Les fouilles de Minet-el-Beida et de Ras-Shamra, quatrième campagne (printemps 1932). *Syria* 14: 93-127.

1938 Les fouilles de Ras Shamra-Ugarit, neuvième campagne (printemps 1937). *Syria* 19: 193-255.

1939 *Ugaritica: études relatives aux découvertes de Ras Shamra.* Première série. Mission de Ras Shamra III. Paris: Paul Geuthner.

1945 La contribution de la Syrie ancienne à l'invention du bronze. *JEA* 31: 92-95.

1948 *Stratigraphie comparée et chronologie de l'Asie occidentale. (IIIᵉ et IIᵉ millénaires).* London: Oxford University.

1949 *Ugaritica II: nouvelles études relatives aux découvertes de Ras Shamra.* Mission de Ras Shamra V.

Paris: Paul Geuthner.

1978 *Ugaritica VII*. Mission de Ras Shamra XVIII. Bibliothèque archéologique et historique 99. Leiden: E. J. Brill.

Schirmer, Wulf.

1969 *Die Bebauung am Unteren Büyükkale-Nordwesthang in Boğazköy. Ergebnisse der Untersuchungen der Grabungscampagnen, 1960-1963. WVDOG* 81. Berlin: Gebr. Mann.

Schmidt, Erich F.

1932 *The Alischar Hüyük: Seasons of 1928 and 1929.* Part I. OIP 19. Researches in Anatolia IV. Chicago: University of Chicago.

Schumacher, G.

1889 Recent Discoveries in Galilee. *PEFQ*: 68-78.

Selimkhanov, I. R.

1962 Spectral Analysis of Metal Articles from Archaeological Monuments of the Caucasus. *PPS* 28, N.S.: 68-79.

Seton Williams, M. V.

1953 A Painted Pottery of the Second Millennium from Southern Turkey and Northern Syria. *Iraq* 15: 56-68.

1954 Cilician Survey. *AS* 4: 121-74.

1961 Preliminary Report on the Excavations at Tell Rifaᶜat. *Iraq* 23: 68-87.

Smith, Robert Houston.

1962 *Excavations in the Cemetery at Khirbet Kūfīn, Palestine*. London: Bernard Quaritch.

1973 *Pella of the Decapolis*. Vol. I: *The 1967 Season of the College of Wooster Expedition to Pella*. The College of Wooster. London: William Clowes.

Smith, Sidney.

1940 *Alalakh and Chronology*. London: Luzac and Company.

1945 Middle Minoan I-II and Babylonian Chronology. *AJA* 49: 1-24.

Smith, William Stevenson.

1965 *Interconnections in the Ancient Near East: A Study of the Relationships between the Arts of Egypt, the Aegean, and Western Asia*. New Haven and London: Yale University.

1969 Influence of the Middle Kingdom of Egypt in Western Asia, especially in Byblos. *AJA* 73: 277-81.

Sollberger, Edmond.

1968 A Tankard for Atta-Hušu. *JCS* 22: 30-33.

Speiser, E. A.

1933 The Pottery of Tell Billa. *MJ* 23: 249-82.

1935 *Excavations at Tepe Gawra*. Vol. I: *Levels I-VIII*. Philadelphia: University of Pennsylvania.

Starr, Richard F. S.

1937 *Nuzi: Report on the Excavations at Yorgan Tepa near Kirkuk, Iraq*. Vol. II: Plates. Cambridge, Mass.: Harvard University.

1939 *Nuzi: Report on the Excavations at Yorgan Tepa near Kirkuk, Iraq*. Vol. I: Text. Cambridge, Mass.: Harvard University.

Stern, Ephraim, and Saltz, Diane Lynn.

1978 Cypriote Pottery from the Middle Bronze Age Strata of Tel Mevorakh. *IEJ* 28: 137-45.

Stewart, James R.

1974 *Tell el ᶜAjjūl: The Middle Bronze Age Remains*. SIMA 38, ed. Hanna E. Kassis. Göteborg: P. Åström.

Stronach, D. B.

1957 The Development and Diffusion of Metal Types in Early Bronze Age Anatolia. *AS* 7: 89-125.

Stuckenrath, Robert, Jr., and Ralph, Elizabeth K.

1965 University of Pennsylvania Radiocarbon Dates VIII. *Radiocarbon* 7: 187-99.

Sukenik, E. L.

1948 Archaeological Investigations at ᶜAffūla. *JPOS* 21: 1-79.

Sussman, Varda.

1966 Middle Bronze Age Burial Caves at Moza. *ᶜAtiqot* 3: 40-43 (Hebrew series).

Swift, Gustavus F., Jr.

1958 *The Pottery of the ᶜAmuq Phase K to O, and its Historical Relationships*. Ph.D. Dissertation, University of Chicago. Chicago.

Thompson, R. Campbell, and Hamilton, R. W.

1932 The British Museum Excavations on the Temple of Ishtar at Nineveh, 1930-31. *LAAA* 19: 55-116.

Thompson, R. Campbell, and Mallowan, M. E. L.

1933 The British Museum Excavations at Nineveh, 1931-32. *LAAA* 20: 71-186.

Thompson, Thomas L.

1970 The Dating of the Megiddo Temples in Strata XV-XIV. *ZDPV* 86: 38-49.

1974 *The Historicity of the Patriarchal Narratives: The Quest for the Historical Abraham*. Beiheft zur Zeitschrift für die alttestamentliche Wissenschaft. 133. Berlin: Walter de Gruyter.

Thureau-Dangin, F., and Dunand, M.

1936 *Til-Barsib*. Bibliothèque archéologique et historique. Tome XXIII. Paris: Paul Geuthner.

Toombs, Lawrence E.

1976 The Stratification of Tell Balâṭah (Shechem). *BASOR* 223: 57-59.

Toombs, Lawrence E., and Wright, G. Ernest.

1961 The Third Campaign at Balâṭah (Shechem). *BASOR* 161: 11-54.

1963 The Fourth Campaign at Balâṭah (Shechem). *BASOR* 169: 1-60.

Trigger, Bruce G.

1968 The Determinants of Settlement Patterns. In *Settlement Archaeology*, ed. K. C. Chang. Palo Alto, Calif.: National Press Books. 53-78.

Tufnell, Olga.

1958 *Lachish IV (Tell Ed-Duweir): The Bronze Age*. Text and Plates. London: Oxford University.

1962 The Courtyard Cemetery at Tell El-ᶜAjjul, Palestine. *Bulletin of the Institute of Archaeology*. University of London. No. 3: 1-37.

1969 The Pottery from Royal Tombs I-III at Byblos. *Berytus* 18: 5-33.

1973 The Middle Bronze Age Scarab-seals from burials on the mound at Megiddo. *Levant* 5: 69-82.

Tufnell, Olga, and Ward, W. A.

1966 Relations between Byblos, Egypt and Mesopotamia at the End of the Third Millennium B.C. *Syria* 43: 165-241.

van Loon, Maurits.

1969 New Evidence from Inland Syria for the Chro-

nology of the Middle Bronze Age. *AJA* 73: 276-77.
1979 1974 and 1975 Preliminary Results of the Excavations at Selenkahiye Near Meskene, Syria. In *Archaeological Reports from the Tabqa Dam Project: Euphrates Valley, Syria*, ed. David Noel Freedman. AASOR 44. Cambridge, Mass.: American Schools of Oriental Research. 97-112.

Veenhof, K. R.
1972 *Aspects of Old Assyrian Trade and its Terminology*. Studia et Documenta 10. Leiden: E. J. Brill.

Vincent, L. -H.
1947 Une grotte funéraire antique dans l'Ouadi et-Tin. *RB* 54: 269-82.

Vogel, J. C., and Waterbolk, H. T.
1972 Gröningen Radiocarbon Dates X. *Radiocarbon* 14: 6-110.

von der Osten, Hans Henning.
1937a *The Alishar Hüyük, Seasons of 1930-32*. Part I. OIP 28. Researches in Anatolia VII. Chicago: University of Chicago.
1937b *The Alishar Hüyük, Seasons of 1930-32*. Part II. OIP 29. Researches in Anatolia VIII. Chicago: University of Chicago.
1956 *Svenska Syrien Expeditionen 1952-1953*. I: *Die Grabung von Tell es-Ṣaliḥiyeh*. Skrifter Utgivna av Svenska Institutet I. Lund: CWK Gleerup.

Waechter, J.; Göguş, Sabahat; and Seton Williams, V.
1951 The Sakce Gözü Cave Site 1949. *TTK Bell* 15: 193-201.

Watson, Patty Jo.
1965 The Chronology of North Syria and North Mesopotamia from 10,000 B.C. to 2000 B.C. In *Chronologies in Old World Archaeology*, ed. Robert W. Ehrich. Chicago: University of Chicago. 61-100.

Webley, D.
1972 Soils and Site Location in Prehistoric Palestine. In *Papers in Economic Prehistory*, ed. E. S. Higgs. London: Cambridge University. 169-80.

Weill, Raymond.
1939 Notes sur les noms asiatiques des "Textes d'Exécration" égyptiens du Moyen Empire. *Mélanges syriens offerts à René Dussaud*. Vol. II. Paris: Paul Geuthner. 947-58.

Welker, Marian.
1948 *The Painted Pottery of the Near East in the Second Millennium B.C. and its Chronological Background*. *TAPS* 38, Pt. 2. Philadelphia: Lancaster. 185-328.

Weinstein, James M.
1974 A Statuette of the Princess Sobeknefru at Tell Gezer. *BASOR* 213: 49-57.
1975 Egyptian Relations with Palestine in the Middle Kingdom. *BASOR* 217: 1-16.

Williams, Bruce.
1975 *Archaeological and Historical Problems of the Second Intermediate Period*. Ph.D. Dissertation, University of Chicago.

Wilson, John A.
1969 The Story of Sinuhe; Middle Kingdom Egyptian Contacts with Asia; The Inscription of Khu-Sebek, Called Djaa. In *Ancient Near Eastern Texts Relating to the Old Testament*, ed. James B. Pritchard. 3rd ed. with Supplement. Princeton: Princeton University. 18-22; 228-30.

Woolley, C. Leonard.
1914 Hittite Burial Customs. *LAAA* 6: 87-98.
1934 *Ur Excavations*. Vol. II: *The Royal Cemetery*. Text and Plates. London: Oxford University.
1955 *Alalakh: An Account of the Excavations at Tell Atchana in the Hatay, 1937-1949*. London: Oxford University.

Wright, G. Ernest.
1961 The Archaeology of Palestine. In *The Bible and the Ancient Near East. Essays in Honor of William Foxwell Albright*, ed. G. E. Wright. Garden City, N.Y.: Doubleday. 73-112.
1965 *Shechem: The Biography of a Biblical City*. New York: McGraw-Hill.
1966 Review of *Excavations at Jericho*. Vol. II, by K. M. Kenyon. *Antiquity* 40: 149-50.

Wright, G. Ernest, *et al.*
1965 The Fifth Campaign at Balâṭah (Shechem). *BASOR* 180: 7-41.

Wright, G. R. H.
1968 Tell el-Yehūdīyah and the Glacis. *ZDPV* 84: 1-17.

Yadin, Yigael.
1972 *Hazor*. The Schweich Lectures of the British Academy. London: Oxford University.
1973 The Tell Beit Mirsim G-F Alleged Fortifications. *BASOR* 212: 22-25.
1975 *Hazor: the rediscovery of a great citadel of the Bible*. Jerusalem: Weidenfeld and Nicholson.
1977 Nature of the Settlements in Eretz-Israel in the Middle Bronze IIA and the Problem of the Fortifications at Aphek. *Eretz-Israel* 13: 91-105 (Hebrew).
1978 The Nature of the Settlements During the Middle Bronze IIA Period in Israel and the Problem of the Aphek Fortifications. *ZDPV* 94: 1-23.

Yadin, Yigael, *et al.*
1958 *Hazor I*. Jerusalem: Magnes.
1960 *Hazor II*. Jerusalem: Magnes.

Yadin, Yigael, and Shiloh, Yigael.
1971 Hazor. *IEJ* 21: 230.

Yakar, Jak.
1979 Troy and Anatolian Early Bronze Age Chronology. *AS* 29: 51-67.

Young, T. Cuyler, Jr.
1969 The Chronology of the Late Third and Second Millennia in Central Western Iran as Seen from Godin Tepe. *AJA* 73: 287-91.

NOTE ON FIGURES

The pottery drawings are all adapted from the publication sources given in the description of the figures. A verbal description of the decoration is given only for figures 10-18 which include only pottery from Megiddo. The primary reason for this is that in the publication of the Megiddo pottery the drawing of a vessel may not correspond to the verbal description for the individual vessel from a particular tomb. In such cases, the verbal description given here does not agree with the vessel's depiction but should be correct for the example from the indicated tomb group. Verbal descriptions of the other vessels illustrated and their fabric are not included due to considerable inconsistencies in (and sometimes lack of) such information in the original publication—a situation which could not be resolved without personal visual inspection of all the illustrated vessels.

The drawing of figure 9 is based on the unpublished plans of the Megiddo expedition. I would like to thank the Oriental Institute of the University of Chicago and the archivist, Ronnie Burbank, for permission to include this information here. "N.S." indicates that the scale of the drawing could not be determined.

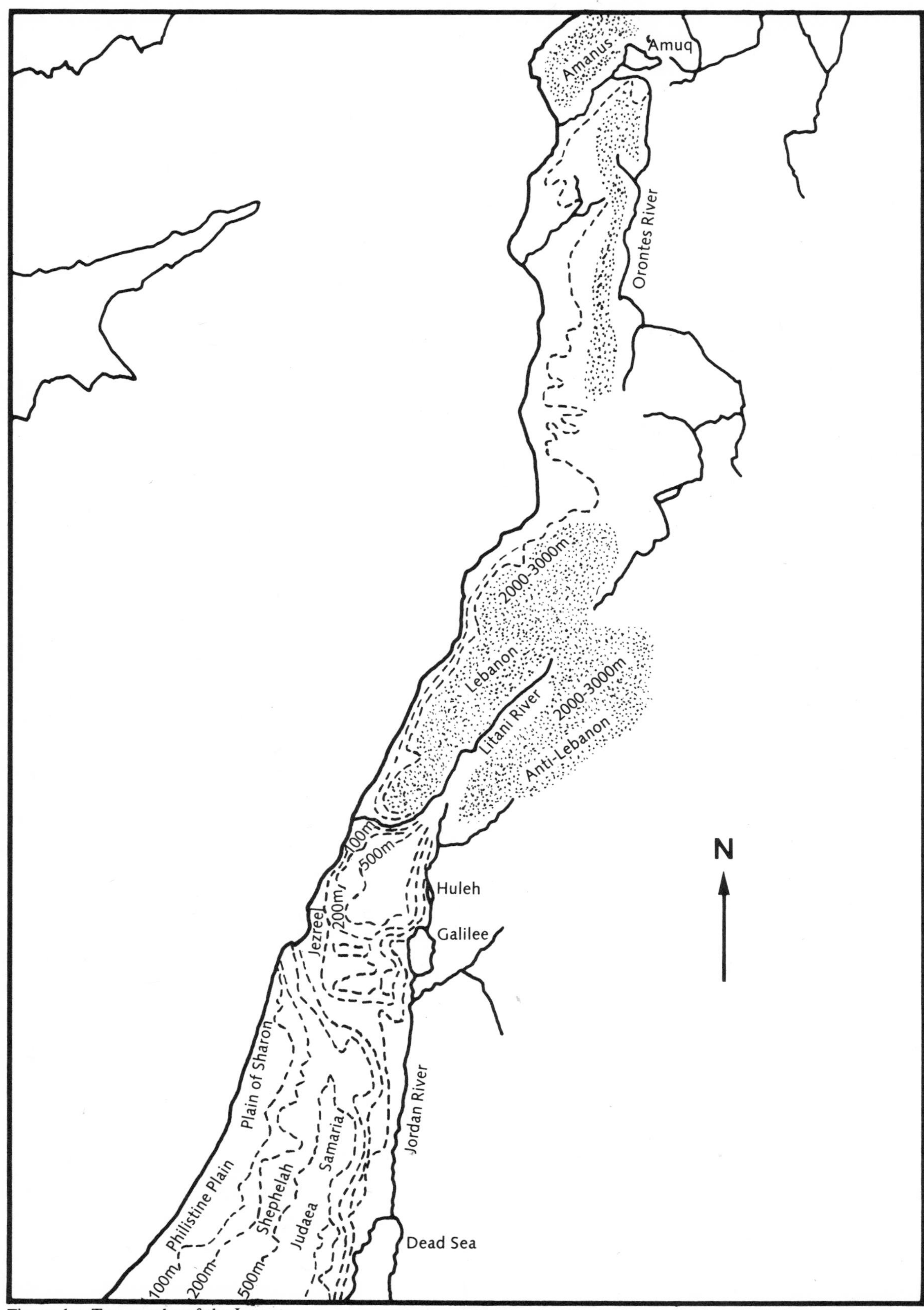

Figure 1: Topography of the Levant
Scale 1:2,500,000

Figure 2: Trade Routes in the Assyrian Colony Period

-------- routes Assur to Kaniš via Maraş or Malatya
-.-.-.-.- routes Assur to Kaniš via Ergani Maden
.... routes to Ebla, Palmyra and Tarsus

Sites:

1. Kültepe (Kaniš)
2. Boğazköy (Ḫattuša)
3. Alişar (Ankuwa?)
4. Acemhüyük (Purušḫaddum?)
5. Tarsus
6. Tell Mardikh (Ebla)
7. Palmyra
8. Tuttul
9. Harran
10. Assur
11. Tell Shemshara (Šušarra)
12. Yorgan Tepe (Nuzi, Ga.Sur)
13. Babylon

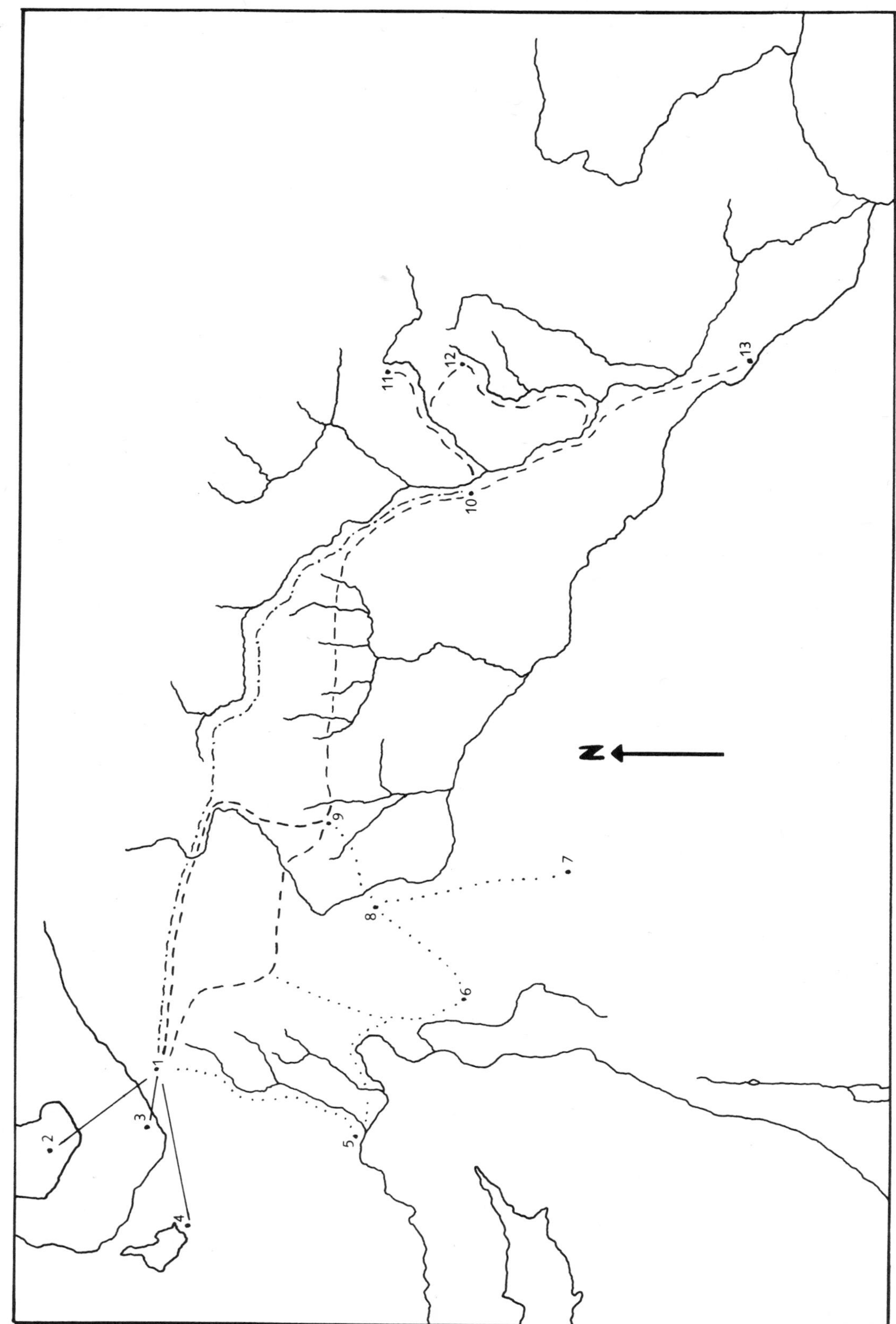

Figure 2: Trade Routes in the Assyrian Colony Period

Figure 3: Trade Routes in the Mari Period

-.-.-.-.-	The Road to Emar
....	The Dream-Book Route
---------	Suggested Tin Routes
-..-..-..	Alternate direct route, Mari to Qatna via the Syrian Desert

Sites:

1. Kültepe (Kaniš)
2. Boğazköy (Ḫattuša)
3. Alişar (Ankuwa?)
4. Acemhüyük (Purušḫaddum?)
5. Atçana (Alalakh)
6. Ras Shamra (Ugarit)
7. Dan (Laiš)
8. Hazor
9. Megiddo
10. Aphek
11. Byblos
12. Qatna
13. Palmyra
14. Tell Mardikh (Ebla)
15. Aleppo (Ḫalab/Iamḫad)
16. Emar
17. Tuttul
18. Harran
19. Chagar Bazar (Šubat-Enlil?)
20. Mari
21. Ekallatum
22. Assur
23. Tell Shemshara (Šušarra)
24. Mankisum
25. Rapiqum
26. Tell Asmar (Ešnunna)
27. Sippar
28. Babylon
29. Larsa
30. Susa

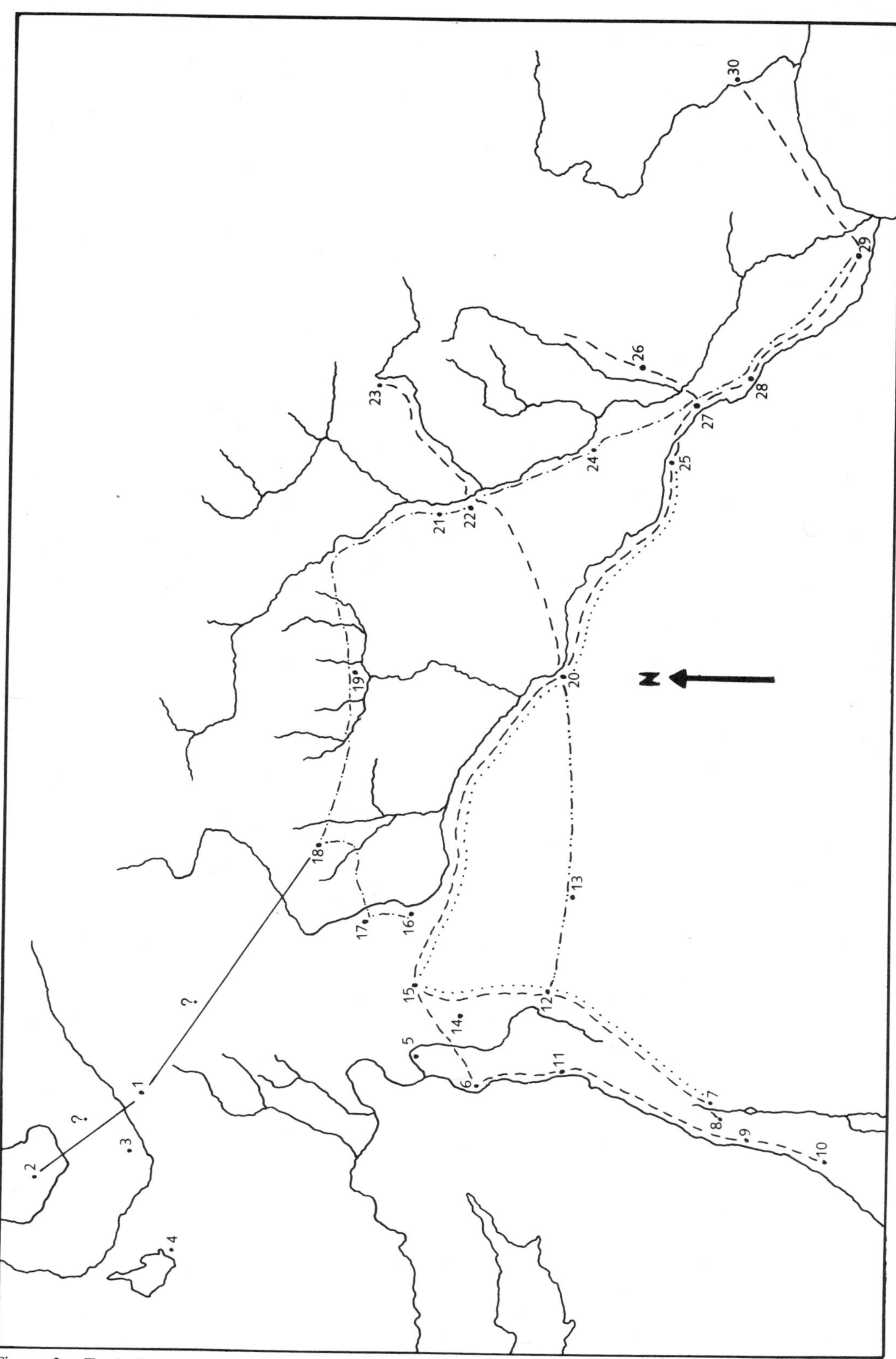

Figure 3: Trade Routes in the Mari Period

Figure 4: Sites of the MB I Period in the Levant

1. Megiddo
2. Aphek (Ras el-^{c}Ain)
3. Tell Beit Mirsim
4. Tell el-^{c}Ajjul
5. Tell ed-Duweir (Lachish)
6. Tell el-Hesi
7. Tell Nagila
8. Dhahrat el-Humraiya
9. Neby Rubin
10. Beth-shemesh
11. Gezer
12. Wadi et-Tin
13. Khirbet Kufin
14. Moza
15. El-Jib (Gibeon)
16. Bethel
17. ^{c}Ain es-Samiyeh/Sinjil
18. Tell es-Sultan (Jericho)
19. Shechem
20. Tell el-Far^{c}h (N.)
21. Beth-shan
22. Kfar Szold/Ginosar
23. Hazor
24. Tel Dan
25. Tel Kedesh
26. Tur^{c}an
27. Affula
28. Tel Zeror
29. Tel Poleg
30. Barqai
31. Mevorach
32. Akko
33. Nahariya
34. Achzib
35. Sidon: Kafer Djarra
Lebe^{c}a
Ruweise
Majdalouna
36. Beirut/Sin el-Fil
37. Amrith
38. Byblos
39. Ugarit
40. Tell Simiriyan
41. Tell Sukas
42. Kāmid el-Lōz
43. Tell es-Salihiyyeh
44. Hama
45. Qatna
46. Osmaniye
Dnebi
47. Selimiye
48. Tell ^{c}As
49. Khan Sheikhoun
50. Tell Masin
51. Yabrud
52. Tell et-Tin
53. Tell Mardikh (Ebla)
54. Judeideh
55. Tell Ta^{c}yinat
56. Atçana (Alalakh)
57. Pella
58. Fo^{c}ara

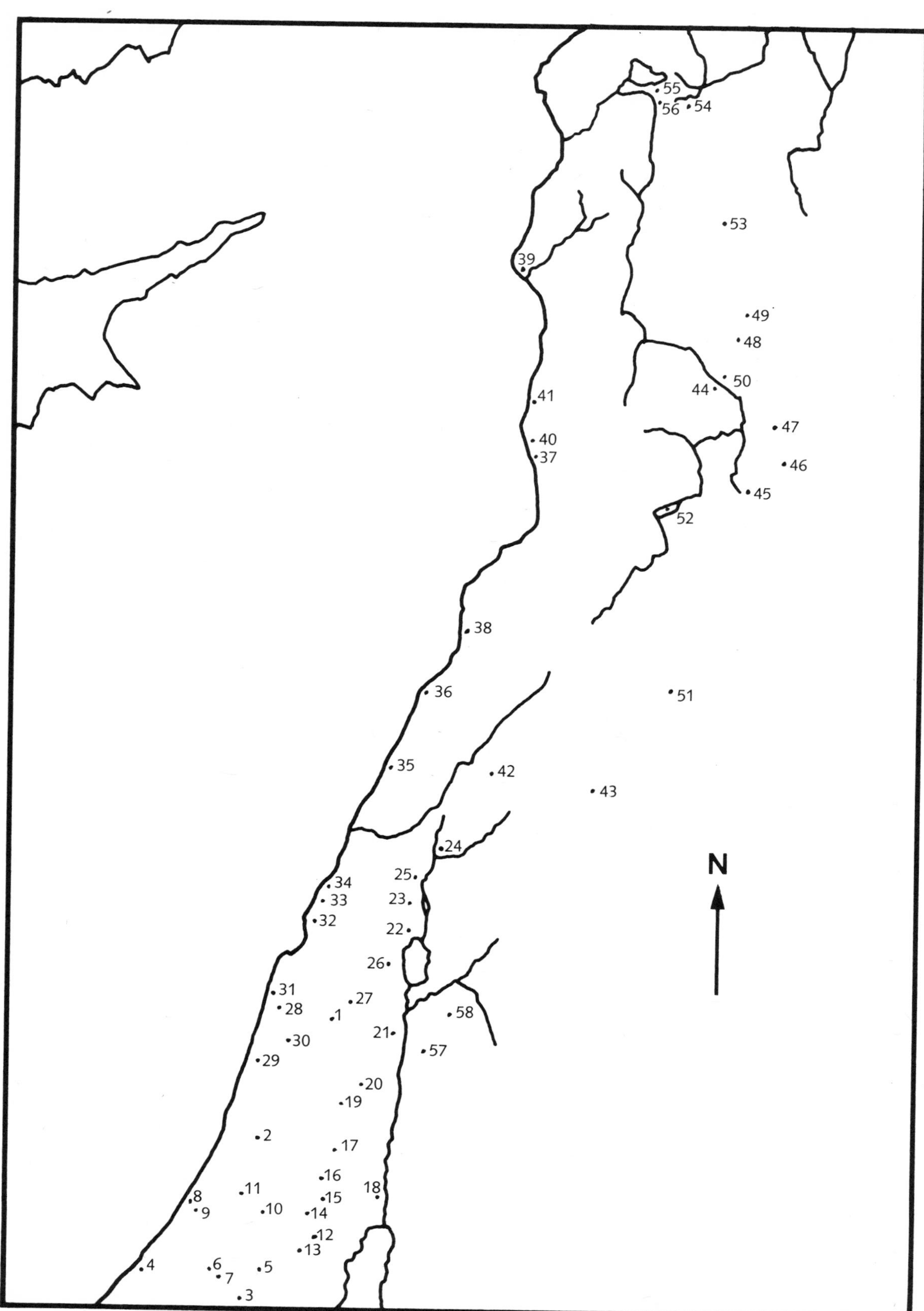

Figure 4: Sites of the MB I Period in the Levant
Scale 1:2,500,000

Figure 5: Sites of Mesopotamia and Anatolia

Anatolia:
1. Kültepe (Kaniš)
2. Boğazköy (Ḫattuša)
3. Alaca Hüyük
4. Alişar Hüyük (Ankuwa?)
5. Acemhüyük (Purušḫaddum?)
6. Gordion
7. Mersin
8. Tarsus
9. Sakcegözü
10. Gaziantep

Northern Syria:
11. Tell Rifa[c]at
12. Aleppo
13. Tadmur/Palmyra
14. Tell Selenkahiye
15. Carchemish
16. Tell Ahmar
17. Harran
18. Tell Chuera
19. Tell Fakhariyah
20. Chagar Bazar
21. Tell Brak

Mesopotamia and Iran:
22. Mari
23. Baghouz
24. Tell al-Rimah (Karana)
25. Nineveh
26. Tepe Gawra
27. Tell Billa
28. Dinkha Tepe
29. Tell Shemshara (Šušarra)
30. Yorgan Tepe (Nuzi)
31. Assur
32. Tell Asmar
33. Khafajeh
34. Ishchali
35. Kish
36. Nippur
37. Larsa
38. Ur
39. Telloh
40. Susa

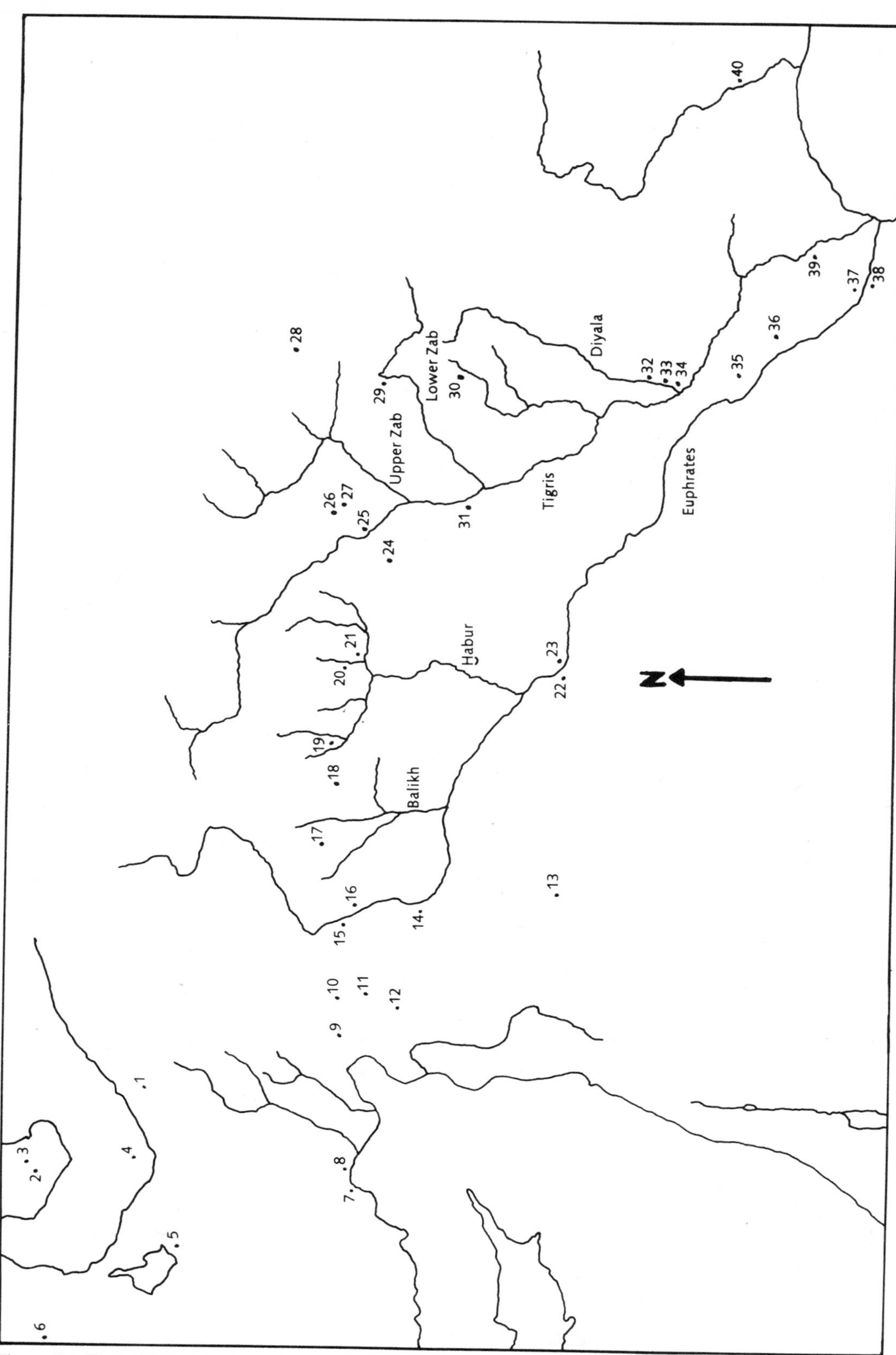

Figure 5: Sites of Mesopotamia and Anatolia

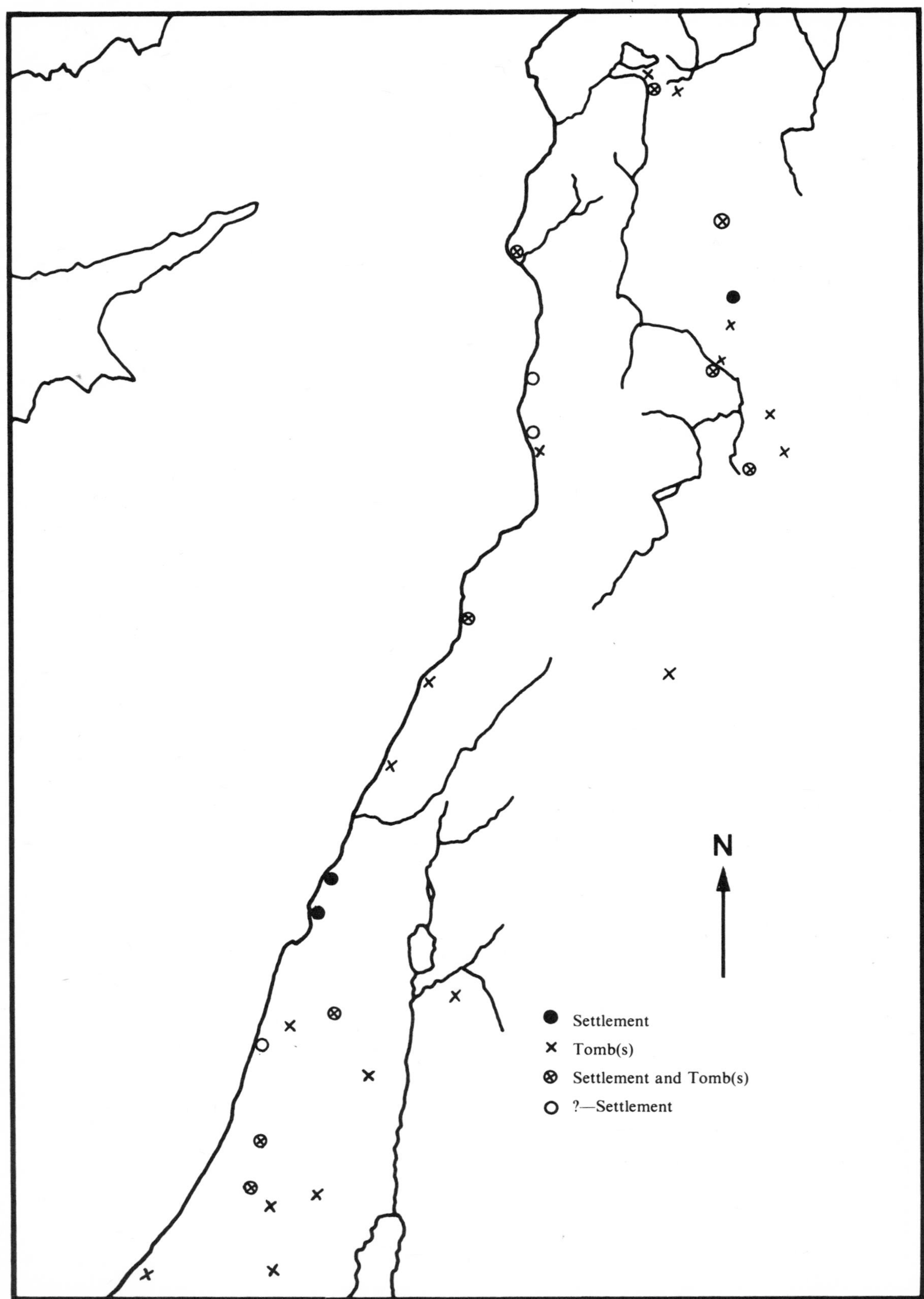

Figure 6: Sites of the MB IA Period
Scale 1:2,500,000

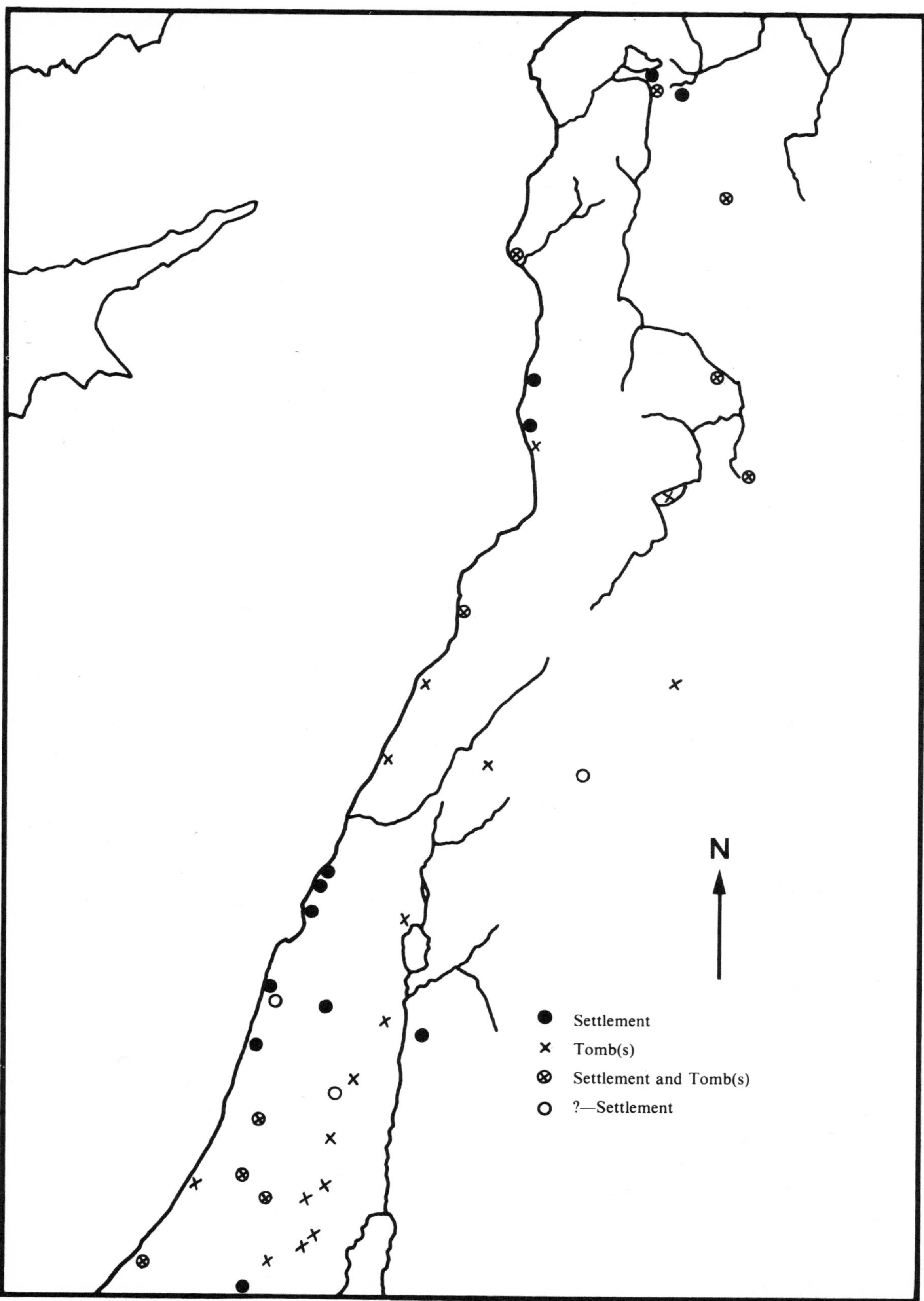

Figure 7: Sites of the MB IB Period
Scale 1:2,500,000

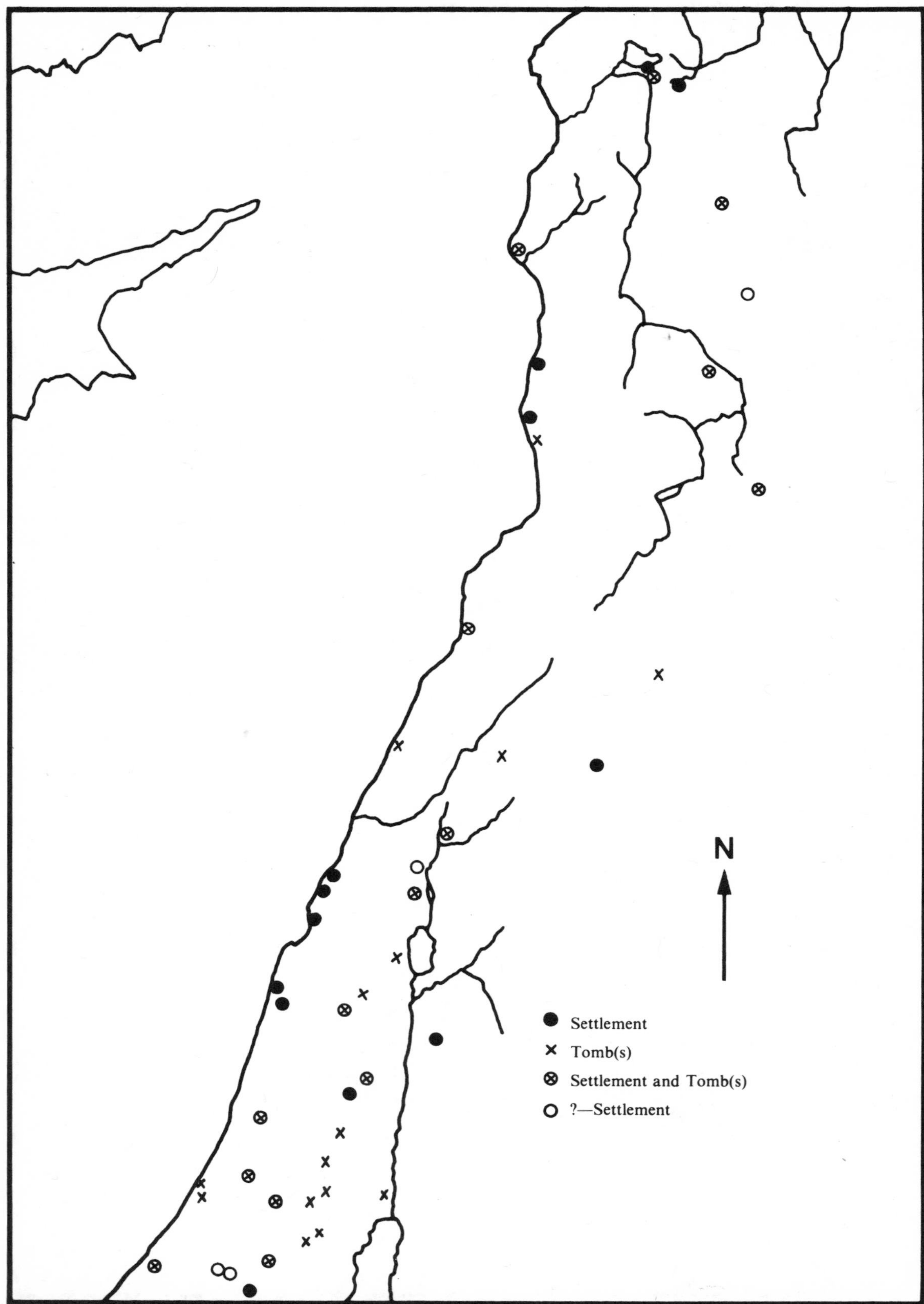

Figure 8: Sites of the MB IC Period
Scale 1:2,500,000

Figure 9 follows.

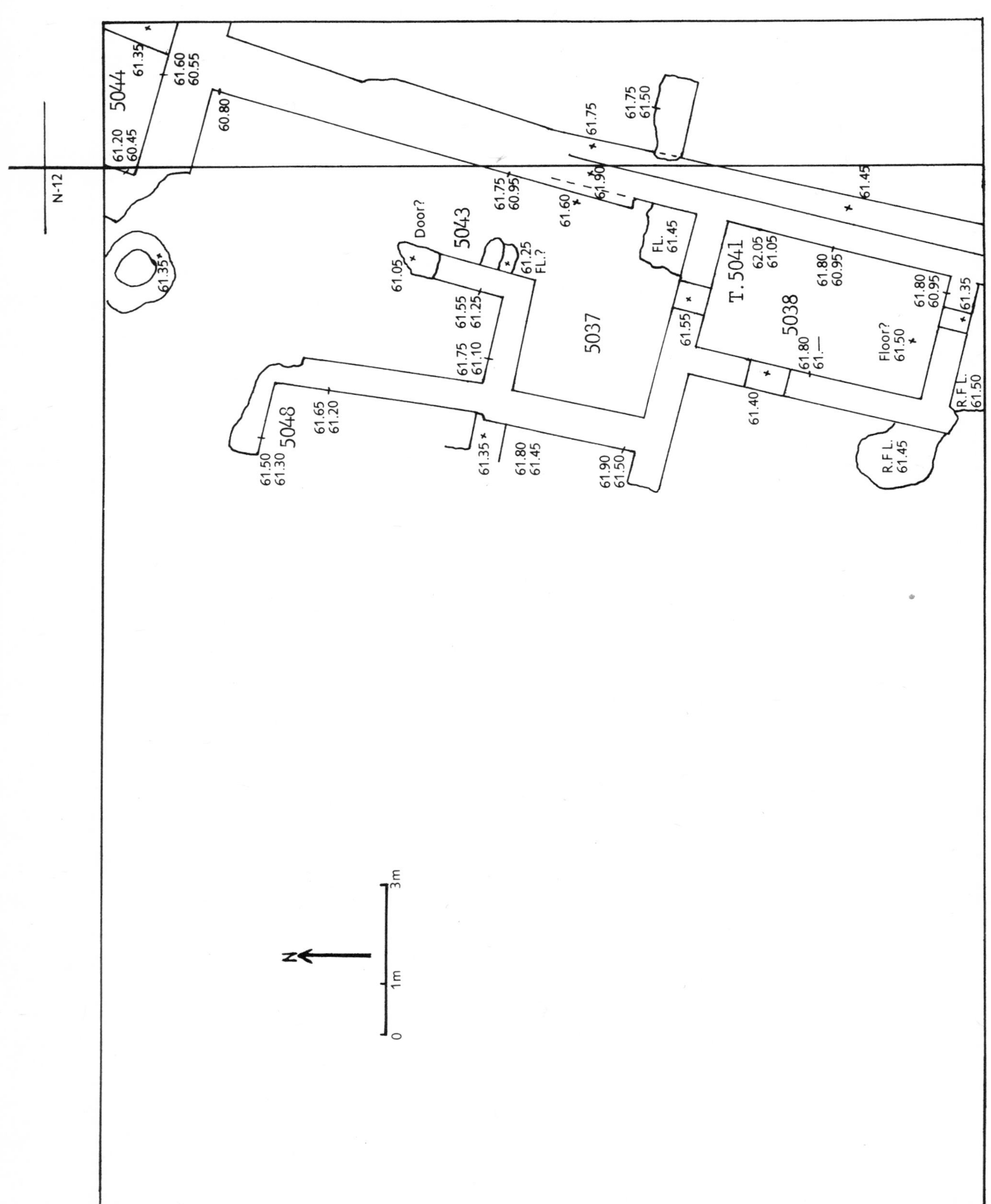

Figure 9: Superposition of Loci in Square N 12, Area BB, West, Megiddo
(Left) from plan 56 "Stable" ("Stratum XII")

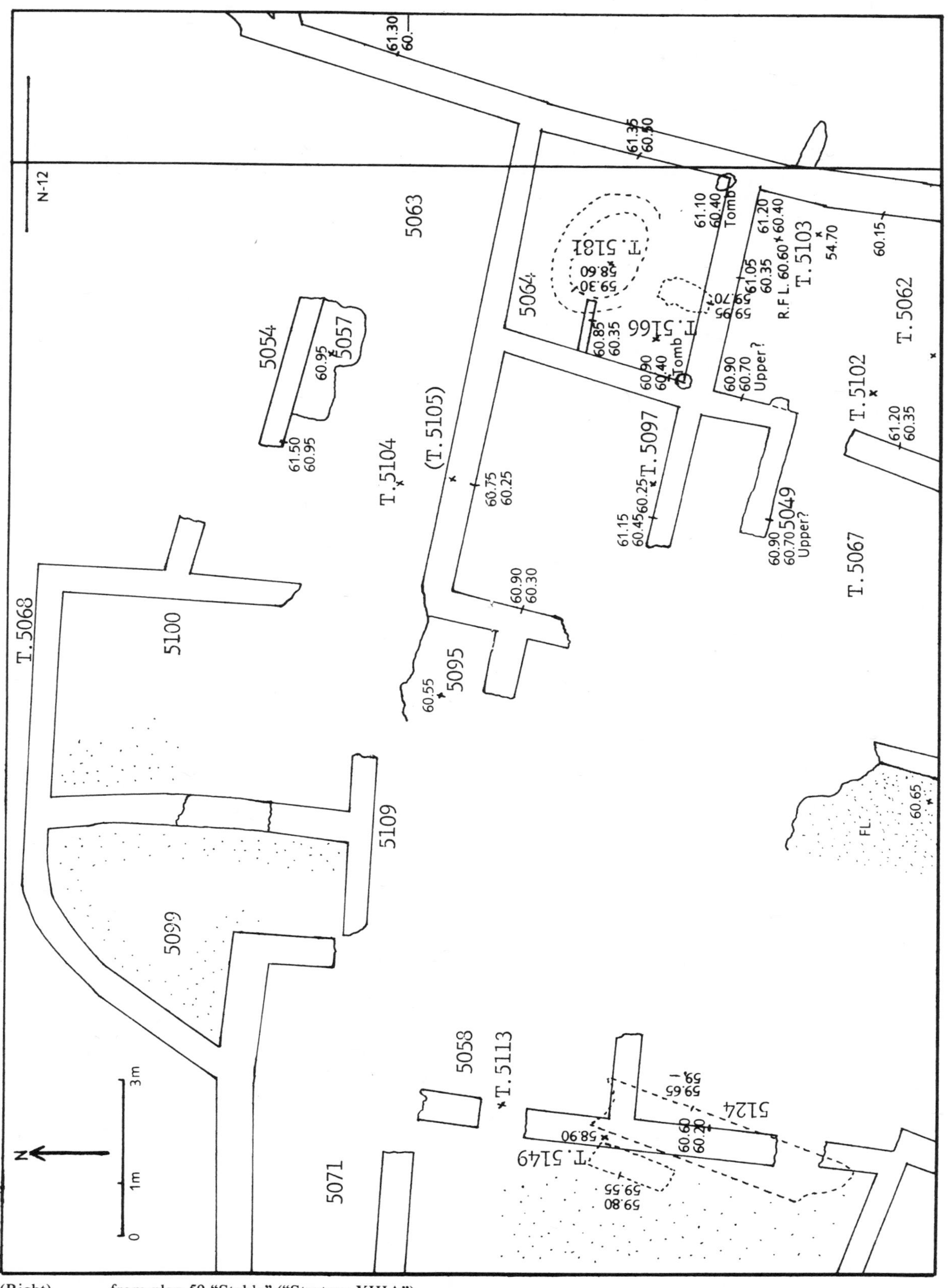

(Right) —— from plan 59 "Stable" ("Stratum XIIIA")
------ from plan 61 "Stable" ("Strata XIIIB, XIV and XV")

Figure 10: Pottery from Megiddo, Area BB, West, Stratigraphically Assigned to Phases 1/2 and 2

Phase 1/2
Tomb 5181:

1. Jar with band-painted decoration	1:5	Loud 1948: pl. 12:22
2. Jar with band-painted decoration	1:5	Loud 1948: pl. 12:20
3. Jug with red wash and burnish	1:5	Loud 1948: pl. 10:12
4. Jug with red wash and burnish	1:5	Loud 1948: pl. 11:17
5. Jug with red wash and burnish	1:5	Loud 1948: pl. 10:17
6. Bowl with red wash, burnish on rim	1:5	Loud 1948: pl. 14:17

Tomb 5149:

7. Jar with band-painted decoration	1:5	Loud 1948: pl. 8:8

Phase 2
Tomb 5180:

8. Jug with red wash and burnish	1:5	Loud 1948: pl. 10:4
9. Jug with red painted decoration	1:5	Loud 1948: pl. 11:13

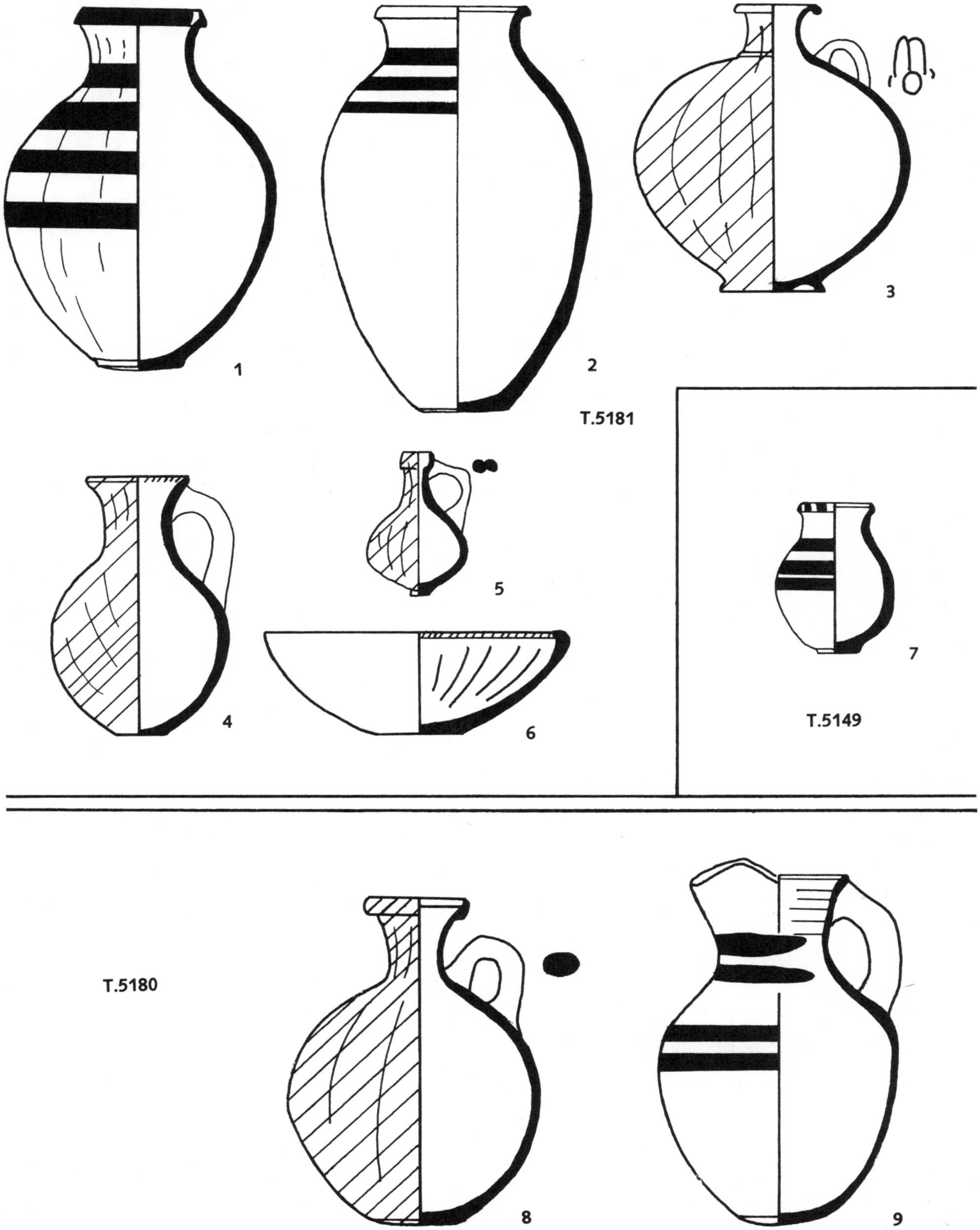

FIGURE 10

1

2

3

T.5181

4

5

6

7

T.5149

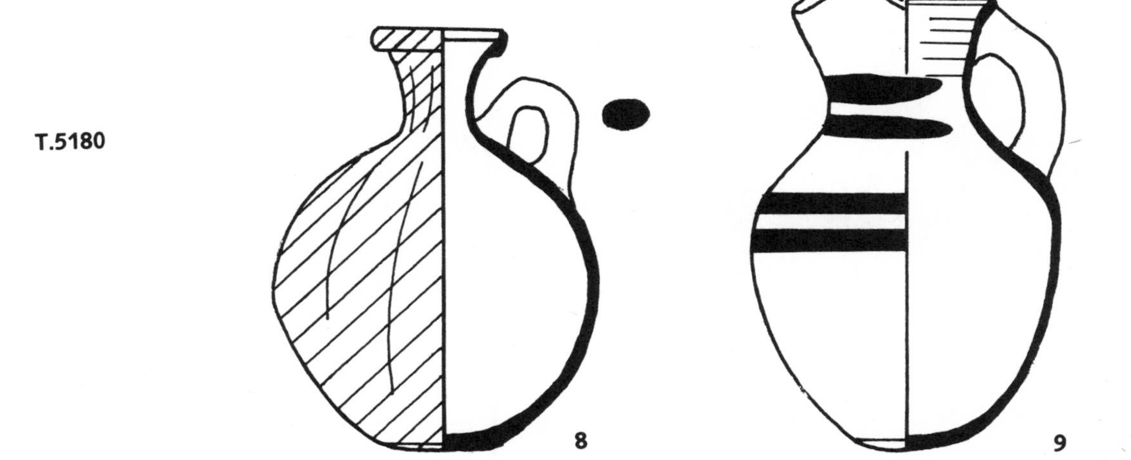

Figure 11: Pottery from Megiddo, Area BB, East, Stratigraphically Assigned to Phase 1/2

Tomb 3143:		
1. Jar	1:5	Loud 1948: pl. 12:16
2. Jug with red wash and burnish	1:5	Loud 1948: pl. 10:21
3. Bowl with red wash on rim	1:5	Loud 1948: pl. 14:6
4. Bowl (one example with red wash outside and over rim, vertical burnish)	1:5	Loud 1948: pl. 14:24
5. Bowl with red wash on rim	1:5	Loud 1948: pl. 14:38
Tomb 3171:		
6. Bowl with spiral burnish inside	1:5	Loud 1948: pl. 9:4
7. Jug with red wash and burnish	1:5	Loud 1948: pl. 7:18
Tomb 3150:		
8. Jug with red and black decoration	1:5	Loud 1948: pl. 11:21
Tomb 3148:		
9. Jug with orange-to-red wash and vertical burnish	1:5	Loud 1948: pl. 12:3
10. Jug with red wash and burnish	1:5	Loud 1948: pl. 12:6
11. Bowl with red wash on rim and spiral burnish inside	1:5	Loud 1948: pl. 14:17

1
2
3
4
5
T.3143
6
7
T.3171
8
T.3150
9
10
11
T.3148

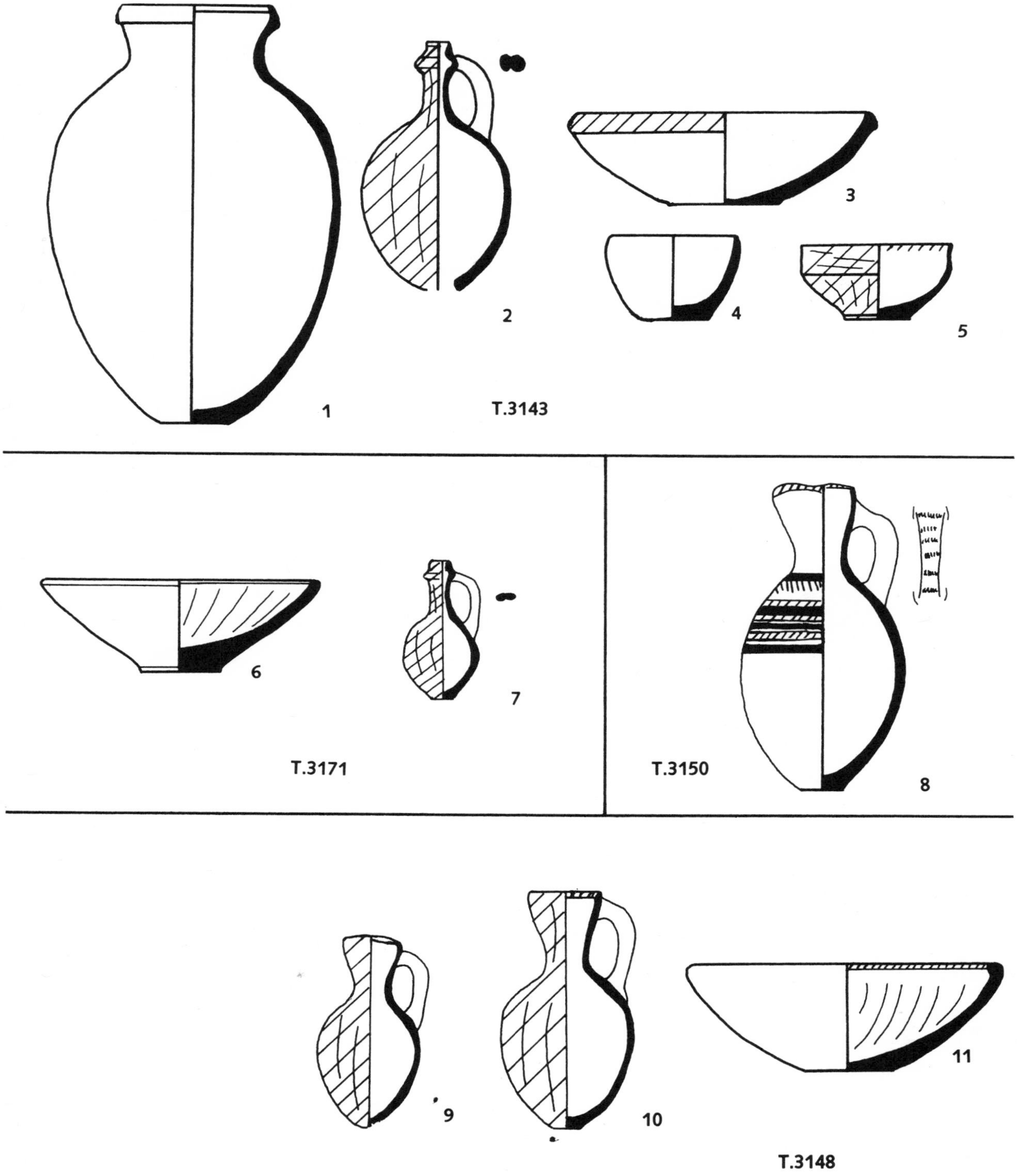

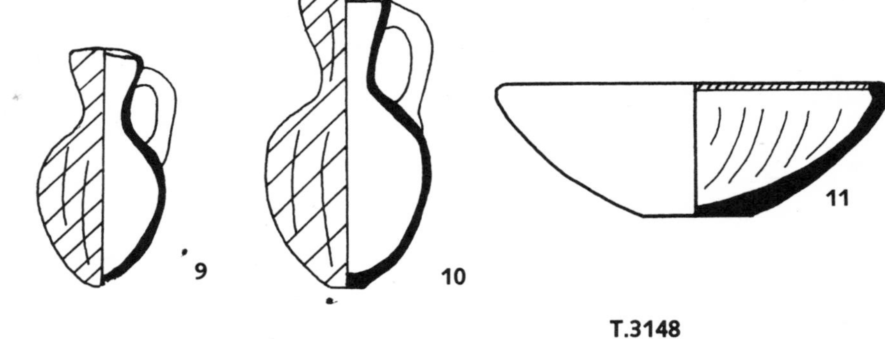

Figure 12: Pottery from Megiddo, Area BB, West, Stratigraphically Assigned to Phase 3

Locus 5054:		
1. Jar	1:5	Loud 1948: pl. 18:6
Locus 5101:		
2. Bowl (handmade)	1:5	Loud 1948: pl. 19:14
Locus 5076:		
3. Bowl with red wash and burnish	1:5	Loud 1948: pl. 19:6
Locus 5034:		
4. Jug	1:5	Loud 1948: pl. 17:11
Locus 5064:		
5. Jug	1:5	Loud 1948: pl. 17:3
6. Jug with red wash and burnish	1:5	Loud 1948: pl. 17:17
Locus 5049:		
7. Jug	1:5	Loud 1948: pl. 17:25
Tomb 5183:		
8. Jug with red painted decoration	1:5	Loud 1948: pl. 11:18
9. Bowl with red wash on rim (one example with spiral burnish inside)	1:5	Loud 1948: pl. 14:12
Tomb 5275:		
10. Mug with red wash and burnish	1:5	Loud 1948: pl. 11:6
11. Mug with red wash and burnish	1:5	Loud 1948: pl. 11:8
12. Jug with burnished exterior	1:5	Loud 1948: pl. 12:3
Tomb 5097:		
13. Jug	1:5	Loud 1948: pl. 17:21
14. Jug with traces of burnish	1:5	Loud 1948: pl. 17:5
Tomb 5103:		
15. Jar	1:10	Loud 1948: pl. 18:3
16. Jug with comb finish	1:5	Loud 1948: pl. 17:13
17. Jug with red wash and burnish	1:5	Loud 1948: pl. 17:24
18. Bowl with red wash and irregular burnish	1:5	Loud 1948: pl. 19:4
19. Bowl with red wash on rim	1:5	Loud 1948: pl. 19:7

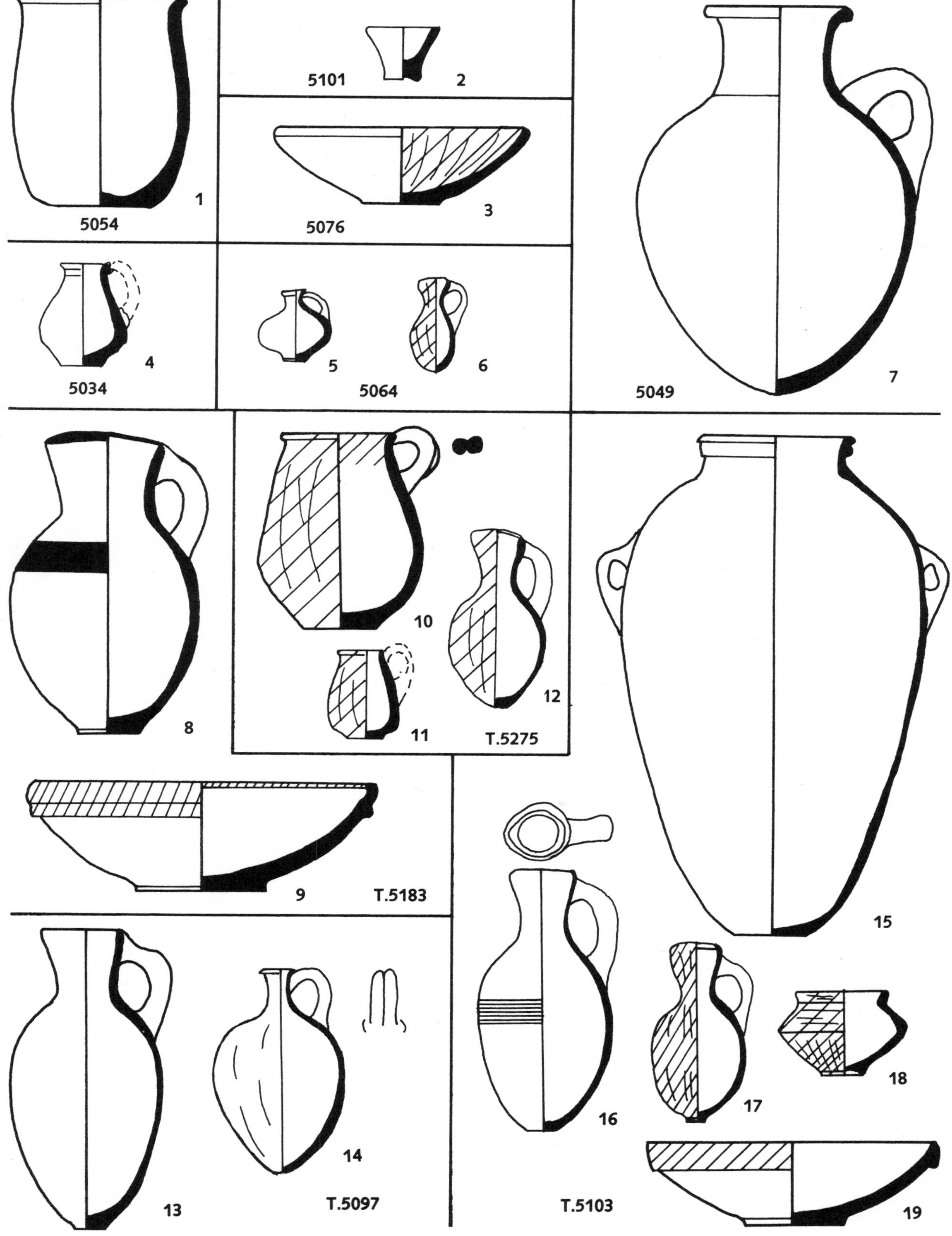
5054
1
5101
2
5076
3
5034
4
5
6
5064
5049
7
8
10
12
11
T.5275
9
T.5183
15
16
17
18
13
14
T.5097
T.5103
19

Figure 13: Pottery from Megiddo, Area BB, East, Stratigraphically Assigned to Phase 3

Tomb 3141:

1.	Jug with red wash and burnish	1:5	Loud 1948: pl. 19:23
2.	Jug with red painted decoration	1:5	Loud 1948: pl. 20:6
3.	Jug with basket handle; orange wash and irregular burnish	1:5	Loud 1948: pl. 20:18
4.	Bowl with red decoration on rim	1:5	Loud 1948: pl. 21:7
5.	Bowl with red wash on rim, spiral burnish inside	1:5	Loud 1948: pl. 21:17
6.	Bowl with red wash on rim	1:5	Loud 1948: pl. 22:6

Tomb 3147:

7.	Jug with red wash and vertical burnish outside	1:5	Loud 1948: pl. 10:1
8.	Jug with red decoration, comb finish	1:5	Loud 1948: pl. 11:22
9.	Jug with red wash and burnish	1:5	Loud 1948: pl. 12:5
10.	Bowl with red wash and burnish	1:5	Loud 1948: pl. 15:11
11.	Bowl with horizontal burnish on rim and spiral inside	1:5	Loud 1948: pl. 14:8
12.	Bowl with red wash and burnish, double bar handle	1:5	Loud 1948: pl. 15:12

Tomb 3168:

13.	Jug with red decoration	1:5	Loud 1948: pl. 11:20
14.	Bowl	1:5	Loud 1948: pl. 14:11

FIGURE 13

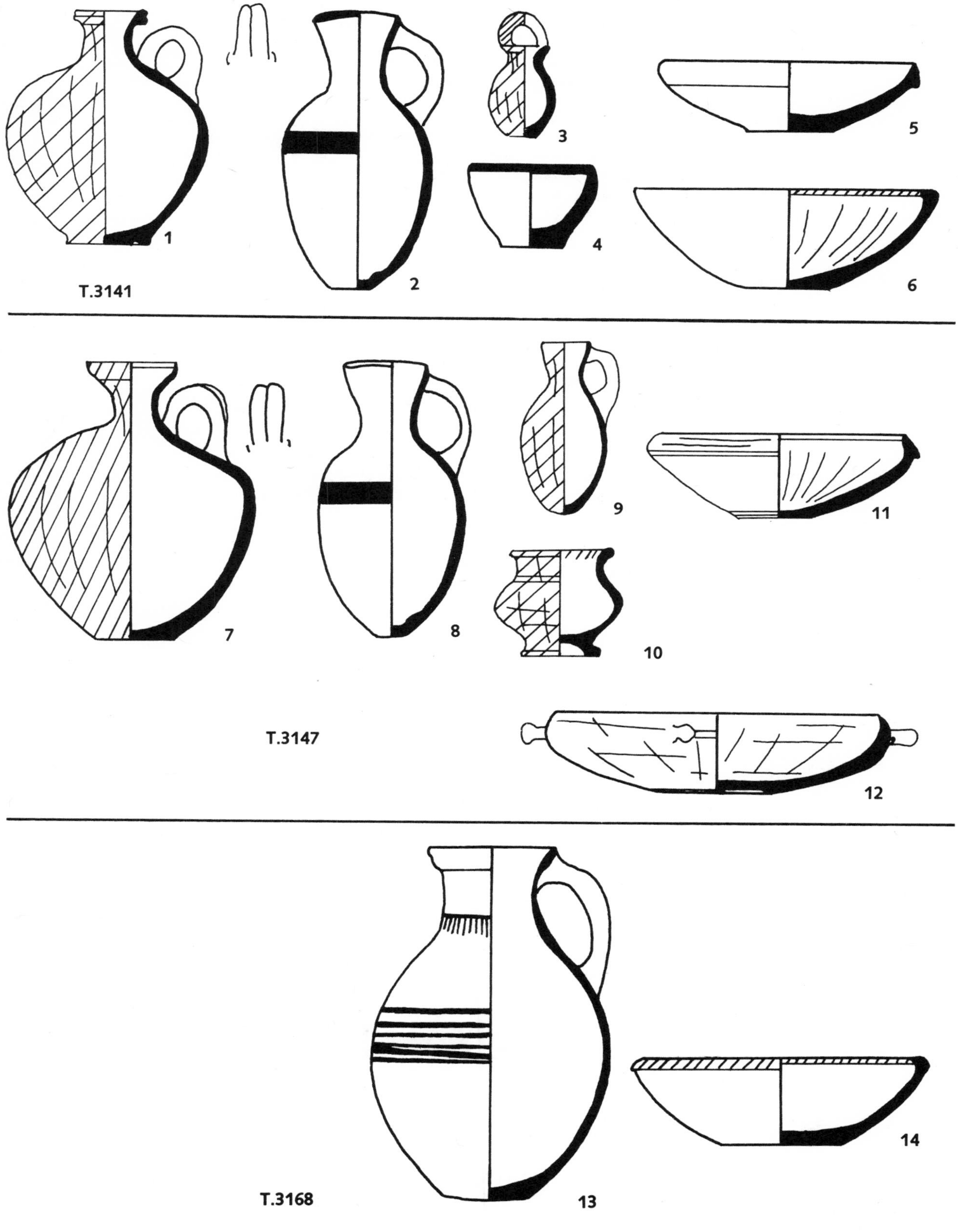

1 3 5 4 6

T.3141 2

9 11

7 8 10

T.3147 12

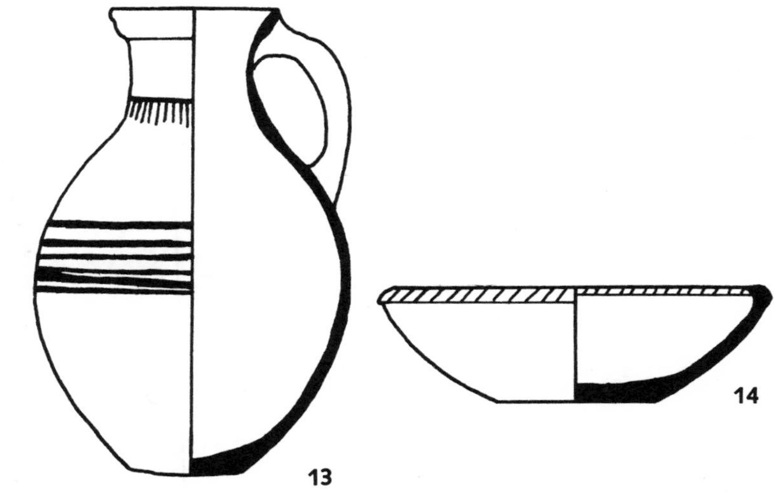

T.3168

Figure 14: Pottery from Megiddo, Area BB, East, Stratigraphically Assigned to Phase 3 (continued)

Tomb 3125:		
1. Bowl	1:5	Loud 1948: pl. 21:14
2. Bowl with spiral burnish inside	1:5	Loud 1948: pl. 21:19
3. Jug with vertical burnish	1:5	Loud 1948: pl. 19:24
4. Jug with triple handle	1:5	Loud 1948: pl. 19:21
Tomb 3140:		
5. Jug with red wash and burnish	1:5	Loud 1948: pl. 20:16
6. Juglet with red wash and burnish	1:5	Loud 1948: pl. 20:15
7. Bowl with red wash and burnish	1:5	Loud 1948: pl. 21:6
8. Bowl	1:5	Loud 1948: pl. 21:13
Tomb 3130:		
9. Jug	1:5	Loud 1948: pl. 19:30
10. Jug with horizontal burnish	1:5	Loud 1948: pl. 19:22
11. Bowl	1:5	Loud 1948: pl. 21:16
Tomb 3109:		
12. Mug	1:5	Loud 1948: pl. 20:17
13. Jug, well burnished outside	1:5	Loud 1948: pl. 19:21
14. Jug with brown red wash and well burnished outside	1:5	Loud 1948: pl. 19:28
15. Bowl	1:5	Loud 1948: pl. 21:9
16. Jar	1:5	Loud 1948: pl. 21:1
17. Jug	1:5	Loud 1948: pl. 20:8
18. Cooking-Bowl	1:5	Loud 1948: pl. 22:7

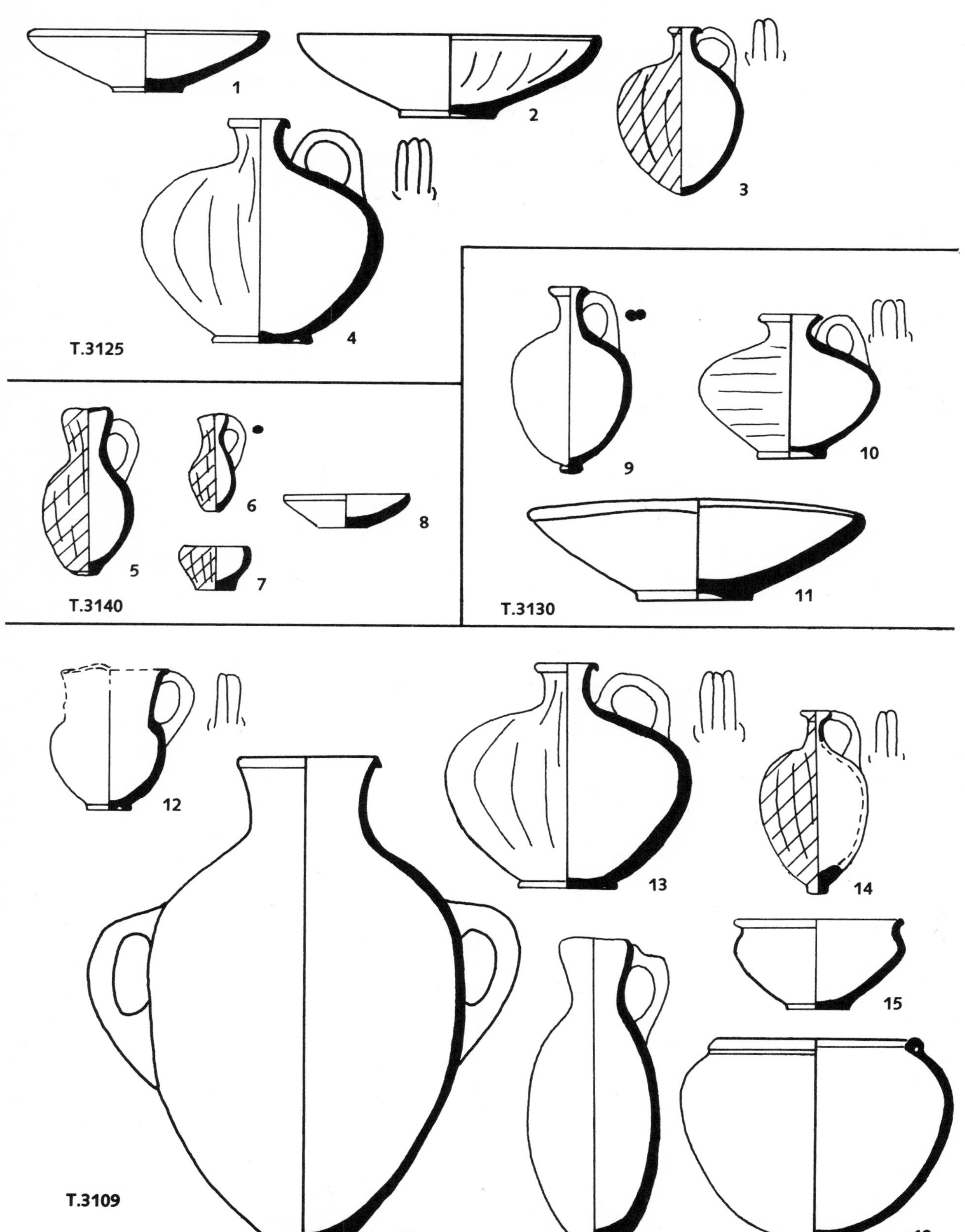
1
2
3
4
T.3125
9
10
11
T.3130
5
6
7
8
T.3140
12
13
14
15
16
17
18
T.3109

Figure 15: Pottery from Megiddo, Area BB, West, Stratigraphically Assigned to Phase 4

Locus 5043:		
1. Goblet with comb finish outside	1:5	Loud 1948: pl. 26:18
Locus 5048:		
2. Jug, Cypriote, handmade, burnish, black decoration	1:5	Loud 1948: pl. 26:16
Tomb 5104:		
3. Mug with red and black decoration	1:5	Loud 1948: pl. 17:10
4. Bowl	1:5	Loud 1948: pl. 19:11
Tomb 5134:		
5. Jug, Cypriote, handmade, black wash, burnish, red decoration	1:5	Loud 1948: pl. 26:14
Tomb 5137:		
6. Jug	1:5	Loud 1948: pl. 24:20
7. Jug	1:5	Loud 1948: pl. 25:6
Tomb 5186:		
8. Jug with red wash and burnish	1:5	Loud 1948: pl. 10:15
9. Jug with red wash and burnish outside and over rim	1:5	Loud 1948: pl. 10:8
10. Bowl	1:5	Loud 1948: pl. 14:8
11. Bowl with red wash and burnish	1:5	Loud 1948: pl. 14:33
12. Bowl with red wash on rim	1:5	Loud 1948: pl. 14:36
Tomb 5252:		
13. Jug with red wash, well burnished outside	1:5	Loud 1948: pl. 17:15
14. Bowl with red wash and burnish outside	1:5	Loud 1948: pl. 19:3
Tomb 5088:		
15. Jug with burnish outside	1:5	Loud 1948: pl. 17:9

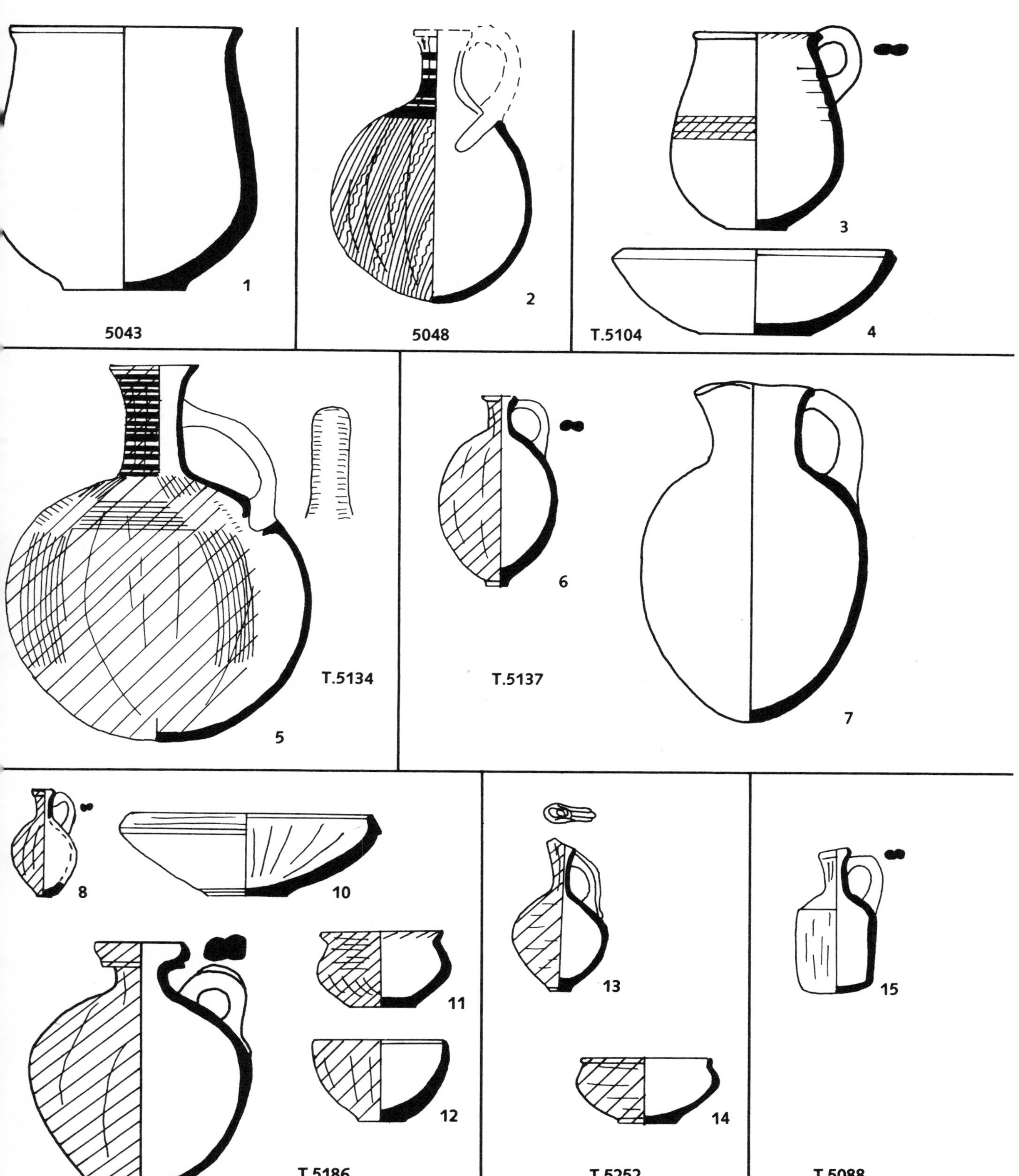
1
5043
2
5048
3
4
T.5104
5
T.5134
6
T.5137
7
8
10
9
11
12
T.5186
13
14
T.5252
15
T.5088

Figure 16: Pottery from Megiddo, Area BB, West, Stratigraphically Assigned to Phase 4 (continued)

Tomb 5178:		
1. Bowl with red wash on rim, spiral burnish inside	1:5	Loud 1948: pl. 14:12
2. Bowl (two examples, one with red wash on rim)	1:5	Loud 1948: pl. 14:5
3. Bowl with red wash and burnish	1:5	Loud 1948: pl. 14:37
4. Bowl with red wash and burnish	1:5	Loud 1948: pl. 15:2
5. Bowl with red wash and burnish outside and over rim	1:5	Loud 1948: pl. 14:34
6. Jug with red wash and burnish outside and over rim	1:5	Loud 1948: pl. 10:11
Tomb 5242:		
7. Bowl	1:5	Loud 1948: pl. 29:19
8. Jug, rough burnish outside	1:5	Loud 1948: pl. 23:17
Tomb 5254:		
9. Bowl	1:5	Loud 1948: pl. 29:21
10. Bowl	1:5	Loud 1948: pl. 29:23
11. Jug, irregularly burnished outside	1:5	Loud 1948: pl. 23:4
12. Bowl	1:5	Loud 1948: pl. 29:19
Tomb 5241:		
13. Jug with red wash and well burnished outside	1:5	Loud 1948: pl. 24:21
Tomb 5152:		
14. Bowl with red wash and horizontal burnish outside	1:5	Loud 1948: pl. 19:3
15. Jar with red wash and burnish	1:5	Loud 1948: pl. 18:5
16. Bowl, spiral burnish inside	1:5	Loud 1948: pl. 19:9
17. Jug with red wash and burnish	1:5	Loud 1948: pl. 17:1
18. Jug with red wash and burnish	1:5	Loud 1948: pl. 17:23
Tomb 5259:		
19. Bowl	1:5	Loud 1948: pl. 29:16
20. Bowl (three examples)	1:5	Loud 1948: pl. 28:13
21. Bowl	1:5	Loud 1948: pl. 29:19
22. Jug with brown pink wash and irregular burnish outside	1:5	Loud 1948: pl. 24:3
23. Jug	1:5	Loud 1948: pl. 26:4
24. Jug	1:5	Loud 1948: pl. 24:13
25. Jug	1:5	Loud 1948: pl. 25:22
26. Jug	1:5	Loud 1948: pl. 25:14

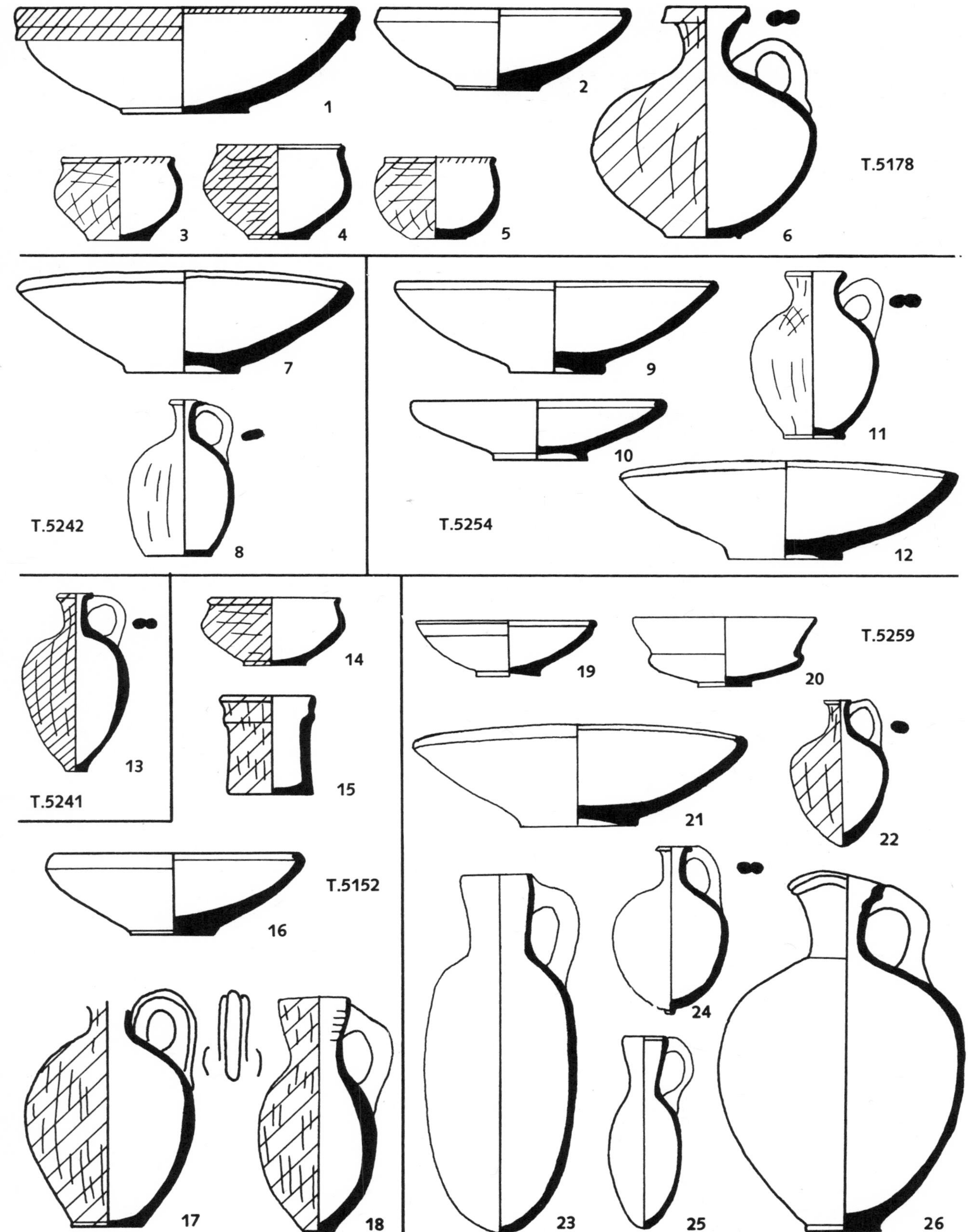
1
2
6
T.5178
3
4
5
7
9
11
8
10
T.5242
T.5254
12
13
14
15
T.5241
19
20
T.5259
21
22
T.5152
16
24
17
18
23
25
26

Figure 17: Pottery from Megiddo, Area BB, West, Stratigraphically Assigned to Phase 4 (continued)

	Scale	Reference
Tomb 5142:		
1. Jug	1:5	Loud 1948: pl. 23:8
2. Jug	1:5	Loud 1948: pl. 23:7
3. Jug	1:5	Loud 1948: pl. 26:2
4. Bowl	1:5	Loud 1948: pl. 28:3
5. Bowl	1:5	Loud 1948: pl. 29:19
6. Jug with orange wash, well burnished outside	1:5	Loud 1948: pl. 24:17
7. Jug with traces of orange wash and burnish outside	1:5	Loud 1948: pl. 24:4
Tomb 5274:		
8. Jug	1:5	Loud 1948: pl. 26:4
9. Jug with red wash and burnish	1:5	Loud 1948: pl. 24:14
10. Jug with thick red wash and burnish outside	1:5	Loud 1948: pl. 24:13
11. Jug with green buff slip	1:5	Loud 1948: pl. 23:8
Tomb 5261:		
12. Jug, traces of burnish outside	1:5	Loud 1948: pl. 24:16
13. Jug	1:5	Loud 1948: pl. 26:4
Tomb 5179:		
14. Bowl with red wash on rim, spiral burnish inside	1:5	Loud 1948: pl. 14:16
15. Jug with red wash and burnish	1:5	Loud 1948: pl. 11:17

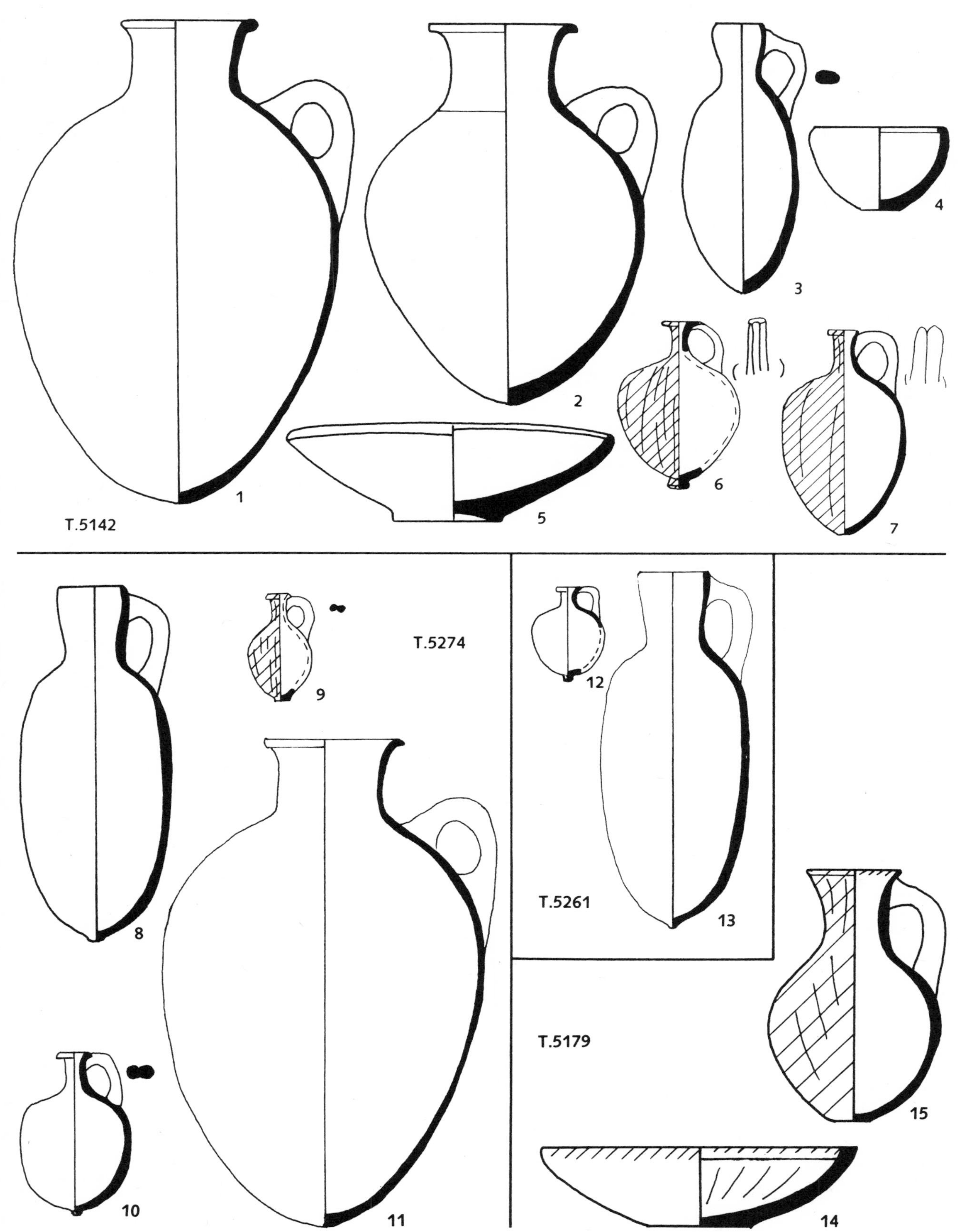
1
2
3
4
5
6
7
T.5142
8
9
T.5274
10
11
12
13
T.5261
T.5179
14
15

Figure 18: Pottery from Megiddo, Area BB, East, Stratigraphically Assigned to Phase 4

Tomb 3144:		
1. Jug	1:5	Loud 1948: pl. 12:11
2. Jug with thick red wash and vertical burnish outside	1:5	Loud 1948: pl. 12:7
3. Jug with thick brown red wash and vertical burnish outside	1:5	Loud 1948: pl. 10:20
4. Bowl with spiral burnish inside	1:5	Loud 1948: pl. 14:7
Tomb 3146:		
5. Bowl with red wash and spiral burnish inside	1:5	Loud 1948: pl. 22:2
6. Jug with red wash and spaced vertical burnish outside	1:5	Loud 1948: pl. 19:31
Tomb 3155:		
7. Jug with red wash and burnish	1:5	Loud 1948: pl. 10:2
8. Jug with red wash and burnish	1:5	Loud 1948: pl. 10:3
9. Bowl with orange red wash and vertical burnish	1:5	Loud 1948: pl. 14:31
10. Bowl	1:5	Loud 1948: pl. 14:1
Tomb 2146:		
11. Jar with red spiral decoration	1:5	Loud 1948: pl. 21:2
Tomb 3157:		
12. Jug with dark red wash and burnish	1:5	Loud 1948: pl. 10:14
13. Bowl with red wash on rim	1:5	Loud 1948: pl. 14:11
14. Jug with red wash and vertical burnish outside (two examples)	1:5	Loud 1948: pl. 11:12
Tomb 3093:		
15. Jug	1:5	Loud 1948: pl. 20:9
16. Jug with orange wash and well burnished outside	1:5	Loud 1948: pl. 19:25
17. Jug	1:5	Loud 1948: pl. 20:11
18. Bowl (=T. 3093)	1:5	Loud 1948: pl. 21:14
19. Bowl	1:5	Loud 1948: pl. 21:18
20. Bowl with red wash on rim, spiral burnish inside (two examples)	1:5	Loud 1948: pl. 22:3
Tomb 2151:		
21. Jug with red decoration, pinched rim	1:5	Loud 1948: pl. 20:7
22. Jug	1:5	Loud 1948: pl. 20:12
23. Bowl, red wash on rim	1:5	Loud 1948: pl. 21:20
24. Bowl with red decoration	1:5	Loud 1948: pl. 21:7

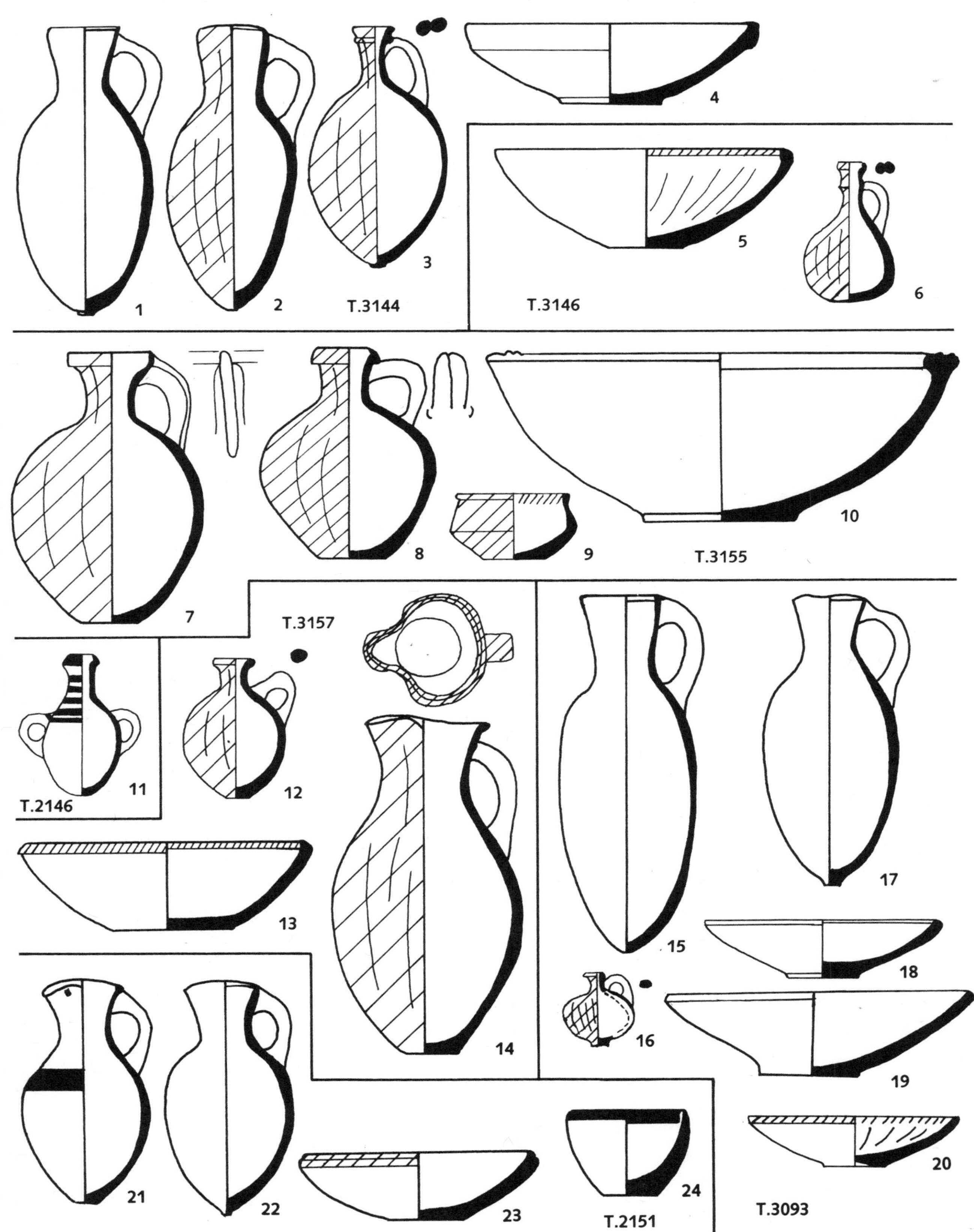

1
2
T.3144
3
4
5
6
T.3146
7
8
9
10
T.3155
T.3157
11
T.2146
12
13
14
15
16
17
18
19
20
21
22
23
24
T.2151
T.3093

Figure 19: Jars with Painted Decoration

1.	Jar	1:5	Megiddo, =T. 5130	Loud 1948: pl. 12:21
2.	Jar	1:5	Megiddo, T. 5167	Loud 1948: pl. 8:9
3.	Jar	1:5	Megiddo, E=T. 5147	Loud 1948: pl. 13:5
4.	Jar Neck	1:5	Aphek, T. 7	Beck 1975: fig. 3:7
5.	Jar Neck	1:5	Aphek, T. 7	Beck 1975: fig. 3:9
6.	Jar Neck	1:5	Aphek, T. 7	Beck 1975: fig. 3:10
7.	Jar	1:5	Chagar Bazar	Mallowan 1937a: fig. 21:8
8.	Jar	1:5	Tepe Gawra, Stratum V	Speiser 1935: pl. LXXI:161
9.	Jar	1:5	Tell Billa, Stratum 4	Speiser 1933: pl. LIX:4
10.	Jar	1:8	Tarsus	Goldman 1956: fig. 374: No. 888
11.	Jar	1:8	Tarsus	Goldman 1956: fig. 374: No. 887
12.	Jar	1:10	Hama, Grave VI	Fugmann 1958: pl. X: 5B398

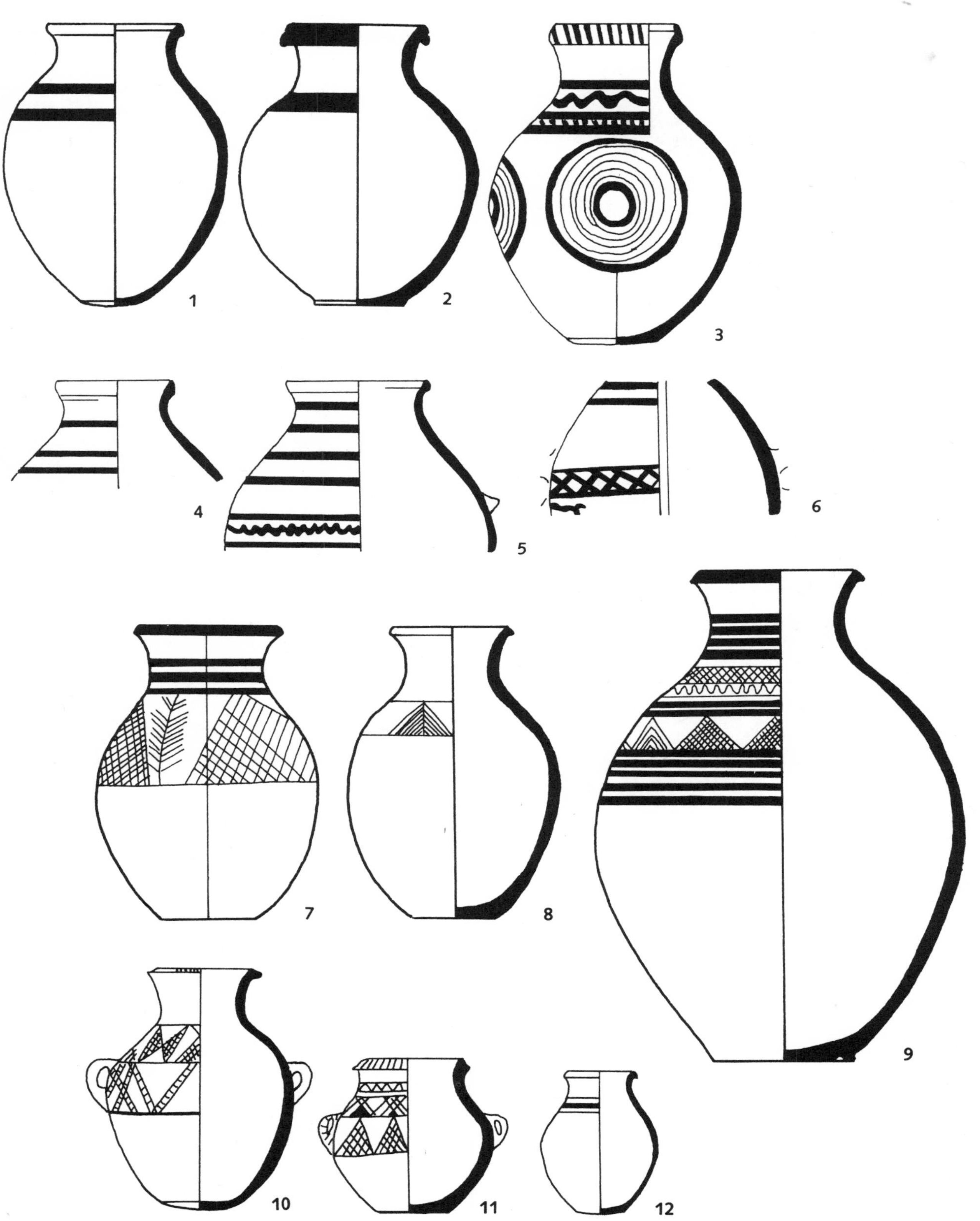
1
2
3
4
5
6
7
8
9
10
11
12

Figure 20: "Eye" Jugs

1. Jug	N.S.	ʿAmuq, Phase L	Swift 1958: fig. 1:2
2. Jug	1:4	Tarsus	Goldman 1956: pl. 370:No. 857
3. Jug	1:5	Alalakh	Woolley 1955: pl. CXV: Type 70
4. Jug	N.S.	Qatna, Tomb I	du Mesnil du Buisson 1927: fig. 47
5. Jug	1:3	Mersin	Garstang 1953: fig. 148:10
6. Jug	N.S.	Alalakh, Level XII	Woolley 1955: pl. XCI
7. Jug	1:4	Mersin	Seton Williams 1953: fig. 3:5

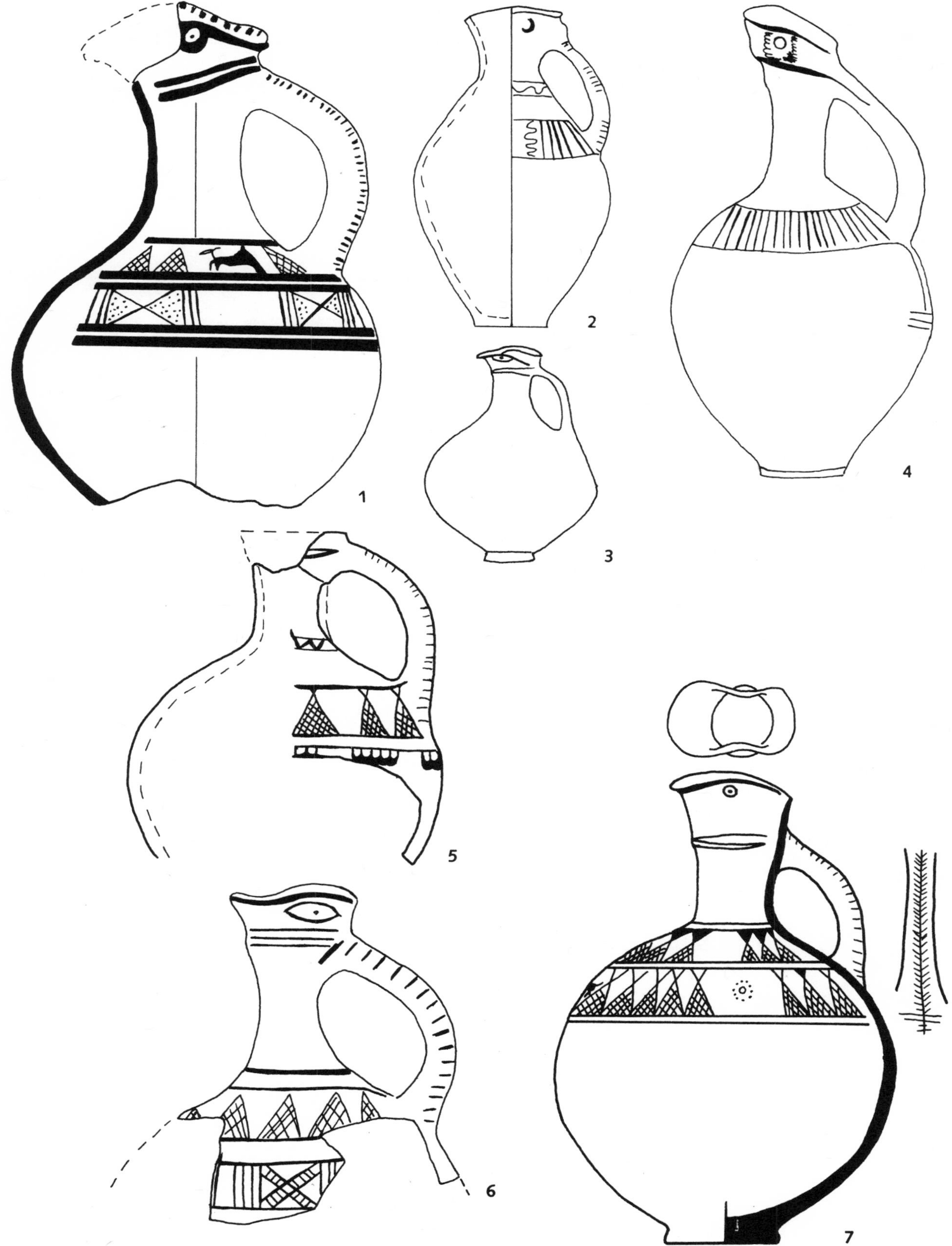
1
2
3
4
5
6
7

Figure 21: Jugs with Painted Decoration

1. Jug	1:4	Ugarit, U.M. 2	Schaeffer 1949: fig. 131:16
2. Jug	1:4	Ugarit	Schaeffer 1949: fig. 108:22
3. Jug	1:2	Kültepe	T. Özgüç 1950: pl. LXXIX: 617
4. Jug	1:8	Tarsus	Goldman 1956: pl. 369:No. 859
5. Jug	1:8	Gezer, Cave III 30	Macalister 1912a: 298, fig. 158:7
6. Jug	1:6	Tell el-ʿAjjul	Petrie 1931: pl. XLVIII: 57H5
7. Jug	1:6	Aphek	Schaeffer 1948: fig. 149:4
8. Jug	1:5	Megiddo, T. 911D	Guy 1938: pl. 31:21
9. Jug	1:5	Megiddo, T. 911D	Guy 1938: pl. 31:19
10. Jug	1:4	Ayia Paraskevi	Seton Williams 1953: fig. 3:3

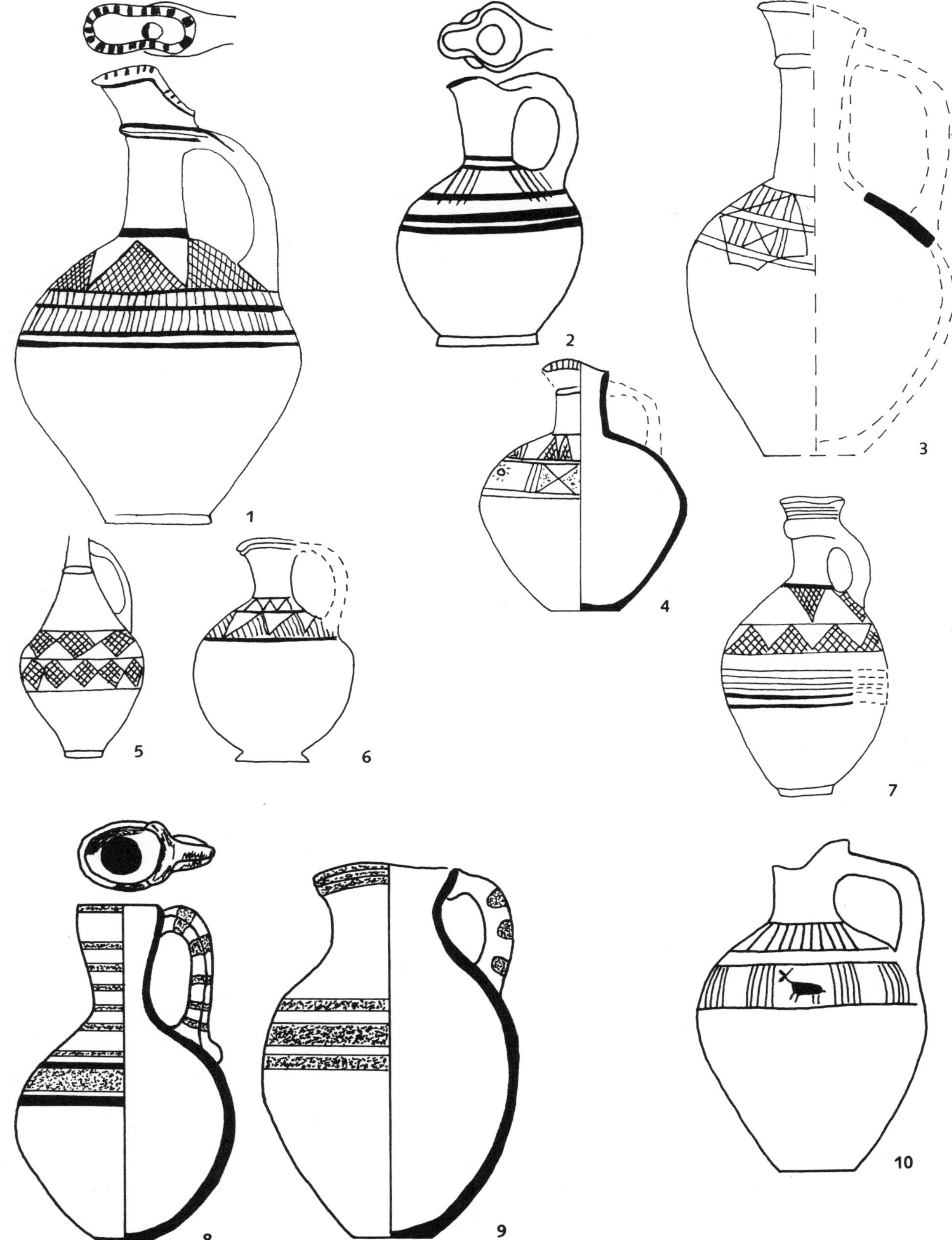
1
2
3
4
5
6
7
8
9
10

Figure 22: "Stepped-Rim" and Collarette Juglets with Painted Decoration

1.	Juglet	1:5	Ginosar, T. 4	Epstein 1974: fig. 14:1
2.	Juglet	1:5	Ginosar, T. 4	Epstein 1974: fig. 14:2
3.	Juglet	1:5	Ginosar, T. 4	Epstein 1974: fig. 14:3
4.	Juglet	1:5	Ginosar, T. 4	Epstein 1974: fig. 14:4
5.	Juglet	1:5	Kfar Szold	Epstein 1974: fig. 1:5
6.	Juglet	1:5	Aphek, T. 43	Beck 1975: fig. 14:8
7.	Juglet	1:5	Megiddo, =T. 4010	Loud 1948: pl. 19:33
8.	Juglet	1:1	Nahariya	Ben-Dor 1950: fig. 16:No. 325
9.	Juglet	1:2	Ginosar, T. 1	Epstein 1974: fig. 5:10
10.	Juglet	1:5	Ugarit	Schaeffer 1949: fig. 100:26
11.	Juglet	1:5	Ugarit	Schaeffer 1949: fig. 100:20
12.	Juglet	N.S.	Kafer Djarra, T. 66	Guigues 1938: pl. III:bl
13.	Juglet	1:4	Byblos	Dunand 1939: fig. 236:No. 3928
14.	Juglet	1:2	Ginosar, T. 4	Epstein 1974: fig. 14:5

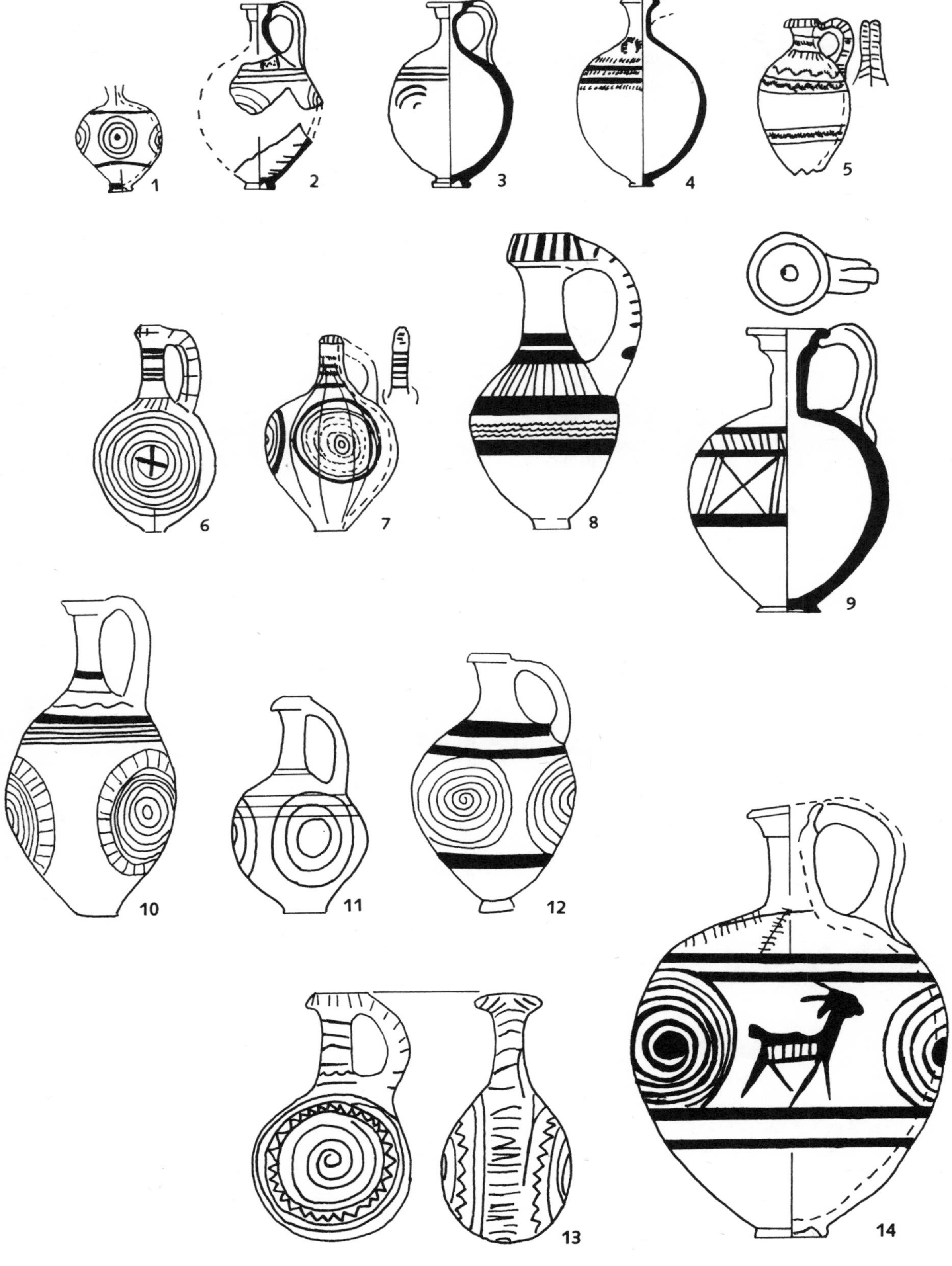
1
2
3
4
5
6
7
8
9
10
11
12
13
14

Figure 23: Bowls with Painted Decoration

1.	Bowl	1:3	Mersin, Level XI	Garstang 1953: fig. 143:1
2.	Bowl	1:3	Mersin, Level XI	Garstang 1953: fig. 148:1
3.	Bowl	1:3	Mersin, Level XI	Garstand 1953: fig. 148:2
4.	Bowl	1:3	Mersin, Level XI	Garstang 1953: fig. 144:3
5.	Bowl	1:3	Mersin, Level XI	Garstand 1953: fig. 144:15
6.	Bowl	N.S.	Alalakh, Level XII	Woolley 1955: pl. XCI: ATP/47/149
7.	Bowl	2:5	Alalakh	Woolley 1955: pl. CX:Type 23a
8.	Bowl	2:5	Alalakh	Woolley 1955: pl. CX:Type 23b
9.	Bowl	2:5	Alalakh	Woolley 1955: pl. CX:Type 23c
10.	Bowl	1:5	Alalakh	Woolley 1955: pl. CXX: Type 119
11.	Bowl	N.S.	ʿAmuq, Phase K	Swift 1958: fig. 1
12.	Bowl	1:4	Tarsus	Seton Williams 1953: fig. 4:8
13.	Bowl	1:4	Tarsus	Seton Williams 1953:fig. 4:11
14.	Bowl	1:4	Kültepe	Seton Williams 1953: fig. 4:3
15.	Bowl	1:4	Qatna (beneath the "Coupole de Loth")	du Mesnil du Buisson 1927: pl. LXXIX:No. 45
16.	Bowl	1:4	Yenice (Cilicia)	Seton Williams 1953: fig. 2:7
17.	Krater	1:4	Ugarit	Schaeffer 1932: fig. 12:10
18.	Krater	1:4	Mersin	Seton Williams 1953:fig. 2:12
19.	Bowl	1:2	Tell Taya, Level IV	Reade 1968: pl. LXXXVII:26
20.	Bowl	2:5	Chagar Bazar, Level 1	Mallowan 1937a: fig. 23:1
21.	Bowl	2:5	Nippur	McCown and Haines 1967: pl. 88:18
22.	Bowl	1:5	Nippur	McCown and Haines 1967: pl. 88:23
23.	Bowl	1:3	Nineveh	Thompson and Hamilton 1932: pl. LIV:5

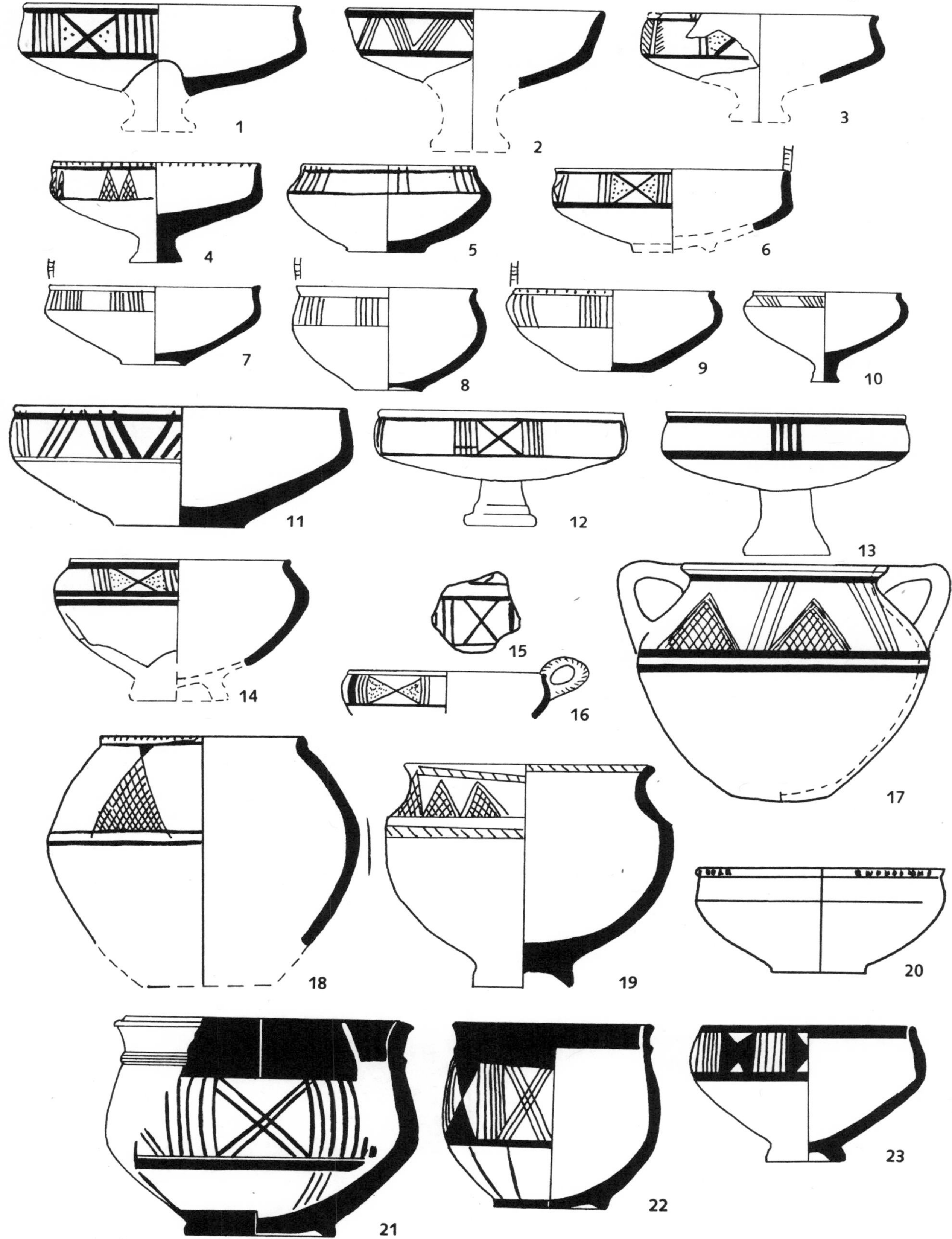
1
2
3
4
5
6
7
8
9
10
11
12
13
14
15
16
17
18
19
20
21
22
23

Figure 24: Bowls with Red-Cross Painted Decoration

1. Bowl	1:5	Tell Beit Mirsim, Stratum F	Albright 1933: pl. 5:5
2. Bowl	1:5	Wadi et-Tin	Vincent 1947: 279: fig. 6:18
3. Bowl	1:5	Tel Poleg	Gophna 1973: fig. 5:4
4. Bowl	1:7	Aphek	Ory 1937: 107:2B
5. Bowl	1:4	Gezer, T. 1	Macalister 1912b: pl. LXI:16
6. Bowl	N.S.	Alalakh, Level XIIb.	Woolley 1955: pl. XCI:ATP/47/119
7. Bowl	N.S.	Alalakh, Level XIIb	Woolley 1955: pl. XCI:ATP/47/152
8. Bowl	1:5	Alalakh	Woolley 1955: pl. CXI:Type 34
9. Bowl	ca. 1:8	Qatna (beneath the "Coupole de Loth")	du Mesnil du Buisson 1927: pl. LXXIX:44
10. Bowl	ca. 1:8	Qatna (beneath the "Coupole de Loth")	du Mesnil du Buisson 1927: pl. LXXIX:43
11. Bowl	1:5	Tell el-Far^{c}ah (N.), Tomb W	Mallet 1973: pl. 23:3

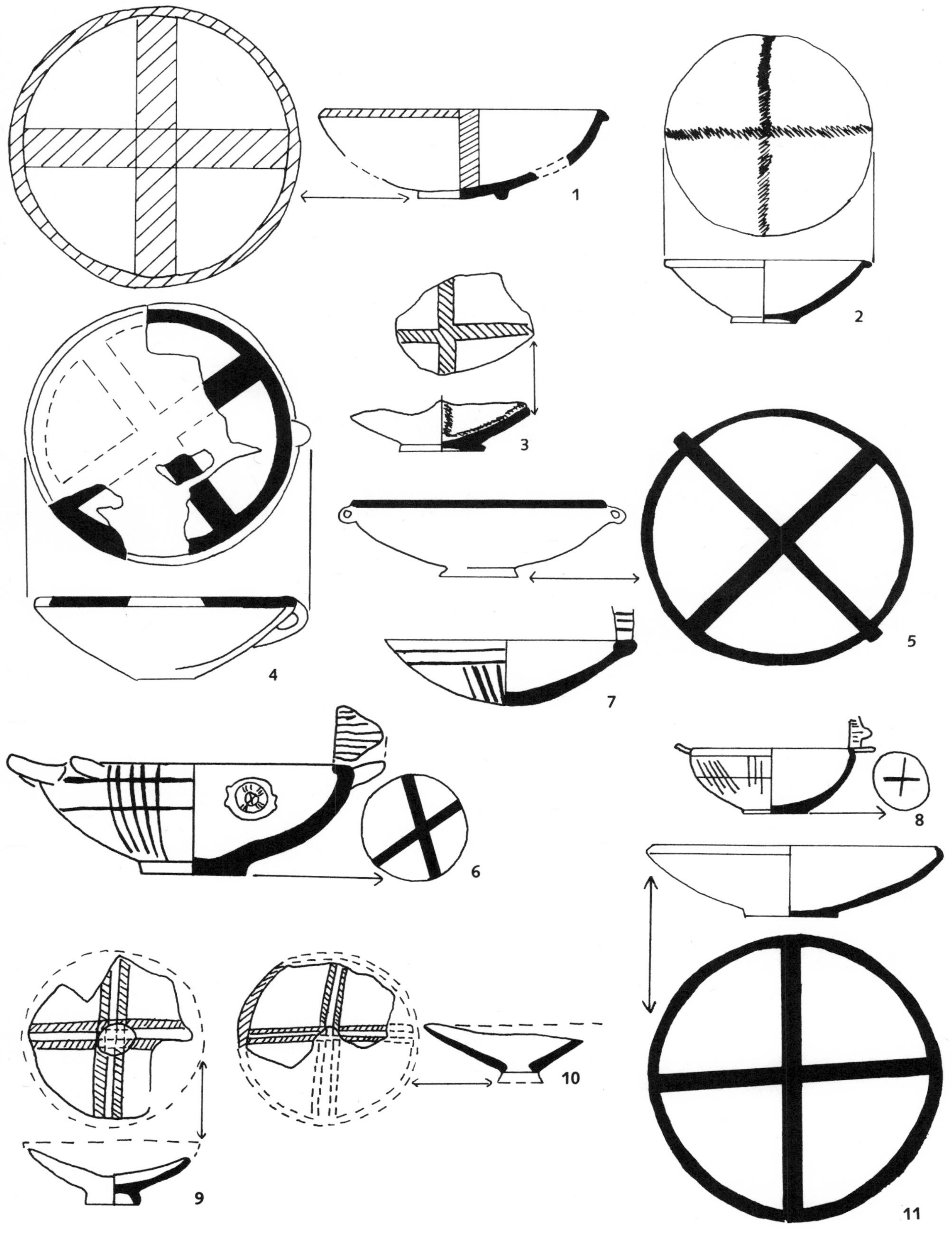
1
2
3
4
5
7
6
8
9
10
11

Figure 25: Imported and/or Imitation Cypriote Jugs and Juglets

1.	Jug	1:4	Dhahrat el-Humraiya, Grave 2/3	Ory 1948: fig. 4
2.	Juglet	1:4	Dhahrat el-Humraiya, Grave 2/3	Ory 1948: fig. 5
3.	Juglet	1:5	Megiddo, T. 3128	Loud 1948: pl. 26:13
4.	Juglet	1:5	Lachish, T. 129	Tufnell, 1958: pl. 79:813
5.	Juglet	1:5	Beth-shemesh	Amiran 1969: pl. 37:10
6.	Jug	1:5	Ginosar, T. 4	Epstein 1974: fig. 15:9
7.	Jug	1:5	Ugarit, U.M. 2/early 3	Schaeffer 1949: fig. 131 6
8.	Jug	1:5	Ugarit, U.M. 2	Schaeffer 1949: fig. 131:9
9.	Juglet	1:5	Ugarit, U.M. 2	Schaeffer 1949: fig. 131:3
10.	Jug	1:5	Ugarit, U.M. 2/early 3	Schaeffer 1949: fig. 131:8
11.	Juglet	1:4	Dhahrat el-Humraiya, Grave 13	Ory 1948: fig. 14
12.	Jug	1:4	Gezer, T. 1	Macalister 1912b: pl. LXII:51
13.	Jug	1:5	Ugarit, U.M. 2	Schaeffer 1949: fig. 131:7
14.	Juglet	1:5	Ugarit, U.M. 2	Schaeffer 1949: fig. 131:4
15.	Sherd	1:5	Lachish	Tufnell 1958: fig. 3:174
16.	Jug	1:5	Ugarit, Cave LV	Schaeffer 1938: fig. 26:Za
17.	Juglet	1:5	Ugarit, Cave LV	Schaeffer 1938: fig. 26:Y
18.	Zoomorphic Jug	1:5	Ugarit, U.M. 2	Schaeffer 1949: fig. 106:10
19.	Jug	1:5	Ugarit, Cave XXXVI	Schaeffer 1938: fig. 6:E

1
2
3
4
5
6
7
8
9
10
11
12
13
14
15
16
17
18
19

Figure 26: Goblets

1. Goblet	1:5	Megiddo, Locus 5054	Loud 1948: pl. 18:6
2. Goblet	1:5	Megiddo, T. 5104	Loud 1948: pl. 17:10
3. Goblet	1:6	Tell el-ᶜAjjul	Petrie 1932: pl. XXIX:31V7/OC990
4. Goblet	2:3	Qatna, T. 1	du Mesnil du Buisson 1927: fig. 54
5. Goblet	1:4	Aphek	Ory 1937: 119:101
6. Goblet	1:4	Aphek	Iliffe 1936: 125:76
7. Goblet	1:4	Aphek	Ory 1937: 108:5
8. Goblet	1:4	Gezer, T. 1	Macalister 1912b: pl. LXII:34
9. Goblet	N.S.	Byblos	Dunand 1950: pl. XCII:No. 15836; Dunand 1958: 803, fig. 919
10. Goblet	1:3	Byblos, Royal Tomb III	Tufnell 1969: fig. 4:47
11. Goblet	1:3	Byblos, Royal Tomb II	Tufnell 1969: fig. 4:46
12. Goblet	1:5	Alalakh	Woolley 1955: pl. CXVII: Type 94b
13. Goblet	1:5	Alalakh	Woolley 1955: pl. CXVII: Type 94a
14. Goblet	2:5	Kültepe, Level Ib	T. Özgüç 1959: fig. 60
15. Goblet	1:5	Alişar	von der Osten 1937b: pl. IV: c2478

1
2
3
4
5
6
7
8
9
10
11
12
13
14
15

Figure 27: Goblets (continued)

1.	Goblet	1:5	Tepe Gawra, Stratum IV	Speiser 1935: pl. LXXIII:190
2.	Goblet	2:5	Tell Billa, Stratum 4	Speiser 1933: pl. LVII:2
3.	Goblet	1:5	Chagar Bazar, Level 1	Mallowan 1937a: fig. 19:3
4.	Goblet	1:5	Chagar Bazar, Level 1	Mallowan 1936: fig. 14:13
5.	Goblet	2:5	Tell Jidle, Level 3	Mallowan 1946: fig. 11:11
6.	Goblet	1:4	Tell Jidle, Level 3	Mallowan 1946: fig. 10:13
7.	Goblet	2:5	Tell Brak	Mallowan 1947: fig. 73:7
8.	Goblet	2:5	Tell Brak	Mallowan 1947: fig. 73:5
9.	Goblet	2:5	Telloh	de Genouillac 1936: pl. 33:996
10.	Goblet	2:5	Nuzi	Starr 1937: pl. 63A
11.	Goblet	2:5	Tell Asmar	Delougaz 1952: pl. 153: B.236.300
12.	Juglet	2:5	Nippur	McCown and Haines 1967: pl. 95:6
13.	Goblet	1:5	Dinkha Tepe	Hamlin 1971: pl. I:12

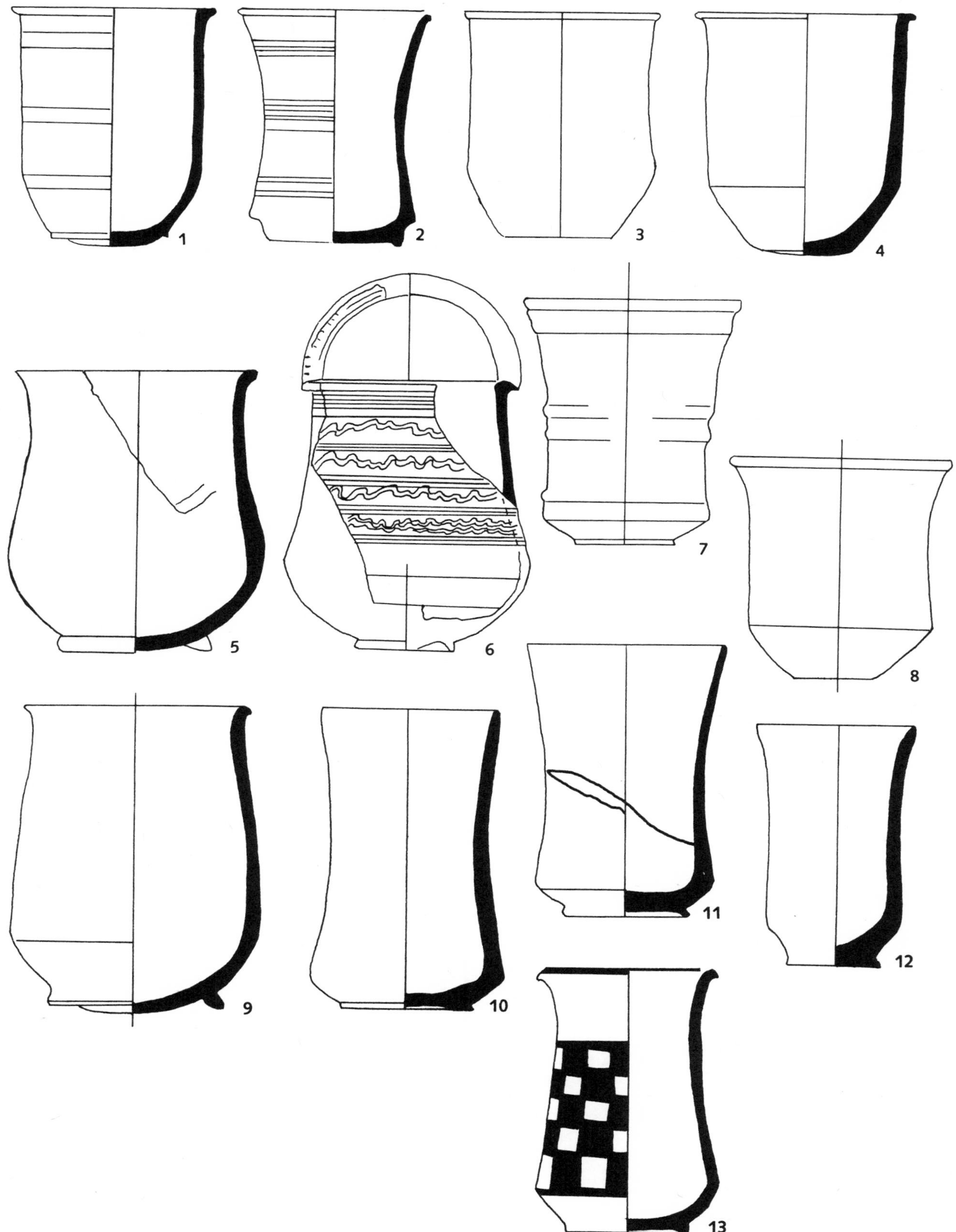
1
2
3
4
5
6
7
8
9
10
11
12
13

Figure 28: Jars

1.	Jar	1:5	Gibeon, T. 58	Pritchard 1963: fig. 64:9
2.	Jar	1:5	Gibeon, T. 58	Pritchard 1963: fig. 64:10
3.	Jar	1:5	Tell el-Far^{c}ah (N.), Tomb B	de Vaux and Steve 1948: fig. 11:1
4.	Jar	1:5	Megiddo, T. 5156	Loud 1948: pl. 13:4
5.	Jar	1:5	Beth-shemesh, T. 2	Grant 1929: 155, No. 134
6.	Jar	1:5	Lachish, T. 1513	Tufnell 1958: pl. 78:804
7.	Jar	1:5	Barqai	Gophna and Sussman 1969: fig. 4:12
8.	Jar	1:2	Dinkha Tepe	Hamlin 1971: pl. I:11
9.	Jar	1:5	Chagar Bazar	Mallowan 1936: fig. 14:10
10.	Jar	1:5	Chagar Bazar	Mallowan 1936: fig. 14:5
11.	Jar	1:5	Tepe Gawra, Stratum VI	Speiser 1935: pl. LXIX:135
12.	Jar	1:5	Tell Billa, Stratum 4, T. 42	Speiser 1933: pl. LVIII:9

1
2
3
4
5
6
7
8
9
10
11
12

Figure 29: Carinated Bowls

1. Bowl	1:5	Megiddo, T. 5121	Loud 1948: pl. 14:39
2. Bowl (metal)	1:2	Byblos ("Montet Jar")	Tufnell and Ward 1966: fig. 9:207
3. Bowl (metal)	1:2	Byblos ("Montet Jar")	Tufnell and Ward 1966: fig. 9:209
4. Bowl	2:5	Chagar Bazar, Level 1	Mallowan 1937a: fig. 16:1
5. Bowl	2:5	Chagar Bazar, Level 1	Mallowan 1937a: fig. 16:2
6. Bowl	2:5	Chagar Bazar, Level 1	Mallowan 1937a: fig. 16:3
7. Bowl	1:5	Megiddo, T. 3109 and T. 3107	Loud 1948: pl. 21:9
8. Bowl	1:5	Megiddo, T. 4110	Loud 1948: pl. 15:9
9. Bowl	1:5	Alalakh	Woolley 1955: pl. CX: Type 24
10. Bowl	1:5	Alalakh	Woolley 1955: pl. CIX: Type 7b
11. Bowl	N.S.	Yabrud	Assaf 1967: pl. II:2
12. Bowl	1:2	Tarsus	Goldman 1956: fig. 368: No. 767
13. Bowl	1:5	Alaca Hüyük, Level IV	Koşay and Akok 1966: pl. 109:e267
14. Bowl	1:5	Alişar	von der Osten 1937b: pl. IV: d2829
15. Bowl	1:4	Tell al-Rimah	Oates 1970: pl. IX:3
16. Bowl	1:4	Assur (Old Assyrian)	Haller 1954: pl. 2:n
17. Bowl	1:4	Assur (Old Assyrian)	Haller 1954: pl. 2:o
18. Bowl	1:4	Assur (Old Assyrian)	Haller 1954: pl. 2:p
19. Bowl	2:5	Nuzi	Starr 1937: pl. 62R
20. Bowl	1:5	Tell Asmar	Delougaz 1952: pl. 170: C.142.310

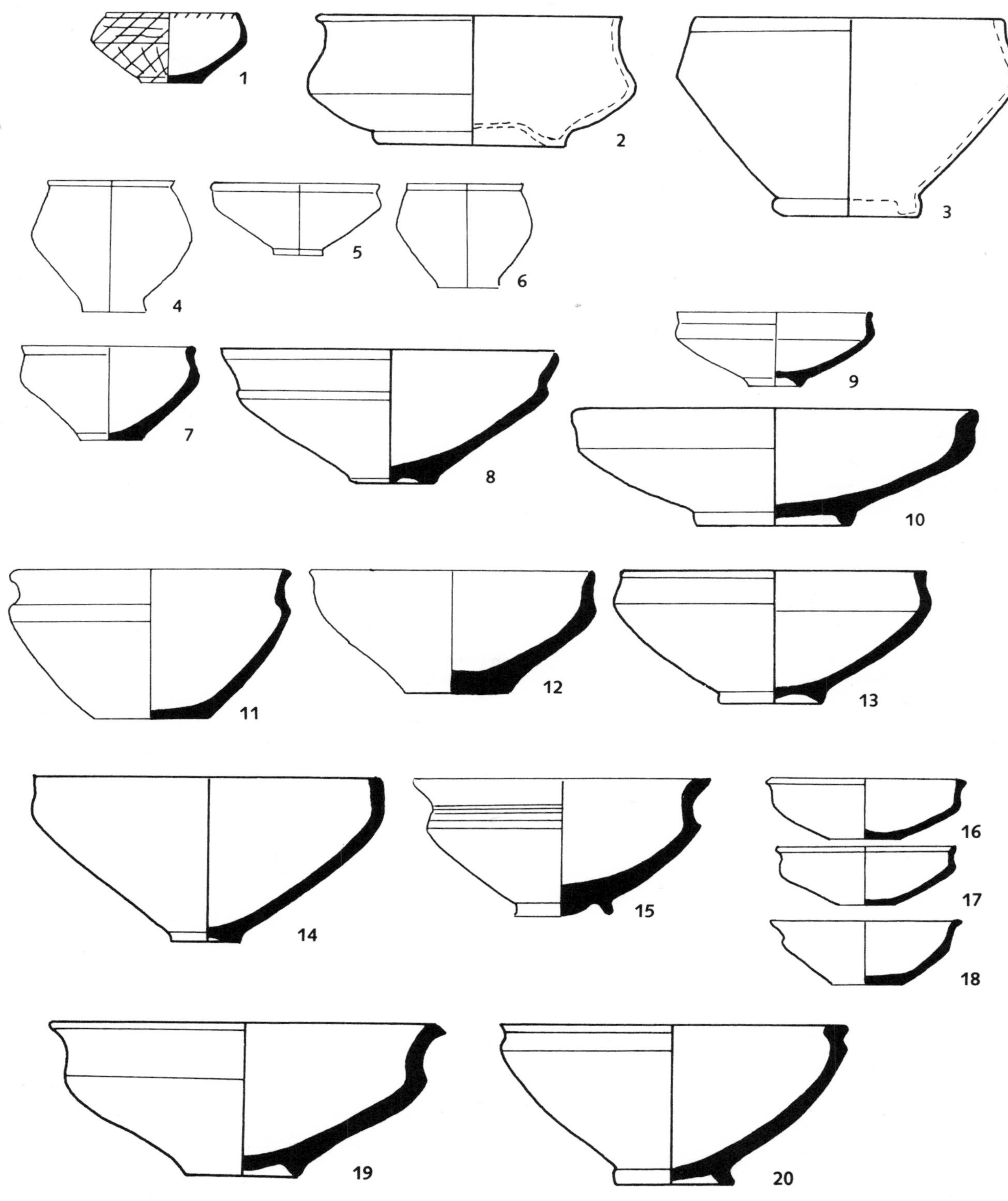
1
2
3
4
5
6
7
8
9
10
11
12
13
14
15
16
17
18
19
20

Figure 30: Bowls

No.	Type	Scale	Site	Reference
1.	Bowl	1:5	Megiddo, T. 5171	Loud 1948: pl. 14:28
2.	Bowl	1:5	Megiddo, T. 4046	Loud 1948: pl. 14:27
3.	Bowl	N.S.	Baghouz	du Mesnil du Buisson 1948: pl. LXXIX:Z220
4.	Bowl	N.S.	Baghouz	du Mesnil du Buisson 1948: pl. LXXIX:Z211
5.	Bowl	N.S.	Baghouz	du Mesnil du Buisson 1948: pl. LXXIX:Z28
6.	Bowl	1:5	Aphek, T. 427	Beck 1975: fig. 11:1
7.	Bowl	1:5	Aphek, T. 436	Beck 1975: fig. 11:6
8.	Bowl	1:5	Aphek, T. 428	Beck 1975: fig. 12:1
9.	Bowl	1:5	Aphek, T. 428	Beck 1975: fig. 12:2
10.	Bowl	1:5	Ginosar, T. 1	Epstein 1974: fig. 7:6
11.	Bowl	1:5	Ginosar, T. 1	Epstein 1974: fig. 7:9
12.	Bowl	1:5	Ginosar, T. 1	Epstein 1974: fig. 7:10
13.	Bowl	1:5	Ginosar, T. 1	Epstein 1974: fig. 7:11
14.	Bowl	2:5	Chagar Bazar, Level 1	Mallowan 1936: fig. 17:3
15.	Bowl	2:5	Chagar Bazar, Level 1	Mallowan 1936: fig. 17:1
16.	Bowl	1:5	Megiddo, T. 3147 and T. 2152	Loud 1948: pl. 15:12
17.	Bowl	1:5	Megiddo, T. 5167	Loud 1948: pl. 9:3
18.	Bowl	1:5	Megiddo, T. 3162	Loud 1948: pl. 15:15
19.	Bowl	1:5	Aphek, Locus 450	Beck 1975: fig. 4:17
20.	Bowl	1:5	ᶜAin es-Samiyeh	Dever 1975a: fig. 3:4
21.	Bowl	N.S.	Baghouz	du Mesnil du Buisson 1948: pl. LXXIX:Z269
22.	Bowl	N.S.	Baghouz	du Mesnil du Buisson 1948: pl. LXXX:Z137
23.	Bowl	1:4	Acemhüyük	Emre 1966: fig. 26

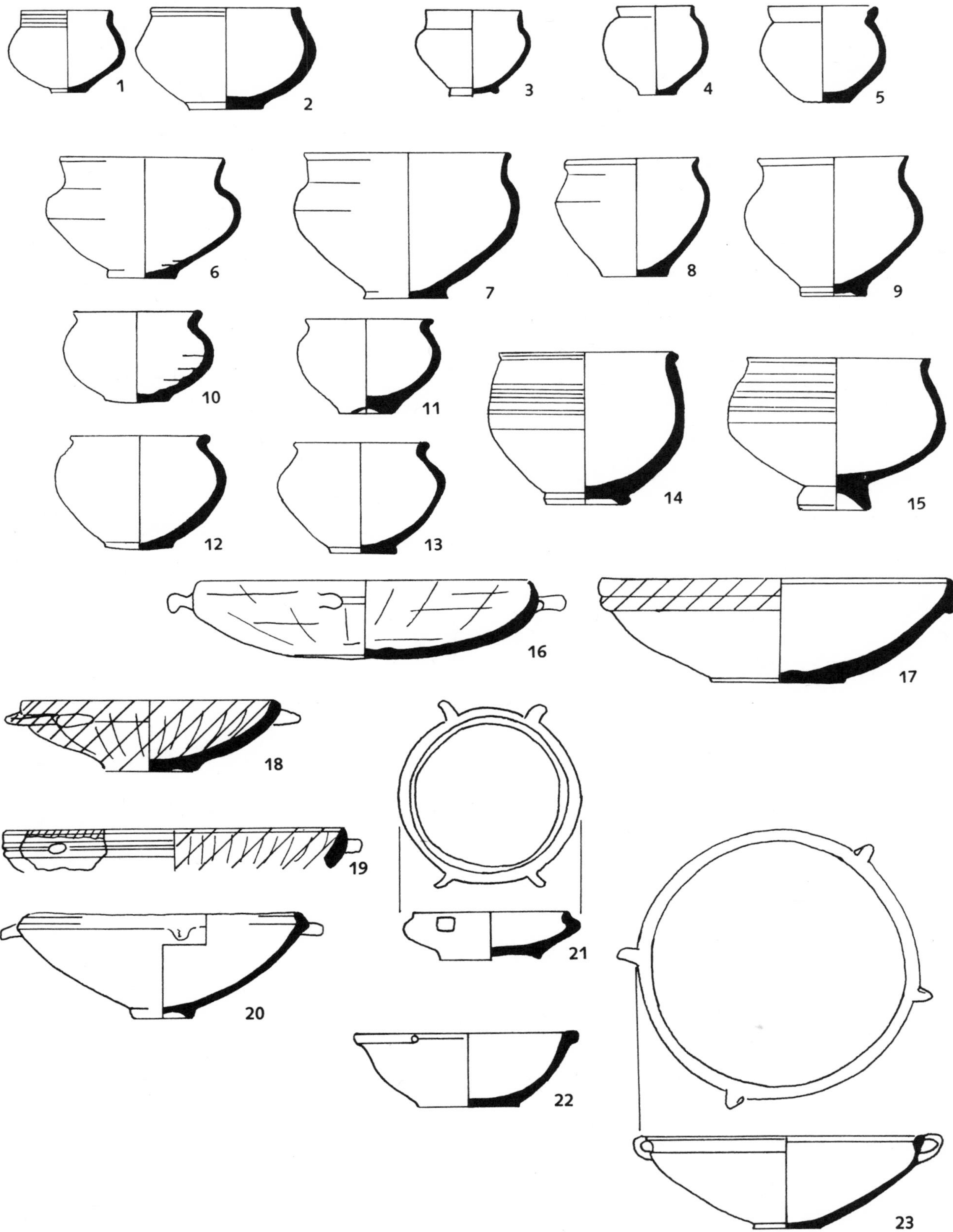
1
2
3
4
5
6
7
8
9
10
11
12
13
14
15
16
17
18
19
20
21
22
23

Figure 31: Jugs with Plain and Pinched Rims

1. Jug	1:4	Acemhüyük	Emre 1966: fig. 17
2. Jug	1:4	Acemhüyük	Emre 1966: fig. 16
3. Jug	1:5	Alişar	von der Osten 1937b: pl. V: b1678
4. Jug	1:5	Alaca Hüyük, Level IV	Koşay and Akok 1966: pl. 110:f37
5. Jug	1:5	Alaca Hüyük, Level IV	Koşay and Akok 1966: pl. 110:f2
6. Jug	1:4	Gordion, Burial H 25	Mellink 1956: pls. 13e, 27a
7. Jug	1:5	Megiddo, T. 4112	Loud 1948: pl. 20:4
8. Jug	1:5	Megiddo, T. 4110	Loud 1948: pl. 11:10
9. Jug	1:5	Megiddo, T. 5259	Loud 1948: pl. 25:14
10. Jug	1:5	Megiddo, T. 3157	Loud 1948: pl. 11:12
11. Jug	1:5	Megiddo, T. 5171	Loud 1948: pl. 11:11
12. Jug	1:5	Megiddo, T. 3151	Loud 1948: pl. 7:16
13. Jug	1:5	Megiddo, T. 2145	Loud 1948: pl. 25:8

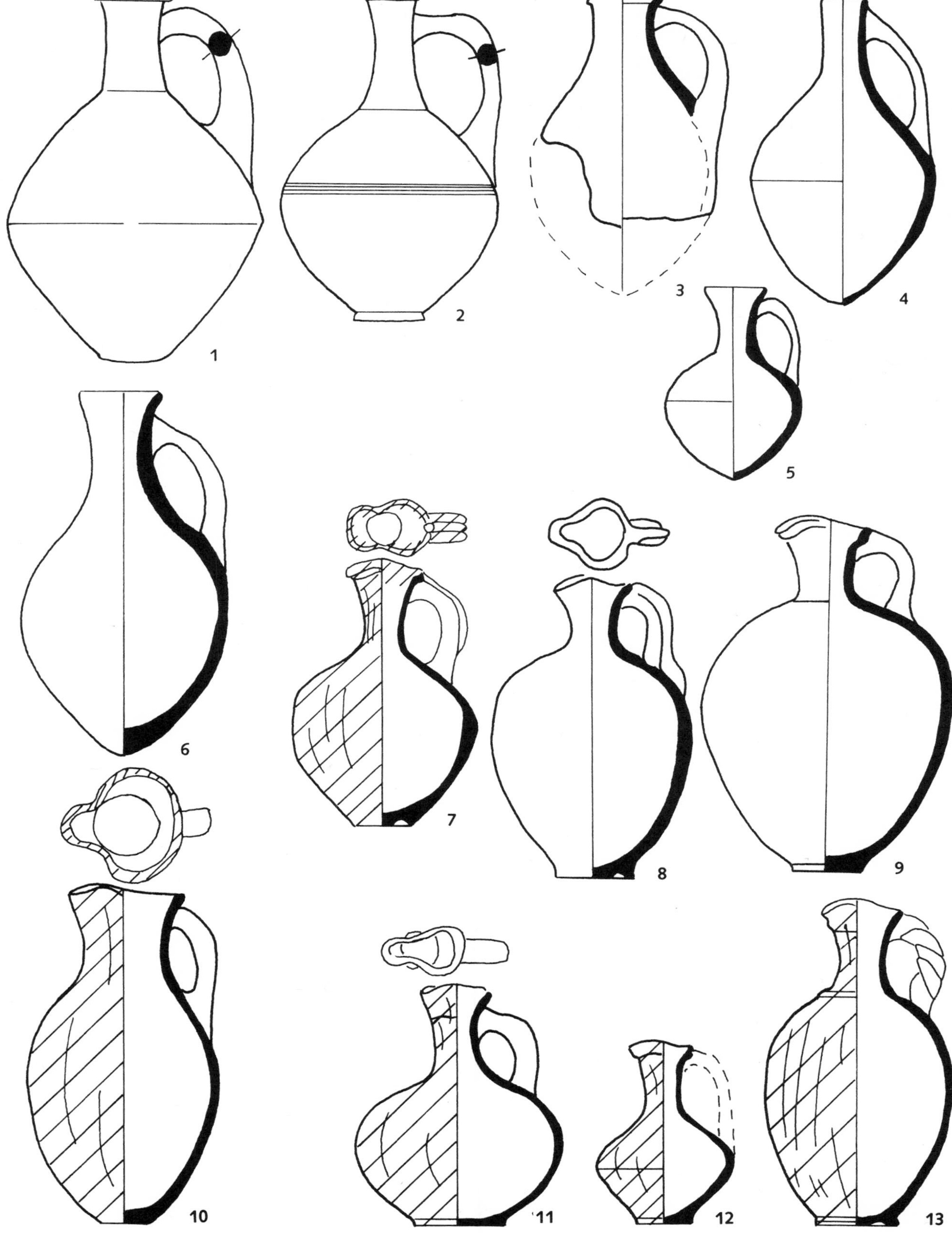
1
2
3
4
5
6
7
8
9
10
11
12
13

Figure 32: Jugs with Pinched Rim

1.	Jug	1:5	Lachish, T. 1504	Tufnell 1958: pl. 86:995
2.	Jug	1:5	Barqai	Gophna and Sussman 1969: fig. 4:1
3.	Jug	1:5	Barqai	Gophna and Sussman 1969: fig. 4:3
4.	Jug	1:5	Tell el-Far^cah (N.), T. 16	de Vaux 1955: fig. 2:4
5.	Jug	1:5	Tell el-Far^cah (N.), T. 16	de Vaux 1955: fig. 2:7
6.	Jug	1:5	Tell el-Far^cah (N.), T. 16	de Vaux 1955: fig. 2:6
7.	Jug	1:5	Tell el-Far^cah (N.), T. 16	de Vaux 1955: fig. 2:5
8.	Jug	1:8	Gezer, Cave III 30	Macalister 1912a: fig. 158:1
9.	Jug	1:4	Gezer, T. 1	Macalister 1912b: pl. LXIII: 68
10.	Jug	1:5	Alaca Hüyük	Koşay and Akok 1966: pl. 109:k157
11.	Jug	1:5	Alişar	von der Osten 1937b: pl. V: c2735
12.	Jug	1:5	Alişar	von der Osten 1937b: pl. IV: 3154
13.	Jug	1:5	Alişar	von der Osten 1937b: pl. IV: d2957
14.	Jug	1:2	Tarsus	Goldman 1956: fig. 369:852
15.	Jug	1:2	Tarsus	Goldman 1956: fig. 369:848
16.	Jug	1:2	Tarsus	Goldman 1956: fig. 369:849
17.	Jug	1:5	Kültepe, Level II	Emre 1963: fig. 10:Kt m/k69
18.	Jug	1:3	Byblos, Royal Tombs	Tufnell 1969: fig. 5:50
19.	Jug	1:4	Mari	Parrot 1959: fig. 84:905
20.	Jug	1:5	Kültepe, Level II	Emre 1963: fig. 10:Kt e/k74

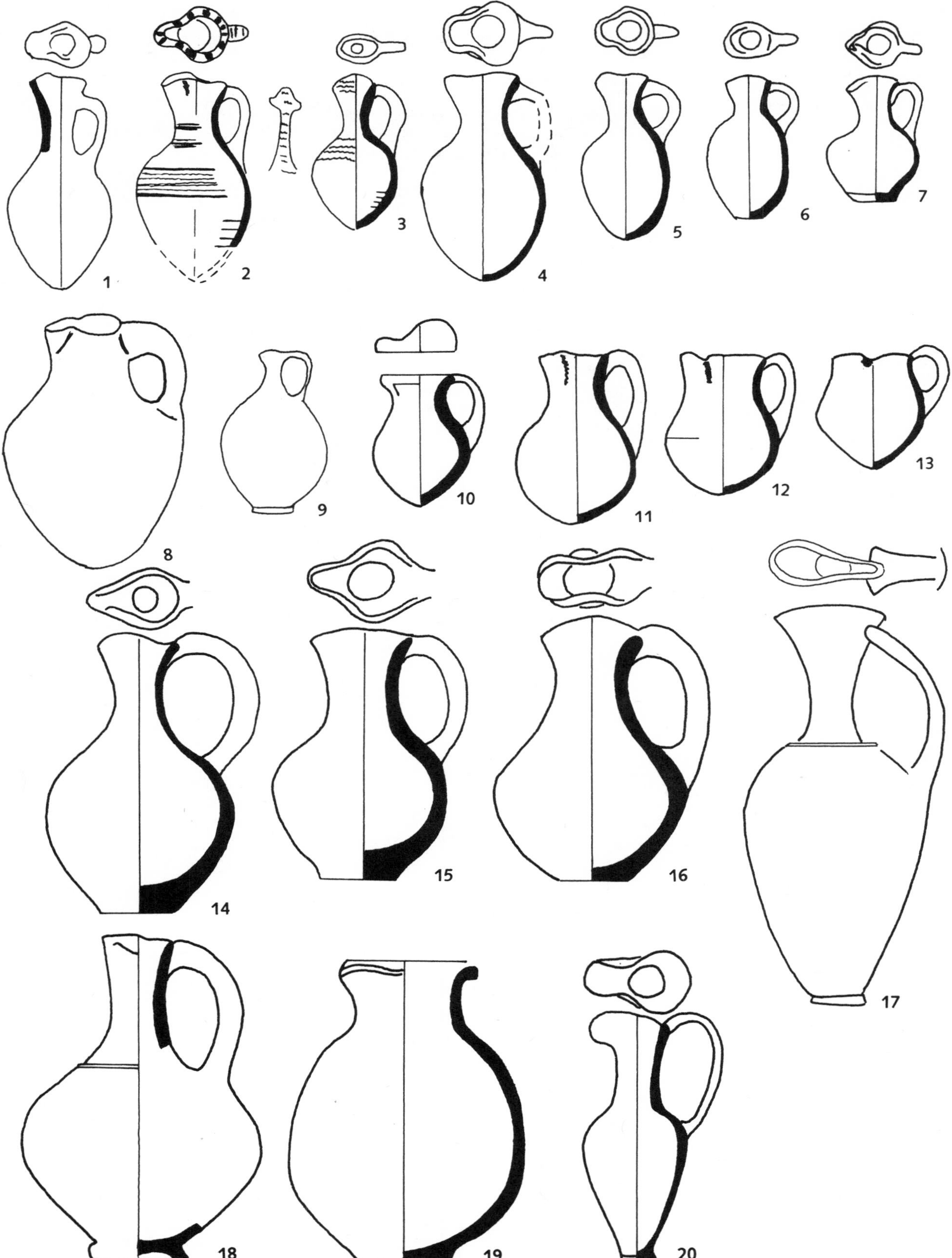
1
2
3
4
5
6
7
8
9
10
11
12
13
14
15
16
17
18
19
20

Figure 33: Jugs with Rising or Spouted Rim

1.	Jug	1:5	Megiddo, T. 5106	Loud 1948: pl. 25:12
2.	Jug	1:5	Megiddo, T. 5121	Loud 1948: pl. 11:2
3.	Jug	1:5	Megiddo, T. 5114	Loud 1948: pl. 16:2
4.	Jug	1:5	Megiddo, T. 5090	Loud 1948: pl. 17:14
5.	Jug	1:5	Aphek, Locus 400	Beck 1975: fig. 10:3
6.	Jug Spout	2:3	Nahariya	Ben-Dor 1950: fig. 25
7.	Jug Spout	2:3	Nahariya	Ben-Dor 1950: fig. 25
8.	Jug	1:4	Wadi et-Tin	Vincent 1947: pl. V:6
9.	Jug	N.S.	Ugarit	Schaeffer 1948: fig. 52A
10.	Jug	1:3	Byblos, Royal Tombs	Tufnell 1969: fig. 5:52
11.	Jug	1:4	Alişar	Schmidt 1932: pl. XII:b 1671
12.	Jug	1:4	Gordion	Mellink 1956: pl. 13c, 26d
13.	Jug	1:5	Alaca Hüyük, Level IV	Koşay and Akok 1966: pl. 109:e150

1
2
3
4
5
6
7
8
9
10
11
12
13

Figure 34: Bottles

1.	Bottle	1:6	Aphek	Iliffe 1936: 25:74
2.	Bottle	1:5	Beth-shemesh, T. 2	Grant 1929: 129, 153, No. 239
3.	Bottle	1:5	Wadi et-Tin	Vincent 1947: fig. 4:4
4.	Bottle	1:5	ʿAin es-Samiyeh	Dever 1975a: fig. 3:5
5.	Bottle	1:2	Qatna ("Coupole de Loth")	du Mesnil du Buisson 1935a: fig. 16:4
6.	Bottle	1:8	Dhahrat el-Humraiya, Grave 21	Ory 1948: fig. 21
7.	Bottle	2:5	Alalakh	Woolley 1955: pl. CXXII: Type 137
8.	Bottle	1:4	Byblos, Royal Tombs	Tufnell 1969: fig. 5:51
9.	Bottle	N.S.	Baghouz	du Mesnil du Buisson 1948: pl. LXXVII:Z260
10.	Bottle	1:3	Mari	Parrot 1959: fig. 88:874
11.	Bottle	2:5	Chagar Bazar, Grave 151, early Level 1	Mallowan 1937a: fig. 15:13

1
2
3
4
5
6
7
8
9
10
11

Figure 35: Biconical and Trefoil-Rimmed Mugs

1.	Mug	1:4	Aphek, Grave 4	Ory 1937: 118:88
2.	Mug	N.S.	Byblos	Montet 1929: pl. CXLVI:934
3.	Mug	N.S.	Byblos	Dunand 1958: fig. 1153:18926
4.	Mug	N.S.	Byblos	Dunand 1958: fig. 1054:17692
5.	Mug	1:4	Kültepe, Level II	Emre 1963: fig. 10:Kt h/k129
6.	Mug	1:5	Alişar	von der Osten 1937b: pl. IV: e26
7.	Mug	1:2	Boğazköy, Level IVd, Büyükkale	Fischer 1963: pl. 82:675
8.	Mug	1:4	Kültepe, Level II or Ib	Fischer 1963: fig. 13:2
9.	Mug	1:4	Alişar	Fischer 1963: fig. 13:3
10.	Mug	1:4	Kültepe, Level II	Fischer 1963: fig. 13:4
11.	Mug	1:2	Acemhüyük	Emre 1966: fig. 63
12.	Mug	1:2	Acemhüyük	Emre 1966: fig. 64
13.	Mug	1:5	Megiddo, T. 3122	Loud 1948: pl. 25:4
14.	Mug	1:5	Megiddo, T. 4107	Loud 1948: pl. 25:5
15.	Mug	1:5	Megiddo, T. 4099	Loud 1948: pl. 25:3
16.	Mug	1:3	Kültepe, Level Ib	Emre 1963: fig. 11:Kt e/k97
17.	Mug	1:4	Jericho	Garstang 1932: pl. 32:8
18.	Mug	1:5	Ginosar, T. 4	Epstein 1974: fig. 15:2
19.	Mug	1:3	Acemhüyük	Emre 1966: fig. 12

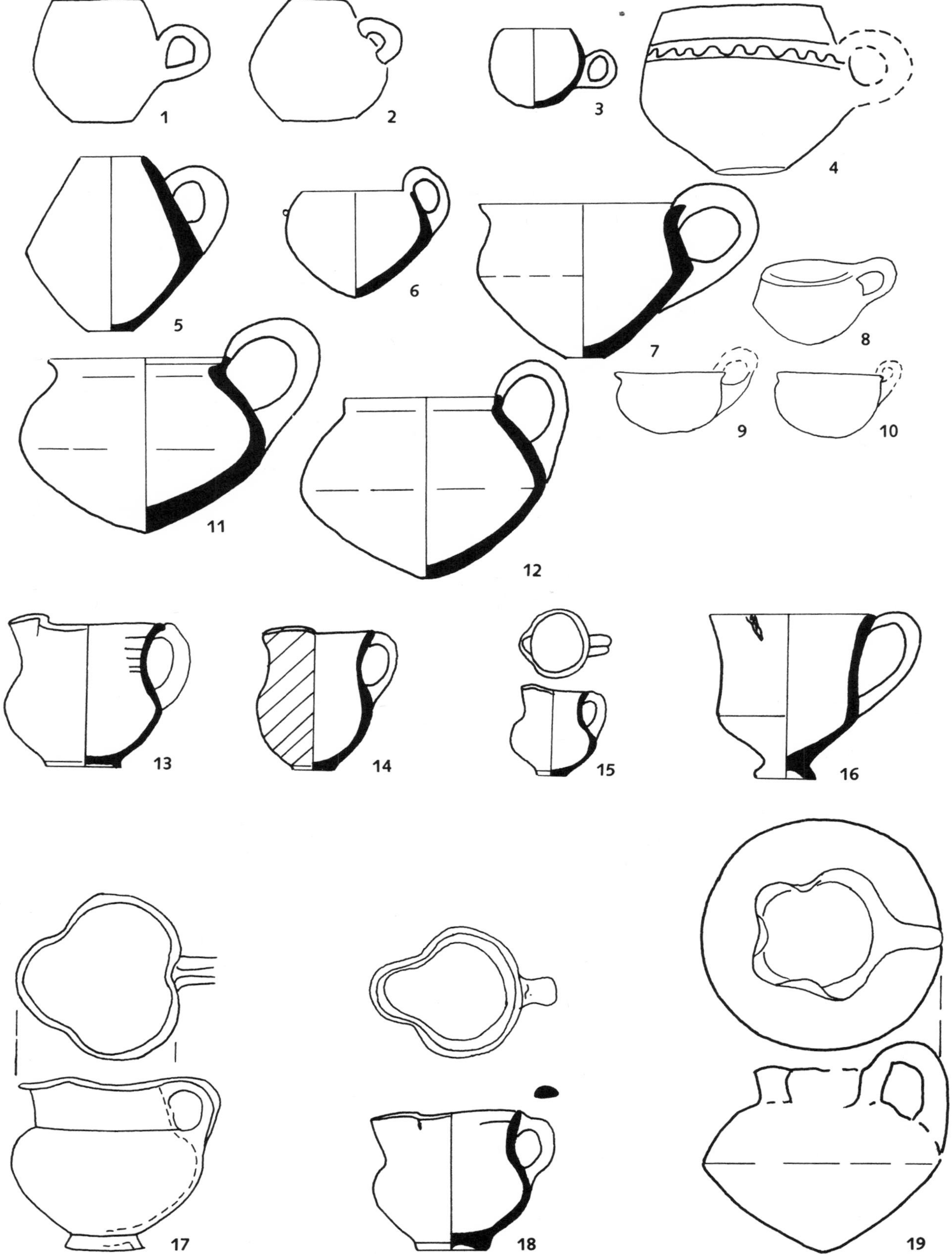
1
2
3
4
5
6
7
8
9
10
11
12
13
14
15
16
17
18
19

Figure 36: Duckbill Axes

1. Axe	1:2	ᶜAin es-Samiyeh	Dever 1975a: fig. 1:4
2. Axe	1:2	Beirut	Greenwell 1902: fig. 15 (British Museum W.G. 844)
3. Axe	N.S.	Esh-Shejara	Schumacher 1889: fig. 15
4. Axe	N.S.	Provenance unknown, in the Lyons Museum (similar to an axe from Tell et-Tin)	Gautier 1895: fig. 10
5. Axe	2:3	Ugarit, U.M. 2	Schaeffer 1932: pl. XIII:4
6. Axe	3:4	Beth-shan, T. 92	Oren 1971: fig. 2:4
7. Axe	2:3	Baghouz	du Mesnil du Buisson 1948: pl. LX:Z305
8. Axe	2:3	Kültepe, Level II	T. Özgüç 1959: fig. 64
9. Axe	2:3	Izmir Region	Przeworski 1967: pl. XXI:5

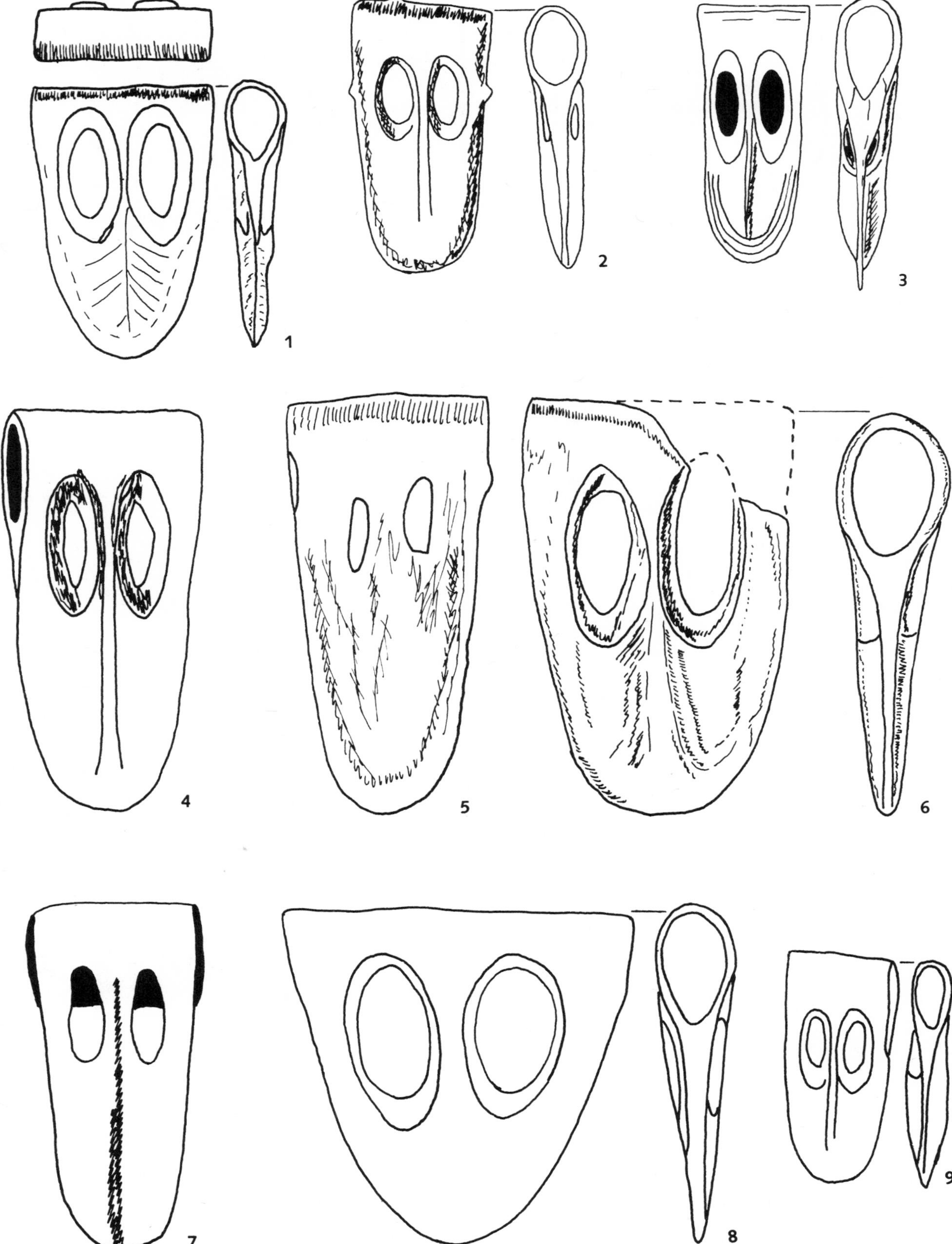
1
2
3
4
5
6
7
8
9

Figure 37: Chisel-Axes

1.	Axe	1:2	Megiddo, T. 911D	Guy 1938: fig. 173:1
2.	Axe	1:2	Megiddo, T. 911D	Guy 1938: fig. 173:2
3.	Axe	1:2	Megiddo, T. 3168	Loud 1948: pl. 182:1
4.	Axe	1:2	Moza, Cave No. 2	Sussman 1966: fig. 3:2
5.	Axe	1:2	ᶜAin es-Samiyeh	Dever 1975a: fig. 1:7
6.	Axe	1:10	Gibeon, T. 31	Pritchard 1963: fig. 34:4
7.	Axe	1:5	Tell el-ᶜAjjul, T. 1015	Tufnell 1962: fig. 4:1c
8.	Axe	1:4	Kafr Malik	Maxwell-Hyslop 1949: pl. XXXV:24 (British Museum W.G. 876)
9.	Axe	1:4	Khirbet Kufin, T. 3, Upper Stratum, Chambers 3-4	Smith 1962: pl. XIII:7
10.	Axe	1:4	Khirbet Kufin, T. 3, Upper Stratum, Chambers 3-4	Smith 1962: pl. XIII:6
11.	Axe	1:2	Ginosar, T. 1	Epstein 1974: fig. 7:15
12.	Axe	N.S.	Kafer Djarra, T. 74	Guigues 1938: fig. 95d
13.	Axe	N.S.	Kafer Djarra, T. 74	Guigues 1938: fig. 95e
14.	Axe	N.S.	Kafer Djarra, T. 66	Guigues 1938: fig. 70

FIGURE 37

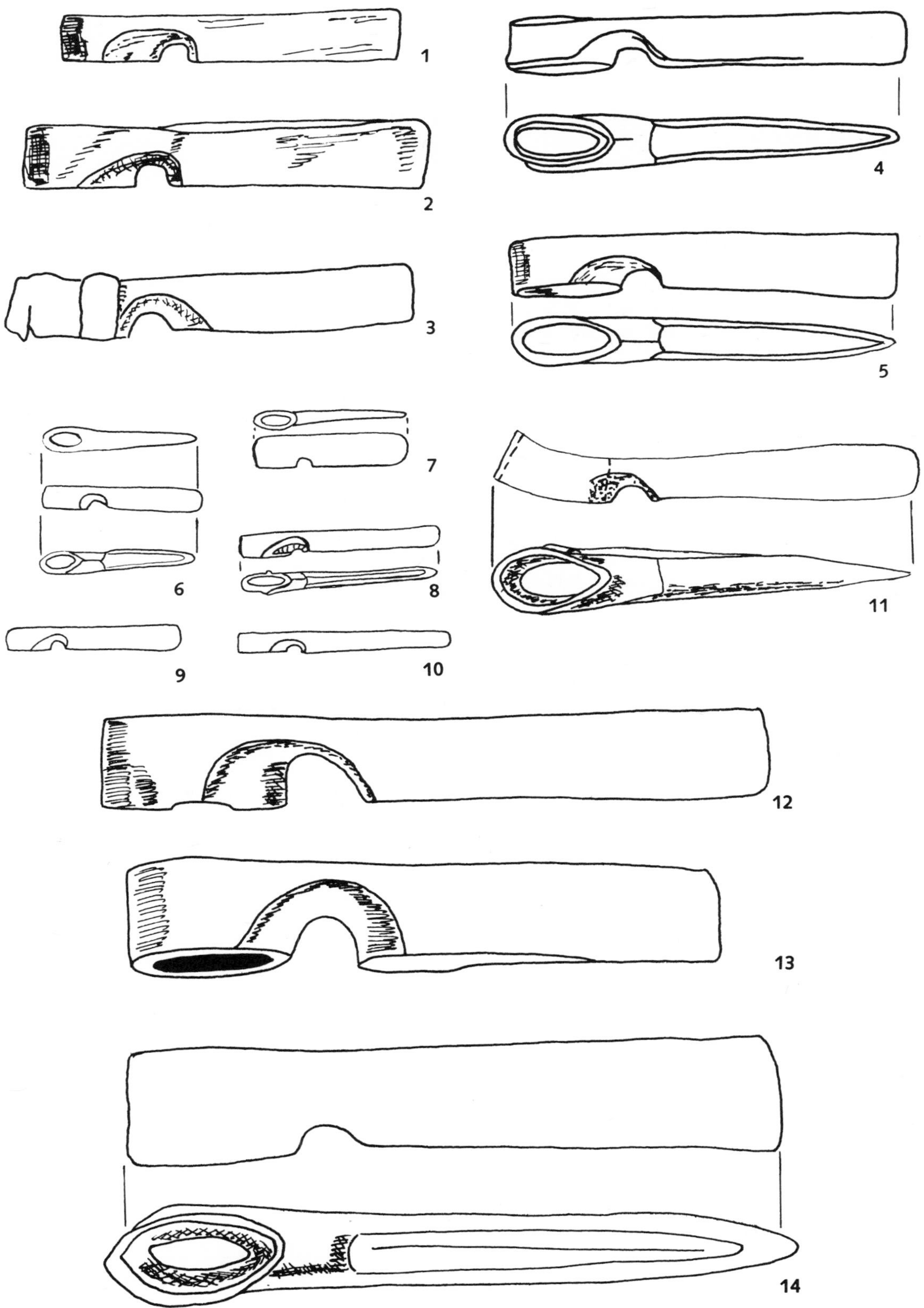

Figure 38: Spearheads

1.	Spearhead	1:2	Megiddo, T. 911D	Guy 1938: fig. 170:3
2.	Spearhead	1:2	Megiddo, T. 911D	Guy 1938: fig. 170:4
3.	Spearhead	1:2	Barqai	Gophna and Sussman 1969: fig. 4:14
4.	Spearhead	1:2	Barqai	Gophna and Sussman 1969: fig. 4:13
5.	Spearhead	1:2	Nahariya	Dothan 1956: pl. 4D
6.	Spearhead	1:2	Ginosar, T. 1	Epstein 1974: fig. 7:14
7.	Spearhead	1:2	Ginosar, T. 4	Epstein 1974: fig. 18:1
8.	Spearhead	1:2	Kfar Szold	Epstein 1974: fig. 4:10
9.	Spearhead	1:2	Sinjil	Dever 1975a: fig. 3:2
10.	Spearhead	1:2	Sinjil	Dever 1975a: fig. 3:3
11.	Spearhead	1:2	ʿAin es-Samiyeh	Dever 1975a: fig. 1:2
12.	Spearhead	1:2	Byblos	Montet 1929: pl. CXLIX: 942
13.	Spearhead	1:2	Kültepe, Level Ib	T. Özgüç 1959: fig. 66
14.	Spearhead	1:2	Kültepe, Level II	T. Özgüç 1959: fig. 67
15.	Spearhead	1:2	Kültepe, Level Ib	T. Özgüç 1959: fig. 68
16.	Spearhead	1:2	Chagar Bazar	Mallowan 1947: pl. LV:16
17.	Spearhead	1:2	Chagar Bazar	Mallowan 1947: pl. LV:10
18.	Spearhead	1:2	Baghouz	du Mesnil du Buisson 1948: pl. LXI:Z143
19.	Spearhead	2:3	Alişar	von der Osten 1937b: fig. 291:d2447

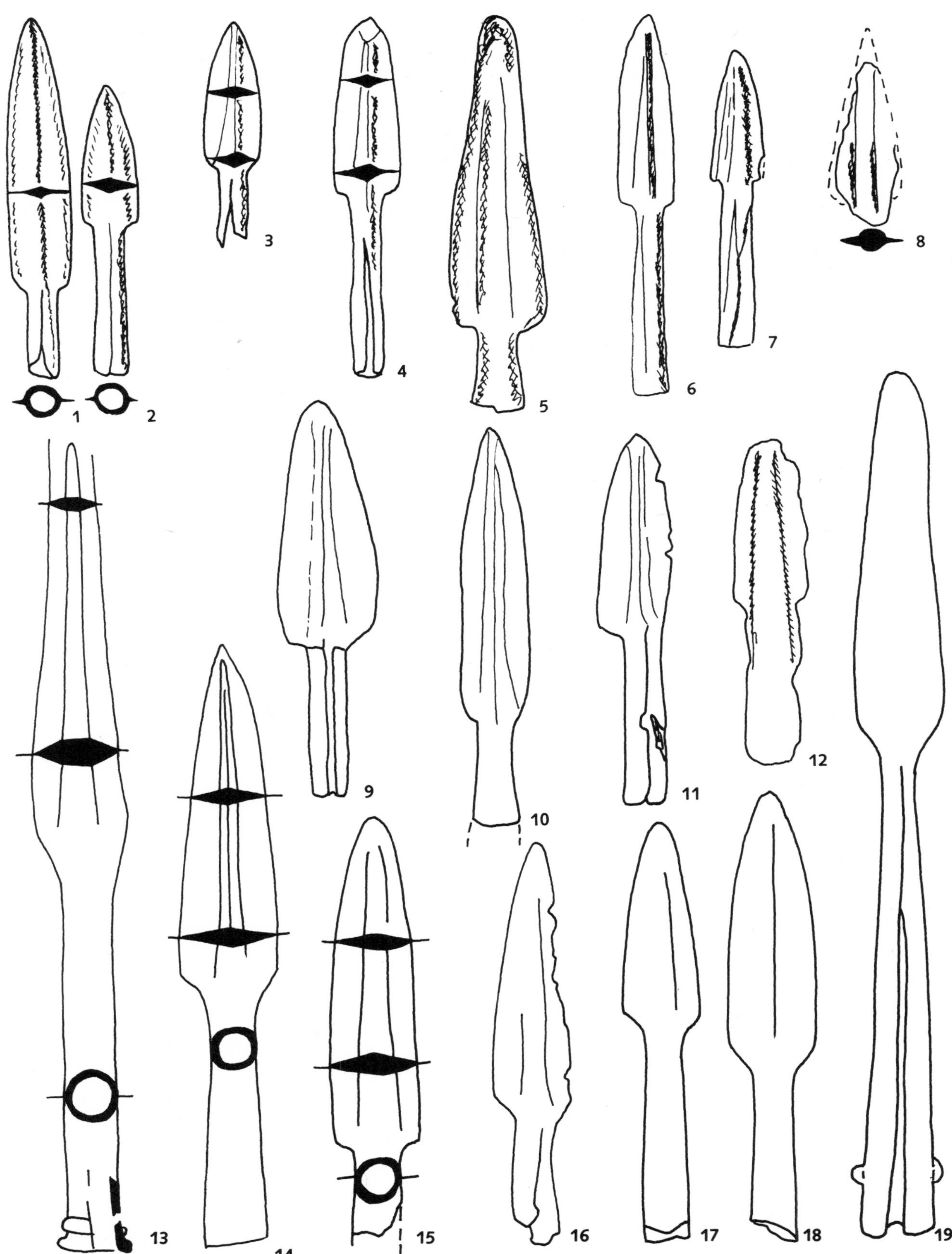
1
2
3
4
5
6
7
8
9
10
11
12
13
14
15
16
17
18
19

Figure 39: Simple Daggers

1.	Dagger	1:2	Ugarit, U.M. 2	Schaeffer 1932: pl. XIII:6
2.	Dagger	1:2	Ugarit, U.M. 2	Schaeffer 1932: pl. XIII:6
3.	Dagger	1:2	Megiddo, T. 912D	Guy 1938: pl. 133:6
4.	Dagger	1:2	Boğazköy, Level Ia, North-west Slope	Schirmer 1969: pl. 46:247
5.	Dagger	2:5	Chagar Bazar, Grave 167	Mallowan 1937a: fig. 13:4
6.	Dagger	2:5	Chagar Bazar, Grave 143	Mallowan 1937a: fig. 13:5
7.	Dagger	1:2	Moza	Sussman 1966: fig. 3:1
8.	Dagger	1:2	Megiddo, T. 911D	Guy 1938: fig. 171:5
9.	Dagger	1:2	Baghouz	du Mesnil du Buisson 1948: pl. LX:Z305
10.	Dagger	1:2	Baghouz	du Mesnil du Buisson 1948: pl. LX:Z193
11.	Dagger	1:2	Baghouz	du Mesnil du Buisson 1948: pl. LX:Z95

FIGURE 39

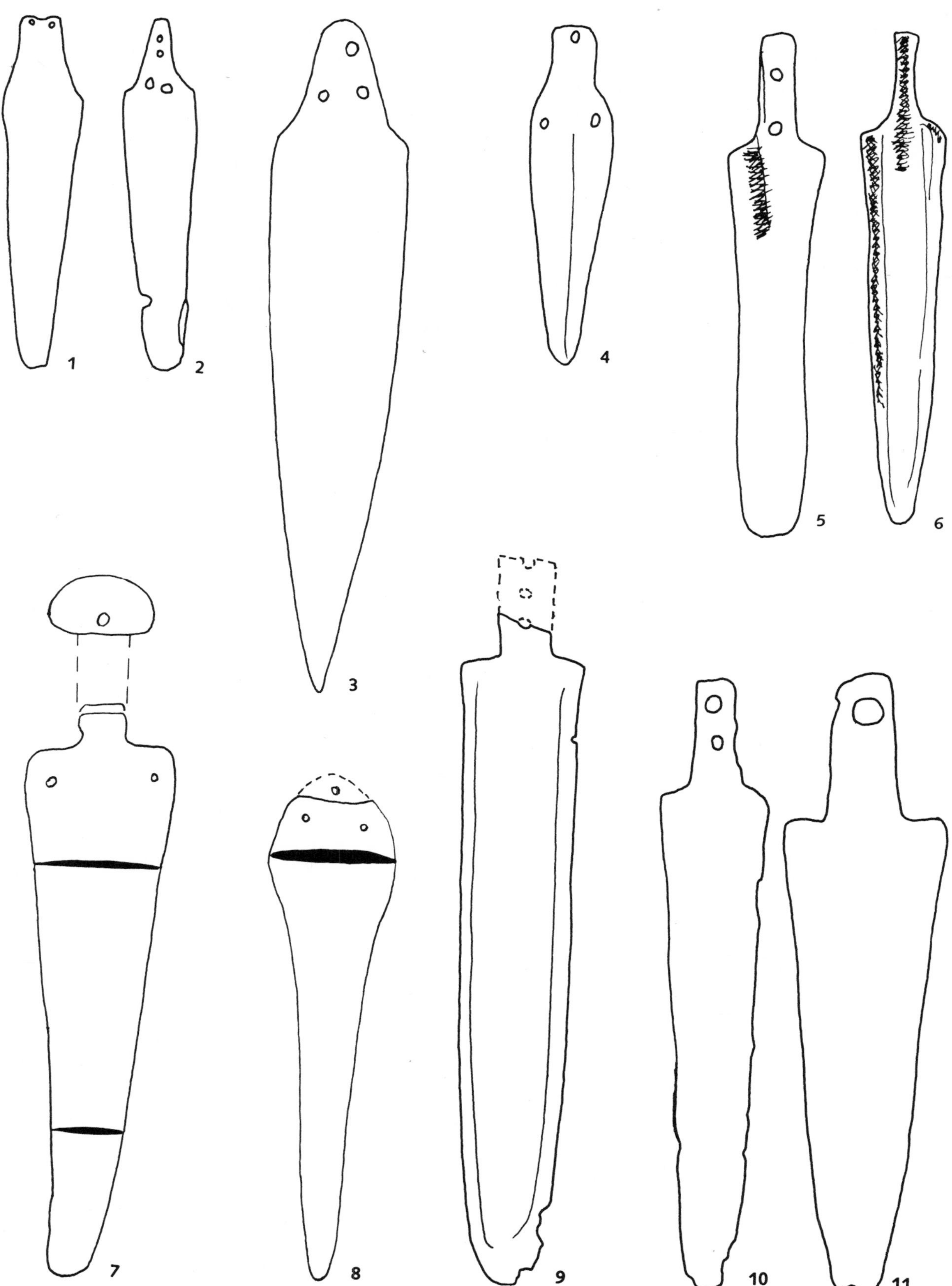

Figure 40: Veined Daggers

1.	Dagger	1:2	Megiddo, T. 911D	Guy 1938: fig. 171:6
2.	Dagger	1:2	Megiddo, T. 911A1	Guy 1938: pl. 118:5
3.	Dagger	1:2	ᶜAin es-Samiyeh	Dever 1975a: fig. 1:1
4.	Dagger	1:2	Sinjil	Dever 1975a: fig. 3:1
5.	Dagger	N.S.	Wadi et-Tin	Vincent 1947: pl. VII, left
6.	Dagger	1:4	Tell et-Tin	Gautier 1895: fig. 9, center
7.	Dagger	1:2	Tell el-Farᶜah (N.) Tomb AD	de Vaux 1962: fig. 4:1
8.	Dagger	3:4	Beth-shan, T. 92	Oren 1971: fig. 2:1

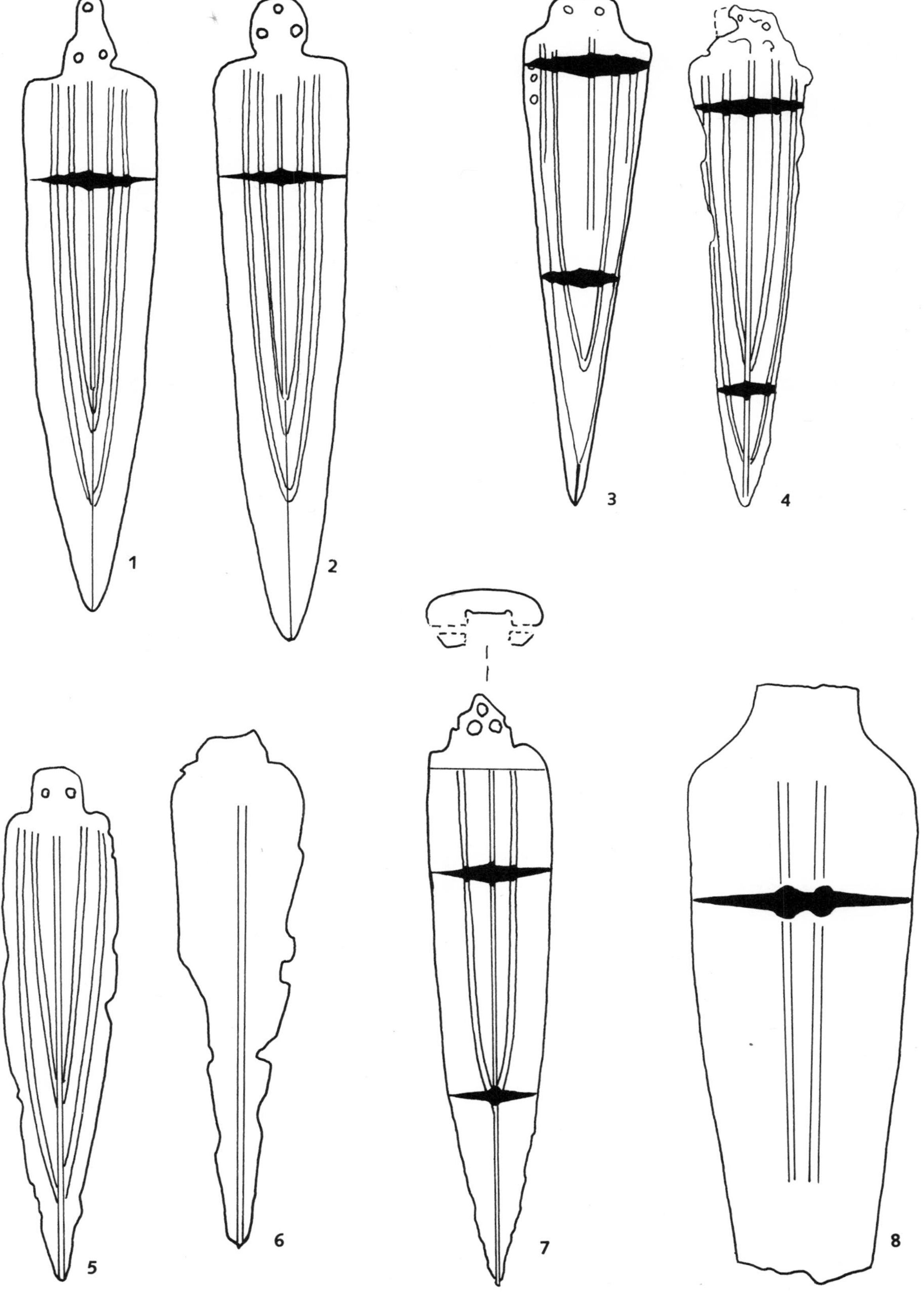
1
2
3
4
5
6
7
8